The Best Places
to Launch
a Career

Fast Track

The Best Places
to Launch
a Career

Lindsey Gerdes

New York   Chicago   San Francisco
Lisbon   London   Madrid   Mexico City   Milan
New Delhi   San Juan   Seoul   Singapore
Sydney   Toronto

Copyright ©2008 by McGraw-Hill. All rights reserved. Printed in the United States of America. Except as permitted under the United States Copyright Act of 1976, no part of this publication may be reproduced or distributed in any form or by any means, or stored in a database or retrieval system, without the prior written permission of the publisher.

1 2 3 4 5 6 7 8 9 0 DOC/DOC 0 9 8

ISBN 978-0-07-149655-1
MHID   0-07-149655-6

McGraw-Hill books are available at special quantity discounts to use as premiums and sales promotions, or for use in corporate training programs. To contact a representative, please visit the Contact Us pages at www.mhprofessional.com.

This book is printed on acid-free paper.

Contents

Acknowledgments

Completing this book has been a two-plus-year process that started with a scribbled brainstorm for a new ranking and culminated in the publication of this book; it has involved the help of numerous talented contributors. First and foremost, I would like to thank my manager, Louis Lavelle, who has provided me with invaluable guidance and support—not to mention substantial hands-on involvement—throughout this endeavor from the beginning. I would also like to thank Frank Comes for his continued mentorship and encouragement. I am also grateful for John Byrne and Steve Adler's support of the "Best Places" project and the book from their earliest stages. Elizabeth Weiner and Fred Jesperson contributed valuable oversight and expertise from the start, while Geoff Gloeckler has long provided helpful advice and support, and my former supervisor, Deborah Stead, has always been an encouraging and understanding "Best Places" supporter.

I have enjoyed collaborating with Patricia O'Connell, Arthur Eves, and Ira Sager and their team to develop online content for the ranking over the past two years. I also look forward to the continued involvement of, and guidance from, a new team, including Mary Kuntz, Robin Ajello, and Susan Berfield, that has now begun oversight of the project.

I have also benefited from the expertise of our various partners in this endeavor. A special thanks to Universum Communications CEO Claudia Tattanelli and her team for their longtime involvement and numerous contributions; to Cambria Consulting; and to the many employees at the "Best Places" organizations and the career services officers who have provided valuable feedback, expertise, and other information for the rankings and the book.

I'm sincerely grateful for the contributions of my capable right-hand (wo)men Sophia Asare, Sonal Rupani, and Kristen Fiani, who have all played integral roles in the completion of this book. Thanks to Erica Pelzek, Maha Atal, Jenna Goudreau, and Tania Loghmani for generously volunteering to pitch in when extra help was needed. I'm also indebted to my amazing parents and sister, extended family, and friends, whose support has been invaluable.

Most pointedly, I would like to acknowledge Leah Spiro, Ruth Mannino, and Morgan Ertel for their invaluable vision, oversight, and dedicated hard work in making this book a reality. Many thanks to all!

Introduction

Bringing Sanity to an Overwhelming Process

When I was graduating from Stanford University in 2003, the economy was in the midst of a prolonged economic downturn that had started two years earlier. Many of my friends had a tough time finding jobs—many didn't—and among my circle a kind of macabre humor took hold. At our graduation ceremony, we wore placards spelling out U-N-E-M-P-L-O-Y-E-D (I can lay claim to putting the "L" in "unemployed," quite literally) for our "Wacky Walk," a school tradition in which graduating seniors parade around the school's stadium in crazy costumes before commencement.

We felt pretty clever at the time. However, it took only a month after I moved back home into a tiny, cramped apartment with my parents, who were renovating their house, for my jobless plight to seem a lot less entertaining. It definitely spurred me to put my job search into high gear. I plowed through articles and research and increased my networking efforts (as uncomfortable as I sometimes found "schmoozing"). I even upgraded my résumé and my interview attire. Unfortunately, this approach led only to greater frustration. I spent my days putting out so many feelers that I didn't make any headway in one real direction. I had never worked that hard to feel that guilty, unproductive, and lazy, even as I devoted increasingly more time and money to the process of not finding work.

As this book was going to press, the situation for today's grads wasn't all that different. Trillions had disappeared from global stock markets without a trace, the financial sector was in turmoil, and the U.S. economy appeared to be slipping into a recession. Meanwhile, the job outlook for new college grads had suddenly turned markedly worse. One widely watched survey of employers—the National Association of Colleges and Employers Job Outlook 2008—had rosy news in September 2007: an expected 16% year-over-year increase in hiring for new college grads. But just six months later, that figure was down to 8%—making the class of 2008 the first in five years to graduate without a double-digit hiring increase.

The most important thing you should know about a highly competitive labor market is that knowledge matters. If you're a young job seeker reading this, you have probably come across numerous resources related to your job quest—"how-to" guides, career search Web sites, and online message boards, to name just a few. Why would *Business Week* create yet another career tool to add to an overcrowded market? It's simple: you need a resource that will simplify and clarify your search, not add to your confusion.

Searching for your first job or internship can be a daunting process. When it is informed only by scattered bits of data obtained from countless—and often questionable—sources of information, as it was in my case, it can feel even more overwhelming.

In the book in your hands, *Business Week* provides you with a concrete starting point for your search: solid, statistically based profiles of 94 top entry-level employers that are drawn from *Business Week*'s 2007 ranking of the "Best Places to Launch a Career." You will also find useful information on the recruiting, pay, benefits, training, and mentorship opportunities these top-ranked employers provide. This hardly means that these are the only solid, high-quality entry-level employers out there, or that every reader will find an employer among these pages that fits ideally with his or her interests and objectives. However, there's a very good chance that this book will have a meaningful impact on your job search in one way or another.

> *You need a resource that will simplify and clarify your search, not add to your confusion.*

Perhaps it's that one interview tip from a recruiter Q&A in an organization's profile that helps you ace an interview, or maybe you become interested in a new industry after reading profiles on those companies.

Something for Everybody

Students from rural liberal arts colleges and big state universities, graduates with degrees in disciplines from engineering to philosophy, will all find potential options in this book's pages. There's something for every undergraduate and young professional, no matter what your school or your major. The "Best Places" list features employers in 15 different private industries—Accounting, Consulting, Consumer Goods, Energy, Financial Services, Hospitality, Insurance, Internet, Investment Banking, Manufacturing, Pharma/Health, Retail, Technology, Telecommunications, and Transportation—as well as some in the public sector—Nonprofit/Government.

We also have a geographically diverse group of employers headquartered across the United States, and even a handful of organizations based in other countries, including the United Kingdom, The Netherlands, France, and even Bermuda.

All 94 employer profiles focus on the United States, with data from 2006 on the organization's U.S. hiring and entry-level salaries and benefits, training, perks, and retention numbers. However, we try to provide a global outlook on the company's lines of business and overall strategy, financial results, and any significant expansion of the company.

The Millennial Generation—and the Employers Who Love (Well, at the Very Least, Need) Them

The much-maligned Millennial Generation is increasingly important to employers. With the mass exodus of Baby Boomers from upper management jobs, many employers need to refill the talent pipeline, and fast. For example, Lockheed Martin, a huge organization, expects to lose more than 40% of its workforce by 2014. When I visited the $42 billion defense contractor's high-security, pristine corporate headquarters in Bethesda, Maryland, the posters plastered across the wall weren't announcements of current contracts or Human Resources updates. They were advertisements for an upcoming seminar exploring how Gen Y and other age groups could better communicate and work together.

In the book in your hands, BusinessWeek provides you with a concrete starting point for your search.

Because the Millennials are so important, employers are pulling out all the stops to recruit them. Two other defense contractors, Raytheon and Boeing, are good examples. Boeing is trying to improve its lukewarm five-year retention rate for new college grads, now at 59%, by making improvements to its mentoring program to make sure they don't get lost in the shuffle as a result of organization shake-ups caused by new acquisitions. "We want to be more deliberative in making sure that every new college hire actually has a group of people [he or she] can develop a relationship with and select a mentor," says Rick Stephens, senior VP of human resources and administration at Boeing. "They [the mentors] can really help coach that new college hire and nurture [them] in a little bit of a different way than a manager." Boeing is currently shifting from a largely informal mentoring network that was spread throughout the company to a more centralized, formal mentoring strategy.

The tech industry is taking a different tack. It's attracting Millennials the old-fashioned way: with money. The tech industry offers the best starting salaries of any industry, with average entry-level pay, bonuses not included, of more than $70,000. That's one reason why tech giants like IBM, Google, and Microsoft are so well represented at the top of our list. Another reason: all three companies are hotly pursuing computer science majors, but all three also hire graduates in many different majors. Microsoft hires approximately 10% of its entry-level staffers from undergraduate business programs, while Google plucks 15% of its young hires from liberal arts majors. IBM turns to economics majors to fill 16% of its slots.

But money isn't the only tool in the tech recruiting arsenal. Universum Communications CEO Claudia Tattanelli says that traditional heavyweights, like IBM and Microsoft, have made huge strides in providing mentoring programs, affinity groups, and diversity initiatives because of what might be called the "Google effect." "They realized they were losing. Google is forcing both of them to completely change," says Tattanelli.

The search engine behemoth Google is a good example of how a company can use a vast array of perks to attract members of this new generation. Rapid growth certainly helped make the company popular with students and career services directors. Google has doubled the size of its workforce annually over each of the past few years and is currently hiring approximately 500 new employees a month, many of whom are recent graduates in their mid- to late twenties. But the Google advantage doesn't end there. An innovative culture, financial success, and impressive employee perks, including free lunches and on-site massages, are also big factors in its popularity. Perhaps the most popular perk is that all employees are allowed to devote one day a week to developing new ideas. Similar innovation initiatives are in place elsewhere in the tech world. Recent initiatives at IBM include the introduction of ThinkPlace, an online suggestion box whose aim is to help the com-

Best Internship Pay*	Average Compensation
1. British Petroleum America	$16,500
2. Intel	$16,000
3. International Business Machines Corporation	$15,000
4. JPMorgan Investment Bank	$14,288
5. Hewlett-Packard	$13,071

*Undergraduate summer internship compensation, including pay, housing/food allowances, bonuses, etc.

Most Internships	Number of 2006 Internships
1. Walgreen Co.	2,902
2. PricewaterhouseCoopers	2,807
3. International Business Machines Corporation	2,805
4. Ernst & Young	2,245
5. General Electric	2,200

pany cull the best ideas from its global workforce. Microsoft's approach is creating an inviting, collaborative environment at its Seattle, Washington, campus. Employees there have access to Ping-Pong tables in the lobbies and gourmet coffee machines across campus.

Accounting: A Surprisingly 'Sexy' Employer

Huge demand, such as Google's, sometimes helps push a company to the top of the ranking, but it also works for entire industries, even some you wouldn't expect. During the good times, accountants used to be spoofed as bean counters—dutiful, middle-aged, gray-suited men with considerable analytical expertise but little charisma. But in our 2007 ranking, the industry suddenly became sexy, dominating the very top of the list.

Why did the accounting firms do so well? Enormous demand. The Sarbanes-Oxley Act, a 2002 overhaul of corporate regulations prompted by a series of financial scandals, has so greatly increased the need for accounting services that the firms are facing an epic talent shortage. Although the number of U.S. students graduating from college with accounting degrees has risen almost 29% since 2002, the accounting firms are also competing with high-paying,

There's something for every undergraduate and young professional, no matter what your school or your major.

bonus-giving investment banks, as well as with major corporations. So the Big Four are falling all over themselves to win the favor of Gen Y. "The ability to recruit and retain younger workers will become critical," says Barry Salzberg, CEO of Deloitte LLP. "In many ways, Gen Y is our future." Accounting and consulting firm Deloitte LLP estimates that it will need to hire as many as 50,000 new employees in the next five years alone.

Necessity, in this case the need to recruit and retain a huge pool of talent, has been the accounting firm's mother of invention. Ernst & Young uses Facebook to

Best Intern-to-Full-time Conversion*	
1. Ernst & Young	98%
2. Grant Thornton	97%
3. Protiviti	95%
4. KPMG	95%
5. Raytheon	92%

*Percentage of undergraduate interns who received full-time offers multiplied by percentage of undergraduate interns with full-time offers who accepted them.

let prospective employees talk freely with real ones. Deloitte is planning to show a rap video about office life—made by interns—to give students a realistic view of the company. And PricewaterhouseCoopers has just launched an online recruiting campaign that includes a faux sitcom. Called "The Firm," it features real employees acting out scenarios in which the female Gen Y star has awkward interactions with older employees. That's right: real older employees. Senior partner Bob is "kinda scary," and Blake, a senior associate, apparently "smells." Says Amy Thompson, PricewaterhouseCooper's national director of campus recruiting, "We hear all the time that students are interested in what it's like in the workplace. This is a funny way to talk about a serious subject."

Attracting Community-Minded Employees

When it comes to Millennials, employers are keenly aware of the competition. And one group that is getting an increasing amount of attention from this community-minded cohort is the government and nonprofit sector. Born between 1982 and 2000, the Millennials began entering the workforce in 2004, and in many cases took detours through organizations like Teach for America and the Peace Corps before heading off for jobs in corporate America.

Teach for America, the nonprofit organization founded by a Princeton University senior to recruit college grads to teach in low-income communities across the United States for two-year commitments, jumped a jawdropping 33 spots in 2007 to No. 10 on the strength of its popularity with this generation. Today, 16 companies—including GE, Google, and Deloitte—partner with Teach for America, allowing students to start their jobs after a two-year teaching stint with the organization. JPMorgan Investment Bank even gives students their signing bonuses up front and offers summer programs to keep them involved with the company while they are teaching.

Bob Corcoran, vice president of corporate citizenship at GE, says that his company's partnership with Teach for America is a win-win. "We [GE and TFA] look for the same types of people—people who want to make a difference, people who have good leadership qualities and who truly want to jump in and lead something. Teachers do that everyday," Corcoran explains. "When these students come out of college and they defer to take on these roles, they learn how to lead. And Teach for America gets some great students who otherwise would have been nervous to jump out of their discipline and teach."

Internship Fever: It's Sweeping the Nation . . . the On-Campus Recruitment Nation, That Is!

For many Millennials, the path to their first permanent job after college will not start at an on-campus recruiting event, but with an internship, either in the summer after their junior year or the summer after graduation. Increasingly, such work opportunities are becoming three-month try-outs. For students, they're a way to test drive a job before committing to it; for employers, they're a way to see how a prospective employee performs before making a job offer.

Because the Millennials are so important, employers are pulling out all the stops to recruit them.

This increased focus on undergraduate internships is reflected in the numbers. According to the 2007 NACE Recruiting Benchmarks Survey, 62% of all entry-level hires have internship experience, up from 49.5% 10 years earlier. Interestingly, on average, nearly a third of all entry-level hires at the employers on *Business Week's* 50 "Best Internships" list had once interned at their new full-time employers. There's good reason for this preference for former interns. Universum's Tattanelli says studies on retention have shown that employees who start out as interns usually stick around a company longer.

Best Long-Term Prospects

Highest 3-Year Retention Rate*	
1. British Petroleum America	97%
2. St. Jude Medical	96%
3. UPS	94%
4. Vanguard	93%
5. AT&T	93%

*Percentage of entry-level employees hired in 2003 that are still with their employer at the end of 2006

For companies in industries like accounting and investment banks, where there is intense competition for top students from top schools with specific skill sets or majors, getting to the best students as early as possible is a prime concern. Many are starting their internship recruiting earlier—freshman and sophomores—as a result. "There are simply not enough really good students," says Jean Wyer, a principal at the No. 1 internship employer on our list, Big Four accounting firm Price-waterhouseCoopers.

Necessity, in this case the need to recruit and retain a huge pool of talent, has been the accounting firm's mother of invention.

Many students do internships during the school year, in addition to the summer—a practice that can quickly lead to burnout. Samantha Chen, now a junior majoring in finance and marketing at New York University's Stern School of Business, began interning at a major investment bank the summer after her freshman year and continued interning there part-time during her sophomore year. "I felt like people here [at Stern] were so accomplished, and I needed to do something instead of being home for the summer and lifeguarding or working at the restaurant," says Chen, 20, who ultimately regretted her decision. "I could handle it, but my school work suffered a little bit, and social life was nonexistent."

The Methodology behind the Rankings

Compiling the "Best Places to Launch a Career" ranking that this book is based upon requires surveys of career services directors, students, and employers themselves.

First, we surveyed career services directors at over 60 U.S. colleges to learn which employers were tops on their list. We then asked those employers to complete a survey on their hiring, pay, benefits, and training programs, which we then compared with those of others in the same industry. Finally, we obtained from Universum Communications, a Philadelphia research company, the results of its 2007 survey of 44,000 U.S. undergraduates who were asked to identify their five most desirable employers. The employer survey counts for 50% of the final ranking, while the career services directors and student surveys count for 25% each.

To compile the "50 Best Internships" ranking, we started out with the nearly 100 employers included in the 2007 "Best Places to Launch a Career" ranking. First, we eliminated those employers that did not complete the internship section of the Best Places survey satisfactorily. The remaining organizations were judged based on three criteria. First, we determined each employer's internship score by weighing how well the company performed in the following areas: number of undergraduate interns (10%), hourly wage (15%), total pay (15%), percentage of entry-level hires

Employers with the Best Entry-Level Pay and Bonuses

Top Signing Bonus	Average/Entry-Level Hire
1. Lehman Brothers	$12,000
2. British Petroleum America	$10,625
3. Capital One Financial	$9,000
4. Hewlett-Packard	$8,750
5. UBS	$8,500

Best Entry-Level Pay*	$70,000 and Above
1. Microsoft	88%
2. Hewlett-Packard	70%
3. Cisco Systems	57%
4. Abbott Laboratories	31%
5. International Business Machines Corporation	26%

*Percentage of entry-level hires with a starting salary of $70,000 or above

Best Performance Bonus	Average Amount
1. JPMorgan Investment Bank	$68,000
2. Lehman Brothers	$50,000
3. Merrill Lynch & Co.	$25,000
4. Deutsche Bank	$24,000
5. Constellation Energy	$9,200

who had been interns (15%), percentage of interns receiving full-time job offers (15%), and percentage of interns who were extended full-time job offers that accepted (30%). Combined, those six items contributed 50% of the final internship ranking. Each company's "Best Places to Launch a Career" ranking counted for an additional 25% of the final ranking. The final 25% was supplied by Universum Communications' survey of undergraduate students, which identifies the most popular internship programs.

Navigating the Employer Profiles

The book's 94 profiles are designed as "cheat sheets" for when you apply for an actual position at a company. We compiled enough company information to allow you to skim a company's profile in under five minutes and still sound knowledgeable in an interview.

We've also included breakdowns of the companies that offer the most competitive pay, spend the most on entry-level training, and are the most competitive to get a job offer from, along with a host of other factors.

Insights from each company's rising superstars, recruiting executives, and entry level employees are also included in a brief Q&A section at the end of each profile. Furthermore, each profile includes a "Sound-Off" section. This is where anonymous current and former interns and employees from these organizations provide tips, tidbits, and honest feedback about their overall experience at the employer. We compiled these quotes from a number of sources, including *BusinessWeek* and Universum surveys, reader comments and discussion forums on the BusinessWeek.com web site, and our own employee sources at individual companies.

Studies on retention have shown that employees who start out as interns usually stick around a company longer.

Finally, a word about the information itself. With few exceptions, all of the statistical data—including salaries, retention rates, selectivity, and diversity—was self-reported by the companies. It is for calendar year 2006. The remainder of the information is based on *BusinessWeek* research. Information in the section called "The Stats" is for the parent company, except where noted, and the most recent available at press time. In the section called "The Stand-Out Perks," where dollar amounts are listed for reimbursement of educational and relocation expenses, they are maximums. In the section called "The Starting Gate," the data on "% of interns at each grade level" is based on each school year and the summer that *preceded* it (for example, seniors include students who intern during the summer after junior year). Unless otherwise noted, the market cap is Bloomberg data from the market's close on December 31, 2007.

The Best Places
to Launch
a Career

Deloitte LLP

1633 Broadway
New York, NY 10019
Phone: 212-489-1600
Fax: 212-489-1687
Web Addresses: www.deloitte.com;
www.careers.deloitte.com/studentgrad.
aspx

The Company

- One of accounting's Big Four, Deloitte LLP offers a wide range of accounting and business consulting services, including auditing and tax consultancy, to clients around the world. It currently has four subsidiaries in operation: Deloitte LLP, Deloitte Consulting LLP, Deloitte Financial Advisory Services LLP, and Deloitte Tax LLP.

- Deloitte LLP is one of approximately 70 member firms organized under Deloitte Touche Tohmatsu, which operates as a Swiss Verein (association). Each member firm is considered a separate and independent legal entity.

- In the wake of the Enron scandal, regulators pushed for accounting industry reform and stepped up efforts to prohibit firms from providing auditing and consulting services to the same client. Deloitte competitors like KPMG and Ernst & Young abandoned their consultancies. Deloitte, however, opted to hold on to its booming practice.

FAST FACTS

"Best Places to Launch a Career"
 Rank: 1
"Best Internships" Rank: 3
Full-Time Salary: $50,000–$54,999
Entry-Level Hires: 1,995
Top College Major: Business
3-Year Retention Rate: 50%
Stock Ticker: N/A (privately owned)

This consulting arm continues to be a lucrative business for Deloitte and accounts for approximately 25% of the firm's sales.

The Suits

James H. Quigley: CEO, Deloitte Touche Tohmatsu
Barry Salzberg: CEO, Deloitte LLP
Sharon Allen: Chairman of the Board, Deloitte LLP

The Stats

2007 sales: $23.1 billion ($9.8 billion in U.S.)
2007 net income: N/A
Market cap: N/A
Employees: 146,000 (40,000 in U.S.)
Locations: 665 offices in 135 countries
Major competitors: Ernst & Young LLP, PricewaterhouseCoopers, KPMG
Largest operating units: N/A

 **The Story**

1845: William Welch Deloitte starts an accounting firm in London but moves the company's core business to auditing for the Great Western Railroad by the end of the decade

1890: First branch of Touche, Niven & Co. opens in New York City

1913: Income tax implemented for first time, driving up demand for accountants and boosting Deloitte's business

1933: The Securities Act requires public corporations to file independently certified registrations and reports; a year later, the Securities and Exchange Commission (SEC) is created to administer this legislation

1952: Touche, Niven, Bailey & Smart is created in a merger; the new entity becomes the first major accounting firm to automate bookkeeping

1960: The firm is renamed Touche, Ross, Bailey & Smart because of its ties with Canadian organization Ross

1989: Deloitte Haskins Sells joins Touche Ross and forms Deloitte & Touche

1990: The organization's name changes once more to Deloitte Touche Tohmatsu; Tohmatsu comes from Tohmatsu Awoki & Co., a company that had merged with Touche Ross in 1975

1993: Deloitte launches its Initiative for the Retention and Advancement of Women

1999: Deloitte appoints its first Chief Diversity Officer and launches a diversity and inclusion initiative

2003: Deloitte is ordered to pay $23 million over claims of negligence while auditing Kentucky Life Insurance

2005: Deloitte is ordered by the SEC to pay a $50 million fine for improper audit charges brought by former client Adelphia Communications Corp.

2007: Barry Salzberg replaces James Quigley as Deloitte LLP CEO on June 1; Quigley becomes CEO of Deloitte Touche Tohmatsu

The Skinny

Most important to recruiters: Communication skills, analytical skills, college GPA

Selectivity: 1 of 25 applicants hired in 2006, down from 1 of 10 applicants hired in 2005

Diversity of entry-level workforce: 43% minority; 48% female

Facts to know:

- In their first year at the firm, entry-level hires get only 8 paid vacation days, but they're immediately bumped up to 38 days of paid time off during their second year at the firm.

- Coaching & Career Connections is an internal program that provides employees with confidential career coaches, self-assessment tests, training courses, and other resources.

The Starting Gate

Undergraduate internships: 1,165

Duration of summer internship: 10 weeks

Average total compensation: $9,400

Interns by grade level:
Freshman 1%
Sophomore 2%
Junior...2%
Senior 53%
College graduate 42%

Interns who receive full-time job offers: 87%

Interns who are extended full-time job offers that accept: 92%

The Sliding Scale

Entry-level hires who had been interns: 88%

Most important performance measurements in entry-level hire: Learning ability, team player, effort

Entry-level hires receiving signing bonuses: 73%

Average entry-level signing bonus: $3,826

Entry-level hires receiving performance bonuses: None

Average performance bonus during first year: N/A

The Stand-Out Perks

- Educational expenses reimbursement ($10,000)

- Full and partial graduate school sponsorship

- Relocation compensation ($10,000)

- Employee discounts on car purchases, computers, and electronics

The Skills

- Two to five days of live, instructor-led orientation and one to three days more that are role-specific

- All Analyst Program for new consultants, which lasts two to six weeks

- Firmwide formal mentorship program for all entry-level employees

The Sound-Off

- "While Deloitte offers a fun internship, it also gives a realistic view of work in public accounting. Many other firms do not." —*Brigham Young senior**

- "Most people, like myself, burn out after three years or so of extremely long hours (especially during the busy season)." —BW *Discussion Forum*

- "It's hard work and often frustrating, but, since joining Deloitte four years ago, my salary has tripled and is likely to triple again in the next 3 to 5 years." —BW *Discussion Forum*

*Data: Universum Communications

THE RECRUITER SPOTLIGHT

Name: Diane L. Borhani
Job: U.S. National Campus Recruiting Leader

Wackiest technique used by a job applicant: *One recruiter had a candidate send a home video in pajamas and his laptop stating why he was the top candidate. In the video, he shared childhood pictures and had his mom say that he was the best candidate out there. No, the person did not get hired.*

Interview tips for readers/faux pas to avoid: *Candidates should always be respectful and polite to everyone they meet throughout the process, from the receptionist to the security staff to the interview teams. The interview and recruiting process is a two-way street, but it is important to remember that you should strive to impress everyone you meet. It is important to display the utmost professionalism in your appearance and in the interactions you have with everyone. Articulating your appreciation for everyone's time and consideration goes a long way.*

Ernst & Young LLP

5 Times Square
New York, NY 10036
Phone: 212-773-3000
Fax: 212-773-6350
Web Addresses: www.ey.com;
www.ey.com/Careers

The Company

- Big Four member Ernst & Young is ranked third in revenue behind PricewaterhouseCoopers and Deloitte Touche Tohmatsu. The firm has offices in 140 countries and brings together a worldwide team of Ernst & Young professionals to provide companies with assurance, tax, transaction, and advisory services. Ernst & Young has implemented a global industry sector strategy, which works to anticipate market trends, identify the implications, and develop points of view on the industry's most demanding issues.

- Ernst & Young is well known for starting the most prestigious entrepreneurial honor in the world, the annual Entrepreneur of the Year award. The competition began in the United States in 1986 and has expanded to 40 countries.

- Ernst & Young is the "Americas area" member firm of Ernst & Young Global Limited. The Americas area Managing Partner is Stephen R. Howe, Jr.

FAST FACTS

"Best Places to Launch a Career"
  Rank: 3
"Best Internships" Rank: 2
Full-Time Salary: $50,000–$54,999
Entry-Level Hires: 3,250
Top College Major: Business
3-Year Retention Rate: 49%
Stock Ticker: N/A (privately owned)

The Suits

James Turley: Chairman and CEO
John Ferraro: COO
Jeffery Dworken: Global Managing Partner of Operations and Finance
Sue Frieden: Global Managing Partner of Quality and Risk Management
Pierre Hurstel: Global Managing Partner of People
Herman Hulst: Global Managing Partner of Client Service and Accounts

The Stats

2007 sales: $21.1 billion
2007 net income: N/A
Market cap: N/A
Employees: 130,000
Locations: 140 countries, with 700 locations in Africa, Asia, Australia, the Caribbean, Europe, and North and South America

Major competitors: Deloitte, PricewaterhouseCoopers, KPMG

Largest operating units: N/A

📖 The Story

1881: A bookkeeper named A. C. Ernst cofounds the firm Ernst & Ernst with his brother Theodore in Cleveland, Ohio

1906: Arthur Young establishes his accounting firm in Chicago, Illinois

1979: The European offices of Arthur Young join several large local European firms, which themselves become member firms of Arthur Young International

1989: The two firms combine to form Ernst & Young

1999: Cendant agrees to pay $2.8 billion and Ernst & Young agrees to pay $335 million to settle a class-action suit for accounting fraud that occurred in April 1998

2000: Ernst & Young sells off its consultancy

2003: Former client HealthSouth deems auditing services negligent; sues the firm for failing to uncover accounting fraud

2006: Mitchell & Titus LLP (the United States' largest minority-owned accounting firm) announces that it will join Ernst & Young as a member firm

2007: After launching the first company-sponsored group on Facebook.com in 2006, Ernst & Young attracts more than 11,000 members to its Facebook group

The Skinny

Most important to recruiters: College major, communication skills, leadership skills

Selectivity: 1 of 3 applicants hired in 2006, up from roughly 1 of 5 applicants hired in 2005

Diversity of entry-level workforce: 35% minority; 50% female

Facts to know:

- Internships culminate in a four-day Leadership Conference, where interns from around the world attend seminars, participate in team-building exercises, and network with firm leaders and their peers.

- Ernst & Young recently reported its best retention rates in the past 10 years. Also, in 2006 over 500 people who had left the firm came back to work at Ernst & Young.

The Starting Gate

Undergraduate internships: 2,245

Duration of summer internship: 8 to 10 weeks

Average total compensation: $9,000

Interns by grade level:
Sophomore 5%
Junior...15%
Senior 55%
College graduate 25%

Interns who receive full-time job offers: 98%

Interns who are extended full-time job offers that accept: 92%

The Sliding Scale

Entry-level hires who had been interns: 40%

Most important performance measurements in entry-level hire: Being a team player, analytical skills, learning ability

Entry-level hires receiving signing bonuses: 75%

Average entry-level signing bonus: $2,250

Entry-level hires receiving performance bonuses: 4%

Average performance bonus during first year: $3,500

The Stand-Out Perks

- Full and partial graduate school sponsorship
- 15 paid vacation days
- Unlimited time off for religious observances and illness
- Charitable gift match ($7,500)
- Firm-initiated relocation compensation
- Employee discounts on car rentals, gym memberships, cell phones/ service, insurance, cultural events, and publications

- Laptops for all professionals, with 24/7 technical assistance
- Concierge service to help manage personal issues, legal concerns, child care, etc.

The Skills

- Formal two-day orientation program
- Formal mentorship program (100% of entry-level hires participate)
- New staff will attend an average of 15 days of formal training their first year

The Sound-Off

- "I learned a lot about the profession during my internship with the company." —*SUNY Binghamton senior**
- "I have worked at Ernst & Young for over nine years now, and I continue to have great opportunities at the firm, as well as opportunities presented outside of the firm. Often people leave their first job too soon! Find a mentor, work hard, and learn as much as you can. Your career is 30 to 40 years long. Don't just 'launch'; ride the wind." —BW *Discussion Forum*

*Data: Universum Communications

THE RECRUITER SPOTLIGHT

Name: Janice Smith
Job: Development Coach and Trainer

What have you done to address the new generation entering the workplace?: *There has been an increasing number of requests from managers who are looking to learn how to coach Generation Y. We have a workshop— it's one of the more popular offerings—introducing the dynamics of the three generations and helping them [managers] appreciate that within three years, Generation Y is going to make up more than half [of the workforce]. What we're doing is helping to build awareness around what this generation needs and values.*

On whether Generation Yers have a groupthink mentality and lack leadership capabilities: *We see the exact opposite. This is a generation, from our perspective, that feels ready to take on challenging leadership roles. They've been in leadership roles long before they even came to our organization. It's important to let them tap into this. We want to ensure that everybody has a voice. We may not accept everyone's ideas and opinions. If everyone feels their ideas and opinions are heard, though, with that level playing field, absolutely, leaders will emerge.*

Grant Thornton LLP

175 W. Jackson Blvd.
Chicago, IL 60604
Phone: 312-856-0001
Fax: 312-565-4719
Web Addresses:
www.grantthornton.com;
www.grantthornton.com/careers

The Company

- Grant Thornton LLP is the U.S. member firm of Grant Thornton International, a global network of independently owned and managed accounting and consulting firms. Grant Thornton International boasts 521 offices in 113 countries and clients in industries including financial services, the global public sector, and technology.

- Based on feedback it gathers from 2,000 of its clients, Grant Thornton LLP issues an annual report that includes how it benchmarks against its top competitors (an independent research firm also surveys Grant Thornton LLP's clients for the same data). Grant Thornton's tax and audit clients ranked the firm ahead of its Big Four competitors in the 2005 results.

- In the wake of accounting-related scandals like Enron, Grant Thornton created a five-point plan on how the firm and its peers should try to restore the public's trust in the accounting profession.

FAST FACTS

"Best Places to Launch a Career"
  Rank: 73
"Best Internships" Rank: N/A
Full-Time Salary: $50,000–$54,999
Entry-Level Hires: 570
Top College Major: Business
3-Year Retention Rate: 77%
Stock Ticker: N/A (privately owned)

The Suits

David C. McDonnell: CEO of Grant Thornton International
Ed Nusbaum: CEO of Grant Thornton LLP
Shelley Stein: COO of Grant Thornton LLP
Fred Walz: CFO of Grant Thornton LLP

The Stats

2007 sales: $3.5 billion (1.1 billon in the U.S.)
2007 net income: N/A
Market cap: N/A
Employees: 27,861 worldwide
Locations: 113 countries, 521 offices worldwide (Grant Thornton LLP has 50 offices in the United States)

Major competitors: Ernst & Young, KPMG, PricewaterhouseCoopers, Deloitte

Largest operating units: N/A

📖 The Story

1924: Alexander Richardson Grant opens Alexander Grant & Co. in Chicago

1961: National Chicago office opens as net revenues surpass $5 million

1969: Alexander Grant & Co. forms an international alliance with British firm Tansley Witt; both firms keep their names, but the larger governing body is called Alexander Grant Tansley Witt

1979: The alliance between Alexander Grant & Co. and Tansley Witt ends when Tansley Witt is acquired by Arthur Andersen

1980: Alexander Grant & Co. and 49 other accounting firms around the world form Grant Thornton International

1985: Grant becomes the nation's ninth-largest accounting firm after a merger with Fox & Co.; the firm also finds itself embroiled in numerous lawsuits this year (and one partner is even sent to jail) when, after its client E.S.M. Government Securities folds, Grant Thornton is accused of falsifying the bankrupt company's financial statements

1986: Alexander Grant & Co. and British firm Thornton Baker change names to Grant Thornton to reflect their affiliation

2002: In the wake of accounting-related scandals like Enron, Grant Thornton creates a five-point plan to help restore faith—and public trust—in the accounting profession

2007: Grant Thornton LLP reports 2007 fiscal year revenue of over $1 billion—up 17% from the prior year's numbers

The Skinny

Most important to recruiters: Leadership skills, work experience, college GPA

Selectivity: N/A

Diversity of entry-level workforce: 27% minority; 51% female

Facts to know:

- LEADS is a learning/leadership development program designed to guide entry-level hires that are fresh out of college from campus to partner. The program provides access to Grant Thornton University online performance and learning tools and business book summaries.

- Entry-level hires must work for at least two years before they are eligible for their first promotion.

- Grant Thornton's 5-year retention rate (76%) is just one percentage point below its 3-year retention rate. 3- and 5-year retention rates far exceed those posted by the Big Four competitors.

The Starting Gate

Undergraduate internships: 379

Duration of summer internship: 10 weeks

Average total compensation: $8,737

Interns by grade level:
Junior...15%
Senior 50%
College graduate 35%

Interns who receive full-time job offers: 97%

Interns who are extended full-time job offers that accept: 87%

The Sliding Scale

Entry-level hires who had been interns: 27%

Most important performance measurements in entry-level hire: Effort, learning ability, organizational skills

Entry-level hires receiving signing bonuses: 65%

Average entry-level signing bonus: $2,356

Entry-level hires receiving performance bonuses: 93%

Average performance bonus during first year: $1,850

The Stand-Out Perks

- 27 paid vacation days

- Educational expenses reimbursement

- Relocation compensation

- 48 days paid maternity leave; 7 days paid paternity leave for birth, adoption, and placement for adoption

The Skills

- Five-day orientation program that includes face-to-face training modules and online- and computer-based training resources

- Entry-level hires have access to a formal leadership program called LEADS

- Formal mentorship program (100% of entry-level hires participate)

The Sound Off

- "What I like most is the people and emphasis on work–life balance. The only con is that entering a firm straight out of undergrad is a big step in regards to the amount of information you must learn and memorize." —*Grant Thornton accountant*

- "The firm attracts fun and interesting people who are able to thrive and excel in a low-stress environment. Given the tedious nature of the world of audit this perk is very much appreciated." —*Grant Thornton consultant*

THE SUPERSTAR SPOTLIGHT

Name: Jarod Allerheiligen

Job: Office Managing Partner—Wichita, Kansas

On keeping the "big picture" in mind: *Each day contains surprises and a variety of operational decisions made on short notice, but I allocate at least 30 minutes each day to thinking about topics that are not of immediate concern to our practice that particular day or month.*

On the importance of flexibility: *I like the flexibility I have in my job. I spend extra time in the morning at home preparing my kids for school, and I also like to go running during a very long lunch hour several times a week. I make up the time at other times of day using the firm's technology to work at home or by BlackBerry someplace else.*

On his personal mantra: *Hard work, humility, discipline, and persistence are, in my view, the key traits that have helped me. There are no secrets to success as far as I am concerned.*

On how to define a leader: *You do not have to be president of an organization or captain of a team to be a leader. Nobody has to appoint you a leader, either. Anyone at any level of an organization or a team can be a leader. Be the person others look to in times of crisis, or the person who is sought after for his views on events of importance. That is what Grant Thornton is looking for in young people. People who are not afraid to think independently and act accordingly with confidence are the true leaders.*

KPMG LLP

345 Park Ave.
New York, NY 10154
Phone: 212-758-9700
Fax: 212-758-9819
Web Addresses: www.kpmg.com;
www.kpmgcampus.com/campus/

The Company

- KPMG may be the smallest of the Big Four accounting firms (in terms of revenue, at least), but it is still a giant by most standards: With over 120,000 employees worldwide (and 22,000 in the United States specifically), KPMG has hired 2,500 new U.S. college graduates annually for the past few years.

- Founded after the merger of Peat Marwick International and Klynveld Main Goerdeler in 1987, KPMG International, a Swiss cooperative, consists of a sprawling network of firms in 145 countries that provide audit, tax, and advisory services to clients in various industries, including media, pharmaceutical, and banking. It is structured into three operating regions: the Americas; Asia/Pacific; and Europe, Middle East, and Africa.

- KPMG spun off its consulting practice, KPMG Consulting, in 2000. The resulting company, Bearing-Point is also profiled among our "Best Places to Launch a Career."

FAST FACTS

"Best Places to Launch a Career"
  Rank: 11
"Best Internships" Rank: 5
Full-Time Salary: $50,000–$54,999
Entry-Level Hires: 2,962
Top College Major: Business
3-Year Retention Rate: 59%
Stock Ticker: N/A (privately owned)

The Suits

Timothy P. Flynn: Chairman of KPMG International
Michael P. Wareing: CEO of KPMG International
John B. Harrison: Chairman of KPMG's Asia/Pacific region
Timothy P. Flynn: Chairman of KPMG's Americas region
Ben van der Veer: Chairman of KPMG's Europe, Middle East, and Africa region

The Stats

2007 sales: $19.8 billion ($5.4 billion in the United States)
Net income: N/A
Market cap: N/A
Employees: 123,000 (22,000 in the United States)
Locations: 145 countries
Major competitors: Deloitte, PricewaterhouseCoopers, Ernst & Young

Largest operating units:*

Audit ....$9.4 billion
($2.6 billion in U.S.)
Tax ....$4.0 billion
($1.2 billion in U.S.)
Advisory ....$6.4 billion
($1.5 billion in U.S.)

*2007 sales

 The Story

1870: William Barclay Peat joins the Robert Fletcher & Co. accounting firm in London

1891: Robert Fletcher & Co. changes name to William Barclay Peat & Co.

1897: New York City accounting firm Marwick, Mitchell & Co. is founded by James Marwick and Roger Mitchell

1911: William Barclay Peat & Co. and Marwick, Mitchell & Co. merge to form what will later be known as Peat Marwick International

1987: KPMG is founded after a merger between Peat Marwick International (PMI) and Klynveld Main Goerdeler (KMG)

2002: The federal government files suit against KPMG for its cooperation in arranging tax shelters for customers involving the posting of artificial losses to reduce their taxes

2005: Though neither admitting nor denying the allegations made by the Securities and Exchange Commission (SEC), KPMG agrees to a $22.5 million settlement with the SEC related to former client Xerox's improper accounting

from 1997 to 2000, in what at the time was the biggest financial settlement between an auditor and a regulator

2007: Timothy Flynn succeeds Sir Michael Rake as chairman of KPMG International

The Skinny

Most important to recruiters: College major, college GPA, communication skills

Selectivity: 1 of every 3 applicants hired in 2006, roughly the same as in 2005

Diversity of entry-level workforce: 33% minority; 49% female

Facts to know:

• In 2007, KPMG increased its allotted number of internships by more than 350 slots.

• A national intern training program is held each winter and summer to help prepare students for successful internships; interns are also sent abroad for a four-week International Intern Exchange Program.

The Starting Gate

Undergraduate internships: 1,871

Duration of summer internship: 8 to 10 weeks

Average total compensation: $8,550

Interns by grade level:
Freshman 1%
Sophomore 1%
Junior...1%
Senior 50%
College graduate 47%

Interns who receive full-time job offers:
95%

Interns who are extended full-time job offers that accept: 87%

The Sliding Scale

Entry-level hires who had been interns: 71%

Most important performance measurements in entry-level hire: Analytical skills, learning ability, team player

Entry-level hires receiving signing bonuses: 69%

Average entry-level signing bonus: $2,848

Entry-level hires receiving performance bonuses: 10%

Average performance bonus during first year: $3,500

The Stand-Out Perks

- 25 paid vacation days

- Educational expenses reimbursement ($8,511 on average per employee in 2006)

- Offices close at 3 p.m. on Fridays in the summer and 5-day July 4 weekend

- In addition to their annual pension, new hires below manager level receive a one-time $5,000 pension credit that vests after 5 years

The Skills

- Two-day orientation that includes computer training, guest speakers, diversity exercises, team-building exercises, and facilities tour

- Audit, Tax, and Advisory new hires expected to attend core curriculum of courses to prepare them for supervisory responsibilities

- Formal mentorship program (100% of entry-level hires participate)

The Sound-Off

- "Experienced personnel are always willing to provide a word of advice and encouragement to younger professionals." —*Young employee*

- "There are many opportunities for cross-functional rotations; if I wanted to move over to the tax practice from audit, or vice versa, I could. You're not locked into one discipline." —*Young employee*

- "I'm able to balance my personal life. A flexible schedule not only makes my life less stressful, but also enables me to be more efficient at work." —*Young employee*

THE ENTRY-LEVEL SPOTLIGHT

Name: Jennifer Ross
Job: Tax Associate

Perks of the job: *Very cool benefits. Cake Day, hot breakfast every Friday, happy hours, incredible vacation package, gift baskets sent to your doorstop, ACC tournament party every year . . . they know we work hard, so they make a big effort to compensate for it.*

Wacky workplace behavior: *One weird thing is how well you get to know your cube neighbors and the funny things you experience, whether it's overhearing someone plan a birthday party for her dog or doing lunges down the hall late at night when you need a break. We laugh and joke constantly.*

Why choose KPMG: *The opportunities here at KPMG are endless. There are many different specializations and offices all over the world, and each employee is encouraged to find his or her best fit. I also believe the well-known clients contribute to the company being a top entry-level employer. You are treated well, and I think word has gotten out.*

Briefly describe the firm's culture: *The work culture at KPMG is what drew me to the company. I have built great relationships with many coworkers. The leaders of the firm truly care for the staff and take an interest in our careers. Open communication is a key component of the culture here; my supervisors encourage me to speak up if there is a problem or if I am unhappy with a particular situation or project I'm working on. There is a lot of flexibility, as long as you get your work done. That's what matters.*

PricewaterhouseCoopers

PricewaterhouseCoopers LLP
300 Madison Ave.
24th Floor
New York, NY 10017
Phone: 646-471-4000
Fax: 813-286-6000
Web Addresses: www.pwc.com;
www.pwc.tv

The Company

- Gaining its full multisyllabic name after a 1998 merger, PricewaterhouseCoopers (PwC) generates the most revenue of the Big Four firms.

- The accounting giant operates throughout the United States, and its global organization has member firms in 150 countries.

- PwC offers assurance, business advisory, and tax services to major corporations in a wide variety of industries and to entities within the public sector.

- For the past two years, PwC has engaged in a "Month of Community" during June. Nearly 30,000 U.S. partners and staff have pitched in over 100,000 volunteer hours to community service projects. The firm looks to continue the initiative in June 2008.

FAST FACTS

"Best Places to Launch a Career"
  Rank: 2
"Best Internships" Rank: N/A
Full-Time Salary: $50,000–$54,999
Entry-Level Hires: 3,744
Top College Major: Business
3-Year Retention Rate: 58%
Stock Ticker: N/A (privately owned)

The Suits

Samuel A. DiPiazza, Jr.: Global CEO
Dennis Nally: U.S. Chairman and
  Senior Partner
Robert Moritz: U.S. Assurance Leader
Rick Stamm: U.S. Tax Leader
Juan Pujadas: U.S. Advisory Leader

The Stats*

2007 revenues: $7.5 billion
2006 net income: N/A
Market cap: N/A
Employees: 31,631 (as of June 30, 2007)
Locations: Offices located throughout the United States, with member firms in 150 countries
Major competitors: Deloitte, Ernst & Young, KPMG, McKinsey, Accenture
Largest operating units: N/A
*Data: PwC USA

The Story

1849: Samuel Lowell Price sets up a financial services business in London

1854: William Cooper establishes his own practice in London, which seven years later becomes Cooper Brothers

1865: Price, William Hopkins Holyland, and Edwin Waterhouse join forces in partnership

1874: Holyland drops out of the partnership, and the firm's name changes to Price, Waterhouse and Co.

1898: Robert H. Montgomery, William M. Lybrand, Adam A. Ross Jr., and his brother T. Edward Ross form Lybrand, Ross Brothers, and Montgomery

1957: Cooper Brothers and Co. (U.K.-based), McDonald, Currie, and Co. (Canada-based), and Lybrand, Ross Brothers, and Montgomery (U.S.-based) are merged to form Coopers and Lybrand

1982: Price Waterhouse World Firm is formed

1990: Coopers and Lybrand merges with Deloitte, Haskins, and Sells in a number of countries around the world

1998: Worldwide merger of Price Waterhouse and Coopers and Lybrand creates the firm currently known as PricewaterhouseCoopers

2002: PricewaterhouseCoopers' partners approve the sale of PricewaterhouseCoopers Consulting to IBM

2007: Agrees to pay $225 million to settle a class-action lawsuit brought by Tyco International shareholders in response to the alleged management fraud uncovered at Tyco in 2002. (PwC was its auditor.)

The Skinny

Most important to recruiters: College major, college GPA, communication skills

Selectivity: 1 of 7 applicants hired in 2006, down from 1 of 6 applicants hired in 2005

Diversity of entry-level workforce: 37% minority; 50% female

Facts to know:

- Prospective hires are given a behavioral-based interview to determine whether they possess PwC's 10 core competencies (which range from contributing to team success to demonstrating change agility).

- PwC's Internship Development Program, which is run through the Disney Institute, provides interns with a four-day curriculum tailored specifically to PwC's environment.

The Starting Gate

Undergraduate internships: 2,807

Duration of summer internship: 8 to 10 weeks

Average total compensation: $9,800

Interns by grade level:
Sophomore 2%
Junior...5%
Senior 70%
College graduate 23%

Interns who receive full-time job offers: 88%

Interns who are extended full-time job offers that accept: 87%

The Sliding Scale

Entry-level hires who had been interns: 41%

Most important performance measurements in entry-level hire: Performance against 10 internal core competencies

Entry-level hires receiving signing bonuses: 89%

Average entry-level signing bonus: $3,300

Entry-level hires receiving performance bonuses: 47%

Average performance bonus during first year: $3,600

The Stand-Out Perks

- Educational expenses reimbursement ($10,000)

- Full and partial graduate school sponsorship

- Charitable gift match ($7,500)

- 15 to 22 paid vacation days

- 12 to 18 weeks of paid maternity leave

The Skills

- 15-day orientation program

- Genesis Park, a professional development program, which lasts 22 weeks and includes a five-month residency program in Washington, D.C., or Berlin

- Formal mentorship program (100% of entry-level hires participate)

The Sound-Off

- "The [internship] training is so in-depth, hands-on, and they really care. We go to Disney World to interact with students all over the country." —*Bryant University junior**

- "The most competitive internship to get accepted to. You are treated as a staff employee." —*SUNY Binghamton junior**

- "There is nothing fun about working 12-hour days for $45,000 a year!" —BW *Discussion Forum*

- "PwC claims that 100% of its new hires work in 'open workspaces.' If you consider a four-person windowless conference room an open workspace, then I guess this could be somewhat accurate." —BW *Discussion Forum*

- "I interned at PwC, and I had a great experience. I learned a lot, and I had a great team. But your experience really does depend on the team that you are in." —BW *Discussion Forum*

*Data: Universum Communications

THE ENTRY-LEVEL SPOTLIGHT

Name: Penelope Moreno
Job: Assurance Associate

Describe your interview process: *I started a little earlier and went on dozens of interviews. I just wanted to make sure I had many options. What made PwC the overall winner was its reputation, [and] also its devotion and commitment to its people. Even in the campus activities that we had, it was on a whole different level.*

Briefly describe your current position, work environment, etc.: *I'm an assurance associate, [working] mostly [in] audit. I work in the technology group. My main client is IBM. What gets me excited is the people I work with. We make sure that we have fun. I also appreciate the diversity of the firm. I don't mean only color and gender—two important things—but diversity in beliefs and points of view. [In] the group of people I work with now, many are 30 years my senior, and [they are] from Denmark, Brazil, France, and more.*

Accenture

1345 Avenue of the Americas
New York, NY 10105
Phone: 917-452-4400
Fax: 917-527-9915
Web Addresses: www.accenture.com;
www.careers.accenture.com

The Company

- Accenture is the largest consulting firm in the world. The company, which also provides technology and outsourcing services, employs approximately 175,000 people in 49 countries and posted $19.7 billion in revenue for the 2007 fiscal year ending August 31, 2007.

- The firm is looking to expand its international presence even further; it is setting its sights on markets in India, and hopes to increase its number of employees there by 30%.

- The firm, once the consulting arm of professional services giant Andersen Worldwide Société Coopérative (AWSC), officially changed its name to Accenture in 2001 after it broke with AWSC (see timeline for more details).

- Accenture's worldwide headquarters is in Hamilton, Bermuda (one of its stateside office addresses is provided in the information above).

FAST FACTS

"Best Places to Launch a Career"
  Rank: 8
"Best Internships" Rank: 16
Full-Time Salary: $55,000–$59,999
Entry-Level Hires: 1,040
Top College Major: Engineering
Relocation Expenses Reimbursed: Yes
Stock Ticker: ACN

The Suits

William D. Green: Chairman and
  CEO
Stephen J. Rohleder: COO
Pamela J. Craig: CFO

The Stats

2007 sales: $19.7 billion
2007 net income: $1.2 billion
Market cap: $27.3 billion
Employees: 175,000
Locations: Americas, Asia Pacific, Europe, Middle East, Africa
Major competitors: BearingPoint, McKinsey, IBM Global Services
Largest operating units:
Products ....$4.9 billion
Communications and
  High Tech ....$4.6 billion
Financial Services ....$4.4 billion
Resources ....$3.2 billion
Public Service ....$2.6 billion

The Story

1913: Arthur Andersen is founded in Chicago

1989: Andersen Consulting is officially established

1991: Andersen Consulting is hired by BP Exploration for one of its first major outsourcing assignments

1997: Andersen Consulting formally requests arbitration to sever all contractual ties to AWSC, charging that its parent company has failed to honor a noncompete arrangement that would ensure that its members weren't going up against Andersen Consulting for business

1999: Joe W. Forehand becomes CEO

2000: Arbitration is settled; Andersen Consulting and AWSC officially sever ties

2001: Andersen Consulting is renamed Accenture on January 1; Accenture becomes a public company and is listed on the NYSE in July

2004: William D. Green becomes CEO

2005: Accenture purchases North American healthcare practice Capgemini, as well as Media Audits, a leader in the measurement of return on advertising investments

2006: Purchases life insurance software provider NaviSys, consulting firm Random Walk, and leading IT firm Pecasso

2007: Acquires strategy consulting firm The George Group, defense consulting firm Gestalt LLC, workforce performance capability company H.B. Maynard & Co., and Corliant, a consulting firm that focuses on enterprise networking services and capabilities

The Skinny

Most important to recruiters: College major, college GPA, analytical skills

Selectivity: 1 of 10 applicants hired in 2007 and 2006

Diversity of entry-level workforce: N/A% minority; 41% female

Facts to know:

- Rising senior interns attend a 3-day leadership conference, which includes team-building exercises, networking opportunities, panel discussions, and presentations.

- All employees are assigned a career counselor, who conducts biannual meetings with the individual and offers guidance throughout the year.

- Accenture has a St. Charles, Illinois, campus dedicated to employee retreats, orientation, and training. Entry-level hires spend 2 weeks of their 5-week orientation in St. Charles.

The Starting Gate

Undergraduate internships: 183

Duration of summer internship: 10 to 12 weeks

Average total compensation: $9,400

Interns by grade level:
Junior 22%
Senior 78%

Interns who receive full-time job offers: 91%

Interns who are extended full-time job offers that accept: 71%

 ## The Sliding Scale

Entry-level hires who had been interns: 6%

Most important performance measurements in entry-level hire: Quality, analytical skills, learning ability

Entry-level hires receiving signing bonuses: 55%

Average entry-level signing bonus: $3,767

Entry-level hires receiving performance bonuses: 85%

Average performance bonus during first year: $1,500

The Stand-Out Perks

- 25 paid vacation days
- Relocation compensation
- Charitable gift match ($5,000)
- Employee discount program

The Skills

- 25-day orientation program
- Formal mentorship program (100% of entry-level hires participate)

The Sound-Off

- "The [internship] program was very formal and well organized. Also, they allow you to become part of the team with client interaction, social events, etc." —*University of Iowa senior*

- "A strong achievement culture that ensures those who can't keep up don't stick around." —*Anonymous Accenture employee*

- "Sixty-to-90 hour work weeks are not uncommon. Good place to get a start, but be ready to bust it." —*Anonymous Accenture employee*

- "Everyone new and experienced is assigned a career counselor, an upper-level manager who serves as a mentor. In addition, the company invests millions of dollars each year to send its employees to its training center in Illinois and has a vast amount of training materials online. The roles are often stressful … but as a place to start your career, the experiences gained here can't be beat." —*Accenture employee*

*Data: Universum Communications

THE RECRUITER SPOTLIGHT

Name: John Campagnino
Job: Global Director of Recruitment

Most inappropriate interview behavior: *When hiring for some of our roles, we do behavioral interviews. They're a great opportunity for candidates to tell us about themselves and something that happened in their past. A lot of times what happens is that people come in and are asked questions, and they relate these intensely personal stories. It's a little bit frightening and awkward, and so fantastically inappropriate for a business setting. Use your judgment when you're relating things from your past.*

Tips on how to recover from an interview faux pas: *We all live very connected, busy lives. All of our interviewers have been in similar situations—real life does interrupt sometimes. Turn your phone off, and apologize if you need to. However, if you were being interviewed and your cell phone went off and you proceeded to have a conversation, then that would be a problem. It's all how you handle it.*

Ultimate do/don't in applying to your company: *It's all about judgment, the judgment about what kind of stories to relate and how to act; it all comes down to good business etiquette. Also, people should take the opportunity to understand the company's background and what the company they're interviewing with does. Accenture does so many things, and we give people every opportunity to understand how we make money and to learn about the diversity of opportunities that exist within the organization, as well as our commitment to diversity and inclusion and corporate citizenship. So do make sure you have a good understanding of the organization you're interviewing with.*

BearingPoint

1676 International Dr.
McLean, VA 22102
Phone: 703-747-3000
Fax: 703-747-3215
Web Addresses:
www.bearingpoint.com;
www.bearingpoint.com/careers

The Company

- The former consulting arm of accounting powerhouse KPMG, BearingPoint was spun off from its parent company in 2000. This global management and IT consulting firm now assists clients in managing technology transitions and with regulatory compliance issues.

- Although it provides regulatory compliance consulting services, since 2004 BearingPoint itself has continually filed its financial reports months late. Its lack of transparency—along with recent bonds it has defaulted on—may be why BearingPoint's stock price hit a record low in September 2007.

- Change may be in the air: on December 3, 2007, BearingPoint filed its Form 10-Q for the third quarter of 2007, making it up-to-date in its SEC periodic reports. BearingPoint also named a new president and CEO, F. Edwin Harbach, an industry veteran.

FAST FACTS

"Best Places to Launch a Career"
  Rank: 83
"Best Internships" Rank: 38
Full-Time Salary: $45,000–$49,999
Entry-Level Hires: 1,344
Top College Major: Business
Dress Code: Business casual
Stock Ticker: BE

The Suits

Roderick C. McGeary: Chairman
F. Edwin Harbach: President and CEO
Judy A. Ethell: Executive VP and CFO
Christopher M. Formant: Executive VP of Global Financial Services

The Stats*

2007 sales: $2.6 billion
2007 net income: –$375 million
Market cap: $978.7 million
Employees: 17,000+
Locations: 37 countries worldwide
Major competitors: Accenture, Deloitte, CGI Group Inc., Perot Systems Corp.
Largest operating units†:
Consulting Services ....$2.6 billion
*Preliminary 2007 results
†2007 sales

The Story

1987: KPMG is founded when Peat Marwick International (PMI) and Klynveld Main Goerdeler (KMG) merge

2000: Amid growing concerns that providing auditing and consulting services for the same client creates conflicts of interest, many accounting firms spin off their consulting practices; KPMG Consulting splits from KPMG

2001: KPMG Consulting goes public on the NYSE; it's renamed Bearing-Point in 2002 and starts trading under ticker BE

2005: Former Oracle CFO Harry L. You is brought on board as CEO to try to fix BearingPoint's tangled financial operations

2005: SEC launches investigation into BearingPoint's accounting practices

2006: BearingPoint partners with Google to create search solutions to help organizations find internal data more easily

2006: A New York court finds BearingPoint in default on $200 million in bonds

2007: Wins a $20 million contract to help the Kosovo government strengthen its economy

2007: Awarded $50 million contract for new Missouri motor vehicle technology project

The Skinny

Most important to recruiters: College major, analytical skills, communication skills

Selectivity: N/A

Diversity of entry-level workforce: N/A% minority; 40% female

Facts to know:

- BearingPoint began expanding its campus recruiting efforts to double its number of campus hires in 2007.

- In a collaborative effort with the Yale School of Management, called the "BearingPoint Leadership Program," BearingPoint creates real-world-relevant courses that its employees can take at Yale's New Haven campus.

- New entry-level consultants, for example, are enrolled in a one-week foundations' course through the program.

- Courses are taught by various Yale faculty members, high-ranking BearingPoint professionals, and other instructors.

The Starting Gate

Undergraduate internships: 50

Duration of summer internship: 10 to 12 weeks

Average total compensation: $9,000

Interns by grade level:
Junior..20%
Senior 80%

Interns who receive full-time job offers: 90%

Interns who are extended full-time job offers that accept: 90%

The Sliding Scale

Entry-level hires who had been interns: 5%

Most important performance measurements in entry-level hire: Team player, analytical skills, customer satisfaction

Entry-level hires receiving signing bonuses: N/A

Average entry-level signing bonus: N/A

Entry-level hires receiving performance bonuses: N/A

Average performance bonus during first year: N/A

The Stand-Out Perks

• 20 paid vacation days

• Relocation compensation

• Health plan option of $2,000 annual rolling deposit by company on employee's behalf to be used for medical expenses

• Employee discount program

The Skills

• Two-day orientation program

• One-week BearingPoint Leadership Program at the Yale School of Management

• Formal mentorship program (100% of entry-level hires participate)

THE RECRUITER SPOTLIGHT

Name: Eric Lowery-North

Job: Senior Manager—Campus Recruiting Solutions

Applicants behaving badly: *I have been a witness to some serious examples of poor judgment. Our out-of-town recruits always stay at a hotel the night before their visit, and one gentleman decided to bring his fiancée. The two of them proceeded to take advantage of spa treatments, massages, dry cleaning, and room service. They even cleaned out the minibar and took the bathrobes. Another time two recruits decided to meet some friends in the city at one of the local bars after an icebreaker dinner with BearingPoint employees before their office interview day. When we started at 9 a.m. the next morning, they were missing. After an hour of trying room and cell numbers, we had hotel security enter their rooms. They were passed out under the covers and arrived looking green and reeking of alcohol. I pulled them aside, ended their interviews, and sent them back to their school.*

Advice to students interested in consulting: *Consulting is projected to be one of the fastest-growing industries for the next several years. . . . Taking part in our Summer Internship Program is an invaluable experience in helping determine if consulting is the career for you.*

Worst interview faux pas: *Getting the company name wrong is the most serious offense. If a candidate has not done enough homework on the company to get the name right, that is a major problem. With regard to arriving late, I can understand if there is an extenuating circumstance like illness, a car accident, or a family emergency. I would recommend calling the career services office so that you are able to get the message to the recruiter. However, daily traffic and parking issues on campus are not an excuse. A student should be well aware of these issues. Plan ahead. A ringing cell phone is more of an annoyance than a major faux pas. However, not shutting it off prior to an interview may be considered a lack of attention to detail by some recruiters. Unless you are on an organ recipient list or are an expectant parent, the cell phone should be turned off.*

Why choose BearingPoint: *If you want to sit in a cubicle and be part of a nameless pack, we are not the company for you. But if you are someone who has a passion for ideas, client service, challenging work, and results, then BearingPoint is the best place for you to start your career.*

Booz Allen Hamilton

8283 Greensboro Dr.
McLean, VA 22102
Phone: 703-902-5000
Fax: 703-902-3333
Web Addresses: www.boozallen.com;
www.boozallen.com/careers

The Company

- In 1914, Booz Allen Hamilton founder Edwin Booz created the field of management consulting when, upon realizing that companies would benefit from the services of someone who could provide them with outside, expert, and impartial advice, he opened his practice.

- Clients of the global strategy and technology consulting firm range from leading commercial corporations to government agencies and institutions. Booz Allen provides services in strategy, organization, operations, systems, and technology.

- Recent Booz Allen consulting gigs have included the restructuring of Vodafone, Mediaset's transformation to digital technology, and the reorganization of the U.S. Air Force systems.

- As of spring 2008, Booz Allen was evaluating a strategic opportunity that would enable separation of its global commercial and U.S. government businesses. If a strategic separation of the firm comes to pass,

Booz Allen's commercial business will become a separate company and Booz Allen Hamilton, Inc., will focus exclusively on the U.S. government business. No further details about a possible transaction have been released as of April 1, 2008.

The Suits

Ralph W. Shrader: Chairman and CEO
Douglas G. Swenson: VP and CFO
Horacio Rozanski: VP and Chief Personnel Officer
Shumeet Banerji: President of European Business
Dennis O. Doughty: President of U.S. Government Business
Cesare R. Mainardi: President of North American Commercial Business

The Stats

2007 sales: $4.1 billion
2007 net income: N/A

Market cap: N/A

Employees: 19,000 (17,000 in the United States)

Locations: Operations in 100 offices on six continents

Major competitors: Accenture, BearingPoint, McKinsey

Largest operating units: N/A

The Story

1914: Edwin Booz creates a new industry, management consulting, when he establishes *The Business Research Service* in Chicago, with the aim of providing expert, impartial advice to organizations in need of outside feedback

1925: George W. Fry joins as the firm's second employee

1929: James L. Allen joins as the company's third employee; clients include Goodyear Tire & Rubber, the *Chicago Tribune*, and Montgomery Ward

1940: The secretary of the navy enlists Booz to help prepare the U.S. Navy for war; Booz and Fry clash over the future of the company's government consultancy; Fry eventually leaves to start his own firm

1947: The firm signs its first U.S. Air Force contract—the "Wright Field Job"

1976: After having gone public six years earlier, Booz Allen partners buy back all stock, return the firm to private ownership, and relocate their headquarters to New York City

1987: The firm secures a $100 million contract with NASA

2003: Purchases Gemini Consulting Japan (GCJ) and in doing so doubles the size of its Tokyo office

2007: Booz Allen returns to its traditional structure of government, commercial, and international markets

The Skinny

Most important to recruiters: Communication skills, analytical skills, college major

Selectivity: 1 of 13 applicants hired in 2006, up from 1 in 17 applicants hired in 2005

Diversity of entry-level workforce: N/A

Facts to know:

- Booz Allen may hire its fair share of business majors (26%) for entry-level positions, but techies are also in demand. A full 25% of entry-level hires are computer science majors.

- Booz Allen has developed a Flex-Work Forum that provides employees with information on the appropriate balance and use of its various flexible work options, which include job sharing and part-time employment.

The Starting Gate

Undergraduate internships: 110

Duration of summer internship: 8 weeks

Average total compensation: N/A

Interns by grade level:

Freshman 12%
Sophomore 23%
Junior..55%
Senior 5%
College graduate 5%

Interns who receive full-time job offers: 35%

Interns who are extended full-time job offers that accept: 34%

The Sliding Scale

Entry-level hires who had been interns: 10%

Most important performance measurements in entry-level hire: Analytical skills, enthusiasm, learning ability

Entry-level hires receiving signing bonuses: N/A

Average entry-level signing bonus: N/A

Entry-level hires receiving performance bonuses: None

Average performance bonus during first year: N/A

The Stand-Out Perks

- Educational expenses reimbursement ($5,000)

- 16 paid days off

- 401(k) contribution equal to 10% of salary, whether employee makes contribution or not

- 40 paid days of maternity leave; 5 paid days of paternity leave

- Employee discounts on cell phones/service, insurance, car rentals, and gym memberships.

The Skills

- Three-day orientation program that includes team-building exercises, a tour of the facilities, computer training, and guest speakers

- Formal mentorship program (100% of entry-level hires participate)

The Sound-Off

- "With internships, Booz Allen doesn't discriminate based on your year in school, unlike most companies." —*University of Virginia sophomore**

- "On the Strategy side, Booz Allen can be an awesome place to work. Small teams, loosely defined roles, great brand, interesting work, and easygoing people who hide their Type A personality well make it a lot of fun and a great place to start a career. However, the Consultant program is small, and the learning curve can be steep. Also, since the larger firm is more focused on transformational government work, there's limited budget and less focus on the flashy social aspects that you hear of at other top consulting firms. Overall, great people, great work, great brand, but less glitz." — *Young Booz Allen employee*

*Data: Universum Communications

THE ENTRY-LEVEL SPOTLIGHT

Name: Mimi Harrington
Job: Administrative Professional

Best thing about the job: *As a member of the Community Relations Team, I am able to be involved in many volunteer-driven activities and outreach programs. I'm fortunate to be a part of helping to allocate resources to organizations that help the community. A percentage of my job involves working on the Community Relations Web site, and I've become more "tech savvy" with the aid of training and resources provided by the firm.*

Weirdest/funniest thing encountered at work: *While not necessarily weird or funny, it was unusual to be recruited for a fashion show for an upcoming administrative professionals conference within my first week at the firm. The purpose of the show was to demonstrate work-appropriate attire for the summer. It was unexpected but fun, and it introduced me to many colleagues in a relaxed and informal atmosphere.*

Advice on how an ambitious young professional can get noticed: *Although it is a large company, Booz Allen is structured to recognize and reward individuals. In my opinion, the environment gives a motivated, hard-working individual every opportunity to achieve his or her full potential.*

Navigant Consulting

615 N. Wabash Ave.
Chicago, IL 60611
Phone: 1-800-621-8390
Fax: 312-573-5678
Web Address:
www.navigantconsulting.com

The Company

- Navigant Consulting attends to clients' conflict, performance, and risk issues by combining legal know-how with economic, accounting, technical and industry-specific support. Many of Navigant's corporate clients are in the construction, energy, financial services, insurance, and healthcare industries.

- While Navigant is feeling the effects of the down market, one issue having a negative impact on some businesses' bottom line could, in fact, benefit the company: subprime. Analysts speculate that the company's litigation branches will pick up many new cases in 2008 as a result of the debacle. Navigant also announced plans in fall 2007 to "realign" organizational responsibilities, implementing a more structured system of accountability in real estate management projects.

- Effective January 1, 2007, Navigant created a tuition grant program that provides up to $50,000 in grants to cover employee graduate program pursuits.

FAST FACTS

"Best Places to Launch a Career"
  Rank: 94
"Best Internships" Rank: 49
Full-Time Salary: $50,000–$54,999
Entry-Level Hires: 99
Top College Major: Business
3-Year Retention Rate: 32%
Stock Ticker: NCI

The Suits

William M. Goodyear: Chairman and CEO
Julie M. Howard: President and COO
Scott J. Krentz: Executive VP and CFO
Richard X. Fischer: VP, General Counsel, and Secretary
Jeffrey H. Stoecklein: VP of Corporate Development

The Stats

2007 sales: $767.1 million
2007 net income: $33.4 million
Market cap: $661.6 million
Employees: 2,539
Locations: Offices in 40 cities in North America, Europe, and Asia, including New York, London, Montreal, Hong Kong, and Shanghai; also, offices throughout Latin America, the Caribbean, and India
Major competitors: Huron Consulting, Gartner, CRP International

Largest operating units*:
North American Dispute and
Investigative Services
...............................$324.7 million
North American Business
Consulting Services ..$379.2 million
International Consulting
Operations ....$63.2 million
*2007 sales

The Story

1996: The Metzler Group, a financial
services company, goes public

1996–1999: Metzler acquires a number of subsidiaries, including Peterson
Consulting and Barrington Consulting
Group

1999: The Metzler Group changes its
name to Navigant Consulting, Inc.

2001: Acquires Chambers Associates,
LLC (based in Washington, D.C.), a
public policy consulting firm that specializes in asbestos and bankruptcy
cases

2002–2007: Acquires several complementary firms, including Barrington
Energy Partners and the Hunter Group
(a health-care provider management
consultancy)

The Skinny

Most important to recruiters: Analytical skills, college major, communication skills

Selectivity: N/A

Diversity of entry-level workforce: 5%
minority; 40% female

Facts to know:

- Navigant seeks out solid research
  skills, flexibility, creativity, a high
  level of motivation, analytical and
  organizational skills, and a strong
  ability to work in teams in an ideal
  entry-level candidate.

- Navigant contributes to nonprofit
  organizations that its employees and
  clients are passionate about through
  its foundation, Navigant Consulting Lending A Hand.

The Starting Gate

Undergraduate internships: 64

Duration of summer internship: 10
weeks

Average total compensation: N/A

2006 interns by grade level:
Sophomore 10%
Junior..79%
Senior 8%
College graduate 3%

Interns who receive full-time job offers:
80%

**Interns who are extended full-time job
offers that accept:** N/A

The Sliding Scale

Entry-level hires who had been interns: 13%

Most important performance measurements in entry-level hire: Profitability/margin, sales/revenue, productivity/efficiency

Entry-level hires receiving signing bonuses: 100%

Average entry-level signing bonus: $3,000

Entry-level hires receiving performance bonuses: N/A

Average performance bonus during first year: N/A

The Stand-Out Perks

- Educational expenses reimbursement ($5,250)

- Tuition grant program that provides up to $50,000 in grants to cover employee graduate program pursuits

- Child/elderly care program, in which dependents of Navigant employees receive planned or emergency care program options

- Salary advance of up to $3,000 on top of a new hire's signing bonus to assist with relocation expenses

The Skills

- Two-day formal orientation program, including computer training, tour of the facilities, and guest speakers

The Sound-Off

- "Being part of this company for more than two years, I can safely vouch for the fact that this is a great place to start your career. The work environment is fantastic, the opportunities are many and diverse, and the outlook is one of sustained yet sure growth." —*Navigant employee; BW Discussion Forum*

- "I was surprised at how much fun I continuously have at work. . . . Navigant's culture is 'work hard, play hard' . . . collegial, energetic, entrepreneurial, fast-paced, open, and flexible. The access that you have to your managing directors and directors is really unique." —*Navigant senior consultant*

THE SUPERSTAR SPOTLIGHT

Name: Elizabeth Wegert
Job: Senior Consultant

Briefly describe a typical day: *On the whole, it usually involves connecting with your team or engagement leader on the goals for the day or week. Most of my day is spent on the given task or analysis at hand. As a new hire, I spent a lot of time sitting with my superiors so that I could fully engage and learn all that I could to effectively contribute to the project.*

Best part of the job: *The coolest thing about my job as a consultant at NCI is the variety of projects and industries I have been able to work on in just two years. Further, I genuinely enjoy the people that I work with. The team dynamics and collaboration really make work enjoyable and fun.*

Why choose Navigant: *The diversity of opportunities it affords its professionals. We have seven distinct practice areas, [which give new hires] the opportunity . . . to explore engagements in a multitude of practice areas and industries. Navigant's culture is youthful and energetic, [which] eases [their] transition into the professional world. New hires are able to contribute to engagements from day one. Mentorship is also a key component of our culture and is particularly critical in acclimating to the professional working environment.*

Career advice: *The key to getting noticed at Navigant is having a positive attitude and a strong willingness to learn. Engagement leaders really appreciate a team player, openness, and flexibility. When you are able to say that you gave 110% effort, you will definitely get noticed.*

Protiviti

2884 Sand Hill Rd.
Menlo Park, CA 94025
Phone: 650-234-6000
Fax: 650-234-6998
Web Address: www.protiviti.com

The Company

- Although Protiviti's executive headquarters is a stone's throw from Silicon Valley, accounting (not technology) is the fledgling firm's bread and butter. Protiviti, the youngest employer on our list; is the product of staffing firm Robert Half International's desire to move into the consulting industry. Robert Half started Protiviti, which is one of the company's wholly owned subsidiaries, when, on May 23, 2002, the company struck a deal to hire 760 employees from scandal-plagued Arthur Andersen's audit and business-risk consulting practice and then formed a new wholly owned subsidiary called Protiviti.

- Protiviti provides internal audit, business, and technology-risk consulting services, and its rapid growth has largely been the product of a greater demand for internal audit and business-risk consulting services since Sarbanes-Oxley was passed in July 2002 (legislation enacted in the wake of corporate scandals like Enron, requiring companies to be more transparent and rigorous in their financial reporting). And what Protiviti does, it does well: the company was named to Forrester Research's list of leaders in risk consulting services in 2007.

- Protiviti is an amalgam of the words "professionalism," "proactivity," "independence," and "integrity." The three "I"s of Protiviti were highlighted in the organization's original "Say I" campaign in 2002, which touted Protiviti's singular focus on pleasing its clients. Protiviti's new campaign is "Know Risk. Know Reward."

The Suits*

Harold M. Messmer, Jr.: Chairman and CEO
M. Keith Waddell: Vice Chairman, President, and CFO
Paul F. Gentzkow: President and COO of Staffing Services
*Data for Robert Half International

FAST FACTS

"Best Places to Launch a Career" Rank: 60
"Best Internships" Rank: 41
Full-Time Salary: $50,000–$54,999
Entry-Level Hires: 333
Top College Major: Business
Average Internship Compensation: $8,000
Stock Ticker: RHI

The Stats*

2007 sales: $4.6 billion (Protiviti: $552.3 million)
2007 net income: $296.2 million
Market cap: $4.4 billion
Employees: 15,300 (Protiviti: 3,300 employees)
Locations: 340 cities in 17 countries, with major operations in Australia, China, and Canada (Protiviti: 60 locations in 15 countries throughout the Americas, Asia-Pacific, and Europe)
Largest operating units[†]:
Accountemps....................$1.7 billion
Office Team ....$860.7 million
Robert Half
   Technology..............$425.1 million
Robert Half Management
   Resources ....$618.6 million
Robert Half Finance &
   Accounting..............$444.1 million
Protiviti ....$552.3 million

*Data for Robert Half International

[†]2007 Robert Half International sales; unaudited

The Story

2002: Robert Half International hires 760 partners and professionals from Arthur Andersen, LLP, to perform internal audit consulting services as part of an independent new business, which is later named Protiviti

2003: In response to Homeland Security concerns regarding companies' awareness of and adherence to national security advisory levels, Protiviti collaborates with ASIS International's Commission on Guidelines to develop Threat Advisory System Response Guidelines

2004: Introduces Discoveri, an online tool used for data analysis and mining

2005: Forrester Research names Protiviti a leader in enterprise risk management

2006: Launches operations in India, Brazil, Germany, Canada, and Mexico

2007: Acquires PENTA Advisory Services, LLC, a consulting firm offering litigation and tax-related services

The Skinny

Most important to recruiters: Communication skills, college major, analytical skills

Selectivity: N/A

Diversity of entry-level workforce: N/A

Facts to know:

- Instead of matching employees' 401(k) contributions, Protiviti provides a separate stock incentive benefit to its employees through a discretionary restricted stock grant program issued by Robert Half International, its publicly traded parent company.

- Protiviti doesn't endorse first-year performance bonuses for recent college graduate hires because the firm "believes a performance bonus plan would distract them from developing a baseline foundation of knowledge to succeed."

- Protiviti actively recruited at 65 U.S. undergraduate campuses during the 2006–2007 school year and extended full-time job offers on 64 of those campuses.

The Starting Gate

Undergraduate internships: 101

Duration of summer internship: 8 to 10 weeks

Average total compensation: $8,000

Interns by grade level:
Junior..1%
Senior 83%
College graduate 16%

Interns who receive full-time job offers: 95%

Interns who are extended full-time job offers that accept: 53%

The Sliding Scale

Entry-level hires who had been interns: 15%

Most important performance measurements in entry-level hire: Effort, learning ability, quality

Entry-level hires receiving signing bonuses: 81%

Average entry-level signing bonus: $2,300

Entry-level hires receiving performance bonuses: None

Average performance bonus during first year: N/A

The Stand-Out Perks

- 20 paid vacation days and 9 paid holidays
- Relocation compensation ($2,000)
- Charitable gift match ($1,000)
- Employee discounts

The Skills

- Seven-day orientation program
- Formal mentorship program (100% of entry-level hires participate)

The Sound-Off

- "Protiviti treats its interns like first- and second-year employees, allowing them more hands-on experience than most other firms." —*University of Illinois senior**
- "Great compensation package and awesome culture. Employees are friendly, and a lot of them have come to work for Protiviti after leaving larger firms like Deloitte." —BW *Discussion Forum*
- "They promote a balanced social and work life." —*Colorado State junior**

*Data: Universum Communications

THE RECRUITER SPOTLIGHT

Name: Jessica Harrison
Job: Director of Recruiting of the Central Area

Worst interview faux pas: *While there are many obvious pitfalls to avoid—inappropriate attire, interrupting the interviewer, poor body language, and so forth—candidates should always come prepared. An interviewer can immediately tell when a candidate did not conduct basic research about the company and the position.*

Why choose Protiviti: *Protiviti provides excellent opportunities for individuals interested in working at a company that, while generating more than $500 million annually in global revenues, is still in its infancy. Protiviti started with only 750 individuals in the United States and now has over 2,900 professionals in 60 offices around the globe. You can explore your potential through our training programs and client experiences while building relationships with all levels of Protiviti personnel, including our most senior management.*

Wackiest encounter while recruiting: *One time while recruiting on campus, I was walking to lunch with two of our managing directors. On our way, a group of eight streakers, wearing nothing but tennis shoes, ran right in front of us. It was definitely an awkward moment. I spent the rest of the day hoping that none of them showed up in my interview room!*

General Mills

1 General Mills Blvd.
Minneapolis, MN 55426
Phone: 763-764-7600
Fax: 763-764-7384
Web Addresses:
www.generalmills.com;
www.generalmills.com/corporate/
careers/index.aspx

The Company

- U.S. shoppers purchase on average at least one General Mills product each time they stock up at the grocery store, according to one study. The company is the sixth-largest food corporation in the world, the second-largest cereal producer in the nation, and the creator of America's best-selling cereal, Cheerios.

- General Mills also owns the Betty Crocker and Pillsbury lines, as well as the Chex Mix snack line, Fruit Roll-Ups, and Pop Secret microwave popcorn—not to mention Häagen-Dazs ice cream. At one time General Mills also owned Parker Bros. (maker of Monopoly).

- In June 2007, General Mills shrunk its cereal boxes, and although the price on each box was also lowered, the overall price per ounce actually increased. In July 2007, General Mills also raised prices on Yoplait and Green Giant vegetables. The move helped the company to a fis-

cal first-quarter earnings increase of 8% over its 2007 first-quarter earnings. If ingredients and gas prices continue rising, General Mills has said that more price increases could be on the way.

👔 The Suits

Stephen W. Sanger: Chairman
Kendall J. Powell: CEO
Don Mulligan: Executive VP and CFO
Robert L. Ryan: Director

The Stats

2007 sales: $12.4 billion
2007 net income: $1.1 billion
Market cap: $19.2 billion
Employees: 28,100
Locations: Operates in 100 countries, with offices and centers in more than 30 countries worldwide
Major competitors: Kellogg, Nestlé, Kraft

Largest operating units*:

U.S. Retail........................$8.0 billion
Food Service ....$1.8 billion

*2006 sales

The Story

1877: Brothers Cadwallader and William Washburn partner with John Crosby to create the successful Washburn-Crosby milling company

1921–1924: Washburn-Crosby creates the Betty Crocker persona and introduces Wheaties cereal

1928: General Mills is born after Washburn-Crosby president James Ford Bell merges the company with 26 other mills

1941: Introduces "Cheerioats" cereal, which is later renamed Cheerios

1965: Pillsbury introduces the Pillsbury Doughboy "Poppin' Fresh"; soon after, the company purchases Play-Doh maker Rainbow Crafts and Monopoly board game company Parker Bros.

1990: Seeking to produce cereals globally, General Mills takes part in a joint venture with Nestlé called "Cereal Partners Worldwide"

2001: General Mills acquires the Pillsbury Company

2005: Converts the entire cereal line to whole grains to encourage the health benefits of whole foods and balanced eating

2008: Increases consumer marketing investment by 13% for the third quar-ter of fiscal 2008; net sales jump 12% during this period

The Skinny

Most important to recruiters: Leadership skills, analytical skills, work experience

Selectivity: 1 of 6 applicants hired in 2006, up from 1 of 10 applicants hired in 2005

Diversity of entry-level workforce: 27% minority; 63% female

Facts to know:

- The General Mills Institute offers formal development programs, including the "Core Business Essentials" program for new employees, which is an internal, executive-led introduction to the company. Other institute offerings support employees at critical career transition points (i.e., "Managing People" for new managers and "Managing the Organization" for experienced managers).

- Specialized training for employees in different career paths includes Camp Champ for new marketing professionals, Cereal School for new technical professionals, HR "U" for new human resources professionals, and Financial Seminar Series for new finance professionals.

The Starting Gate

Undergraduate internships: 100

Duration of summer internship: 12 weeks

Average total compensation: $9,216*

Interns by grade level:
Sophomore 2%
Junior...10%
Senior 88%

Interns who receive full-time job offers: 84%

Interns who are extended full-time job offers that accept: 72%

*Varies by year in school and major ($7,350–$12,900/summer).

 ## The Sliding Scale

Entry-level hires who had been interns: 23%

Most important performance measurements in entry-level hire: Productivity/efficiency, learning ability, effort

Entry-level hires receiving signing bonuses: 76%

Average entry-level signing bonus: $3,360

Entry-level hires receiving performance bonuses: 100%

Average performance bonus during first year: $2,070

The Stand-Out Perks

- Full and partial graduate school sponsorship

- Educational expenses reimbursement ($6,000)

- 15 paid vacation days

- Charitable gift match ($30,000)

- Relocation compensation

- Employee discounts

The Skills

- Formal one-day orientation program

- Operations Management Associate Program, which is 72 to 84 weeks in length

- Formal mentorship program

The Sound-Off

- "They offered me the highest [internship] compensation and assisted in transportation and housing expenses. They cover every base." —*Ohio State junior**

- "I interned with them and was given very challenging projects that gave me great experiences and really helped build my résumé." — *Rochester Institute of Technology student**

- "I have accepted an internship because of ... the unexpectedly high number of General Mills employees who contacted me to encourage me to work for the company, etc...." —*Purdue student**

*Data: Universum Communications

THE RECRUITER SPOTLIGHT

Name: Kenneth Charles
Job: Director of U.S. Recruiting

Most creative job application: *A candidate created a full-size Lucky Charms box with her picture on the front and her résumé on the back. The side panels explained why she was a good candidate for us.*

Advice for young prospective employees: *It's all about the people! Candidates should seek out our teams on campus. Get to know our people and you'll know our company. Successful candidates know what they want to do and understand how General Mills can help them achieve their goals.*

How to recover from an interview faux pas: *People can make mistakes when they're stressed. We'll move on and focus on their capabilities. Candidates should always do their homework prior to the interview and appreciate that offers are earned, not given.*

Why young job seekers should choose General Mills: *General Mills is more than the American icon brands you'll work on. It's the quality of the people you'll work with and for. It's the community we've built and the values we share. It's the development you'll receive and the chance to have an impact. There is no better place to launch your career.*

Kraft Foods

Three Lakes Dr.
Northfield, IL 60093
Phone: 847-646-2000
Fax: 847-646-6005
Web Addresses: www.kraft.com;
www.kraft.com/Careers/

The Company

- Kraft Foods is the second-largest food and beverage company in the world. Its eight North American business units—Snacks, Beverages, Canada, Cheese, Grocery, Foodservice, Oscar Mayer, and Pizza—boast brands like Jell-O, DiGiorno, and Oreo.

- Parent company Altria spun off Kraft in spring 2007. Other big changes at Kraft have included its decision to sell off hot-cereal brands, such as Cream of Wheat, and its plan to merge the Post cereal brand with Ralcorp Holdings.

- Kraft is in the midst of a larger three-year turnaround plan put into place by CEO Irene Rosenfield. Not surprisingly, righting the ship has proved bumpy: Kraft's third-quarter 2007 earnings fell 20% from its third-quarter 2006 profits. The company's rocky returns have alarmed (and emboldened) powerful shareholders like Nelson Peltz, leading Kraft to recently select two board picks that were supported by Peltz's Trian Partners.

FAST FACTS

"Best Places to Launch a Career"
   Rank: 89
"Best Internships" Rank: N/A
Full-Time Salary: N/A
Entry-Level Hires: N/A
Stock Ticker: KFT

The Suits

Irene Rosenfeld: Chairperson and CEO
David Brearton: Executive VP of Operations & Business Services
Tim McLevish: Executive VP and CFO
Mary Beth West: Executive President and Chief Marketing Officer
Marc Firestone: Executive VP of Corporate and Legal Affairs and General Counsel

The Stats

2007 sales: $37.2 billion
2007 net income: $2.6 billion
Market cap: $50.5 billion
Employees: 90,000
Locations: 159 manufacturing facilities worldwide in Europe, Asia, and South America
Major competitors: Campbell Soup, ConAgra, Danone, General Mills, Kellogg, Nestlé, PepsiCo, Sara Lee, Unilever

Largest operating units*:
European Union .... $8 billion
Snacks/Cereals .... $6.5 billion
   (North America)
Cheese & Foodservice ...... $6.4 billion
   (North America)
*2007 sales

📖 The Story

1903: J. L. Kraft begins selling cheese to local grocers in Chicago from a horse-drawn wagon

1914: Kraft purchases a manufacturing plant and begins producing processed cheese

1928: Acquires Phenix Cheese Corporation, maker of Philadelphia Brand cream cheese

1945: Maxwell House instant coffee is introduced to consumers in the United States by Kraft

1950: Develops the first commercially successful sliced processed cheese

1981: Oscar Mayer is acquired by General Foods Corporation

1985–1989: Philip Morris Companies Inc. acquires General Foods in 1985 and Kraft in 1988 and merges the two in January 1989 to form Kraft General Foods

1993: Kraft General Foods acquires the U.S. and Canadian cold-cereal business of RJR Nabisco; two years later, Kraft General Foods changes its name to Kraft Foods

2000: Nabisco Holdings is acquired by Altria Group (formerly Philip Morris Companies Inc.) and is integrated into Kraft Foods

2001: Kraft Foods goes public, with Altria Group retaining majority ownership

2007: Kraft Foods is spun off from its parent company, Altria Group; later this year, Kraft sells off its hot-cereal business and announces the pending sale of Post cereal brands

The Skinny

Most important to recruiters: N/A

Selectivity: N/A

Diversity of entry-level workforce: N/A

Facts to know:

- Kraft offers on-site dry cleaning and oil changes for its employees.

- In 2006 Kraft provided $83.3 million in food and financial support to hundreds of nonprofit organizations worldwide through the Kraft Cares global community involvement program. These contributions are intended to promote hunger relief and healthy lifestyles.

🏇 The Starting Gate

Undergraduate internships: 219

Duration of summer internship: 10 to 12 weeks

Average total compensation: N/A

Interns by grade level: Approximately 40% of interns are juniors or younger; the remaining 60% are seniors and college graduates

Interns who receive full-time job offers: N/A

Interns who are extended full-time job offers that accept: N/A

The Sliding Scale

Entry-level hires who had been interns: N/A

Most important performance measurements in entry-level hire: N/A

Entry-level hires receiving signing bonuses: N/A

Average entry-level signing bonus: N/A

Entry-level hires receiving performance bonuses: 100%

Average performance bonus during first year: N/A

The Stand-Out Perks

- Educational expenses reimbursement ($10,000)

- Full graduate school sponsorship

- 401(k) and co-funded pension

- Charitable gift match

- Relocation compensation

- Employee discounts

The Skills

- Formal one-day orientation program that includes guest speakers

- Formal leadership program for entry-level hires that have been with the company for a year or more

The Sound-Off

- "Kraft Foods offered me a very strong [internship] program, where I was able to learn a lot about the company, earn a reasonable salary, and become friends with the internship class and colleagues."
  —*University of Iowa senior**

- "A very good internship program that offers competitive compensation. It also gives the student a defined project to work on. This gives real experience." —*Rutgers senior**

- "They are a major recruiter on my campus and offer lots of opportunities for minority students to create a diverse workplace." —*North Carolina A&T State University senior**

*Data: Universum Communications

THE ENTRY-LEVEL SPOTLIGHT

Name: Courtney Dunn

Job: Associate Engineer in the Global Technology and Quality Group of the Cheese and Dairy Sector

Briefly describe a typical day: *As my projects vary, so does my schedule. On Monday I might catch an early morning flight to Montreal to meet with the production plant staff, monitor production of a new product, and produce several new formulations that I have worked on to determine which will be commercialized. Then on Tuesday I could catch an afternoon flight to Toronto to observe a focus group, which is a group of consumers selected to try my new formulation and give their opinions as to what works and what doesn't. Then I may be back in my Chicago office on Wednesday to review and capture the learnings from the beginning of the week and prepare to update the director and VP of my sector on the progress of my projects during our product showing meeting. The fast pace and changing schedule mean there is no fear of monotony.*

Best part of the job: *I am able to see others enjoy my work. Every time I go into a grocery store, I can see my products on the shelf. At restaurants, sporting events, and practically anywhere else there is food, people are eating products that my coworkers and I have worked on. I love that I am able to personally see that a Kraft product that was directly influenced by me is loved and purchased by millions of families across the country!*

Weirdest/funniest workplace moment: *During my first weeks at Kraft, I was working in the pilot plant (a small-scale facility that allows us to produce products on a much smaller scale than regular production), testing out different formulas. One day when I was finished, I took a look in the mirror and saw that I had cheese everywhere. Immediately I thought back to my childhood, baking with my mother and grandmother, and being covered in flour and frosting when we were all done. That's when it hit me: I get paid to play with food!*

Entry-level insights: *Even as a junior-level employee [she is a 25-year-old Howard University graduate], I have been given a great deal of responsibility. If you work to your full potential, being noticed is inevitable.*

L'Oréal USA

575 Fifth Ave.
New York, NY 10017
Phone: 212-818-1500
Fax: 212-984-4999
Web Addresses: www.loreal.com;
www.lorealusa.com/_en/_us/

The Company

- The L'Oréal Group, the Paris-based parent company of L'Oréal USA, owns 19 global cosmetics brands, including Lancôme, Redken, and the Body Shop International. The company also has managed to buy out more than half of its competitors, from Maybelline and Soft Sheen to Kiehl's and Carson.

- L'Oréal's over 2,800 scientists acquire 500 new patents a year and hold over 35,000 patents worldwide. Since 1989, the company has banned animal testing in its labs.

- In October, the L'Oréal Group reported an 8.6% rise in sales for the first three quarters of 2007 over the same period in 2006. The company, which benefited from the launch of a new Diesel perfume, also affirmed its positive full-year profit and revenue guidance and ended the year strongly. In terms of the U.S. market specifically, L'Oréal has generally outperformed its rivals in 2007. However, the company has warned that the general slowdown in the U.S. marketplace—and unfa-

FAST FACTS

"Best Places to Launch a Career"
 Rank: 35
"Best Internships" Rank: 22
Full-Time Salary: $50,000–$54,999
Entry-Level Hires: 55
Top College Major: Engineering
Formal Training Program: Yes
Stock Ticker: OREP (Paris Stock Exchange)

vorable currency movements in general—could slow L'Oréal USA's continued progress.

The Suits

Jean-Paul Agon: CEO of L'Oréal S.A.
Laurent Attal: President and CEO of L'Oréal USA

The Stats

2007 sales: 17.1 billion euros
2007 net income: N/A
Market cap: N/A
Employees: 60,851 employees in 58 countries
Locations: Headquartered in France, with products sold in Western Europe, North America, and Asia
Major competitors: Estée Lauder, Chanel, Shiseido, Revlon, Bath and Body Works, Johnson & Johnson

Largest operating units*:
Professional Products 2.4 billion euros
Consumer Products ..8.3 billion euros
Luxury Products........3.9 billion euros
Active Cosmetics ......1.2 billion euros
The Body Shop ......787 million euros
Dermatology ....368 million euros
*2007 sales

📖 The Story

1907: Scientist Eugene Schueller establishes L'Oréal

1953: L'Oréal SA sets up a licensee in the United States called Cosmair, Inc.

1994: Cosmair becomes a wholly owned subsidiary of L'Oréal SA and changes its name to L'Oréal USA

1996: Acquires Maybelline

1998: Acquires Soft Sheen

2000: Acquires skin care line Kiehl's and hair products makers Matrix and Carson

2002: Acquires hair products line ARTec

2005: Acquires skin-care products line SkinCeutical

2007: Acquires salon hair-product maker PureOlogy

The Skinny

Most important to recruiters: Leadership skills, analytical skills, communication skills

Selectivity: 1 of 100 applicants hired in 2006, roughly the same as in 2005

Diversity of entry-level workforce: 56% minority; 60% female

Facts to know:

- The internship program is the main pipeline to full-time hires. L'Oréal's current global CEO started his career at L'Oréal as an intern. The current global chairman of L'Oréal and the CEO of L'Oréal USA were also recruited on their college campuses.

- Entry-level hires may be sent to work outside the United States after just two years with the company.

🐎 The Starting Gate

Undergraduate internships: 109

Duration of summer internship: 10 to 13 weeks

Average total compensation: $10,300

Interns by grade level:
Junior..10%
Senior 90%

Interns who receive full-time job offers: 40%

Interns who are extended full-time job offers that accept: 78%

The Sliding Scale

Entry-level hires who were interns: 58%

Most important performance measurements in entry-level hire: Learning ability, leadership skills, creativity

Entry-level hires receiving signing bonuses: N/A

Average entry-level signing bonus: N/A

Entry-level hires receiving performance bonuses: N/A

Average performance bonus during first year: N/A

The Stand-Out Perks

- Educational expenses reimbursement

- Full graduate school sponsorship

- 10 paid vacation days and 2 paid days off for religious observance

- 401(k), co-funded pension, and profit-sharing plans (profit-sharing program can add up to three weeks of pay onto employee's yearly income)

- Charitable gift match (must be educational in nature)

- Relocation compensation ($10,000)

- Employee discounts

The Skills

- Formal five-day orientation program

- Management Development Program, which consists of two to five rotations and lasts 72 to 144 weeks; includes rotations in different fields, such as Sales, Finance, Manufacturing, and so on

- Formal mentorship program (50% of entry-level hires participate)

The Sound-Off

- "Their internship program is very well advertised and well respected. Also, it is challenging, allows you to learn a lot about the field you are working in, and offers a chance for future employment." —*Lehigh junior**

- "They provide housing, pay interns well, and also hire many interns for full time. —*Cornell junior**

- "L'Oréal USA was the best internship program I participated in. They gave us challenging projects, networking opportunities with upper management, and training sessions (presentation and project management), and also planned fun social events for the interns. — *Carnegie Mellon senior**

*Data: Universum Communications

THE RECRUITER SPOTLIGHT

Name: Diane Lewis
Job: VP of Talent Recruitment, L'Oréal USA

The wackiest thing encountered during recruiting: *A one-hour slide show of a candidate's accomplishments.*

Advice for young job seekers: *Do your homework. Look at our Web site, visit our stores, look at advertising, try our products. Show your passion while interviewing!*

If a candidate's cell phone rings during an interview, is it possible for him/her to recover? Any other faux pas to avoid? *As long as they don't answer their cell phone, it is okay. Other faux pas include chewing gum, mispronouncing brand names, and having no questions.*

Why choose L'Oréal: *To work in an innovative and diverse environment with so many opportunities. We give people amazing opportunities to work on different brands in various distribution channels in different places around the world. You can truly build your entire career within one company here at L'Oréal.*

Nestlé USA

800 N. Brand Blvd.
Glendale, CA 91203
Phone: 818-549-6000
Fax: N/A
Web Addresses: www.nestleusa.com;
www.nestlejobs.com

The Company

- Nestlé USA is a subsidiary of Vevey, Switzerland–based Nestlé S.A., (LSE: NESNQ) the world's largest food company. It all started in the 1860s with entrepreneur Henri Nestlé's desire to provide a nutritious product to a malnourished baby who couldn't breast-feed. What resulted was the first baby food ever brought to market.

- Nestlé S.A. has introduced a number of other important "firsts" to the consumer goods market, including evaporated milk, instant coffee, dry pet food, and milk chocolate, to name just a few.

- Today, Nestlé brands include the following: Nestlé Toll House, Nestlé Nesquick, Nestlé Coffee-Mate, Nestlé Good Start, Stouffer's, Lean Cuisine, Hot Pockets and Lean Pockets brand sandwiches, Nescafé, Nescafé Taster's Choice, Nestlé Juicy Juice, Buitoni, PowerBar, Nestlé Crunch, Nestlé Butterfinger, and Wonka.

FAST FACTS

"Best Places to Launch a Career" Rank: 62
"Best Internships" Rank: 46
Full-Time Salary: $40,000–$44,999
Entry-Level Hires: 36
Top College Major: Engineering
3-Year Retention Rate: 55%
Stock Ticker: NESNQ (London Stock Exchange)

The Suits

Brad Alford: Chairman and CEO
Kim Lund: GLOBE Executive and Chief Information Officer
Dan Stroud: Senior VP and CFO

The Stats*

2007 sales: $8.25 billion
2007 net income: N/A
Market cap: N/A
Employees: 15,500 employees in the United States
Locations: 20 manufacturing facilities, 5 distribution centers, 12 sales offices across the country
Major competitors: Kraft Foods, Mars
Largest operating units: N/A
*Data: Nestlé USA

The Story

1866: Henri Nestlé creates the world's first commercially marketed baby food

1875: Jules Monnerat purchases the Nestlé Company from Henri Nestlé

1929: Nestlé acquired Peter's Chocolate, which specializes in chocolate for bakers; the founder of Peter's Chocolate uses Nestlé's condensed milk to create the world's first milk chocolate

1939: Debuts the world's first instant coffee, Nescafé

1958: Launches Friskies, the world's first dry cat food

1961: Introduces Coffee-Mate, the world's first nondairy powdered coffee creamer

1981: Stouffer's frozen foods which was acquired by Nestlé in 1973, introduces the popular calorie-conscious Lean Cuisine brand

1985: Acquires the Carnation Company

2000: Acquires PowerBar; Nestlé also celebrates 100 years of operating in the United States

2001: Acquires Purina Pet Care

2002: Acquires Hot Pockets and Lean Pockets

2003: Acquries Dreyer's Grand Ice Cream

2006: Acquires Jenny Craig, a weight-management company

2007: Acquires Novartis Medical Nutrition and announces an agreement to acquire Gerber

The Skinny

Most important to recruiters: Leadership skills, analytical skills, communication skills

Selectivity: N/A

Diversity of entry-level workforce: 4% minority; 45% female

Facts to know:

- In 2007, entry-level hiring at Nestlé USA nearly quadrupled over the prior year's numbers.

- Of the 91 Nestlé U.S.A. employees that are at a VP level or higher, 54 have more than 20 years of experience at the organization

- Roughly 55% of college-educated employees receive full-time salaries between $40,000 and $44,999, and 45% are paid in the $50,000-to-$54,499 range.

- Employees with graduate degrees receive full-time salaries of around $70,000 and above.

The Starting Gate

Undergraduate internships: 21

Duration of summer internship: 10 to 12 weeks

Average total compensation: $9,174

Interns by grade level:
Senior 100%

Interns who receive full-time job offers: 67%

Interns who are extended full-time job offers that accept: 64%

The Sliding Scale

Entry-level hires who had been interns: 21%

Most important performance measurements in entry-level hire: Team player, productivity/efficiency, creativity

Entry-level hires receiving signing bonuses: 8%

Average entry-level signing bonus: $5,500

Entry-level hires receiving performance bonuses: 83%

Average performance bonus during first year: $3,200

The Stand-Out Perks

- Educational expenses reimbursement ($2,500)

- Partial graduate school sponsorship

- 12 paid vacation days for first-year employees; 15 paid vacation days for employees that have been with the company between two and five years

- 401(k) plan with company match of up to 4% of salary

- Employee discounts

The Skills

- One-day orientation program with guest speakers, diversity exercises, team-building exercises, tour of the facilities, and overview of company history, structure, and brand portfolio

- No formal mentorship or leadership development program

The Sound-Off

- "I went through this summer internship program, and it offered me a variety of projects that helped me to acclimate to the working environment." —*University of Illinois senior**

- "Nestlé offers the best internship program because there is a strong chance of being hired for a full-time position." —*University of Missouri/Columbia junior**

- "Nestlé has been a great place to start in logistics because, as a function, it is crucial for Nestlé and its success. We are trained very well and then are expected to perform at a high level, which is the way I think it should be. Once training is finished, there is a sink-or-swim period, and I think that gives entry-level employees an opportunity to shine and be noticed. Also, Nestlé does a good job of exposing new hires to all of the business functions, so you can take responsibility for your career path. I would recommend this company to anyone in any major." —*Current entry-level employee*

*Data: Universum Communications

THE SUPERSTAR SPOTLIGHT

Name: Fabiola Pereyra
Job: Category Development Manager in the Beverage Division

Best part of the job: *Being creative! I launched a new product in eight months (from concept to launch) and created a unique advertising campaign to support it. This was after my first year as a marketing associate. When I say I launched it, I don't mean that I took a passive functional role. I was the lead on the project. I made it happen. I don't think you'll get that experience so quickly at other companies.*

Biggest surprise you've encountered: *I think the weirdest thing has been how flat and nonhierarchical Nestlé is. I find it odd that our chairman and CEO knows me. He takes the time to meet all of us and knows what brands we're working on. I know he's a busy man, so I think that's a little weird!*

Advice for young professionals: *Make an impact! People sit at their desk waiting for someone to notice them; it's not going to happen. When you get to a marketing job at a CPG company, one thing is clear: your peers are very bright. They're all MBAs with great experience. What will differentiate you is making sure that people know who you are. Get to know people in all areas; volunteer to lead projects; volunteer on corporate initiatives; just get noticed!*

Nike Inc.

One Bowerman Dr.
Beaverton, OR 97005
Phone: 503-671-6453
Fax: 503-671-6300
Web Addresses: www.nike.com/nikebiz/
nikebiz.jhtml?page=0; www.nike.com/
nikebiz/nikebiz.jhtml?page=30

The Company

- In recent years, athletic-gear giant Nike has diversified through a number of progressive acquisitions, including luxury designer Cole Haan, sneaker designer Converse, and teen lifestyle brand Hurley.

- After fielding sweatshop labor allegations for nearly a decade, Nike became the first apparel company to publicly reveal its entire supply chain structure in its 2004 Corporate Responsibility Report, detailing actions that were being taken to halt any abuses.

- In December 2004, founder and longtime CEO Phil Knight stepped aside and named outsider William Perez as his successor. Perez left the company after only 13 months as a result of strategic differences. Nike veteran Mark Parker was appointed as the company's new CEO in February 2006, but Knight remains active in shaping the company's vision (and operations) as chairman.

FAST FACTS

"Best Places to Launch a Career" Rank: 55
"Best Internships" Rank: 42
Top College Major: Business
Average Internship Compensation: $10,000
Entry-Level Minority/Female Hires: 55%
Graduate School Sponsorship: Partial
Stock Ticker: NKE

- In 2007, to celebrate the 25th anniversary of its classic Air Force 1 shoe brand, Nike launched a new version and an ad campaign called "Second Coming: Our Game. Our Time," featuring current NBA stars Kobe Bryant and LeBron James.

The Suits

Phillip Knight: Chairman
Mark Parker: President and CEO
Charlie Denson: President of Nike Brand
Lewis Bird: President of Subsidiaries
Donald Blair: VP and CFO
Trever Edwards: VP of Global Brand and Category Management

The Stats

2007 sales: $16.3 billion
2007 net income: $1.5 billion

Market cap: $32 billion

Employees: 30,200

Locations: On top of its 200-plus factory stores, 100-plus offices, and 479 factories worldwide, Nike owns facilities in Tennessee, North Carolina, and the Netherlands

Major competitors: Adidas, New Balance, Columbia Sportswear, K-Swiss, Oakley

Largest operating units*:

Footwear ....$8.5 billion
Athletic Apparel ....$4.6 billion
Equipment/Other ....$3.2 billion
*2007 sales

The Story

1964: Phil Knight and his former University of Oregon track coach Bill Bowerman found Blue Ribbon Sports (BRS) to import and sell the Tiger running shoe from Japan

1971: The Swoosh trademark is designed

1978: BRS officially changes its name to Nike

1980: Nike becomes a publicly traded company on the New York Stock Exchange

1988: Launches the "Just Do It" tagline; the company also acquires Cole Haan and begins its expansion into other apparel brands

2004: Designs LiveStrong bracelets for the Lance Armstrong Foundation

2006: Teams up with Apple to launch Nike+, which pairs Apple's iPod technology with Nike running shoes, enabling runners to listen to music and track their speed and burned calories as they exercise

The Skinny

Most important to recruiters: College GPA, work experience, leadership skills

Selectivity: N/A

Diversity of entry-level workforce: 45% minority; 55% female

Facts to know:

- The Adrenaline summer internship program, which included 200 interns from 70 schools in 2007, gives students hands-on experience in virtually every area within Nike, from sports marketing and logistics to product development and information technology. Most positions are located at Nike World Headquarters.

- Nike actively recruited at 11 U.S. undergraduate campuses during the 2006–2007 school year but extended full-time job offers on only 2 of these campuses.

The Starting Gate

Undergraduate internships: 111

Duration of summer internship: 10 weeks

Average total compensation: $10,000

Interns by grade level:

Sophomore 1%
Junior..34%
Senior 23%
College graduate 26%

Interns who receive full-time job offers: 15%

Interns who are extended full-time job offers that accept: 90%

The Sliding Scale

Entry-level hires who had been interns: N/A

Most important performance measurements in entry-level hire: N/A

Entry-level hires receiving signing bonuses: N/A

Average entry-level signing bonus: N/A

Entry-level hires receiving performance bonuses: N/A

Average performance bonus during first year: N/A

The Stand-Out Perks

- Educational expenses reimbursement ($5,000)

- Partial graduate school sponsorship

- Charitable gift match ($5,000)

- Relocation compensation

- Employee discounts

- Nike World Headquarters' 178-acre campus has an exercise center, running trails, and playing fields

The Skills

- Formal three-day orientation program, including guest speakers, diversity exercises, team-building exercises, and a tour of the facilities

- Career Decision Making, a half-week leadership program

- Marketing Development Program, a formal leadership program that consists of four to six rotations and lasts 18 to 30 weeks

The Sound-Off

- "They have the best facilities and job opportunities, they have the best corporate culture, and they give responsibility and encourage innovation and creativity on the part of their interns." —*University of North Carolina at Chapel Hill senior**

- "They provide competitive [internship] compensation, a great hands-on learning experience, as well as access to the Nike company store. They make you feel not as an intern only, but as a full member of their corporate team." —*Babson junior**

- "There is a constant stream of conversation, really about anything. It's amazing how often thoughts from these random conversations come up later and become projects." —*Nike employee*

*Data: Universum Communications

THE SUPERSTAR SPOTLIGHT

Name: Ricky Engelberg
Job: Asia Pacific Digital Marketing Director

Briefly describe a typical day: *It's tough to classify. There is always work on current and future projects that might range from athlete marketing campaigns like LeBron James to shoe launches like Nike Free to Nike+ runner outreach in Tokyo. Occasions like a shoe coming out the next month have immediate timelines, and you also help identify new opportunities and figure out how to address them as you go.*

Best part of the job: *(1) Nike is extremely entrepreneurial. At their core, most of the great projects at Nike have a tiny group of people championing them. Eventually the entire company embraces them, but there is always a small group of people with an idea that a new project can be traced back to. (2) I absolutely love the global network of friends you develop pretty quickly. When I look at all of the amazing cities I've been in for meetings, shoots, or work trips, it's staggering, but it is really normal at Nike. (3) You work in something so tangible with a complete element of surprise to it. We might have fully complete plans for a launch of a new shoe, and then LeBron goes and scores 48 points in Game Five. Everyone knows we need to get something out to the world as quickly as possible and make something great happen. Nothing is ever over at Nike.*

Your mantra for success: *Never say that something can't be done. Nike is a place where things happen so quickly that it's tough to even feel like you rise through the ranks fast [Engelberg, 29, interned at Nike in '99 and '00 and has been promoted three times since joining full-time in '02]. The company flattens out pretty quickly. If someone does something on a project that's great, then everyone will know. Once you prove yourself, the opportunities are endless.*

Tips for ambitious young employees: *Be passionate about something or, ideally, a lot of things. Diversity of interests is such an integral part of generating new ideas. To quote one of our Nike maxims, "Be a sponge."*

Philip Morris USA

6601 W. Broad St.
Richmond, VA 23230
Phone: 804-274-2000
Fax: 804-484-8231
Web Addresses:
www.philipmorrisusa.com;
www.pmusa.com/careers

The Company

- Philip Morris USA (PM USA) is the country's largest tobacco product manufacturer and the maker of the United States' most popular cigarette brand, Marlboro. (Other PM USA labels include Parliament, Virginia Slims, and Basic.) Until recently, Philip Morris USA, Philip Morris International, Philip Morris Capital Corporation, and Kraft Foods were all subsidiaries of Altria Group, a holding company that also has a stake in brewing giant SABMiller. However, Altria recently announced plans to focus on the lucrative U.S. tobacco business, spun off Kraft in 2007, and announced that it would do the same with Philip Morris International in 2008.

- In October 2007, PM opened a $350 million Richmond-based research center to develop new technologies that improve its current products and lead to innovative new products.

- Although Altria's operating income remained strong in 2007, taxes and other charges have crippled net earnings—and could continue to do so to an even greater degree: Philip Morris has been battling a proposed 156% federal tax increase on cigarettes but it did not occur in 2007.

The Suits

Michael E. Szymanczyk: Chairman and CEO
John R. Nelson: President of Operations and Technology
Howard A. Willard: Executive VP of Strategy, Business Development and IS
Craig A. Johnson: Executive VP of Sales and Brand Management
David R. Beran: Executive VP and CFO

The Stats*

2007 sales: $73.8 billion
2007 net income: $9.8 billion
Market cap: N/A
Employees: 10,790 (PM USA only)

Locations: Richmond, VA headquarters; Cabarrus County, NC factory; sales force presence in all 50 states (PM USA only)

Major competitors: Carolina Group, Commonwealth Brands, Reynolds America

Largest operating units[†]:

PM USA ....$18.5 billion
PM International............$49.9 billion

*Unless otherwise noted, data is for parent company Altria

[†]2007 sales

📖 The Story

1847: Philip Morris opens a tobacco shop in London, England

1902: Philip Morris & Co. Ltd is incorporated in New York City

1924: Introduces Marlboro to the cigarette market

1965: The Federal Cigarette Labeling and Advertising Act mandates that cigarette companies place health warnings on their products

1967: Reorganizes into three internal divisions: Domestic, International, and Industrial

1969: Philip Morris Inc. acquires Miller Brewing Company

1983: Philip Morris USA becomes the biggest cigarette company in the United States

1988: Philip Morris Companies acquires Kraft

2000: Acquires Nabisco which becomes part of Kraft Foods

2002: Sells Miller Brewing Company to South African Breweries, but retains a stake in the company

2003: Philip Morris Companies changes its name to Altria Group

2007: Altria spins off Kraft; the company also announces a planned spin-off of Philip Morris International

The Skinny

Most important to recruiters: Leadership skills, communication skills, ability to handle complex situations

Selectivity: 1 of 265 applicants hired in 2006, roughly the same as in 2005

Diversity of entry-level workforce: 28% minority; 42% female

Facts to know:

- Philip Morris USA funds three diversity scholarship programs.

- Entry-level employees receive a 25% reduction in health-care premiums. Additional benefits include $3,000 in adoption assistance, health-advocate services, and scholarships for dependents. On-site amenities include a medical clinic that provides health screenings, a company store, a hair salon, a fitness center with trainers, shoe shiners, cooking classes, and more.

🎠 The Starting Gate

Undergraduate internships: 173

Duration of summer internship: 10 to 12 weeks

Average total compensation: $8,267

Interns by grade level:
Sophomore 8%
Junior..8%
Senior 84%

Interns who receive full-time job offers: 67%

Interns who are extended full-time job offers that accept: 64%

The Sliding Scale

Entry-level hires who had been interns: 21%

Most important performance measurements in entry-level hire: Leadership skills, communication skills, ability to handle complex situations

Entry-level hires receiving signing bonuses: 5%

Average entry-level signing bonus: $2,000

Entry-level hires receiving performance bonuses: 67%

Average performance bonus during first year: $4,000

The Stand-Out Perks

- Full graduate school sponsorship
- Educational expenses reimbursement
- 15 paid vacation days
- Profit sharing of 10 to 15% of base salary after the employee has been with the company for one year

- Charitable gift match ($30,000)
- Relocation compensation
- Employee discounts

The Skills

- Discovery Days, a formal three-day orientation program
- Leadership Forums, a one-week leadership program
- Engineering Leadership Development Program, which consists of three rotations and lasts 286 weeks

The Sound-Off

- "Incredible learning experiences, leadership opportunities, etc."
  —*James Madison senior**
- "Great internship. I was part of a team working on a large project in the company. I was looked at as equal to those who were full-time."
  —*VA Tech senior**
- "Philip Morris offers great pay and excellent benefits, even to interns. Full-time employment is almost guaranteed if you do a good job as an intern." —*Penn State senior**

*Data: Universum Communications

THE ENTRY-LEVEL SPOTLIGHT

Name: Samuel Jamison
Job: Associate Technology Analyst

On defending employment by a tobacco company: *I often get asked by college [Virginia Commonwealth University] acquaintances and family members, "How can you work for a tobacco company?" My response is always in reference to the way that Philip Morris USA treats its employees. I've never seen a company that values its employees as much as Philip Morris does, as it relates to benefits, perks (employee appreciation days), and so on. Another reason I can work for a tobacco company is the way the company puts its mission into action. The first part of our mission states, "Our goal is to be the most responsible, effective, and respected developer, manufacturer, and marketer of consumer products," and our actions are guided by that. Philip Morris USA has put programs and departments in place to prevent youth smoking and youth access to our products. We've also taken steps to assist adult tobacco consumers who choose to no longer smoke or use our products by creating a QuitAssist Program, which is a resource pool that provides those adult consumers with expert information from public health authorities on how to quit smoking. How could you not work for a company with those values?*

Tips for ambitious young employees trying to get ahead: *The best way for ambitious young people to get noticed at Philip Morris USA [Jamison is 23] is to have conversations with their managers about their development plan and use those conversations and advice to position themselves for new opportunities within the company. It's all about letting management know what your aspirations are within the company and taking on those new opportunities. That's what will get you noticed here at Philip Morris USA.*

Procter & Gamble

1 Procter & Gamble Plaza
Cincinnati, OH 45202
Phone: 513-983-1100
Fax: 513-983-9369
Web Addresses: www.pg.com;
www.pg.com/jobs/sectionmain.jhtml

The Company

- Where can you find a pharmaceutical company, a cosmetics company, and a food products company all in one? The answer is Procter & Gamble (P&G), the world's number one maker of household goods. Popular product lines such as Herbal Essences, Olay, and Cover Girl draw graduates interested in careers in brand management.

- The company has grown exponentially over the years through a series of key market innovations, such as Bounce and Pert Plus Shampoo, and a number of strategic acquisitions, including P&G's purchase of Gillette in 2005.

- P&G has been experiencing some executive shuffling in the last year, undergoing a drastic corporate overhaul in May 2007 that split up Gillette and divided its operations into three global units: Beauty Care, Global Health and Well Being, and Household Care.

Fast Facts

"Best Places to Launch a Career" Rank: 66
"Best Internships" Rank: 43
Entry-Level Hires: 323
Top College Major: Engineering
3-Year Retention Rate: 70%
5-Year Retention Rate: 60%
Stock Ticker: PG

The Suits

A.G. Lafley: Chairman, President, and CEO
Susan E. Arnold: Vice Chairperson of P&G Beauty and Health
Bruce L. Byrnes: Vice Chairperson of P&G Household Care
Robert A. McDonald: Vice Chairperson of Global Operations
Clayton C. Daley, Jr.: CFO

The Stats

2007 sales: $76.5 billion
2007 net income: $10.3 billion
Market cap: $228 billion
Employees: 138,000
Locations: Offices in over 80 countries worldwide, with products available in 140 countries
Major competitors: Johnson & Johnson, Kimberly-Clark, Unilever, Bristol-Myers Squibb, Energizer Holdings

Largest operating units*:

Beauty ....$23.0 billion
Fabric and Home Care ..$19.0 billion
Baby and Family Care ....$12.7 billion
Health Care ....$9.0 billion
Snacks/Coffee/Pet Care ....$4.5 billion
Blades/Razors ....$5.2 billion
Duracell/Braun ....$4.0 billion

*2007 sales; doesn't include a $963 million loss listed under "Corporate"

The Story

1837: William Procter and James Norris Gamble start selling soap and candles in Cincinnati, Ohio

1879: Gamble develops Ivory soap

1890: Procter's son, also named William Procter, becomes the first president of P&G

1911: P&G introduces Crisco, an all-vegetable shortening that is a cheaper and healthier alternative to butter and traditional cooking oils

1946: Tide laundry detergent, "the washing miracle," is introduced

1972: Creates Bounce, the first fabric-softener sheet

1992: Creates Pantene Pro-V, one of the world's best-selling lines of shampoo

2001: Acquires hair color leader Clairol and introduces Crest Whitestrips to the market

2005: P&G and Gillette merge, which adds shaving and grooming products, Oral-B dental care, and Duracell batteries to P&G's portfolio

2007: P&G splits up newly acquired Gillette into three global business units

The Skinny

Most important to recruiters: Analytical skills, leadership skills, communication skills

Selectivity: 1 of 333 applicants hired in 2006, roughly the same as in 2005

Diversity of entry-level workforce: 37% minority; 50% female

Facts to know:

- Of P&G's 199 senior executives (VP level and higher), 152 have been with the company for 20 years or longer. In addition, more than 100 former P&Gers have gone on to leadership positions at other companies, including General Electric CEO Jeff Immelt, eBay CEO Meg Whitman, Boeing CEO Jim McNerney, Philip Morris USA CEO Michael Szymanczyk, and Microsoft CEO Steve Ballmer.

- P&G's profit-sharing program is one of the oldest continuous programs of its kind in U.S. industry.

The Starting Gate

Undergraduate internships: 440

Duration of summer internship: 10 to 14 weeks

Average total compensation: N/A

Interns by grade level:

Freshman 1%
Sophomore 8%
Junior..28%
Senior 63%

Interns who receive full-time job offers:
81%

Interns who are extended full-time job offers that accept: 68%

The Sliding Scale

Entry-level hires who had been interns: 29%

Most important performance measurements in entry-level hire: Analytical skills, leadership ability, being a team player

Entry-level hires receiving signing bonuses: N/A

Average entry-level signing bonus: N/A

Entry-level hires receiving performance bonuses: N/A

Average performance bonus during first year: N/A

The Stand-Out Perks

- Educational expenses reimbursement (after six months of continuous employment)
- Charitable gift match ($5,000)
- Relocation compensation

The Skills

- Formal three-day orientation program, including leadership exposure, guest speakers, diversity exercises, team-building exercises, facilities tour, benefits overview, and company policies and practices overview

- Formal mentorship program (100% of entry-level hires participate)

The Sound-Off

- "Very receptive and welcoming to student candidates. I was even invited to see what one of its plants is like. All [of my] expenses [were] paid by the company." —*Cornell junior**

- "The [internship] program offers you projects of the same caliber a full-time employee would tackle. Compensation is excellent; good comaraderie." —*Purdue senior**

- "P&G is the best place to start your career for three reasons: its people, its training, and its track record. Your coworkers are a refreshing oxymoron … some of the sharpest minds you will ever meet, but also some of the most well-rounded people. The time and resources the company devotes to your training is truly astounding, but there is a reason for this. History has proven that this investment in training works." —*P&G account manager, Customer Business Development*

*Data: Universum Communications

THE RECRUITER SPOTLIGHT

Name: Bill Reina
Job: Director of Global Talent Supply

Wackiest behavior encountered in recruiting: *Recently, a candidate that we interviewed for a management position sent us 25 pizzas and a variety of other gifts from his school store. It was quite a sight, seeing all the pizzas delivered. We tried to arrange for them to be given to the local food bank, as we don't accept gifts from candidates, or anyone else for that matter. The place smelled like pizza all afternoon.*

Why choose P&G: *P&G is one of the premier—if not the premier—consumer products companies in the world. The company earned this position by creating innovative brands, attracting very talented people, and developing great leaders. Most people who are interested in the industry will at least consider P&G. Some do it thinking that P&G is a terrific training ground and way to launch their career, [and they have] no intention of staying. Others see P&G's build-from-within staffing system, combined with its global breadth and varied businesses, as the ideal place to be able to grow and change jobs, locations, and even careers within the same company. While the vast majority of P&Gers decide to stay for a career with the company, many of those who don't stay become leaders in other firms. In fact, among Fortune 500 companies, only General Electric has more alumni in CEO positions than P&G.*

Sherwin-Williams Co.

101 Prospect Ave. NW
Cleveland, OH 44115
Phone: 216-566-2000
Fax: 216-566-3670
Web Addresses: www.sherwin-williams.com; www.sherwin-williams.com/careers

The Company

- Sherwin-Williams, the first company to make "DIY" (do-it-yourself) paint jobs possible, is the largest manufacturer and distributor of paints, coatings, industrial finishes, and supplies in North America. Sherwin-Williams paint jobs include the country's yellow school buses, the red coating on the Golden Gate Bridge, the floor finishes in the White House, and the intensely colorful NASCAR vehicles.

- The company realigned its business segments in 2006 into three main operating units: the Paint Stores Group, the Consumer Group, and the Global Group. While the Paint Stores Group handles the Sherwin-Williams branded products that are sold in the company's over 3,000 North American stores, the Consumer Group manages a number of acquired paint brands, including Dutch Boy, Pratt & Lambert, Martin-Senour, Dupli-Color, Krylon, Thompson's, and Minwax.

- Sherwin-Williams has a shareholder-friendly policy of paying out 30% of earnings in dividends—an amount that had increased for 28 consecutive years as of 2006.

The Suits

Christopher M. Connor: Chairman and CEO
John G. Morikis: President and COO
Cynthia D. Brogan: VP and Treasurer
Sean P. Hennessy: Senior VP of Finance and CFO

The Stats*

2007 sales: $8 billion
2007 net income: $615.6 million
Market cap: $7.3 billion
Employees: 30,767
Locations: 3,046 stores in North America, with products available in more than 20 countries globally

Major competitors: ICI Paints in North America, Azko Nobel N.V., PPG Industries

Largest operating units[†]:

Paint Stores ....$5 billion
Consumer Group ....$1.3 billion
Global Group ....$1.7 billion

*Unaudited 2007 results
[†]2007 sales

The Story

1866: Henry A. Sherwin becomes a partner in paint ingredient supplier Truman, Dunham & Co.

1870: The Truman, Dunham partnership dissolves; replaced by Sherwin, Williams & Co.

1878: After developing and patenting the resealable tin can, the company launches its first ready-mixed paint

1884: Sherwin-Williams Co. is incorporated

1964: Sherwin-Williams is listed on the New York Stock Exchange

2002: The company opens its first factory in China

2006: Paint manufacturers (Sherwin-Williams included) are found guilty of creating a "public nuisance" with their lead-paint products in the state of Rhode Island; while the company's Rhode Island appeal is pending, six other rulings (jury or judicial finding) have all been in Sherwin-Williams' favor

2007: Earnings increase again, despite a difficult housing market that sees double-digit declines in sales of existing homes

The Skinny

Most important to recruiters: Leadership skills, communication skills, work experience

Selectivity: 1 of 20 applicants hired in 2006, down from 1 of 18 applicants hired in 2005

Diversity of entry-level workforce: 20% minority; 22% female

Facts to know:

- Sherwin-Williams promotes almost exclusively from within (approximately 90%). Furthermore, nearly 20% of Sherwin-Williams' top executives began their careers as management trainees at the company, and 10% of Sherwin-Williams' VP-level employees are 40 years old or younger.

- Entry-level hires that start out as trainees travel with district managers on field visits to stores/customers. In two to three years, these trainees are empowered by the company to manage a $1 million store.

The Starting Gate

Undergraduate internships: 349

Duration of summer internship: 8 to 18 weeks

Average total compensation: $4,410

Interns by grade level:

Junior..25%
Senior 75%

Interns who receive full-time job offers: 23%

Interns who are extended full-time job offers that accept: 92%

The Sliding Scale

Entry-level hires who had been interns: 30%

Most important performance measurements in entry-level hire: Quality, customer satisfaction, productivity/efficiency

Entry-level hires receiving signing bonuses: None

Average entry-level signing bonus: N/A

Entry-level hires receiving performance bonuses: 95%

Average performance bonus during first year: $3,600

The Stand-Out Perks

- 401(k) with company match of up to 6% of salary and co-funded pension

- Educational expenses reimbursement ($5,250)

- Partial graduate school sponsorship

- 10 paid vacation days

- Health plan with dental and vision coverage

- Relocation compensation ($3,000)

- Charitable gift match ($5,000)

The Skills

- One-day orientation program, including computer training, guest speakers, team-building exercises, ergonomics training, and a tour of the facilities

- Management Trainee Program that consists of one to four rotations and lasts six to eight weeks

The Sound-Off

- "I have very good benefits and also the pay is very acceptable for an entry-level position. There is also the potential to make very large bonuses if your store performs well. I am currently an assistant manager. The only negative that I would have to say is that even though you have been with the company for a while, your base pay will not go up that high; but the bonus potential is enormous." —*Young Sherwin-Williams employee*

THE ENTRY-LEVEL SPOTLIGHT

Name: Aamir Bharmal

Job: Inventory Analyst of the Stores Group in the Midwestern Division

Briefly describe your company's work culture: *Sherwin-Williams primarily promotes from within. [Bharmal is 23 years old.] That is why entry-level employees are promoted so quickly. I was in my first position for only 11 months before I was promoted. However, during those 11 months, I gained a tremendous amount of experience and made a great amount of contacts across the whole company.*

Best part of the job: *The aspect of my job that I enjoy most is the traveling. Since Sherwin-Williams is such a large company and I work for our Midwestern Division Office, I regularly travel to anywhere between Cleveland and Seattle.*

Advice for ambitious young employees: *Despite this being such a large company, it is extremely easy for an ambitious individual to get noticed. In almost every position available, the employee is exposed to and regularly communicates with members of upper management across all divisions of the company. If you're not shy, you will succeed.*

Discuss your job: *When I first started with the company in July 2006, right out of college [Indiana University], I was hired as a field auditor. On any given day, I would travel, analyze financial reports, train store managers on store operations, communicate audit findings to district, division, and corporate management, and type up audit reports to be reviewed by district, division, and corporate management.*

Unilever

U.S. Headquarters
800 Sylvan Ave.
Englewood Cliffs, NJ 07632
Phone: 201-567-8000
Fax: N/A
Web Addresses: www.unileverusa.com;
www.unileverusa.com/ourcompany/
careers/

The Company

- Axe, "all," Ben & Jerry's, Dove personal care products, Hellmann's, Knorr, Lipton, Popsicle, Promise, Q-Tips, Slim-Fast, Sunsilk, and Vaseline are just a few products from Unilever, which operates in the food, home, and personal care categories. The multinational corporation has two parent companies that are based in the Netherlands and England—Unilever NV in Rotterdam and Unilever PLC in London.

- At the start of the millennium, Unilever launched a five-year "Path to Growth" plan. The company has now shifted gears with a new "One Unilever" program focused on improving margins. It has streamlined the business by creating a single operating company per country. Additional streamlining includes cutting 20,000 jobs globally and considering the sale of its slow-growing businesses such as its North American laundry unit.

- Unilever voluntarily decided to no longer use size 0 models in its advertising, and initiated Dove's innovative, buzz-generating "Real Beauty" campaign, a series of advertisements that featured nonairbrushed women of very different ages and body types.

The Suits

Patrick Cescau: Group CEO
James A. Lawrence: CFO
Kees van der Graaf: President of European Division
Ralph Kugler: President of Home and Personal Care
Manvinder Singh "Vindi" Banga: President of Foods
Michael B. Polk: President of the Americas
Kevin Haveluck: President of the United States Division

The Stats

2006 sales: 39.6 billion euros
2006 net income: 4.7 billion euros
Market cap: N/A
Employees: 179,000
Locations: 47 countries, with major offices in New Jersey, the United Kingdom, and the Netherlands
Major competitors: Kraft Foods, Frito-Lay, Cargill Inc., Mars Inc., Tyson Foods
Largest operating units*:
Foods ....21.3 billion euros
Home/Personal........18.3 billion euros
*2006 sales

The Story

1884: Family grocery store owner William Lever produces Sunlight Soap and brands it as a Lever and Co. product

1894: Creates Lifebuoy soap; Lever Brothers goes public after undergoing a company renaming in 1890

1917: Acquires Pear Soap; works with Jurgens and Van den Bergh margarine companies, which leads Lever Brothers to move into the margarine arena with the launch of Planters

1930: Lever Brothers and Margarine Unie merge, officially establishing Unilever

1954–1955: Introduces Dove soap in the United States, as well as "fish fingers" and Sunsilk shampoo in the United Kingdom

1961: Unilever acquires Good Humor ice cream

1978: Acquires National Starch in what was at the time the largest acquisition by a European company in the United States; National Starch specializes in starch, organic chemicals, and adhesives

1983: Launches Axe body spray for men in France

1989: Acquires Calvin Klein and Elizabeth Arden/Faberge

1993: Acquires Breyers Ice Cream in the United States

1998: Launches a sustainability agricultural program

2000: Acquires Best Foods in the second-largest cash acquisition in history; acquires Slim-Fast and Ben & Jerry's

2005: Axe becomes the top-selling male deodorant in the United States three years after its launch; Unilever also sells its cosmetics business this year, in addition to some of its frozen foods

The Skinny

Most important to recruiters: Analytical skills, leadership skills, communication skills

Selectivity: N/A

Diversity of entry-level workforce: N/A

Facts to know:

- Unilever's formal internship program includes meeting with company presidents, store visits, and AC Nielsen training.

- Almost half of Unilever's top executives (VP level and above) have been with the company for 20 years or more.

The Starting Gate

Undergraduate internships: 42

Duration of summer internship: 8 to 16 weeks

Average total compensation: $7,500

Interns by grade level:
Junior...100%

Interns who receive full-time job offers: 50%

Interns who are extended full-time job offers that accept: 78%

The Sliding Scale

Entry-level hires who had been interns: 40%

Most important performance measurements in entry-level hire: Analytical skills, leadership ability, sales/revenue

Entry-level hires receiving signing bonuses: 100%

Average entry-level signing bonus: $3,000

Entry-level hires receiving performance bonuses: 100%

Average performance bonus during first year: $2,400

The Stand-Out Perks

- Educational expenses reimbursement (up to two classes per semester)
- Alternative work arrangements
- Able to use two vacation days to spend a full week serving the community
- Full graduate school sponsorship
- 401(k) with company match of up to 5% of salary
- Charitable gift match ($10,000)
- Backup care for children/elders at subsidized rate of $2 per hour for up to 120 hours per year

The Skills

- Formal one-day orientation program
- Supply Chain Management Program, which consists of two to four rotations and lasts 52 to 200 weeks
- Formal mentorship program

The Sound-Off

- "I had a co-op there for a seven-month period and enjoyed it. I would recommend it to others. Competitive salary, challenging assignments, and great feedback."
  —*Rensselaer Polytechnic senior**

*Data: Universum Communications

THE ENTRY-LEVEL SPOTLIGHT

Name: Matt Algar

Job: Customer Demand and Replenishment Planning Analyst in the Supply Chain Management Program

Why choose Unilever: *The company has positions both nationally and internationally in virtually every aspect of business. Unilever also provides a fantastic supplemental learning environment designed to enhance professional skills beyond those gained on the job—a big advantage for someone beginning their career. After graduating with a degree in Supply Chain, I found a perfect fit within Unilever's Supply Chain Management Program. The program is designed to provide broad experience and exposure to Unilever's supply chain through three complementary rotations, each ranging from 12 to 18 months.*

The workplace culture: *Unilever employees are extremely passionate about their work. The culture is relaxed without losing professionalism and challenges while maintaining a fun atmosphere. Unilever is extremely active in environmental and community projects, and many employees choose to participate in local volunteer efforts.*

Best part of the job: *The ability to work with globally recognized brands and have a positive impact on millions of consumers.*

Most off-the-wall corporate practice: *The company recently underwent a major systems convergence. It was a very busy time for employees, and many were working unusually long hours. To maintain morale, Unilever set up stress-relief rooms with board games, table sports, video games, and ice cream. This type of effort says a lot about Unilever's culture and the priority the company places on the well-being of its employees.*

BP America

British Petroleum America
501 Westlake Park Blvd.
Houston, TX 77079
Phone: 281-366-2000
Fax: N/A
Web Addresses: www.bp.com;
www.bp.com/careers/us

The Company

- Over the last century, British Petroleum (BP) has grown from a small-time oil company to a global energy group. Today, BP produces 3.9 million barrels of oil a day and operates 25,000 gas stations worldwide.

- Six brands make up the BP family, including the convenience store brand ampm and the global automotive lubricant maker Castrol.

- Lauded as an environmental good guy in a much-maligned industry, BP suffered blows to its image in 2006 when evidence surfaced suggesting that safety lapses were probably behind a deadly accident in BP's Texas City refinery. Additional safety concerns then forced the company to shut down one of its largest oil fields in Alaska. This was the start of a difficult end to the illustrious career of CEO Lord John Browne, one of the United Kingdom's most revered business leaders. BP's 2007 third-quarter results were the worst since 1993, but the com-

pany is counting on its new, well-regarded CEO, Tony Hayward, to right the ship.

 ## The Suits

Tony Hayward: Group CEO
David Allen: Group Chief of Staff
Iain Conn: CEO of Refining and
    Marketing
Byron Grote: CFO
Andy Inglis: CEO of Exploration and
    Production

The Stats

2007 sales: $284.4 billion
2007 net income: $20.8 billion
Market cap: N/A
Employees: 97,600
Locations: BP actively explores oil in
    26 countries, and its products and
    services are available in over 100
    countries

Major competitors: Exxon Mobil, Shell

Largest operating units*:

Exploration and Production
...................................$57.9 billion

Refining and Marketing
...................................$251.5 billion

Gas, Power and Renewables
...................................$21.7 billion

Other Business and Corporate
...................................$42.3 billion

*2007 sale; financial data provided by Capital IQ

📖 The Story

1909: The Anglo-Persian Oil Company Limited is established in England; the company's first oil discovery is in the Middle East

1922: The company goes public

1954: The Anglo-Persian Oil Company Limited is renamed the British Petroleum Company Limited

1969: BP discovers oil in Alaska and begins drilling shortly thereafter

1987: Standard Oil of Ohio becomes a wholly owned subsidiary of BP

1998: BP merges with Amoco; all Amoco locations are either closed or renamed BP

2000: Atlantic Richfield Company and Burmah Castrol join the BP family

2005: A fatal blast at BP's Texas City–based refinery kills 15 people and injures 170; BP launches BP Alternative Energy, a venture focused on generating low-carbon energy

2006: After discovering signs of heavy corrosion, BP shuts down one of its biggest oil fields in Alaska, raising gasoline prices to record highs; BP then announces plans to invest $500 million over the next 10 years in researching alternative fuels for transportation

2007: Scandal-plagued CEO John Browne steps down and Tony Hayward takes the position

2008: Group Chief of Staff David Allen announces he will retire in March of 2008

The Skinny

Most important to recruiters: College major, motivation, college GPA

Selectivity: 1 of 30 applicants hired in 2006, up from 1 of 16 applicants hired in 2005

Diversity of entry-level workforce: 33% minority; 34% female

Facts to know:

- BP has an early experience program for every new hire in every segment of the company. The Exploration & Production segment, for example, features Challenge, a program consisting of an induction event with university hires all over the globe, a variety of work experiences, and extensive training opportunities.

🏇 The Starting Gate

Undergraduate internships: 214

Duration of summer internship: 12 weeks

Average total compensation: $16,500

Interns by grade level:
Junior...19%
Senior 61%
College graduate 20%

Interns who receive full-time job offers: 84%

Interns who are extended full-time job offers that accept: 90%

The Sliding Scale

Entry-level hires who had been interns: 39%

Most important performance measurements in entry-level hire: Learning ability, effort, creativity

Entry-level hires receiving signing bonuses: 100%

Average entry-level signing bonus: $10,625

Entry-level hires receiving performance bonuses: 100%

Average performance bonus during first year: $6,924

The Stand-Out Perks

- 10 paid vacation days and 8 paid holidays

- Unlimited time off for religious observances

- Employee discounts

- Relocation compensation ($10,000)

- Charitable gift match ($5,000)

The Skills

- Six-day orientation program

- Challenge, an entry-level training program consisting of three to five rotations and lasting three years

- Formal mentorship program (100% of entry-level hires participate)

The Sound-Off

- "They had very challenging projects and a lot of activities for the interns." —*UCLA senior**

- "BP really does care about the environment. This makes it easy to stand up for my company if I'm ever on the firing line." —*Employee in Integrated Supply & Trading*

- "BP is very supportive of diversity in the workplace, safety, and women who are starting families or having additional children. This company makes promises and keeps those promises!" —*Employee in Exploration Geology*

*Data: Universum Communications

THE ENTRY-LEVEL SPOTLIGHT

Name: Tracy Porter

Job: Process Engineer in BP's Carson Refinery (Carson, CA)

Why BP is an attractive entry-level employer: *BP helps new hires by giving them significant training in their first year. . . . BP has a great education program if you are interested in getting a master's or an MBA. There are many possible paths I can take in my career. BP is also very competitive in pay and benefits, and I do enjoy many perks, such as an on-site gym, travel for training, social events, great benefits, and a very new office facility with a café and everything centrally located.*

Briefly describe a typical day: *Sometimes I am in my office or in meetings all day, working on solving problems using simulation tools, data analysis, or modeling calculations in Excel. Other days I put on my protective personal equipment (PPE) and spend the entire day out in the refinery. Every day brings something a little different, which I really enjoy.*

Best part of the job: *One of the cool things about my job is how many young, enthusiastic people I get to work with every day. Some people believe that the oil industry is supported primarily by older male workers, but that is not the case. There definitely is an age gap, but about half of my group is age 30 or under.*

Advice on how an ambitious young hire can get noticed: *The career philosophy at my refinery is, "If you want to do it, let us know." Our managers want to know what we're interested in, and they will assist you in developing the skills you need to take the path you are interested in.*

Constellation Energy

750 East Pratt St.
Baltimore, MD 21202
Phone: 410-783-2800
Fax: 410-783-3629
Web Addresses:
www.constellation.com;
www.constellation.com/careers

The Company

- Constellation Energy is the nation's largest competitive supplier of electricity to commercial and industrial customers, and it is also the nation's largest wholesale power seller. Through its regulated utility—Baltimore Gas and Electricity—Constellation Energy delivers electricity to 1.2 million electric and 640,000 natural gas residential customers in central Maryland.

- Constellation's businesses include Constellation Energy Commodities Group, Constellation NewEnergy, Constellation NewEnergy Gas Division, Constellation Energy Generation Group, Baltimore Gas and Electric (BGE), Fellon-McCord & Associates (an energy consulting and management services provider), Constellation Energy Projects & Services Group, and BGE Home.

- In the past few years, Constellation has invested $190 million into emissions-reducing equipment and upgrades; the company has also worked to improve its employee safety record.

The Suits

Mayo A. Shattuck: Chairman, President, and CEO
Thomas V. Brooks: Executive VP of Constellation Energy
Thomas F. Brady: Executive VP of Corporate Strategy
Michael J. Wallace: President of Constellation Energy Generation Group
Irving B. Yoskowitz: Executive VP and General Counsel

The Stats

2007 sales: $21.2 billion
2007 net income: $822 million
Market cap: $18.5 billion
Employees: 10,231

Holdings: Operates 78 electricity units generating 8,700 megawatts; also oversees 23,907 miles of distribution lines, 1,300 miles of transmission lines, and 6,586 miles of gas mains

Locations: 42 states and 8 countries

Major competitors: Allegheny Energy, Duke Energy, NJ Resources, PSEG, Dynegy, Chesapeake Utilities

Largest operating units*:

Merchant Energy............$18.7 billion
Regulated Electric ....$2.5 billion
Regulated Gas ....$963 million
Other nonregulated........$250 million
*2007 sales

The Story

1816: Rembrandt Pearle and three partners found Gas Light Company of Baltimore, the U.S.'s first gas utility. Operates for 50+ years before merging with local competitors to become Consolidated Gas Co.

1906: Consolidated Gas, U.S. Electric Light, and Brush Electric Light merge to form Consolidated Gas Electric Light and Power Company

1920s: Consolidated switches from using mostly hydroelectric power to utilizing steam power

1955: Consolidated is renamed Baltimore Gas and Electric Company (BGE)

1967: BGE announces plans for its first nuclear power plant

1985: BGE founds its own holding company, Constellation Holdings, and begins investing in nonutility and independent power developments

1989–1990: BGE shuts down its nuclear power generators for repairs, a move that ultimately costs the company $458 million

1999: Constellation Energy Group, a holding company for BGE and Constellation Enterprises, is formed after deregulation legislation passes in Maryland

2002: Acquires AES New Energy, a commercial and industrial energy company

2003: Acquires Alliance Energy Services; Fellon-McCord & Associates; and the electricity division of Dynegy Canada

2004: Several Constellation businesses are consolidated to form NewEnergy-Gas Division

2005: Constellation Energy and FPL Group announce their plans for a merger

2006: The proposed FPL/Constellation merger is called off as a result of legislative holdups

The Skinny

Most important to recruiters: College major, communication skills, analytical skills

Selectivity: 1 of 4 applicants hired in 2006, up from 1 of 5 applicants hired in 2005

Diversity of entry-level workforce: 21% minority; 38% female

Facts to know:

- Constellation actively recruited at 15 U.S. undergraduate campuses during the 2006–2007 school year and extended job offers on 12 of those campuses.

- Career Planning workshops (Career Power) help new employees plan their careers and development within the company.

The Starting Gate

Undergraduate internships: 152

Duration of summer internship: 8 to 12 weeks

Average total compensation: $6,000

Interns by grade level:
Freshman 23%
Sophomore 9%
Junior...24%
Senior 30%
College graduate 14%

Interns who receive full-time job offers: 75%

Interns who are extended full-time job offers that accept: 75%

The Sliding Scale

Entry-level hires who had been interns: 50%

Most important performance measurements in entry-level hire: Productivity/efficiency, learning ability, leadership ability

Entry-level hires receiving signing bonuses: 17%

Average entry-level signing bonus: $3,950

Entry-level hires receiving performance bonuses: 86%

Average performance bonus during first year: $9,200

The Stand-Out Perks

- Educational expenses reimbursement

- Full graduate school sponsorship

- 15 paid vacation days

- Charitable gift match ($2,000)

- Relocation compensation ($5,000)

- Discounts on car rentals, gym, cell phones/service, insurance, and cultural events

The Skills

- Formal one-day orientation program

- Two-week-long Constellation Management Development Program

The Sound-Off

- "Constellation showed incredible flexibility and class in allowing me out of my employment agreement to attend business school, and we've decided to take up the employment conversation again when I finish. Needless to say, I have a very high opinion." —*Future employee*

THE RECRUITER SPOTLIGHT

Name: Adrienne Alberts
Job: Senior Human Resources Consultant

Memorable recruiting experiences: *During my nine years in recruiting, there are two experiences that remain quite memorable. The first was a student who thought it appropriate to interview in a three-piece suit and flip flops; the overall presentation was not what it should have been. The second situation involved a student who submitted a résumé with a comic strip on the bottom. While the comic strip was funny, it was inappropriate.*

Advice for young prospective employees looking to join your company: *The first piece of advice I would give is to be proactive. No matter the organization that you are considering for employment, be sure to do your homework. Find out about the company, culture, community involvement, etc. Be sure to participate in events held on your campus or in your community. Take the opportunity to network with individuals in the organization or alumni from your institution. It is about more than good grades; you need to stand out among the competition.*

Other interview faux pas that candidates should try to avoid: *The biggest thing to avoid is getting so nervous that you forget to be yourself. There is a good deal of information available to help you learn how to answer interview questions and prepare for an interview. Do your homework, and you will be prepared. But remember that it is important to be yourself. Also, remember that the interview is a unique opportunity to decide if the organization is a good fit for you. Avoid getting so caught up in responding that you don't stop and listen about the company. This information will be critical as you decide if you want to pursue the opportunity.*

Why choose Constellation: *Constellation Energy is a dynamic and exciting organization that values and respects its customers, employees, and the communities in which we operate. We're an industry leader that continues to grow and innovate. Not only do we recognize the value of attracting and retaining top talent, but we are committed to employee engagement and development.*

Duke Energy

526 South Church St.
Charlotte, NC 28202
Phone: 704-594-6200
Fax: 704-382-3814
Web Addresses: www.duke-energy.
com; www.duke-energy.com/careers/

The Company

- Duke Energy Corporation is one of North America's largest electric utility holding companies. The energy giant supplies electricity to 4 million utility customers in five U.S. states and Latin America.

- The company also supplies natural gas to half a million gas utility customers in Ohio and northern Kentucky. Its 2006 merger with Cinergy Corp. gave Duke an additional 1.7 million U.S. customers located in the Midwest.

- Duke's natural gas businesses were spun off into an independent, publicly traded company called Spectra Energy in early 2007.

- Duke owns effectively half of Crescent Resources LLC, a joint real estate venture with Morgan Stanley Real Estate Fund. Crescent manages land holdings and develops commercial and residential real estate projects primarily in the southeastern region of the United States.

FAST FACTS

"Best Places to Launch a Career"
 Rank: 80
"Best Internships" Rank: N/A
Full-Time Salary: $35,000–$39,999
Entry-Level Hires: N/A
Top College Major: Science
3-Year Retention Rate: 61%
Formal Mentorship Program: Yes
Stock Ticker: DUK

The Suits

James E. Rogers: Chairman, President, and CEO
Henry B. Barron Jr.: Group Executive and Chief Nuclear Officer
Lynn J. Good: Group Executive and President of Commercial Businesses
David L. Hauser: Group Executive and CFO
Marc E. Manly: Group Executive and Chief Legal Officer

The Stats

2007 operating revenue: $12.7 billion
2007 net income: $1.5 billion
Market cap: $25.4 billion
Employees: 25,600 (as of 2006)
Locations: Though headquartered in Charlotte, North Carolina, Duke provides energy to customers in North Carolina, South Carolina, Indiana, Kentucky, and Ohio, and

internationally in Argentina, Brazil, Ecuador, El Salvador, Greece, Guatemala, Peru, and Saudi Arabia

Major competitors: AEP, Constellation Energy Group, Progress Energy

Largest operating units*:

U.S. Franchised Electric
and Gas ....$9.7 billion
Commercial Power ....$1.9 billion
International Energy ....$1.1 billion
Other ....$167 million

*2007 sales

📖 The Story

1904: James Buchanan Duke founds the company under the name Catawba Power Station to provide hydropower for North Carolina's growing textile industry

1930s–1940s: Growing demand and limited water resources lead Duke Power, as the company became known, to switch to coal-fired power generation during this period

1976: Duke, which has been exploring the possibilities of nuclear power since the 1950s, founds the Institute of Nuclear Power Operations (INPO) to increase public confidence in this energy source

1997: Duke Energy Corporation is formed after a merger between PanEnergy and Duke Power

2002: Acquires Westcoast Energy Inc.

2003: Sells Energy Delivery Services business unit to The Shaw Group Inc.

2006: Merges with energy company Cinergy Corp.

2007: James E. Rogers becomes chairman of Duke, replacing Paul Anderson; natural gas business becomes an independent, publicly traded company called Spectra Energy Corp.

The Skinny

Most important to recruiters: Leadership skills, college GPA, communication skills

Selectivity: N/A

Diversity of entry-level workforce: N/A

Facts to know:

- Nearly half of all top executives have 20-plus years of experience at Duke under their belts.

- All newly hired entry-level leaders take Supervisory Essentials on policies and procedures. New hires starting in leadership roles may also enter the Supervisory Leadership Development Program, which covers policies, planning, work assignment, managing performance, and other issues pertaining to personnel supervision.

🐎 The Starting Gate

Undergraduate internships: 121

Duration of summer internship: 10 to 12 weeks

Average total compensation: N/A

Interns by grade level:
Freshman 16%
Sophomore 30%
Junior..19%
Senior 6%
College graduate 5%
*24% of interns did not indicate their graduation date

Interns who receive full-time job offers: 7%

Interns who are extended full-time job offers that accept: N/A

The Sliding Scale

Entry-level hires who had been interns: N/A

Most important performance measurements in entry-level hire: Being a team player, other qualities depend on job classification

Entry-level hires receiving signing bonuses: N/A

Average entry-level signing bonus: N/A

Entry-level hires receiving performance bonuses: N/A

Average performance bonus during first year: N/A

The Stand-Out Perks

- Allowed to take up to 10 hours off per week for educational or community activities

- Partial and full graduate school sponsorship

- 10 paid vacation days and 3 paid personal days

- Access to co-funded pension and 401(k) with company matching up to 6% of pay

- Charitable gift match to educational institutions ($5,000); for other qualifying public charities, Duke matches 50 cents for every dollar donated

The Skills

- Formal two-day orientation program includes review of code of business ethics, enterprise policies and key procedures, safety principles, and company charter

- One-week leadership program for supervisory new hires; full library of instructor led and e-learning employee development programs

- Formal mentorship program

THE RECRUITER SPOTLIGHT

Name: Beth Britt

Job: Managing Director of Enterprise Staffing

Wacky recruiting technique: *[A candidate] offered to come in "on a trial basis," unpaid, with no guarantee of a full-time job. For a host of reasons, we declined the offer.*

Advice for prospective young hires: *Be sure you're applying for the right reasons, e.g., you love the industry or the particular discipline. Demonstrate that you've done your homework about the company, its position in the market, its history, etc.*

Why choose Duke Energy: *There hasn't in recent years been a more exciting time to join Duke Energy. Our nation has significant challenges ahead in the areas of energy efficiency, carbon reduction, and meeting the energy needs of a growing customer base. Our chairman, president, and CEO (Jim Rogers) is a visible and vocal leader in Washington, D.C. around these issues. Duke Energy is one of the leading utilities in the country, with a long history of providing safe, reliable, and affordable energy. And we are actively looking for the best and brightest talent for areas including engineering, IT, technical and craft, and accounting and finance.*

Exelon

10 South Dearborn St.
Chicago, IL 60603
Phone: 312-394-7398
Fax: 312-394-7945
Web Addresses: www.exeloncorp.com;
www.exeloncorp.com/careers

The Company

- The product of a 2000 merger between Chicago- and Philadelphia-based utility companies, this public utility holding company distributes electricity to over 5 million Illinois and Pennsylvania customers and gas to almost 500,000 people in the Philadelphia area. Exelon's two business segments are Energy Delivery, which consists of northern Illinois electricity provider Commonwealth Edison Company (ComEd) and southeastern Pennsylvania electricity and natural gas provider Philadelphia Electrical Company (PECO) Energy, and Generation, a power producer and wholesale marketer with three operating groups.

- Exelon operates the largest nuclear fleet in the nation. Its 10 stations account for approximately 20% of the U.S. nuclear industry's power capacity.

- Green-friendly job seekers might not gravitate toward the industry in general, but Exelon has embarked

on several recent environmentally friendly ventures, including the launch of the PECO Green Region Grant Program to conserve open spaces and a campaign to reduce greenhouse gas emissions under the EPA's Climate Leaders Program. In April 2007, Exelon's green headquarters received a Leadership in Energy and Environmental Design (LEED®) Platinum Commercial Interiors (CI) certification from the U.S. Green Building Council, becoming the largest office space in the world to be LEED-CI certified at the platinum level.

- Exelon attempted to merge with Public Service Enterprise Group in 2005, which would have created the largest utility company in the United States. Public interest groups had other plans though: state regulatory issues ultimately quashed the deal.

The Suits

John W. Rowe: Chairman, CEO, and President
Frank M. Clark Jr.: Chairman and CEO of ComEd
John F. Young: CFO and Executive VP of Finance and Markets
Randall E. Mehrberg: Executive VP, Chief Administrative Officer, and Chief Legal Officer
Elizabeth Anne Moler: Executive VP of Government and Environmental Affairs and Public Policy

The Stats

2007 sales: $18.9 billion
2007 net income: $2.7 billion
Market cap: $53.9 billion
Employees: 17,800
Locations: Chicago and Philadelphia
Major competitors: Ameren, Dynegy, PPL
Largest operating units*:
Generation ....$10.7 billion
ComEd ....$6.1 billion
PECO Energy ....$5.6 billion
*2007 revenues

The Story

2000: Unicom, a Chicago-based utility company, and PECO Energy, a large utility company in southeastern Pennsylvania, merge and form Exelon Corporation

2001: Exelon Nuclear complies with all of the U.S. Nuclear Regulatory Commission's security measures after September 11, 2001

2004: Completes its exit from the non-core businesses of Exelon Enterprises

2005: Federal Energy Regulatory Commission approves merger of Exelon and Public Services Enterprise Group (PSEG)

2006: Merger with PSEG, which would have created the largest utility company in the United States, falls through because of intense scrutiny and disapproval by public interest groups

2007: The cost of power that ComEd procures for Illinois residential customers increases by approximately 26%; later, ComEd and its parent company, Exelon, (and others) reach a settlement with Illinois policymakers that cuts that increase in half

The Skinny

Most important to recruiters: College GPA, analytical skills, college major

Selectivity: N/A

Diversity of entry-level workforce: 39% minority; 21% female

Facts to know:

- Job seekers should note: entry-level employment opportunities at Exelon are almost exclusively located in the greater Chicago and Philadelphia areas.

- Exelon actively recruited on 25 undergraduate U.S. campuses in the 2006–2007 school year, and ultimately made job offers to students at 16 of those schools.

The Starting Gate

Undergraduate internships: 213

Duration of summer internship: 10 weeks

Average total compensation: $8,095*

Interns by grade level: N/A

Interns who receive full-time job offers: N/A

Interns who are extended full-time job offers that accept: N/A

*Includes hourly rate, overtime and housing stipend

The Sliding Scale

Entry-level hires who had been interns: N/A

Most important performance measurements in entry-level hire: College GPA

Entry-level hires receiving signing bonuses: None

Average entry-level signing bonus: N/A

Entry-level hires receiving performance bonuses: 100%

Average performance bonus during first year: $3,000

The Stand-Out Perks

- Educational expenses reimbursement ($15,000)

- Three weeks vacation plus 18 days for sickness, holiday, and religious observances

- Relocation compensation

- Employee discount plan

The Skills

- Formal, one-day orientation program that includes computer training and a tour of the facilities

- Initial License Training (ILT) that lasts 78 weeks, employees typically receive a 5–10% raise after program completion

- Formal mentorship program (45% of entry-level hires participate)

THE SUPERSTAR SPOTLIGHT

Name: Bob Carroll
Job: Manager of Corporate Strategy

Fill us in on your dizzying climb through the ranks: *I started with Exelon in July 2002 as an analyst within the Customer and Marketing Services department at ComEd, where I served in an operational/process improvement analytical role. I rotated through a couple of other roles (Mobile Data Analyst and Operations Supervisor) before being promoted in October 2003 to Senior Administrator in Customer and Marketing Services. The director whom I worked for at this time asked if I was interested in other opportunities at corporate headquarters. I was ultimately offered a lateral position in July 2004 as an analyst in the department. Since that time, I have been promoted twice within the group, to a Principal Planning Analyst (Senior Level Analyst) in January 2006 and Manager of Corporate Strategy in July 2007, taking on increased responsibilities.*

Describe a typical day: *The wonderful thing about working in Corporate Strategy is that every day is different. In a given work day, I may be engaged in analysis or research in a variety of strategic focus areas, participate in a brainstorming session with team members or business unit leaders, lead a discussion on Exelon's Vision and Strategic Direction with employees, or work with project team members from across the company to successfully deliver recommendations and/or work products at the request of the senior leadership team.*

Best part of the job: *The challenge that comes from working with essentially every part of the organization on both large projects and smaller work assignments over time. By its very nature, Corporate Strategy reaches into everything that Exelon does, which means it is necessary to have a certain level of understanding of the operational, financial, environmental, and employee-related aspects of the company. I am provided a unique opportunity to see the "big picture" and understand how each of Exelon's companies and business units contributes to the direction of our company's vision and strategic goals.*

Any tips for ambitious new entry-level hires: *My advice would be, take every opportunity to engage in formal and informal learning opportunities, including everything from participating in available internal training programs and external industry forums to getting involved in discussions with people in different areas of the company over lunch.*

Shell Oil Company

910 Louisiana, One Shell Plaza
Houston, TX 77210
Phone: 713-241-6161
Fax: N/A
Web Addresses: www.shell.com/;
www.shell.com/careers

The Company

- Shell Oil is a Houston, Texas–based subsidiary of multinational oil company Royal Dutch Shell, which is headquartered in The Hague, Netherlands. Royal Dutch Shell (also known as the Shell Group) is truly a global organization, operating in 130 countries and trading simultaneously on the New York Stock Exchange (NYSE), the Financial Times Stock Exchange (FTSE), and several German exchanges. Shell's $318 billion in 2006 revenues made it the third-largest company in the world.

- Shell's operations are organized into the following businesses: Corporate, Exploration and Production, Gas and Power, Oil Products, Chemicals, and Other industry segments (including Renewables, Hydrogen, CO_2, etc.).

- Shell's third-quarter net profits rose 16% over the third quarter of 2006, although there was a drop in production, and the company warned that its refining operations were weaker than they appeared. Shell is

in the midst of a huge campaign to find new oil and gas reserves and has also invested approximately $1 billion into biofuel research in recent years.

FAST FACTS

"Best Places to Launch a Career" Rank: 86
"Best Internships" Rank: N/A
Entry-Level Hires: 157
Top College Major: Engineering
Entry-Level Hires Who Had Been Interns: 23%
Sponsors Grad School: Partial
Stock Ticker: RDSA

The Suits

Jeroen van der Veer: CEO
Malcom Brinded: Executive Director of Exploration and Production
Rob Routs: Executive Director of Downstream (Oil Products and Chemicals)
Linda Cook: Executive Director of Gas and Power
Peter Voser: CFO

The Stats*

2007 sales: $355.8 billion
2007 reported income: $31.3 billion
Market cap: $106.4 billion (as of March 5, 2008)
Employees: 108,000

Locations: Operates 40 refineries, 50 trade ships, 5,000 miles of pipeline, and 45,000 service stations in 130 countries worldwide

Main competitors: BP Plc, Chevron, ExxonMobil

Largest operating units:[†]

Exploration & Production..$14.7 billion
Gas & Power ....$12.8 billion
Oil Products ....$7 billion
Oil Sands ....$582 million
Chemicals ....$1.7 billion
Other Industry Segments
    and Corporate ....$4.6 billion

*Unaudited 2007 results for the Shell Group
[†]2007 reported income by segment

The Story

1833: Marcus Samuel begins importing oil from Asia into Europe

1897: Samuel's sons rename the firm Shell Transport Company

1901: The Shell logo makes its first appearance

1903–1907: Shell Transport merges with Royal Dutch Petroleum

1914–1918: Royal Dutch Shell provides 80% of the fuel for the British Royal Air Force during World War I

1939: Upon Adolf Hitler's invasion of Holland, Shell relocates its headquarters to Curacao

1950: Shell partners with Ferrari and develops specialized fuels for Formula One race cars

1973: Shell partners with Gulf Oil and purchases nuclear reactors, but the oil

company later sells these interests after an accident at Three Mile Island in 1979

2004: An accounting scandal leads to the departure of Shell Chairman Philip Watts, Oil and Gas Chief Walter van de Vijver, and CFO Judy Boynton; the incident also forces the company to lower its stated oil and gas reserves

2005: Royal Dutch and Shell Trading officially become the Royal Dutch Shell group

2006: Shell is forced to surrender control of its $22 billion Sakhalin-II project in Russia because of pressure from the country's regulators

The Skinny

Most important to recruiters: College major, college GPA, behavioral interview results

Selectivity: 1 of 133 applicants hired in 2006, up from 1 of 265 applicants hired in 2005

Diversity of entry-level workforce: 29% minority; 38% female

Facts to know:

- Shell actively recruited on 23 U.S. undergraduate campuses during the 2006–2007 school year and extended job offers on 19 of those campuses.

- Of the company's top executives (VP level and higher), 50% have been with Shell for 20 years or longer.

The Starting Gate

Undergraduate internships: 146

Duration of summer internship: 8 to 16 weeks

Average total compensation: N/A

Interns by grade level:
Sophomore 5%
Junior..29%
Senior 66%

Interns who receive full-time job offers: N/A

Interns who are extended full-time job offers that accept: N/A

The Sliding Scale

Entry-level hires who had been interns: 23%

Most important performance measurements in entry-level hire: Productivity/efficiency, leadership ability, sales/revenues

Entry-level hires receiving signing bonuses: N/A

Average entry-level signing bonus: N/A

Entry-level hires receiving performance bonuses: N/A

Average performance bonus during first year: N/A

The Stand-Out Perks

- 401(k) and co-funded pension
- Partial graduate school sponsorship

- Educational expenses reimbursement
- 10 paid vacation days, 8 paid holidays, and 5 paid sick days
- Health plan that includes dental and vision coverage
- Employee discounts

The Skills

- One-day orientation
- 30-week BUILD leadership program for nominated new hires
- Formal mentorship program (100% of entry-level hires participate)

The Sound-Off

- "The [internship] projects are challenging, and there is a lot of opportunity to network with other interns, as well as full-time employees. Also, they compensate interns very well." —*Michigan State senior**

- "Shell Oil Company offers internships to freshmen, which the majority of companies don't do." —*Colorado School of Mines student**

- "They pair you [intern] up with a mentor, and they offer a relocation expense package." —*Florida State junior**

*Data: Universum Communications

THE RECRUITER SPOTLIGHT

Name: Cary Wilkins
Job: Director of Recruitment, Americas

Wackiest behavior encountered during recruiting: *Getting a surprising phone call from a parent ready to negotiate his graduate's compensation package, announcing that "we have another offer we are considering." While this may not be too "wacky," it is an intriguing change in the world of recruitment. Parents appear to be taking a stronger role in coaching and assisting their young adult children as they move into their professional careers.*

Advice for a young prospective employee: *Bring a well-rounded résumé to the table. Demonstrate your willingness to contribute academically and beyond the classroom. Shell sees work-life balance as important, so in addition to excelling in academic achievements, we look for candidates who have been involved in community activities and organizations. Overall, your ability to perform and work in a collaborative environment is key to successfully landing a position with Shell.*

If someone arrives late for an interview, is there any way that he or she can redeem him- or herself? *All of us have been in situations that have caused us to be late for an important meeting or event. Redemption comes with honesty and open communication. A candidate [who is] running late should simply contact us to let us know of his or her situation. With that information, we will make changes to schedules and provide other reasonable accommodations to conduct the interview. We recognize that events beyond our control can interrupt even the best-laid plans. Our goal is to make sure that everyone remains safe and that we have the chance to meet with qualified candidates.*

Ameriprise Financial

55 Ameriprise Financial Center
Minneapolis, MN 55474
Phone: 612-671-3131
Fax: 612-671-8880
Web Addresses: www.ameriprise.com;
www.ameriprise.com/amp/global/
careers/careers.asp

The Company

- In 2005, American Express Financial Corporation broke off from its parent company and became Ameriprise Financial, an independent public company with approximately 12,000 advisors and 8,000 employees. Ameriprise provides financial planning, income management, and insurance services to its clients.

- Ameriprise Financial has $466 billion in owned, managed, and administered assets and serves approximately 2.8 million individual, business, and institutional clients nationwide. In addition, the company operates Ameriprise Bank FSB, offering home equity loans, mortgages, and cash management.

- Ameriprise's philanthropic endeavors include funding grants for various national and community arts and theater projects and providing financial education programs.

FAST FACTS

**"Best Places to Launch a Career"
Rank:** 58
"Best Internships" Rank: N/A
Full-Time Salary: $35,000–$39,999
Entry-Level Hires: 2,335
3-Year Retention Rate: 54%
5-Year Retention Rate: 50%
Stock Ticker: AMP

The Suits

James M. Cracchiolo: Chairman and CEO
Walter S. Berman: CFO
William F. Truscott: President of U.S. Asset Management/Distribution and CIO
Brian M. Heath: President of U.S. Advisor Group
Glen Salow: Executive VP of Technology and Operations

The Stats

2007 sales: $8.9 billion
2007 net income: $814 million
Market cap: $12.8 billion
Financial advisors: 12,592
Employees: 8,680
Locations: Throughout the United States
Major competitors: FMR Corp., Principal Financial Group, T. Rowe Price, Franklin Resources Inc.

Largest operating units*:

Advice & Wealth Management
..................................$3.8 billion
Asset Management ....$1.8 billion
Annuities..........................$2.3 billion
Protection ....$2.0 billion
Corporate & Other ....$1.2 billion

*2007 sales; financial data provided by Capital IQ

The Story

1894: John Tapper founds Investors Syndicate insurance company

1940: Investors Syndicate partners with Investors Mutual and soon changes its name to Investors Diversified Services, Inc. (IDS)

1958: IDS Life Insurance is created

1984: American Express acquires IDS Financial Services

1986: IDS acquires Wisconsin Employers' Property Casualty Company and reopens it as IDS Property Casualty Insurance

1994: IDS begins operating under the American Express brand as American Express Financial Corporation

2003: American Express Financial Corporation acquires London's Threadneedle Asset Management Holdings Ltd.

2005: American Express Financial Advisors is renamed Ameriprise Financial, Inc., and the new entity goes public as an independent company on the NYSE

The Skinny

Most important to recruiters: Communication skills, leadership skills, analytical skills

Selectivity: 1 of 14 applicants hired in 2006 (June–December), compared to 1 of 20 hired in 2005

Diversity of entry-level workforce: N/A

Facts to know:

- On average, Ameriprise spends more than $60,000 training its new entry-level hires in their first year.

- The company participates in STEP UP, a Minnesota state-funded internship program for high school students.

- In addition to profit sharing, Ameriprise Financial offers a company stock contribution. Employees are eligible after 60 days with the company and are fully vested after 5 years of service.

The Starting Gate

Undergraduate internships: 25

Duration of summer internship: 10 to 12 weeks

Average total compensation: N/A

Interns by grade level:
Junior...16%
Senior 84%

Interns who receive full-time job offers: N/A

Interns who are extended full-time job offers that accept: N/A

The Sliding Scale

Entry-level hires who had been interns: 1%

Most important performance measurements in entry-level hire: Learning ability, effort, sales/revenues

Entry-level hires receiving signing bonuses: N/A

Average entry-level signing bonus: N/A

Entry-level hires receiving performance bonuses: N/A

Average performance bonus during first year: N/A

The Stand-Out Perks

- Educational expenses reimbursement ($5,000)
- Partial graduate school sponsorship
- Profit-sharing plan
- Charitable gift match ($5,000)
- Relocation compensation ($12,000)

The Skills

- Formal, one-day orientation program, including guest speakers
- Finance Leadership Development Program, which is a rotational, 78-week program for entry-level hires

- Some departments offer their own formal mentorship programs; others offer a buddy program that partners new employees with peers who have been at the company for less than one year

The Sound-Off

- "If you are young and want the world handed to you, this is not the place for you. But if you are looking for a place where you can build a sound financial practice with great support and don't mind a little hard work, this is it. There is no ceiling on your income." —BW *Discussion Forum*

- "On top of the first 20 weeks being minimum wage, you do work 8 a.m. to 8 p.m., plus Saturdays. Using Sundays to catch up on paperwork is not uncommon, because your weekdays and evenings are spent on the phone marketing." —BW *Discussion Forum*

- "I was 22 when I started; I made $82,000 in year one, $79,000 in year two, and $120,000 in year three, and I will finish my fourth year next month with an annual rolling total of $240,000. This is no joke: it takes hard work, commitment, passion, and a no entitlement mentality." —*Ameriprise employee*, BW *Discussion Forum*

- "It offers more opportunities for personal growth and accountability than a mature company would." —*Business analyst in compensation at Ameriprise, age 22*

THE SUPERSTAR SPOTLIGHT

Name: Christopher Matlock
Job: Field VP

Describe your career progression: *I began my career in 2002 at the Phoenix office. . . . I was promoted to district manager in my first year and built a team of advisors that ultimately produced some of our company's best results and retention rates. After three years of consistent performance, I was asked to lead the Las Vegas branch as field vice president. At the time, I was only 25 years old. While I was in Las Vegas, our office grew from 12 advisors (August 2005) to 35 advisors (July 2007). We also led the country in developing, defining, and executing on consistent marketing programs designed to help new advisors have success early in their careers. As a result, I served as a national marketing coach for the Western Region and presented information on marketing and on creating a high-activity, high-productivity culture at several regional conferences. Subsequently, I was offered the opportunity to manage and lead the San Diego branch, where I am today.*

How did you rise through the ranks so quickly? What is your personal mantra?
Early on I realized that there was only one way to win: focus on productivity and people. Businesses must hit revenue and profitability targets, so being productive is essential. However, people are a company's greatest resource. Treat people as individuals and they will often perform at higher levels. The bottom line: work hard to help others succeed and you cannot help but win in the long term.

Advice for young job seekers: *In my perspective, to succeed at Ameriprise Financial, you must be willing to work hard, tackle a tremendous learning curve, and have a genuine desire for success. With those key ingredients, the sky is the limit.*

Capital One Financial

1680 Capital One Dr.
McLean, VA 22102
Phone: 703-720-1000
Fax: 703-205-1755
Web Addresses: www.capitalone.com;
www.capitalone.com/careers/

The Company

- Although Capital One was officially established in 1995, the financial holding company got its start in 1988 as a division of a small bank in Virginia. When the division was spun off as its own credit card company seven years later, founder Richard Fairbank became the chairman and CEO of what is now known as Capital One Financial Corporation, which is the holding company for Capital One Bank, Capital One Auto Finance Inc., and Capital One N.A., all of which offer U.S. retail banking services.

- Credit cards are hardly Capital One's only line of business; the company also offers small business and auto loans, as well as other financial services.

- After taking a hit in the subprime mortgage bust, Capital One announced that it was closing its Greenpoint mortgage unit in August 2007.

FAST FACTS

"Best Places to Launch a Career"
  Rank: 22
"Best Internships" Rank: N/A
Full-Time Salary: $55,000–$59,999
Entry-Level Hires: 190
Top College Major: Engineering
Entry-Level Hires Who Receive
  Signing Bonuses: 100%
Stock Ticker: COF

The Suits

Richard. D. Fairbank: Chairman, CEO, and President
Rob Alexander: Chief Information Officer
Lynn Pike: President of Capital One Banking
Gary L. Perlin: CFO and Principal Accounting Officer
David R. Lawson: President of Capital One Auto Finance
Jory Berson: President of U.S. Card
Larry Klane: President of Global Financial Services

The Stats

2007 sales: $12 billion
2007 net income: $1.6 billion
Market cap: $18.2 billion
Employees: 27,000
Locations: Canada, United Kingdom, United States

Major competitors: American Express, Bank of America, Discover

Largest operating units*:

U.S. Card ....$6.5 billion
Auto Finance ....$567.0 million
Global Financial Services ..$2.1 million
Banking............................$3.1 billion
Other ....$316.2 million

*2007 sales; financial data provided by Capital IQ

 The Story

1988: Richard Fairbank implements his IBS credit card strategy at Signet Bank in Richmond, Virginia

1994: Capital One Financial Corporation is formed as a spin-off of Signet's credit card business; Fairbank becomes the chairman and CEO of Capital One

2004: Fairbank is named a director of MasterCard International's global board of directors

2005: Capital One Financial Corporation becomes a financial holding company

2006: Acquires New York–based North Fork Bancorporation

2007: Capital One's stock price drops by approximately 40% during the year; it rebounds slightly with the Fed's interest rate cuts in the spring of 2008

The Skinny

Most important to recruiters: Analytical skills, college major, work experience

Selectivity: 1 of 45 applicants hired in 2006, up from 1 of 57 applicants hired in 2005

Diversity of entry-level workforce: 60% minority; 19% female

Facts to know:

- Capital One CEO Richard Fairbank makes $1 as his base salary.

- The credit card company aggressively recruits diverse applicants; 60% of Capital One's 2006 hires were minorities.

- Forty-two percent of the financial service company's 2006 entry-level hires were engineering majors.

The Starting Gate*

Undergraduate internships: N/A

Duration of summer internship: 10 to 13 weeks

Average total compensation: N/A

Interns by grade level: N/A

Interns who receive full-time job offers: N/A

Interns who are extended full-time job offers that accept: N/A

*Capital One did not offer a 2006 summer internship program because 2005–2006 full-time hiring needs more than doubled from the previous year; Capital One utilized the summer of 2006 to complete analyses on previous years' programs and revamp the program for the summer of 2007.

The Sliding Scale

Entry-level hires who had been interns: N/A

Most important performance measurements in entry-level hire: Analytical skills, profitability/margin, effort

Entry-level hires receiving signing bonuses: 100%

Average entry-level signing bonus: $9,000

Entry-level hires receiving performance bonuses: 100%

Average performance bonus during first year: $5,750

The Stand-Out Perks

- 15 paid vacation days and 8 paid holidays

- Educational expenses reimbursement and full and partial scholarships available

- Relocation compensation ($3,500)

- Employee discounts for car rentals, gym memberships, and insurance

- Access to 401(k) plan with company match of up to 6% (full vested after two years)

- Access to profit-sharing program fully vested after two years

- Maximum paid maternity leave of 40 days; maximum paid paternity leave of 10 days

The Skills

- Each line of business offers an orientation program, including a business and product overview, a human resources–conducted benefits information session, and social events

- The Finance Rotation Program is a formal leadership program for new hires who have been with the company for a year or more. The program is three rotations and lasts 104 weeks.

THE RECRUITER SPOTLIGHT

Name: Matt Schuyler
Job: Chief Human Resources Officer

A memorable résumé: *We had a candidate send us a link to his online video résumé—he had his own Web page—and [the video showed] the candidate rapping [about] his credentials and why he should be hired.*

Advice for young prospective employees: *Be authentic and be open to feedback. We have a collaborative culture, and we expect our associates to seek and give feedback constantly. Learn how to communicate—e-mails, PowerPoint, Instant Messaging, short presentations, daily dialogue with colleagues—the language of our business includes many channels. Be practical; showing that you have common sense and can get things done makes a big difference in a fast-moving culture. Show that you are okay with change. We are constantly changing, and someone who is change-averse won't fit in well. Be prepared to demonstrate how you exercise good judgment. Everyone makes mistakes, but the judgment you exercise along the way helps you navigate the approach. Ask yourself if there are four key elements in place here before you join us: can you learn, grow, develop, and have fun here? If not, don't join us.*

SunTrust

303 Peachtree St., NE
Atlanta, GA 30308
Phone: 404-588-7711
Fax: 404-332-3875
Web Addresses: www.suntrust.com;
www.suntrust.com/campus

The Company

- SunTrust and its subsidiaries offer clients personal and corporate banking services, including retail banking, credit card issuance, mortgage banking, mutual funds, insurance and asset management, and securities underwriting. All branches and offices are located throughout the southeastern region of the United States.

- SunTrust is the number two owner (behind Berkshire Hathaway) of Coca-Cola Corporation, a fellow Georgia-based enterprise. SunTrust's relationship with the soft drink maker dates back to 1919, when a predecessor of the bank underwrote Coke's initial public offering.

- The corporation's southern hospitality extends even further, as the bank has a private unit for clients involved in motor racing and country music. The corporation also sponsors SunTrust Racing (since 2004) and is the official bank of the Grand American Road Racing Association.

FAST FACTS

**"Best Places to Launch a Career"
Rank:** 75
"Best Internships" Rank: 70
Full-Time Salary: $45,000–$49,999
Entry-Level Hires: 211
Top College Major: Business
3-Year Retention Rate: 48%
Stock Ticker: STI

The Suits

L. Phillip Humann: Executive Chairman
William R. Reed, Jr.: Vice Chairman
James M. Wells, III: President and CEO
Mark A. Chancy: CFO
David F. Dierker: CAO

The Stats

2007 sales: $8.3 billion
2007 net income: $1.6 billion
Market cap: $21.8 billion
Employees: 32,323
Locations: Over 1,600 bank branches located throughout the southern United States, including Alabama, North and South Carolina, Florida, Georgia, Maryland, Tennessee, and Washington, D.C.
Major competitors: Bank of America, Wachovia

Largest operating units*:

Retail Banking ....N/A
Investment Management ....N/A
Commercial Banking ....N/A
Mortgage Services........................N/A
Investment Banking ....N/A

*2007 sales

The Story

1811: The Farmers' Bank of Alexandria (based in Virginia), SunTrust's earliest predecessor, receives a congressional charter to operate

1919: The Trust Company of Georgia serves as the Coca-Cola Corporation's underwriter and gains partial ownership for its services

1934: The First National Bank of Orlando, the predecessor to SunBanks, is chartered

1985: The Trust Company of Georgia and SunBanks merge to form SunTrust Banks, Inc.

1998: Acquires Crestar Financial Corporation and expands into Virginia, Maryland, and Washington, D.C.

1999: Its 27 bank charters are consolidated into the SunTrust Bank of the Federal Reserve

2000: SunTrust consolidates its investment management subsidiaries into Trusco Capital Management

2001: Acquires the institutional business of the Robinson-Humphrey Company, creating the SunTrust Robinson Humphrey Capital Markets division of SunTrust Capital Markets

2002: Acquires Florida-based Huntington Bancshares, a move that adds 59 branches to SunTrust's portfolio

2004: Merger with National Commerce Financial Corporation gives SunTrust a market presence in North Carolina, South Carolina, and Memphis for the first time

2006: SunTrust moves its credit card portfolios to InfiCorpHoldings, Inc.

The Skinny

Most important to recruiters: Analytical skills, communication skills, work experience

Selectivity: N/A

Diversity of entry-level workforce: 43% minority; 36% female

Facts to know:

- SunTrust actively recruited at 30 U.S. undergraduate college campuses during the 2006–2007 school year and extended job offers to students at 23 of those campuses.

- SunTrust's Vacation Policy offers employees vacation hours based on length of service, officer status, salary grade, and exempt/nonexempt status.

The Starting Gate

Undergraduate internships: 74

Duration of summer internship: 12 weeks

Average total compensation: $7,500

Interns by grade level:
Junior...10%
Senior 90%

Interns who receive full-time job offers: N/A

Interns who are extended full-time job offers that accept: N/A

The Sliding Scale

Entry-level hires who had been interns: 8%

Most important performance measurements in entry-level hire: Analytical skills, effort, sales/revenue

Entry-level hires receiving signing bonuses: 100%

Average entry-level signing bonus: $4,000

Entry-level hires receiving performance bonuses: 50%

Average performance bonus during first year: $7,500

The Stand-Out Perks

- Educational expenses reimbursement ($2,500)

- 10 paid vacation days

- 401(k) with a company match of up to 5% of salary

The Skills

- Formal one-day orientation program that includes guest speakers and diversity exercises

- Commercial Banking Associate Training Program, which consists of a maximum of three rotations and lasts 26 weeks

- Formal mentorship program (100% of entry-level hires participate)

The Sound-Off

- "SunTrust is a great place to work! It offers a competitive benefit package, a great incentive program, over a week of paid vacation time after being there only six months, 15 paid sick days, and guaranteed advancement." —BW *Discussion Forum*

- "I work on commission and make exactly what I am worth. SunTrust has been awesome! — BW *Discussion Forum*

- "While it may be a good place to start a career, as a veteran who joined, it was like working in Mayberry RFD. They count tick marks instead of looking at revenues. As long as you look busy and are at your desk from 8:30 a.m. to 5 p.m., they are happy, whether you are a teller or a senior VP." — BW *Discussion Forum*

THE ENTRY-LEVEL SPOTLIGHT:

Name: Carlos A. Medina
Job: Portfolio Specialist in Commercial Banking

Describe a typical day at work: *I set a list of priorities for the upcoming workday. Once I get to the office, I try to take care of those things in the morning before lunch. Meetings are early Monday mornings. I try to get out of the office for lunch as much as I can in order to clear my head and return to the office motivated to tackle new tasks and projects. It helps to break the day in two. The afternoons are for getting ahead on tasks and projects that have deadlines. I typically end my day once I am at a stopping point in my work.*

Best part of the job: *My job is cool because I get to meet prospective business clients, and it is very enjoyable to listen to them explain how they got started with their business and the goals they have for the future.*

Most unexpected experience: *The weirdest thing I have encountered so far is the recurring calls from headhunters who pretend they are clients and call in to whatever phone extension they can get their hands on in order to seek new names for their calling lists.*

Vanguard

P.O. Box 2600
Valley Forge, PA 19482
Phone: 877-662-7447
Fax: N/A
Web Addresses: www.vanguard.com;
www.vanguardcareers.com

The Company

- Vanguard is a client-owned investment management firm with operations in three states and five countries. The company manages a portfolio of $1.3 trillion (90% of which is held in domestic U.S. funds) for 9 million individual and institutional shareholders.

- A pioneer in financial services, Vanguard is credited with developing the first stock and bond index mutual funds and popularizing low-cost investing.

- In the last decade, the company has worked to appeal to a broader investor base, offering new funds and exchange-traded funds (ETFs), launching additional services, and lowering costs.

FAST FACTS

"Best Places to Launch a Career"
  Rank: 33
"Best Internships" Rank: 60
Entry-Level Hires: 1,250
Top College Major: Liberal arts
Rotational Training Program: Yes
3-Year Retention Rate: 93%
Stock Ticker: N/A (privately owned)

The Suits

John J. Brennan: Chairman and CEO
F. William McNabb III: President
Thomas J. Higgins: Treasurer
Heidi Stam: Managing Director,
  General Counsel, and Secretary
George U. Sauter: Managing Director
  and Chief Investment Officer
Ralph K. Packard: Managing Director
  of the Financial Division

The Stats

2007 sales: N/A
2007 net income: N/A
Market cap: N/A
Employees: 12,000 in the United
  States
Locations: Offices in North Carolina,
  Pennsylvania, Arizona, Japan,
  Singapore, Belgium, and Australia
Major competitors: American
  Century, BlackRock, AIM Funds,
  INVESCO

Largest operating units: N/A

Total assets ....$1.3 trillion in U.S. mutual funds*

Number of funds ....150 domestic funds plus additional funds in international markets

*As of December 31, 2007

The Story

1975: Begins operations with a total of 11 funds and $1.8 billion

1976: Opens the world's first indexed mutual fund, First Index Investment Trust (now Vanguard 500 Index Fund)

1986: Launches the first bond index mutual fund for individual investors

1990: Launches the first international stock index mutual funds

1998: Begins serving international investors and opens its first offices in Europe and Australia

1998: Vanguard funds become available to investors in 529 college savings programs thanks to sponsorship by the states of Iowa and Utah

2001: Launches its first ETF, Total Stock Market ETF

2008: Effective March 1, F. William McNabb III becomes president and is set to succeed Jack Brennan as CEO within a year

The Skinny

Most important to recruiters: Communication skills, college GPA, work experience

Selectivity: 1 of 25 applicants hired in 2006, up from 1 of 26 applicants hired in 2005

Diversity of entry-level workforce: 32% minority; 45% female

Facts to know:

- Vanguard's entry-level client relationship associates receive a salary and job-level increase after six months of employment, provided they've completed all job requirements. Employees who provide exemplary service may earn a $250 spot bonus award. Another incentive program makes employees eligible for a $1,000 bonus if they make a lateral move to a different job.

- Vanguard's standard full-time work-week is 37.5 hours. Overtime opportunities vary, depending on job function and business needs.

The Starting Gate

Undergraduate internships: 67

Duration of summer internship: 10 weeks

Average total compensation: N/A

Interns by grade level:
Junior...15%
Senior 85%

Interns who receive full-time job offers: 85%

Interns who are extended full-time job offers that accept: 57%

The Sliding Scale

Entry-level hires who had been interns: 6%

Most important performance measurements in entry-level hire: Productivity/efficiency, profitability/margin, learning ability

Entry-level hires receiving signing bonuses: N/A

Average entry-level signing bonus: N/A

Entry-level hires receiving performance bonuses: None*

Average performance bonus during first year: N/A

* Vanguard provides all employees with a year-end performance review, during which a merit increase is typically awarded for good performance.

The Stand-Out Perks

- Educational expenses reimbursement ($9,000)
- Full and partial graduate school sponsorship
- 401(k) with company match of up to 4% of pay
- Charitable gift match ($7,500)
- Employee discounts

The Skills

- Formal two-day orientation program, including computer training, guest speakers, diversity exercises, team-building exercises, a tour of the facilities, and company video
- Acceleration Into Management (AIM) program, which is rotational and lasts 48 weeks; after completion, participants generally receive a 10 to 15% salary raise
- Technology Leadership Program, which consists of three rotations and lasts 96 weeks
- Other specialty programs for recent graduates, including Analyst and Client Engagement and Acceleration into Financial Professional
- Formal mentorship program

The Sound-Off

- "Vanguard offers a very structured and challenging internship program that requires a great deal of personal thought and involvement and thus promotes higher understanding of the company, as well as the industry." —*Arizona State sophomore**
- "They express a personal interest in you [interns] and the future of your career." —*Howard junior**
- "There are no executive parking spaces, dining rooms, or rest rooms. You can bump into the chairman or a managing director at the lunch line in the Galley (our term for the cafeteria). And it's not that way at a lot of companies." —*Portfolio manager*

*Data: Universum Communications

THE SUPERSTAR SPOTLIGHT

Name: Marlin Brown
Job: Portfolio Manager

Describe your current position: *I'm a portfolio manager in Vanguard's $400 billion fixed-income group. My primary responsibility is to manage two tax-exempt bond mutual funds. Simply put, my job is to decide what to invest in when cash is coming in and what to sell when cash is going out.*

Most enjoyable aspect of the job: *I thrive on the environment of the trading desk. I found a new appreciation for the term "fast-paced work environment" when I moved to the desk in 2000. For example, in the brief window between 9:30 a.m. and 11:00 a.m., the seven members of Vanguard's short-term trading desk can execute more than 75 transactions for our funds. We are in constant contact with the dealer community. The phones ring continually.*

Tips for rising quickly through the ranks: *Even though I had an ultimate goal in mind, I realized that the most important thing I could do was to excel in my current position(s). Before I had even one informational interview or attempted to apply for a position in Vanguard's Fixed Income Group, I spent nearly three years trying to distinguish myself as a strong contributor in the Retail Investor Group. Try to "knock the cover off the ball," no matter where you are currently. Your track record is what will ultimately open up doors for you at Vanguard.*

Wachovia

One Wachovia Center
Charlotte, NC 28288
Phone: 704-374-6565
Fax: N/A
Web Addresses: www.wachovia.com;
www.wachovia.com/careers

The Company

- Wachovia's foresight, including its sale of its home equity divisions before the then-impending subprime mortgage bubble burst, has helped the North Carolina–based bank grow from a largely regional player into the fourth-largest American bank holding company (based on assets) and the third-largest American full-service brokerage firm (based on client assets).

- Wachovia's increasing influence is partially due to its numerous mergers and acquisitions, though these deals have received some scrutiny in the past. Allegations of unethical accounting policies following mergers, as well as the eye-popping compensation of Wachovia power players involved in mergers, have been a persistent cloud over the bank's expansion efforts.

- Wachovia Securities, LCC, and Evergreen Investment Management, two of the corporation's many subsidiaries, offer strategies to clients in fields like fixed-income asset and

FAST FACTS

"Best Places to Launch a Career"
  Rank: 51
"Best Internships" Rank: N/A
Full-Time Salary: $45,000–$49,999
Entry-Level Hires: 275
Top College Major: Business
3-Year Retention Rate: 80%
Stock Ticker: WB

mutual fund analysis, corporate brokerage transactions, and mortgage lending. In addition, Wachovia's personal banking centers are located in 21 states, including those along the Eastern Seaboard, Texas, and California.

The Suits

Ken Thompson: President and CEO
Tom Wurtz: Executive VP and CFO
David Carroll: Head of the Capital Management Group
Ranjana Clark: Senior Executive VP and Chief Marketing Officer
Stan Kelly: Head of Wealth Management
Shannon McFayden: Head of Human Resources and Corporate Relations
Steve Cummings: Senior Executive VP and Head of Corporate and Investment Banking

The Stats

2007 sales: $29.2 billion
2007 net income: $6.3 billion
Market cap: $75.1 billion
Employees: 108,238
Locations: Offices in 21 states (primarily in the eastern and southern regions of the United States), with Wachovia Securities, LLC, boasting offices in 48 states and 40 countries
Major competitors: Citigroup, Bank of America, JPMorgan Chase
Largest operating units*:
General Bank ....$16.6 billion
Corporate and Investment
   Bank ....$5.0 billion
Capital Management ....$7.8 billion
Wealth Management ....$1.5 billion
Parent ....–$1.7 billion
*Financial data provided by Capital IQ

The Story

1753: Moravian settlers in North Carolina name their new land "Wachovia" (the Latin version of the German "Wachau") after the Wachau River

1866: Israel Lash forms the First National Bank of Salem after the North Carolina banking system is largely destroyed by the Civil War

1879: William Lemly, Lash's nephew, moves the bank to Winston (an emerging tobacco and furniture center) and renames it Wachovia National Bank

1968: Wachovia Corporation is formed as a holding company

1985: The U.S. government approves interstate banking; Wachovia merges with First Atlanta and expands outside of North Carolina

1997: Wachovia's global banking services division is formed

1998: Founds underwriting and capital formation markets subsidiary Wachovia Capital Markets

1999: Buys OFFITBANK Holdings, marking the bank's first operations above the Mason-Dixon Line

2001: First Union Corporation buys the former Wachovia Corporation, then changes the subsidiary's name back to Wachovia Corporation

2004: Wachovia loses its bid for MBNA, the credit card issuer, to Bank of America

2006: Sells its home equity loan division to Barclays Bank and acquires Golden West Financial

2007: Buys AG Edwards, creating a 3,300-office chain that oversees $1 trillion in assets

The Skinny

Most important to recruiters: Communication skills, leadership skills, college GPA

Selectivity: 1 of 43 applicants hired in 2006, roughly the same as in 2005

Diversity of entry-level workforce: 43% minority; 62% female

Facts to know:
- In 2006, Wachovia's community-outreach efforts included training more than 26,000 families and

individuals in PC, Internet, and money management skills through Wachovia's financial literacy programs, Money Smart and eCommunitiesfirst.

The Starting Gate

Undergraduate internships: 220

Duration of summer internship: 12 weeks

Average total compensation: $9,000

Interns by grade level:
Freshman 20%
Sophomore 25%
Junior..25%
Senior 25%
College graduate 5%

Interns who receive full-time job offers: 10%

Interns who are extended full-time job offers that accept: 8%

The Sliding Scale

Entry-level hires who had been interns: 13%

Most important performance measurements in entry-level hire: Sales/revenues, learning ability, enthusiasm

Entry-level hires receiving signing bonuses: 50%

Average entry-level signing bonus: $2,500

Entry-level hires receiving performance bonuses: 50%

Average performance bonus during first year: $1,650

The Stand-Out Perks

- Educational expenses reimbursement ($10,000)

- Full and partial graduate school sponsorship

- 15 paid vacation days

- 401(k) plan with company match of up to 6% of salary (3 years to vest)

- Relocation compensation ($5,000)

- Employee discounts

The Skills

- 5-day orientation program

- Formal mentorship program (30% of entry-level hires participate)

The Sound-Off

- "The internship compensation was competitive. They focus intently on personal and professional development skills." —*University of North Carolina at Chapel Hill senior**

- "I [an intern] was really able to get involved in the day to day of the office." —*Ohio State student**

*Data: Universum Communications

THE ENTRY-LEVEL SPOTLIGHT

Name: John Woodward
Job: Financial Center Manager

Advice for young employees on how to get noticed: *At the end of the day, age really doesn't matter. Your performance and your ability to get the job done are what matters. I would have to say that the work ethic of young career moguls coming out of college can't match that of the generation before us. Many come out of college today thinking they will quickly jump the corporate ladder. The truth is, being young in the corporate world, you have a lot to prove, not just in the big tasks, but primarily in the small ones.*

Briefly describe your firm's work culture: *Wachovia Bank is committed to diversity in the workplace, with an emphasis on employee engagement. It prioritizes putting the right people in the right positions and has a strong commitment to work-life balance.*

The weirdest/funniest thing encountered on the job: *My age has definitely created the most awkward moments since I started this position. Blowing Rock, North Carolina, is primarily a community of second-home owners and retirees. I always find it amusing to see the customers' facial expression when they learn of my age [he's 24] and position.*

Wells Fargo

420 Montgomery St.
San Francisco, CA 94163
Phone: 1-800-869-3557
Fax: N/A
Web Addresses: www.wellsfargo.com;
www.wellsfargo.com/careers

The Company

- Wells Fargo specializes in many financial services, including consumer and business banking, venture capital, investment management, and insurance. It is also one of the largest mortgage issuers in the country. In fact, the typical Wells Fargo customer has over five products with the bank, making it the number one U.S. bank by this metric.

- Wells Fargo is the only U.S. bank to receive the Standard & Poor's (like *BusinessWeek*, a division of The McGraw-Hill Companies) "AAA" rating.

- Wells Fargo is the second-largest Small Business Administration lender in the United States. Since 1995, Wells Fargo has loaned $33 billion in funds to women and minority business owners alone. Aside from capital, the bank provides advisory services, like the Webcast "Protecting your Business," which commemorated Small Business Appreciation Month (May 2007).

FAST FACTS

"Best Places to Launch a Career"
  Rank: 41
"Best Internships" Rank: 65
Full-Time Salary: $40,000–$44,999
Entry-Level Hires: 196
Top College Major: Business
3-Year Retention Rate: 70%
Stock Ticker: WFC

The Suits

Richard Kovacevich: Chairman
John G. Stumpf: President and CEO
Howard Atkins: Senior Executive VP and CFO
David A. Hoyt: Senior Executive VP of Wholesale Banking
Mark C. Oman: Chairman of Wells Fargo Home Mortgages

The Stats

2007 sales: $39.4 billion
2007 net income: $8.1 billion
Market cap: $101.3 billion
Employees: 168,000 (159,800 U.S.)
Locations: 3,200 banking branches in 23 western and midwestern U.S. states, with 2,000 mortgage and consumer finance offices nationwide
Major competitors: Bank of America, U.S. Bancorp, Washington Mutual

Largest operating units*:
Community Banking......$25.5 billion
Wells Fargo Financial........$5.5 billion
Wholesale Banking ....$8.3 billion
*2007 sales

The Story

1852: Wells Fargo & Co. Bank is founded

1905: Wells Fargo & Co. Bank officially separates from Wells Fargo & Co. Express

1906: Though its building does not survive the San Francisco earthquake and fire, Wells Fargo's credit does; the bank begins its rebuilding process by expanding its operations throughout the western United States

1910: Expands into the Upper Midwest and Great Lakes regions of the United States, growing to 6,000 locations

1929: Northwestern National Bank of Minnesota combines with Norwest Corporation to form the holding cooperative Banco, as a result of the Great Depression

1983: Banco becomes Norwest once again

1998: Norwest merges with Wells Fargo

2000: Buys mortgage-servicing portfolios from First Union and General Electric Capital, helping Wells Fargo reach the $400 billion mark in mortgage ownership

2005: Buys $34 billion in assets under the management of Strong Financial, a firm facing securities fraud charges, for a bargain-basement price in the $500 to $700 million range

The Skinny

Most important to recruiters: Leadership skills, communication skills, work experience

Selectivity: 1 of 15 applicants hired in 2006, down from 1 of 5 applicants hired in 2005

Diversity of entry-level workforce: 36% minority; 43% women

Facts to know:

• Wells Fargo's online Learning Center is a venue in which all of its employees can register for learning opportunities (with their manager's support) to help strengthen their on-the-job skills, prepare for a new role in Wells Fargo, or learn more about Wells Fargo's businesses.

• The number of undergraduate internships at Wells Fargo has climbed steadily over the past few years, increasing more than 30 since 2005.

The Starting Gate

Undergraduate internships: 167

Duration of summer internship: 8 to 12 weeks

Average total compensation: $10,000

Interns by grade level:
Senior 100%

Interns who receive full-time job offers:
N/A

Interns who are extended full-time job offers that accept: N/A

The Sliding Scale

Entry-level hires who had been interns: 13%

Most important performance measurements in entry-level hire: Learning ability, leadership ability, sales/revenue

Entry-level hires receiving signing bonuses: N/A

Average entry-level signing bonus: N/A

Entry-level hires receiving performance bonuses: 75%

Average performance bonus during first year: $4,150

The Stand-Out Perks

- Educational expenses reimbursement ($5,000)

- Partial graduate school sponsorship

- Charitable gift match ($6,500)

- Relocation compensation

The Skills

- Formal five-day orientation program, including computer training, guest speakers, diversity exercises,

team-building exercises, and a tour of the facilities

- Technology Information Group Leadership Development Program, a formal leadership program that consists of a maximum of two rotations and lasts 52 weeks

- Formal mentorship program (20% of all employees participate)

The Sound-Off

- "I find Wells Fargo to be a truly awesome place to be employed at. Since it is a financial institution, it is slightly more conservative, but I lucked out with my coworkers. I couldn't have asked for a better team or workplace environment!" —BW *Discussion Forum*

- "It is true that Wells Fargo values results over education, but for those that are motivated and successful, it is a great place to start a career." —BW *Discussion Forum (former employee)*

- "I work there now, and I was hired as a part-time teller, even though I have a BA from a major university. It has been nothing but frustration, as nearly all my superiors have GEDs and hardly any college background. What's more, even though I *want* to be full-time and have voiced this many times, since I was hired as part-time, I cannot be full-time." —BW *Discussion Forum*

THE RECRUITER SPOTLIGHT

Name: Elcio Robert Barcelos

Job: VP and Manager of Corporate Recruiting and Employment

Outrageous interview behavior: *I've had candidates show up with their family—husband, wife, kids, mom, etc.—or use their BlackBerries to respond to e-mails during interviews. I even had one individual bring his lunch into the interview because the meeting was scheduled during his "lunch time." Also, one interviewee was pregnant, and her water broke during the interview. We hired her!*

Interview faux pas to avoid: *Dress professionally, and also try on the suit the day before to make sure it fits properly and comfortably. Be respectful of the interviewer's time—don't be too late or too early. If you are running late because of an emergency, call ahead and offer to reschedule.*

Why choose Wells Fargo: *Unlike many companies, Wells Fargo's size and multiple-business structure offer candidates a breadth of career opportunities and career paths. We offer a culture where team members can really challenge themselves and make a positive impact in their community and their industry.*

ARAMARK

1101 Market St.
Philadelphia, PA 19107
Phone: 215-238-3000
Fax: 215-238-3333
Web Addresses: www.aramark.com;
www.aramark.com/careers

The Company

- What began as a scheme to put vending machines in offices has grown into a diverse global services giant responsible for catering at national and state parks, resorts, concert halls, and sports arenas. ARAMARK aims to be a one-stop shop in event planning, facilities management, uniforms, and food services to clients ranging from businesses to schools to hospitals.

- ARAMARK bought out its shareholders in 2007, the second time in its history that it has taken itself private. The company remains the number three American food supplier and the number two American uniform supplier.

- Two acquisitions in recent years have given ARAMARK a stronger presence in China, leading to its selection as the caterer of the 2008 Beijing Olympic Games. This will be the fourteenth time ARAMARK has served at the Olympics since 1968.

FAST FACTS

"Best Places to Launch a Career"
 Rank: 85
"Best Internships" Rank: N/A
Full-Time Salary: $40,000–$44,999
Entry-Level Hires: 425
Top College Major: Culinary Arts/
 Hospitality and Hotel Management
Maximum Annual Education
 Reimbursement: $5,000
Stock Ticker: N/A (privately owned)

The Suits

Joseph Neubauer: Chairman and CEO
L. Frederick Sutherland: Executive VP and CFO
Thomas J. Vozzo: Executive VP and President of Uniform & Career Apparel
Ravi K. Saligram: Executive VP and President of ARAMARK International
Andrew C. Kerin: Executive VP and President of Domestic Food, Hospitality & Facilities

The Stats

2007 sales: $12.4 billion
2007 net income: $30.9 million
Market cap: N/A
Employees: 250,000
Locations: 18 countries worldwide

Major competitors: Cintas, Centerplate, ServiceMaster, UniFirst, ABM Industries

Largest operating units*:

Food & Support Services
(United States) ....$8.4 billion

Food/Support Services
(International) ....$2.3 billion

Uniform/Career Apparel ..$1.7 billion

*2007 sales

The Story

1936: Entrepreneur Davre Davidson teams up with vending machine maker William Fishman to put vending machines into offices across America

1959: Davidson and Fishman officially merge their operations to form Automatic Retailers of America (ARA); ARA goes public one year later

1968: ARA becomes a diverse service company with its entry into food and catering; the entity serves over one million meals at the Mexico City Olympics and changes its name to ARA Services

1984: A management buyout takes ARA off the NYSE and gives management 40% ownership of the company

1990: ARA Services changes its name to ARAMARK

2001: ARAMARK acquires rival ServiceMaster Management Services and returns to the NYSE under the ticker RMK

2004: ARAMARK acquires Beijing-based facility services company Bright China

2006: ARAMARK acquires Beijing-based food services company Golden Collar

2007: Shareholder buyout takes ARAMARK private again

The Skinny

Most important to recruiters: Work experience, communication skills, leadership skills

Selectivity: 1 of 25 applicants hired in 2006, up from 1 of 27 hired in 2005

Diversity of entry-level workforce: 25% minority; 41% female

Facts to know:

- A typical week is 55 hours. Applications and entry-level hires doubled in 2007.

- There are formalized summer internship programs in some of ARAMARK's businesses, most notably ARAMARK Higher Education and ARAMARK Sports and Entertainment.

- ARAMARK recruited on 100 U.S. undergraduate campuses during the 2006–2007 school year and extended job offers to students on 75 of those campuses.

 The Starting Gate

Undergraduate internships: 146

Duration of summer internship: 10 to 12 weeks

Average total compensation: N/A

Interns by grade level:
Freshman 5%
Sophomore 15%
Junior 40%
Senior 25%
College graduate 15%

Interns who receive full-time job offers:
35%

Interns who are extended full-time job
offers that accept: 30%

🏢 The Sliding Scale

Entry-level hires who had been interns:
N/A

Most important performance measurements in entry-level hire: Customer
satisfaction, leadership ability, being a
team player

Entry-level hires receiving signing
bonuses: 4%

Average entry-level signing bonus:
$1,500

Entry-level hires receiving performance bonuses: None

Average performance bonuses during
first year: N/A

The Stand-Out Perks

- Educational expenses reimbursement ($5,000)

- Partial graduate school sponsorship

- Access to 401(k) with company
  match to 6% of pay (fully vested
  after 24 months)

- Charitable gift match ($2,500)

- Relocation compensation

- Employee discounts on car rentals,
  gym memberships, cell phones/
  service, insurance, cultural events,
  publications

The Skills

- Formal 10-day orientation program, including guest speakers,
  diversity exercises, and team-building activities

- ARAMARK sponsors Building
  Leadership Skills, a formal one-week
  leadership program for entry-level
  hires (eligibility determined based
  on recommendation of sponsor)

- Formal mentorship program (100%
  of entry-level hires participate)

The Sound-Off

- "ARAMARK allows interns to have
  real-life responsibilities and gives
  compensation." —*James Madison
  senior**

- "I worked as a cashier there. . . . I
  never saw anybody advance. . . .
  I just saw people quit." —*Former
  ARAMARK employee*

- "Being flexible will certainly get you
  a lot farther." —*Regional VP of
  ARAMARK Business Services*

*Data: Universum Communications

THE SUPERSTAR SPOTLIGHT

Name: Marc Bruno

Job: Regional VP of ARAMARK Business Services

Career highlights: *For the 1996 Summer Games in Atlanta, I oversaw the recruiting, training, and staffing needs for more than 1,500 managers and employees. . . . I had the opportunity to travel to Sydney, Australia, in 1998 to assemble the successful bid for ARAMARK's management of food services for the 2000 Summer Games in that city.*

In 2002, I led ARAMARK's successful bid for the management contract to provide dining services for the athletes at the 2004 Summer Games in Athens.

Current job description: *I oversee hundreds of operations and several thousand employees and managers for $300 million worth of business from the Washington, D.C.–Northern Virginia region through New England. In addition, ARAMARK has once again been awarded the contract to provide food services for athletes, officials, media, and other guests during the 2008 Summer Games in Beijing—set to be the largest sporting event ever in the world—and I am in charge of planning and managing the operations team.*

A typical day on the job: *There is no such thing as a typical day! My day consists of everything from motivating an hourly dishwasher to having coffee with the CEO of a Fortune 500 company. In general, I have to manage, motivate, and lead my teams to help operate our business.*

Your personal mantra: *There are two sayings or quotes that help motivate me. The first is: "If not you, then who?" And the second is a quote from Kim Clark, former dean of Harvard Business School. In my class commencement address, he said, "There's no success at work that compensates for failure at home." As much as you have to work hard to succeed, you have to make sure you have a balance in life and take time to spend with friends and family. I try to live by that as much as possible.*

Harrah's Entertainment

2100 Caesars Palace Dr.
Las Vegas, NV 89109
Phone: 702-407-6000
Fax: 702-407-6037
Web Addresses: www.harrahs.com/
harrahs-corporate/index.html;
www.harrahs.com/harrahs-corporate/
careers-home.html

The Company

- Harrah's is the world's largest gambling company, operating 50 properties in 13 states and 6 countries. The company is actively pursuing capital investments in the United States, Asia, Europe, Latin America, and the Bahamas. In addition to the Harrah's brand, Harrah's Entertainment owns the Caesars and the Horseshoe brands as well as World Series of Poker and Total Rewards.

- Like the gambling industry in general, the Harrah's story is one of rapid buying and selling—the company has appeared on the New York Stock Exchange (NYSE) under four different names since it first went public in 1972.

- January 28, 2008 marked the closing of the purchase of Harrah's Entertainment by private equity firms Apollo Management and TPG for $17.1 billion. This represents the largest acquisition in the gaming industry.

FAST FACTS

"Best Places to Launch a Career" Rank: 36
"Best Internships" Rank: N/A
Full-Time Salary: $35,000–$39,999
Entry-Level Hires: 2,270
Top College Major: Hospitality
3-Year Retention Rate: 25%
Stock Ticker: N/A

The Suits

Gary Loveman: Chairman and CEO
Chuck Atwood: Vice Chairman of the Board
Jonathan S. Halkyard: Senior VP and CFO
J. Carlos Tolosa: President of Eastern Division
Tom Jenkin: President of Western Division
John Payne: President of Central Division

The Stats

2006 sales: $9.7 billion
2006 net income: $535.8 million
Market cap: $16.6 billion
Employees: 85,000
Locations: 50 properties in 6 countries
Major competitors: MGM Mirage, Trump Resorts, Ameristar Casinos, Isle of Capri Casinos, President Casinos, Wynn Resorts, Sands Corporation

Largest operating units*:
Gaming and Hotels ....$9.7 billion
*2006 sales

The Story

1937: Bill Harrah opens his first bingo parlor in Reno, Nevada

1946: The first Harrah's Club is opened

1962: Harrah's opens a 400-room hotel tower in Reno, Nevada

1972: Harrah's becomes a publicly traded company (and the first casino company the NYSE has seen)

1980: Harrah's Casinos is acquired by Holiday Inns

1985: Harrah's Casinos becomes the Holiday Corporation

1989–1990: Holiday Inns brand is acquired by Bass PLC, and all Holiday Corporation brands become the Promus Companies

1995: Promus is renamed Harrah's Entertainment Inc.

2000: The Mohawk Tribe files a lawsuit against Harrah's, charging the company with illegal anticompetitive behavior; a tribal court issues a $1.8 billion judgment against Harrah's. However, the case is still pending in federal court.

2005: Harrah's becomes the world's largest gaming company with its acquisition of the Caesar's casino brand

2005: Harrah's buys casino brands in Spain, the Bahamas, and Slovenia

2008: Harrah's is acquired by TPG and Apollo in a $17.1 billion deal, becoming the seventeenth largest private company in the United States

The Skinny

Most important to recruiters: Analytical skills, communication skills, leadership skills, an upbeat and positive attitude

Diversity of entry-level workforce: 31% minority; 49% female

Facts to know:

- While Harrah's does not have an official internship program, the company offers a variety of internships at its properties and corporate offices. Most internship opportunities at Harrah's are in hospitality roles (Hotel Operation, Food and Beverage, and so on) and information technology.

- Nearly two-thirds of employees have access to on-site fitness facilities. Roughly 70% of employees have access to on-site health care, as well as physical therapy, wellness education, lifestyle coaching, employee assistance programs, and dietary counseling.

The Starting Gate

Undergraduate internships: 70

Duration of summer internship: N/A

Average total compensation: N/A

Interns by grade level:

Junior...25%

Senior 75%

Interns who receive full-time job offers: N/A

Interns who are extended full-time job offers that accept: N/A

⊞ The Sliding Scale

Entry-level hires who had been interns: N/A

Most important performance measurements in entry-level hire: Analytical skills, customer satisfaction, effort, upbeat and positive attitude

Entry-level hires receiving signing bonuses: 1%

Average entry-level signing bonus: $2,259

Entry-level hires receiving performance bonuses: N/A *

Average performance bonus during first year: Varies by position

*Company has doled out close to $150 million in entry-level bonuses since 1999

The Stand-Out Perks

- Educational expenses reimbursement ($2,500)

- Graduate school sponsorship

- Access to 401(k) with company match of up to 3% of pay (fully vested after 60 months)

- Charitable gift match

- Relocation compensation

- Employee discounts

The Skills

- Formal five-day orientation program, including computer training, guest speakers, diversity exercises, team-building exercises, tour of facilities, and customer service training

- College Assistant Manager Program (CAMP), a program consisting of two to eight rotations and lasting 40 to 52 weeks; upon completion, 75 to 99.9% of participants receive permanent offers with an average raise of 5 to 9.9%

- Formal mentorship program (15% of new hires participate)

THE RECRUITER SPOTLIGHT

Name: Susan Hailey

Job: VP, Talent Acquisition

Advice for prospective young employees: *Be confident in your abilities and humble in the way you express yourself. It's the best combination for long-term success. Be aware of your strengths and self-aware of your development areas. Nobody is good at everything. Know what you want to develop, and be excited about learning. Ask about the company culture and how things get accomplished. Being smart is only part of being effective in an organization.*

Why choose Harrah's: *We are in an industry (gaming entertainment) that is poised for double-digit growth over the next few years as the business grows internationally and domestically. Harrah's is the number one player in the industry, with the best-managed organization that values smart, passionate, and innovative leaders. The career growth opportunities for people who fit our culture are tremendous. We value results-oriented individuals who achieve their goals in a collaborative, upbeat and team-oriented manner.*

Wackiest interview behavior encountered: *The candidate who confused our company with another one and kept referring to the other one as the one she wanted to work for in the course of our interview. Even after I clarified that this was "Harrah's" and not "XYZ," she kept saying it!*

Whether it's possible to recover from an interview faux pas, like a ringing cell phone: *Of course people can redeem themselves if their cell goes off! However, they can't redeem themselves if they answer it and proceed to have a conversation! Other faux pas in my book are not knowing anything about the company and not having a real reason for wanting to work here.*

Hyatt Hotels and Resorts

71 S. Wacker Dr.
Chicago, IL 60606
Phone: 312-750-1234
Fax: 312-780-5281
Web Addresses: www.hyatt.com;
www.explorehyatt.jobs/index_flash.php

The Company

- Global Hyatt Corporation is the umbrella organization for eight hospitality brands: Hyatt Regency (for group and leisure travelers), Grand Hyatt (hotels catering to business travelers), Hyatt Resorts (19 vacation resorts in the United States, including Hawaii, and the Caribbean), Park Hyatt (five-star luxury hotels), Andaz (a boutique-inspired brand offering casual luxury), Hyatt Place (sleek, limited-service lodging with high-tech amenities, primarily located in suburbia), Hyatt Summerfield Suites (residential-style suites for extended-stay guests), and Hyatt Vacation Ownership Inc. (U.S. resorts that offer rental and ownership options).

- U.S. Franchise Systems is a Hyatt subsidiary, and it owns the brands Hawthorn Suites hotels and Microtel Inns & Suites.

- In 2005, Hyatt purchased the AmeriSuites hotel chain and began converting these locations into its new Hyatt Place brand. (In order to woo the younger traveler, upgrades to these locations have included wireless Internet services, flat screen TVs, and contemporary furniture.) Hyatt also purchased Summerfield Suites in 2006 and is renovating the properties to fit Hyatt standards.

- Hyatt recently transformed the Great Eastern Hotel in London to fit its new lifestyle luxury brand, Andaz. Hyatt plans to open an Andaz hotel in Austin, Texas, and two more Andaz locations in New York City within the next few years. The hotel chain's ultimate goal is to open 50 Andaz hotels in various locations within the next 5 to 10 years.

FAST FACTS

"Best Places to Launch a Career" Rank: 21
"Best Internships" Rank: 37
Full-Time Salary: Less than $35,000–$45,000*
Entry-Level Hires: 330
Top College Major: Hospitality, culinary, facility management, business
3-Year Retention Rate: 60%
Stock Ticker: N/A (privately owned)
* Depending on location and function

The Suits

Thomas J. Pritzker: Chairman of
  Global Hyatt Corporation
Mark S. Hoplamazian: President and
  CEO of Global Hyatt Corporation

The Stats

2006 sales: $6.4 billion
2006 net income: N/A
Market cap: N/A
Employees: 88,647
Locations: 735 hotels in over 44
  countries
Major competitors: Hilton, Marriott,
  Starwood Hotels and Resorts
Largest operating units: N/A

The Story

1957: Jay Pritzker buys Hyatt House,
located at the Los Angeles International
Airport, from Hyatt von Dehn

1967: Hyatt opens the world's first
atrium hotel, the Hyatt Regency
Atlanta, designed by famed architect
John Portman

1969: The Hyatt Regency Hong Kong,
Hyatt's first international hotel, opens

1979: Hyatt goes private after being a
public company for 12 years

1980: Hyatt introduces two new
brands, the Grand Hyatt and Park
Hyatt; the Hyatt Regency Maui also
opens this year

2005: Global Hyatt Corporation is
formed, consolidating all of Hyatt's
hospitality holdings

2005: The AmeriSuites hotel chain is
acquired by Global Hyatt Corporation
and begins transformation into the new
brand Hyatt Place

2005: Liesel Pritzker settles a 2002 lawsuit against her father and cousins alleging they had misused money from
trusts set up for her and her brother
Matthew; Liesel and Matthew each
receive $280 million in addition to the
money they had been given

2006: Acquires Summerfield Suites

2007: Hyatt's latest brand, Andaz, is
launched; the company opens or converts 100 Hyatt Place hotels

2007: In late December, Warren Buf-
fett's Berkshire Hathaway announces it
will acquire 60% of Mormon Holdings
(125 separate businesses) from the
Pritzker family for $4.5 billion with
plans to buy the remaining 40% over
the next five or six years

The Skinny

Most important to recruiters: Communication skills, work experience,
leadership skills

Selectivity: 1 of 13 applicants hired in
2006, up from 1 of 19 applicants hired
in 2005

Diversity of entry-level workforce:
25% minority; 60% female

Facts to know:

- More than half of all entry-level
  hires who graduate from Hyatt's
  "Ladder Climbers" program receive
  double-digit raises.

- In addition to a Management Training Program for recent U.S. graduates, Hyatt offers an International Management Development Program, a 12-month U.S. training experience for recent international student graduates with degrees in hospitality.

The Starting Gate

Undergraduate internships: 250

Duration of summer internship: 10 to 13 weeks

Average total compensation: $5,400

Interns by grade level:
Freshman 10%
Sophomore 40%
Junior..50%

Interns who receive full-time job offers: 25%

Interns who are extended full-time job offers that accept: 90%

The Sliding Scale

Entry-level hires who had been interns: 25%

Most important performance measurements in entry-level hire: Customer satisfaction, leadership ability, being a team player

Entry-level hires receiving signing bonuses: 100%

Average entry-level signing bonus: $1,000

Entry-level hires receiving performance bonuses: 15%

Average performance bonus during first year: $3,000

The Stand-Out Perks

- Educational expenses reimbursement
- Partial graduate school sponsorship
- 10 paid vacation days
- Charitable gift match (company-sponsored charities only)
- Relocation compensation ($1,000)
- Complimentary hotel rooms and 50% discount on food when staying at Hyatt Hotels and Resorts
- Complimentary associate cafeteria meals
- Employee discounts

The Skills

- Formal two-day orientation program, including guest speakers, diversity exercises, team-building exercises, tour of facilities, service training, and company initiatives
- Hyatt's Management Training Program, which lasts 20 to 52 weeks
- Formal mentorship program (100% of entry-level hires participate)

THE ENTRY-LEVEL SPOTLIGHT

Name: Emily Wong

Job: Human Resources Corporate Management Training Program Participant

Why choose Hyatt: *I think Hyatt is one of the top entry-level employers because it offers a great Corporate Management Training (CMT) program, which gives you the understanding of how the hotel/property operates. You initially rotate throughout each department, thus meeting other associates and learning the operation. After the rotation, you enter the department you are concentrating in and train for a certain number of months. After successfully completing the CMT program, you are then placed into either an Assistant Manager or a Manager position. Hyatt's CMT program definitely gives you the opportunity to build relationships, to be hands-on, and to truly gain an experience that will be advantageous for those seeking a future career with the company. In addition to Hyatt's relocation package, which assists you with movement, it also provides a 14-day stay at the hotel you will be training at while you look for housing.*

Briefly describe a typical day: *As a Human Resources CMT, I will be training in all areas within Human Resources. I am currently in the Associate Relations position, which includes any activity our associates participate in, such as receptions, general meetings, holiday parties, and contests. I work with organizing different events and assisting any associates that sporadically enter the Human Resources office each day. I am responsible for providing them [associates] with information on any upcoming volunteer events, transportation cards, confirmation sheets for comp rooms they have booked, and other such material. And in order to get anything accomplished, I have to multitask each day as best as I can.*

Biggest challenge and how to deal with it: *Working at a property that employs 1,400 associates can be very challenging. Managing others as a recent college graduate is another challenge. Given these two factors, it may seem almost impossible to be noticed. However, the answer is quite simple. Wanting to get noticed at your company plainly begins with smiling and greeting your associates. Acknowledging the people you work with is crucial, no matter what position you or they are in.*

Marriott International

Marriott Drive
Washington, DC 20058
Phone: 301-380-3000
Fax: 301-380-1438
Web Addresses: www.marriott.com;
www.marriott.com/careers

The Company

- Two generations of Marriotts have grown a small food services business into the multibillion global empire this company is today. Founder J. W. Marriott, who was raised in Utah in the Mormon Church, discovered a niche business opportunity in Washington, D.C., when he opened and operated an A&W Root Beer stand after returning home from his two-year mission trip.

- J. W. Marriott, Jr. (Bill), who was instrumental in moving the company in the lodging direction, became CEO in 1972. Today, Marriott International operates such properties as Marriott Hotels and Resorts, Courtyard, Renaissance, Fairfield Inn, and even the luxurious Ritz-Carlton.

- Long priding itself on a people-first culture, with employees focused on good customer service and encouraged to serve their communities, Marriott also has turned its attention to the environment in recent years, pledging to reduce its green-

house emissions by one million tons by 2010.

The Suits

J. W. Marriott, Jr.: Chairman and CEO
William J. Shaw: President and COO
Arne M. Sorenson: CFO, Executive VP, and President of Continental European Lodging
Robert J. McCarthy: President of Global Brand Management for North American Lodging Operations
James M. Sullivan: Executive VP of Lodging Development

The Stats

2007 sales: $13 billion
2007 net income: $751 million*
Market cap: $12.6 billion
Employees: 151,000
Locations: More than 2,800 hotels worldwide, with locations in 18 different countries

Major competitors: Hyatt, Hilton
Largest operating units[†]:

North American
 Full-Service ....$5.5 billion
North American
 Limited-Service ....$2.2 billion
International ....$1.6 billion
Luxury ....$1.6 billion
Timeshare ....$2.1 billion
Corporate and Other........$81 million

*Adjusted income from continuing operations
[†]2007 sales

The Story

1927: J. Willard Marriott opens an A&W Root Beer stand in Washington, D.C.; the stand is later renamed The Hot Shoppe when Mexican food is added to the menu

1957: Marriott opens first hotel, the Twin Bridges Motor Hotel, in Arlington, Virginia

1967: Marriott changes his company name to Marriott Corporation; buys Big Boy restaurants

1976: Opens two Great America theme parks in Gurnee, Illinois, and Santa Clara, California

1993: Company splits into Marriott International (Bill Marriott remains CEO), the current Marriott hotel group, and Host Marriott Corporation (chaired by Richard Marriott), which later splits into two separate companies

1995: Marriott International acquires luxury hotel chain Ritz-Carlton

2005: Sells Ramada International hotels to Cendant

2007: Marriott International opens its 3,000th hotel, a JW Marriott in Beijing, bringing the number of Marriott hotels in China to more than 30

The Skinny

Most important to recruiters: Leadership skills, work experience, communication skills

Selectivity: 1 of 8 applicants hired in 2006, roughly the same as 2005

Diversity of entry-level workforce: 30% minority; 55% female

Facts to know:

• Marriott "associates" as the company calls its employees, average 78 hours of training and 34 hours of professional development each year.

• Although a majority of its young hires are hospitality majors, Marriott has internship and entry-level career opportunities for individuals with backgrounds in numerous disciplines, including engineering and sales and marketing, among others.

The Starting Gate

Undergraduate internships: 374

Duration of summer internship: 8 to 18 weeks

Average total compensation: $5,000

Interns by grade level:
Freshman 10%
Sophomore 25%
Junior......................................55%
Senior 10%

Interns who receive full-time job offers: 10%

Interns who are extended full-time job offers that accept: 97%

The Sliding Scale

Entry-level hires who had been interns: 35%

Most important performance measurement in entry-level hire: Leadership ability

Entry-level hires receiving signing bonuses: 7%

Average entry-level signing bonus: $2,000

Entry-level hires receiving performance bonuses: 13%

Average performance bonus during first year: N/A

The Stand-Out Perks

- Employee discounts on hotel stays and purchases of food and beverages at Marriott-managed retail stores
- Relocation compensation ($4,000)
- 24 paid vacation days
- Educational expenses reimbursement ($5,250)

The Skills

- One-day orientation program called "Enjoy Your Stay," which introduces new associates to the company's history and engages them in team-building exercises
- Formal mentorship program (10% of entry-level hires participate)

The Sound-Off

- "Marriott isn't the right fit for everyone, but it definitely is for me. I can say without doubt that I haven't been bored a single day. It's a job with endless opportunities for advancement. I felt at home from day one and can't imagine leaving. It's rare these days for college graduates to think they're only going to work for one company until retirement, but a year and a half into it, I have no doubt in my mind that I will want to retire here!" —*Marriott employee*

- "The reason I left the company was its lack of concern for hiring and developing quality individuals. I have seen too many fresh college graduates accept an entry-level management position and leave out of frustration." —*Former Marriott entry-level employee*

THE SUPERSTAR SPOTLIGHT

Name: Nawfal Bendefa

Job: VP, International Project Finance & Asset Management

Your rise through the ranks: *I am a 29-year-old Moroccan national currently based at Marriott's London Regional Office. I joined Marriott in January 1999 as a front desk associate at the Orlando World Center Marriott Resort and Convention Center in Florida. It was meant to be a side job while I was studying, but I ended up being able to finance most of my college expenses through Marriott's tuition reimbursement program. In 2003, I transferred to Marriott's international team to take up a finance role in London. I will soon be taking up yet another new challenge within Marriott as vice president of development in Europe, Middle East, and Africa.*

Best part of the job: *I work with a team of translators on the development of hotels, and it is rewarding to look back after a hotel is built and consider that I was part of the team that made it happen. These buildings will be there for a long time, and they are in places around the world that I never thought I would even get to visit one day. I have now worked with Marriott on transactions in the United States, Europe, Asia, the Middle East, and Africa. How's that for a cool job?*

Your career philosophy: *I have learned to rely on two basic things: (1) understanding my strengths and focusing on using them to add value, and (2) understanding the company's strategy and knowing where I fit into the organization and, therefore, how I can contribute to that strategy. I was expecting to find a glass ceiling and a limit to what I could achieve. I have never felt in the past eight years that I have had few chances to succeed.*

The Walt Disney Co.

500 S. Buena Vista St.
Burbank, CA 91521
Phone: 818-560-1000
Fax: 818-560-1930
Web Addresses: www.corporate.disney.
go.com; www.corporate.disney.go.com/
careers

The Company

- The Disney Brothers Cartoon Studio was founded in 1923 when Walter Elias Disney and his brother Roy decided to turn a short film written by Walt about a little girl in a cartoon world—Alice in Wonderland—into a comedy series.

- Today, the Walt Disney Company is a global multimedia empire with four business segments: Studio Entertainment (Miramax, Touchstone, Walt Disney Pictures), Parks and Resorts (a successful cruise line, Disney theme parks), Consumer Products (The Disney Stores, Disney Interactive Studios), and Media Networks (ABC, ESPN, The Disney Channel).

- Former CEO Michael Eisner resigned in September 2005 in the wake of a contentious power struggle and shareholder revolt and his lieutenant, Robert A. Iger, took over.

- In 2007 Disney released *The Secret of the Magic Gourd* in China (the first Disney co-production in the country) and announced a $1.1 billion expansion of Disney's California Adventure.

FAST FACTS

"Best Places to Launch a Career" Rank: 7
"Best Internships" Rank: 7
Full-Time Salary: $50,000–$54,999
Entry-Level Hires: N/A
Top College Major: Business
Interns Who Receive Full-Time Job Offers: 30%
Stock Ticker: DIS

The Suits

Robert A. Iger: President and CEO
Andy Bird: President of Walt Disney International
Alan Braverman: Senior Executive VP, General Counsel, and Secretary
Wes Coleman: Executive VP and Chief Human Resources Officer
Ronald L. Iden: Senior VP of Security

The Stats

2007 sales: $35.5 billion
2007 net income: $7.8 billion
Market cap: $63.3 billion
Employees: 137,000
Locations: Worldwide,; headquarters in Burbank
Major competitors: News Corp., Time Warner, CBS Corp.

Largest operating units*:
Media Networks.............$15.0 billion
Parks and Resorts............$10.6 billion
Studio Entertainment ......$7.5 billion
Consumer Products..........$2.3 billion
*2007 sales

The Story

1923: The Disney Brothers Cartoon Studio is founded

1928: *Steamboat Willie* (with Mickey Mouse) is the first fully synchronized sound cartoon

1937: *Snow White and the Seven Dwarfs*, the first full-length animated film, is released

1950: *Treasure Island*, the studio's first live-action film, is released

1955: Disneyland opens in LA

1971: Walt Disney World Resort opens in Florida

1983: First international theme park, Tokyo Disneyland, is opened

1984: Launches Touchstone Pictures

1991: Releases *Beauty and the Beast*, the only animated film ever nominated for Best Picture Academy Award

1993: Acquires Miramax Films

1995: Forms a partnership with Pixar Animation that results in *Toy Story* and *Finding Nemo*

1996: Acquires Capital Cities/ABC

2006: Pixar Animation is acquired by Disney

The Skinny

Most important to recruiters: Communication skills, leadership skills, talent/experience

Selectivity: N/A

Diversity of entry-level workforce: 26% minority; 43% female

Facts to know:

- Disney refers to its theme park employees as "Cast Members," as they are cast for a role in the Disney Show.

- Disney's benefits program includes pet insurance and a personal assistant network.

The Starting Gate

Undergraduate internships: 1,800

Duration of summer internship: 10 to 12 weeks

Average total compensation: $7,680

Interns by grade level:
Freshman 1%
Sophomore 4%
Junior...80%
Senior 10%
College graduate 5%

Interns who receive full-time job offers: 30%

Interns who are extended full-time job offers that accept: 30%

The Sliding Scale

Entry-level hires who had been interns: 35%

Most important performance measurements in entry-level hire: Productivity/efficiency, profitability/margin, effort

Entry-level hires receiving signing bonuses: None

Average entry-level signing bonus: N/A

Entry-level hires receiving performance bonuses: None

Average performance bonuses during first year: N/A

The Stand-Out Perks

- Capped educational reimbursement for job-related courses

- 10 paid vacation days and 11 paid holidays (includes 2 floating holidays)

- 80 hours of paid sick/personal leave

- "Silver Passes" that grant salaried employees and cast members complimentary admission to Disney Theme Parks for themselves and eligible dependents and/or guests

The Skills

- A formal mentorship program, which varies by business unit

- Orientation programs vary by business unit (1 to 5 days)

- Management Journey leadership program, which lasts half of a week

The Sound-Off

- "They pay their CP [Disney College Program] students dirt and the CPers work the crap jobs, but what a great line on your résumé, and what an amazing experience it is."
  —*SUNY Buffalo senior on internship**

- "ESPN gives opportunities to younger workers, offers lots of advancement, and is one of the best résumé builders in the world."
  —BW *Discussion Forum*

- "I worked for the Walt Disney World Resort and started as a front-line intern in the park. I was able to network with leaders, worked my way up to a full-time position, and eventually moved myself into a salaried role in HR Communications—what I had gone to school for. I was impressed that I wasn't 'just a number' when you consider their size and the number of people they employ. It truly was a great place to start right out of college."
  —BW *Discussion Forum*

- "ESPN production assistants (PAs) are paid $10.68/hour starting. They get a Burger King whopping $1.60 raise after their first 'promotion.' Most PAs are PAs for at least three years before they have any chance of actually being promoted to Assistant Producer." —BW *Discussion Forum*

*Data: Universum Communications

THE RECRUITER SPOTLIGHT

Name: Tracy Montoya
Job: VP, Segment Recruitment

Wackiest encounter with a job applicant: *I will always remember one applicant in particular who had come quite a ways, traveling by bus, including several connections, in full Cinderella dress, including a tiara and "glass" slippers! She had made the entire costume herself as she prepared for a potential interview. Needless to say, we knew she was someone who would always take initiative and who had a passion for the Disney product!*

Biggest "dos" and "don'ts" of applying for a job: *I think the biggest "do" is to be yourself, and let your interests, talents, and experience shine. Our job in recruitment is to find new Cast Members who bring talent, creativity, and diversity into our organization. The more we can meet the true you, the better we can find the perfect role! Likewise, a "don't" would be to give your recruiter answers you think he or she may "want to hear." There isn't really any "right" answer, and we're most interested in getting to know you.*

Aetna

151 Farmington Ave.
Hartford, CT 06156
Phone: 860-273-0123
Fax: 860-273-3971
Web Addresses: www.aetna.com;
www.aetna.com/working

The Company

- Insurance provider Aetna offers health-care, dental, pharmacy, group life, and disability insurance, and employee benefits. The company's more than 17.4 million medical members, 14 million dental members, and 10.9 million pharmacy members have access to a network of more than 800,000 health-care professionals.

- In September 2001, Aetna became the first full-service U.S. insurer to introduce a consumer-directed product to the market. The "Aetna Health Fund"—the official name of the company's growing portfolio of options—allows consumers to take a more active role in determining where their health-care dollars go. (Members generally accrue a certain amount of money per year in a fund or account that they use to pay medical expenses. Any unused dollars roll over to the next year and can be used for future medical issues, as long as the employee remains enrolled in the plan.)

- Aetna attributes solid 2007 financial results, including a 20% increase in operating earnings over 2006 and the 730,000 new medical members it added during 2007 (according to organic net medical membership growth), to a fourfold strategy of segmentation, integration, consumerism, and operations excellence.

The Suits

Ronald A. Williams: Chairman and CEO
Mark T. Bertolini: President and Head of Business Operations
Joseph M. Zubretsky: Executive Vice President and CFO
William J. Casazza: Senior VP and General Counsel

The Stats

2007 sales: $27.6 billion
2007 net income: $1.8 billion
Market cap: $28.9 billion
Employees: 35,173
Locations: Two large offices in Connecticut, one in Pennsylvania, and operations in all 50 states
Major competitors: BlueCross, Cigna, UnitedHealthGroup, WellPoint, Humana
Largest operating units*:
Healthcare .... $24.8 billion
Group Insurance .... $2.1 billion
Large Case Pensions .... $691.5 million
*2007 sales

The Story

1850: Aetna Insurance Company begins selling life insurance policies

1902: Begins selling liability coverage. Progressive reform movement inspires company to develop Accident and Liability department, which handles workmen's compensation issues and, later, workplace property and casualty insurance situations

1936: Sells first group health policy

1944: Becomes the first insurance company to have television commercials; provides insurance coverage for the Manhattan Project

1963: Provides life insurance for the first seven U.S. astronauts

1968: Goes public on the New York Stock Exchange

1986: Provides bonds for the Statue of Liberty's restoration

1996: Acquires U.S. Healthcare, combining its existing health-care business with it to become Aetna U.S. Healthcare; the company's other business units include Aetna Retirement Services, which handles employee retirement benefit services, and Aetna International, which sells insurance products in Latin America and the Pacific Rim

2000: Sells financial services and international businesses to ING to focus more on health and group benefits coverage

2006: John W. Rowe retires; Ronald A. Williams succeeds him as chairman, CEO, and president

The Skinny

Most important to recruiters: Leadership skills, work experience, college major

Selectivity: N/A

Diversity of entry-level workforce: N/A

Facts to know:

- Aetna's selective, unique Sales Professional Group School Training Program has been offered since 1924 (over 100 classes have graduated since then). This E. E. Cammack Group School provides participants with classroom and on-the-job training, a formal career mentor, and networking opportunities with senior management. Aetna also has a formal information technology leadership program and an Actuarial Student Program.

- Women hold 61% of management/supervisory positions at Aetna. Furthermore, 28% of senior leaders are women. Overall, 75% of the population is women. (Named top 10 company by National Association for Female Executives in 2007.)

The Starting Gate

Undergraduate internships: 140

Duration of summer internship: 12 to 14 weeks

Average total compensation: $7,000

Interns by grade level: N/A

Interns who receive full-time job offers: 40%

Interns who are extended full-time job offers that accept: 90%

The Sliding Scale

Entry-level hires who had been interns: N/A

Most important performance measurements in entry-level hire: Leadership skills, analytical skills, quality of work experience

Entry-level hires receiving signing bonuses: 15%

Average entry-level signing bonus: $4,000

Entry-level hires receiving performance bonuses: 90%

Average performance bonus during first year: $1,200

The Stand-Out Perks

- Educational expenses reimbursement ($3,000)

- Partial graduate school sponsorship

- Charitable gift match ($10,000)

- Relocation compensation ($4,000)

- Employee discounts

The Skills

- One-day orientation program that includes computer training

- Actuarial Training Program, a formal leadership program that consists of three to six rotations and lasts three to six years

THE RECRUITER SPOTLIGHT

Name: Nancy L. Untiet
Job: Recruiting Team Lead

Advice for young job seekers: *Do your homework on the company and be well prepared for the interview, as this will be expected because of the easy availability of company information online. Have a clear understanding of the company's business, have knowledge of the specific position you are applying for, and bring a list of written questions to engage in a dialogue with your interviewer as a way to demonstrate your abilities.*

Worst interview faux pas: *Getting the company name wrong, arriving late, and a ringing cell phone are all faux pas. However, depending on the interviewer and the situation, sometimes an interviewee can recover.*

Wackiest technique used by a job applicant: *The most memorable technique a person used to get a job was sending a dozen long-stemmed red roses with the résumé.*

Why recent graduates should choose Aetna: *Aetna offers college students and recent graduates the guidance and opportunities they need to develop their skills and grow their careers in a rewarding environment. At Aetna, we value leadership, creativity, and initiative. If you share those values and our commitment to excellence and innovation, consider a career with Aetna.*

AIG

American International Group
70 Pine St.
New York, NY 10270
Phone: 212-770-7000
Fax: 212-943-1125
Web Addresses: www.aig.com;
www.aig.com/careers

The Company

- An insurance and financial services giant, American International Group (AIG) is broken up into four principal segments: general insurance, life insurance and retirement services, financial services, and asset management. It was one of the first firms in history to profit from insurance underwriting, and AIG subsidiaries are now the largest U.S.-based underwriters of commercial and industrial insurance.

- AIG is truly a global company, with operations in 130 countries and jurisdictions around the world. AIG's roots date back to 1919, when Cornelius Vander Starr set up an insurance agency in Shanghai, China.

- Longtime AIG CEO Hank Greenberg was ousted by the board in 2005 after he was brought up on civil fraud charges stemming from allegations that he manipulated earnings for the firm's clients; AIG settled for $1.6 billion the following year (Greenberg, who denies any wrongdoing, still faces possible charges related to the incident). Despite this contentious parting, Greenberg's holding company SICO still controls roughly 10% of AIG's stock. With the company facing continued weakness in its mortgage unit, Greenberg has aggressively tried to reenter the scene to help shape its future.

The Suits

Martin J. Sullivan: President and CEO

Edmund S. W. Tse: Senior Vice Chairman of Life Insurance

Steven J. Bensinger: Executive VP and CFO

Robert M. Sandler: Executive VP of Domestic Personal Lines

Win Jay Neuger: Executive VP and CIO

The Stats

2007 sales: $110.1 billion
2007 net income: $16.2 billion
Market cap: $147.9 billion
Employees: 116,000
Locations: Operations in more than 130 countries
Major competitors: Allianz SE, AXA, Nippon Life Insurance Company
Largest operating units*:
Life Insurance and Retirement
Services ....$53.6 billion
General Insurance ....$1.7 billion
Financial Services ....–$1.3 billion
Asset Management ....$5.6 billion
*2007 sales

The Story

1919: In Shanghai, China, Cornelius Vander Starr creates American Asiatic Underwriters, the insurance agency that eventually becomes AIG

1926: Starr opens his first U.S. office in New York and names it American International Underwriters; the firm serves as an insurance writer on U.S.–owned risks outside of North America

1939: Because of the World War II conflict overseas, Starr moves his firm's official headquarters to New York

1967: Maurice Greenberg is elected president and CEO; AIG is also incorporated as a company this year

1969: AIG goes public on the New York Stock Exchange

1973: AIG-owned International Lease Finance Corporation is founded and eventually becomes the world's largest aircraft lessor

2005: After being implicated in an accounting scandal, Greenberg steps down as CEO and Martin Sullivan takes the helm

2007: AIG acquires most of Bulgarian Telecommunications Company and Vivatel

The Skinny

Most important to recruiters: Analytical skills, communication skills, college GPA

Selectivity: 1 of 24 applicants hired in 2006, down from 1 of 17 applicants hired in 2005

Diversity of entry-level workforce: 21% minority; 45% female

Facts to know:

- Employees and dependent family members receive discounts on lift tickets, retail items, rental equipment, ski/snowboard school, and lodging at Stowe Mountain Resort, a wholly owned AIG subsidiary.

- AIG offers extensive work-life programming, including a child-care service, adoption assistance, college coaching, and scholarship programs.

The Starting Gate

Undergraduate internships: 87

Duration of summer internship: 10 weeks

Average total compensation: $9,200

Interns by grade level:
Junior..67%
Senior 33%

Interns who receive full-time job offers:
35%

Interns who are extended full-time job
offers that accept: 90%

The Sliding Scale

Entry-level hires who had been interns:
25%

Most important performance measurements in entry-level hire: Produc-
tivity/efficiency, analytical skills, being
a team player

Entry-level hires receiving signing
bonuses: 100%

Average entry-level signing bonus:
$3,000

Entry-level hires receiving performance bonuses: 21%

Average performance bonus during
first year: $2,500

The Stand-Out Perks

- Educational expenses reimburse-
  ment
- Graduate school sponsorship
- Cofunded pension
- Charitable gift match ($2,500)
- Employee discounts

The Skills

- Formal one-day orientation, including guest speakers and an overview
  of the organization

THE ENTRY-LEVEL SPOTLIGHT

Name: Anthony K. Ottati

Job: Training Specialist

Describe your job: *I am a training specialist for the AIG Insurance School. I currently work with a group of 15 domestic trainees who are enrolled in a one-year insurance underwriting training program. I act as program coordinator for all 15 trainees, which means that if any of the trainees have any issues with the development of behavioral or technical underwriting skills, I will work with them. Upon successful completion of the program, the trainees enter AIG as entry-level insurance underwriters.*

Anything about the job that has surprised you: *Training people who are older [Anthony is 22 years old] and have more professional experience than I have is one of the more curious aspects of my job.*

Best part of your work: *I most enjoy the classroom training aspect of the job. I create and present content for a financial analysis class for AIG's insurance underwriters. The presentation, called "Good Account Bad Industry, Bad Account Good Industry," focuses on the importance of monitoring macroeconomic and industry trends when deciding whether or not to underwrite a particular risk. The overall point is that even though a potential insured may seem like a good risk to underwrite based on the company's bottom line, the trajectory of broader industry trends may suggest otherwise. I focus on the recent turmoil in the subprime mortgage/credit markets and the Fed's interest-rate activity. It allows me to utilize my background in economics [a B.A. in Economics from the University of Massachusetts (Amherst) and the University of Constance (Germany) and a minor in International Relations with an E. U. focus] and teach people about a subject about which I am passionate.*

Blue Cross Blue Shield

The Blue Cross and Blue Shield
   Association
225 N. Michigan Ave.
Chicago, IL 60601
Phone: 312-297-6000
Fax: 312-297-6609
Web Addresses: www.bcbs.com;
www.bcbs.com/careers

The Company

- The Blue Cross and Blue Shield Association (BCBSA) is the association for a national federation of 39 independent, community-based, and locally operated Blue Cross and Blue Shield companies.

- Since 1965, BCBS companies have partnered with Medicare and Medicaid to administer health-care coverage to low-income, elderly, and disabled Americans.

- In November 2007, BCBSA signed memorandums of understanding with the People's Republic of China's Central Party School and Counselor's Office of State Council to collaboratively explore ways to advance health-care reform in China.

- In April 2007, BCBSA and 23 BCBS plans resolved a class-action lawsuit that alleged that the plans delayed, denied, or diminished clients' claims for physicians' services. To settle the suit, the plans created a fund of approximately $128 million benefiting some 900,000 physicians and paid approximately $49 million in plaintiffs' legal fees.

- In 2006, BCBSA created Blue Health Intelligence, a database of anonymous claims data on 80 million individuals designed to help analyze health trends.

👔 The Suits

Scott P. Serota: President and CEO
William J. Colbourne: Senior VP of Human Resources and Administration
Mary Nell Lehnhard: Senior VP of Office of Policy and Representation
Maureen E. Sullivan: Senior VP of Strategic Services

The Stats

2007 sales: N/A
2007 net income: N/A

Market cap: N/A

Employees: 880

Locations: Although headquartered in Chicago, Illinois, BCBS also has offices in Washington, D.C.

Major competitors: Aetna, CIGNA, Humana, UnitedHealth Group

Largest operating units: N/A

The Story

1929: The foundation for the modern BCBS plan is laid when the operators of lumber and mining camps make monthly fee-for-service arrangements with physicians in order to treat and cover their employees

1929: The prototype upon which BCBS plans are later based begins in Texas as a prepaid hospital inpatient payment plan for Dallas public school teachers

1933: The first "Blue Cross baby" is born in North Carolina, marking the first birth in the United States that is covered by a family health plan

1946: The Blue Cross Commission is formed; Associated Medical Care Plans, the first national Blue Shield organization, is founded one year later

1960: Associated Medical Care Plans changes its name to the Association of Blue Shield Plans

1965: Medicare and Medicaid programs are created; BCBS continues to process an overwhelming majority of Medicare claims

1976: The Association of Blue Shield Plans changes its name to the Blue Shield Association

1982: The BCBS Association is formed after the separate associations for Blue Cross and Blue Shield merge

1985: The BCBS Association founds the Technology Evaluation Center

1991: A national transplant network, called the Blue Quality Centers for Transplant, is created

1994: BCBS's BlueCard is introduced, enabling members who travel to another service area to receive the benefits of their home plan

2007: The Blue Healthcare Bank is launched after receiving federal regulatory approval to operate as a federal savings bank; the charter allows the bank to provide health-care-related banking services throughout the United States.

The Skinny

Most important to recruiters: Communication skills, analytical skills, work experience

Selectivity: 2 of 3 applicants hired in 2006, up from 1 of 3 applicants hired in 2005

Diversity of entry-level workforce: 56% minority; 70% female

Facts to know:

- BCBS companies collectively cover one in three Americans; in all, roughly 100 million people are insured by BCBS.

- BCBS covers the health-care needs of 57 percent of federal employees and retirees through FEP, the Federal Employee Program.

The Starting Gate

Undergraduate internships: 20

Duration of summer internship: 12 weeks

Average total compensation: $6,338

Interns by grade level:
Sophomore 10%
Junior...80%
College graduate 10%

Interns who receive full-time job offers: 5%

Interns who are extended full-time job offers that accept: 100%

The Sliding Scale

Entry-level hires who had been interns: 2%

Most important performance measurements in entry-level hire: Productivity/efficiency, sales/revenue, analytical skills

Entry-level hires receiving signing bonuses: None

Average entry-level signing bonus: N/A

Entry-level hires receiving performance bonuses: 100%

Average performance bonus during first year: $2,000

The Stand-Out Perks

- Educational expenses reimbursement ($7,200)

- 401(k) plan

- Relocation compensation ($7,500)

- Employee discounts

The Skills

- Formal 12-day orientation program, including computer training, guest speakers, diversity exercises, a tour of the facilities, an explanation of benefits, coaching, and networking

- Passage/Passport Programs, a formal two-week leadership program

- Formal mentorship program (5% of entry-level hires participate)

THE SUPERSTAR SPOTLIGHT

Name: Nat Kongtahworn
Job: Director of Network Strategies of the BCBS Association

Briefly describe a typical day: *It includes working with my team, teams at local BCBS plans, and industry/professional groups on national performance measurement initiatives to improve the quality and affordability of care provided by network physicians and hospitals.*

Coolest thing about the job: *Working with some of the most influential people in the industry to transform health care into a value-based enterprise.*

How he rose so quickly: *[I] identified mentors; recognized [and] seized opportunities; treated others with respect; [and] participated in leadership opportunities outside of work with professional organizations such as the Chicago Health Executives Forum and volunteer organizations like the Make-A-Wish Foundation of Illinois.*

Chubb

15 Mountain View Rd.
Warren, NJ 07059
Phone: 908-903-2000
Fax: 908-903-2027
Web Addresses: www.chubb.com/
corporate/chubb2408.html;
www.chubb.com/careers/chubb1668.
html

The Company

- The Chubb Group of Insurance Companies—an insurance company that provides products ranging from professional and management liability insurance to property and casualty insurance—manages a total asset portfolio of $44 billion for clients in 29 countries.

- Chubb's Employee Referral Program provides a monetary incentive ($1,500 for any position) to Chubb employees for their active participation in attracting and hiring qualified, experienced candidates for professional and support positions. Approximately 30% of new hires come to Chubb through this program.

- Thanks in part to Chubb's "Reach Up, Reach Out, Reach Down" initiative, in a four-year period ending in 2005, the number of women serving as senior vice presidents at the company rose from 16% to 23%, and the number of women serving as executive vice presidents rose from 0% to 17%.

FAST FACTS

"Best Places to Launch a Career" Rank: 39
"Best Internships" Rank: N/A
Full-Time Salary: $45,000–$49,999
Entry-Level Hires: 458
Top College Major: Business
3-Year Retention Rate: 50%
Stock Ticker: CB

The Suits

John D. Finnegan: Chairman, CEO, and President
Michael O' Reilly: Vice Chairman and CFO
Thomas F. Motamed: Vice Chairman and COO
John J. Degnan: Vice Chairman and Chief Administrative Officer
Paul J. Krump: COO of Chubb Commercial Insurance

The Stats

2007 net written premiums: $11.9 billion
2007 net income: $2.8 million
Market cap: $20.9 billion
Employees: 10,800
Locations: With its headquarters in New Jersey, Chubb also occupies 120 offices in 29 countries
Major competitors: ACE, AIG, Travelers, Fireman's Fund

Largest operating units:
Personal Insurance............$3.7 billion
Commercial Insurance......$5.1 billion
Specialty Insurance ....$2.9 billion

📖 The Story

1882: Thomas and Percy Chubb open Chubb & Son, an insurance firm that underwrites cargo in New York City's seaport

1901: Cofounds the New York Marine Underwriters (NYMU)

1967: Chubb & Son becomes the Chubb Corporation after the company purchases Pacific Indemnity

1970: Acquires Bellemead Development, expanding its holdings in real estate

1984: Chubb first appears on the New York Stock Exchange

1985: Scales back on medical malpractice insurance

1991: Chubb Life Insurance Co. of America is founded after the consolidation of three of the company's subsidiaries

1997: Sells its life and health insurance operations and part of its real estate portfolio

1998: Expands into Latin America, buying Venezuela-based Italseguros Internacional

2001: The attack on the World Trade Center on September 11, 2001, results in $3.2 billion in claims ($645 million after reinsurance) for Chubb, the first insurer to announce that its insurance policy covered terrorism and that it wouldn't seek to apply the war risk exclusion

2002: Reserves an additional $700 million for claims related to asbestos

2003: Exits the personal lines insurance business in continental Europe and the credit derivative business of Chubb Financial Solutions

2006: Reports record financial results

The Skinny

Most important to recruiters: Analytical skills, communication skills, leadership skills

Selectivity: 1 of 3 applicants hired in 2006, roughly the same as in 2005

Diversity of entry-level workforce: 25% minority; 64% female

Facts to know:

- Finance, accounting, and actuarial trainees/interns work in New Jersey locations, while underwriting and claims trainees/interns work mainly in larger branch offices.

- Chubb provides tuition assistance for employees working toward department-sponsored industry certifications or other relevant courses. Employees also receive monetary awards for successful completion of department-sponsored education such as the Claims Law Program and Safety Professional Certification.

- Chubb offers a one-time company car allowance of $1,950 (depending on job responsibilities) to assist in the purchase of a vehicle, as well as a commuter benefits plan that makes it possible for employees to save as much as 40% by paying their commuter costs through pre-tax payroll deductions.

The Starting Gate

Undergraduate internships: 65

Duration of summer internship: N/A

Average total compensation: N/A

Interns by grade level:
Freshman 5%
Sophomore 10%
Junior...35%
Senior 50%

Interns who receive full-time job offers: N/A

Interns who are extended full-time job offers that accept: N/A

The Sliding Scale

Entry-level hires who had been interns: 30%

Most important performance measurements in entry-level hire: Analytical skills, learning ability, profitability/margin

Entry-level hires receiving signing bonuses: 10%

Average entry-level signing bonus: $2,520

Entry-level hires receiving performance bonuses: 56%

Average performance bonus during first year: $2,059

The Stand-Out Perks

- Educational expenses reimbursement ($5,100)
- Full and partial graduate school sponsorship
- Charitable gift match ($25,000)
- Relocation compensation
- Employee discounts
- Some Chubb offices have dry-cleaning services, hair and nail salons, restaurants, banks, nursing facilities, and art galleries

The Skills

- Formal ten-day orientation program, including computer training, guest speakers, diversity exercises, team-building exercises, a tour of the facilities, and a review of corporate culture
- Year One at Chubb is a 16-week formal leadership program for entry-level hires

THE RECRUITER SPOTLIGHT

Name: Valerie Aguirre
Job: Senior VP of Talent Acquisition

Biggest interview turn-off: *Some candidates feel compelled to divulge information that isn't necessary. Revealing too much personal information can make the interviewer feel very uncomfortable. For example, sharing an experience about a messy divorce takes away from your ability to sell yourself. The focus should be only on your skills and accomplishments.*

If someone arrives late for an interview, can he or she recover? Any other faux pas to avoid? *Most hiring managers understand that unanticipated traffic jams and emergencies do occur. You should call ahead to explain the delay and ask whether you should still come in or schedule a new appointment. When you arrive for the interview, simply apologize, and, most important, tell the truth. On the other hand, showing up too early will add to your anxiety, as well as make the receptionist and hiring manager uncomfortable. You should arrive about 10 minutes prior to the interview time. Make sure to turn in any paperwork, such as employment applications, that you had received in the mail. Casual dress does not apply to applicants, even if you happen to be interviewing on casual day at a company. An applicant should always dress professionally, from head to toe (no sandals!).*

Why choose Chubb: *You will be joining the premier insurance company in the industry. We're a financially stable organization and offer work/life balance opportunities. Our training programs are superb. Our culture is built around integrity, respect, and fairness for our employees and our customers.*

Liberty Mutual

175 Berkeley St.
Boston, MA 02116
Phone: 617-357-9500
Fax: 617-350-7648
Web Addresses:
www.libertymutual.com;
www.libertymutual.com/careers

The Company

- The Liberty Mutual Group offers auto, home, and life insurance for individuals, as well as commercial insurance for businesses. Liberty is divided into four units—personal markets, commercial markets, agency markets, and international operations. (Passenger auto insurance is Liberty's biggest money-maker.)

- Liberty Mutual is the sixth-largest casualty and property insurer in the United States (based on 2006 written premiums). Liberty Mutual's U.S. brands also include life insurance company Liberty Life and property/casualty business insurer Wausau.

- In 1954, Liberty set up the Liberty Mutual Research Institute for Safety, which studies a wide range of injuries in an effort to improve overall safety conditions.

FAST FACTS

"Best Places to Launch a Career" Rank: 54
"Best Internships" Rank: 52
Full-Time Salary: $45,000–$49,999
Entry-Level Hires: 667
Top College Major: Business
3-Year Retention Rate: 83%
Stock Ticker: N/A (privately owned)

The Suits

Edmund F. Kelly: Chairman, President, and CEO
A. Alexander Fontanes: Executive VP and Chief Investment Officer
Dennis J. Langwell: Senior VP and CFO
Christopher C. Mansfield: Senior VP and General Counsel
Stuart M. McGuigan: Senior VP and Chief Information Officer

The Stats

2007 sales: $26 billion
2007 net income: $1.5 billion
Market cap: N/A
Employees: More than 40,000
Locations: 900 offices in 49 U.S. states and 23 countries in Asia, Europe, and Latin America
Major competitors: AIG, State Farm, Allstate, GEICO, CIGNA

The Story

1912: The Massachusetts Employees' Insurance Association (MEIA) is established as a mutual company that is owned by its policyholders

1917: MEIA changes its name to Liberty Mutual Insurance Company

1937: Liberty expands operation to 48 states

1943: Liberty Mutual opens the nation's first rehabilitation center in Boston

1954: Liberty's Research Center for Safety opens

1967: Liberty International Agency is established to cover domestic policyholders abroad

1985: Liberty Financial Services is founded, marking the organization's entrance into the financial services market

1993: Liberty International Holdings is formed to underwrite risks in international markets

1997: San Diego-based Golden Eagle Insurance acquired by Liberty Mutual

1998: Latinoamericana de Seguros SA in Columbia and Citystate Insurance in Singapore, Hong Kong, and the Philippines are both acquired

1999: Establishes the Center for Disability Research.

2001: Sells off the Liberty Financial Companies and its asset management, annuity, and bank marketing businesses; acquires OneBeacon, boosting its Agency Markets business

2003: Acquires MetLife's Spanish operations and completes purchase of Prudential Financial's personal property and casualty operations in 47 states

2004: Opens its first office in China

2005: Forms Agency Markets division; acquires ING's Property and Casualty operations in Chile

2006: Liberty International Underwriters opens its first offices in the Middle East

2007: Acquires Ohio Casualty Corporation

The Skinny

Most important to recruiters: Communication skills, analytical skills, leadership skills

Selectivity: N/A

Diversity of entry-level workforce: 22% minority; 49% female

Facts to know:

- Of Liberty Mutual's 317 senior executives (VP level and higher), 107 have been with the organization for 20 years or longer.

- Liberty Mutual's entry-level retention statistics are among the highest of the insurers included in *Business-Week's* "Best Places to Launch a Career" list: Liberty's 3-year retention rate is 83%, and its 5-year retention rate is 62%.

The Starting Gate

Undergraduate internships: 326

Duration of summer internship: 8 to 12 weeks

Average total compensation: $6,000

Interns by grade level:
Freshman 2%
Sophomore 3%
Junior..11%
Senior 84%

Interns who receive full-time job offers: 50%

Interns who are extended full-time job offers that accept: 50%

The Sliding Scale

Entry-level hires who had been interns: 45%

Most important performance measurements in entry-level hire: Customer satisfaction, productivity/efficiency, profitability/margin

Entry-level hires receiving signing bonuses: 5%

Average entry-level signing bonus: $2,000

Entry-level hires receiving performance bonuses: 100%

Average performance bonus during first year: $2,250

The Stand-Out Perks

- Educational expenses reimbursement ($6,000)

- Full graduate school sponsorship

- 401(k) with company match of up to 7% of salary, company-funded pension, and profit sharing

- Employee discounts

The Skills

- Formal one-day orientation program that includes computer training and a tour of the facilities

- Fellowship in Finance and Accounting, a rotational leadership program that lasts 104 weeks

The Sound-Off

- "Liberty Mutual has an unbelievable internship program, because the intern is treated as an actual employee." —*Bentley junior**

*Data: Universum Communications

THE ENTRY-LEVEL SPOTLIGHT

Name: Charles Hill

Job: Human Resources Development Program participant

Briefly describe a typical day: *First thing I do is check my e-mail. Then I make a list of everything I need to work on, starting with high-priority [projects] and moving to low-priority [projects]. Some of the high-priority items involve lots of reporting and research. For example, I have an action plan for one big project where I am supposed to complete certain items by Week One, Week Two, and so on. So I work on this for most of the day and respond to any e-mails or calls that come my way. There are several components to the project, so there's always something new. And if my team needs support with anything, I lend a helping hand. There are also projects that come up in my one-on-one meetings with my manager . . . that I will work on, too. Other times, there are training courses I work on, which have to be completed by certain dates.*

Best part of the job: *Right now I'm in the Human Resources Development Program. When I started in June 2006, I was in the Corporate Human Resources Operations Unit. The team camaraderie in the unit was great. I was set up in a quad, so they were definitely a fun group to work with, and whenever you felt swamped, they were willing to help you. Now I am on my first rotation in Corporate Undergraduate University Relations. The work itself is challenging and project-oriented, and you are given a lot of autonomy. I could be traveling to facilitate a college workshop one day, preparing a presentation the following day, and completing reports or writing proposals the day after that.*

Advice for ambitious young employees: *To be noticed at Liberty, you should do a few things. You need to be assertive. Your manager won't know if you are interested in a particular project or skill unless you tell her. Another thing that is equally important is that you can't be afraid to network. One of the individuals you meet could hold your future job in his hands. Finally, you need to make sure that you put 150% into any of the work you do. Stay humble, but still have confidence in the work you produce.*

MetLife

200 Park Ave.
New York, NY 10166
Phone: 212-578-2211
Fax: 212-578-3320
Web Addresses: www.metlife.com;
www.metlife.com/careers

The Company

- MetLife handles $3.6 trillion of life insurance and serves 70 million consumers worldwide. An undisputed U.S. leader, the company is now looking abroad for growth, honing in on emerging markets with high potential for surging demand.

- The company might be best known for being the country's largest life insurer (and for its Snoopy mascot), but MetLife offers a range of other financial services. In addition to life, homeowner's, and auto insurance, the company provides annuities, financial retirement and savings, and retail banking products.

- MetLife Real Estate Investments maintains a portfolio of around $40 billion in real estate projects and financial services. Its rich real estate history dates back to its partial financing of New York City's Rockefeller Center and Empire State Building in the 1930s. More recently, MetLife sold the Sears Tower in Chicago after a brief ownership stint, and also sold New York City's largest residential complexes,

FAST FACTS

**"Best Places to Launch a Career"
  Rank:** 95
"Best Internships" Rank: 29
Full-Time Salary: Less than $35,000*
Entry-Level Hires: 4,253
**Reimbursement for Graduate School
  Expenses:** Full
3-Year Retention Rate: 53%
Stock Ticker: MET
*Nonsales positions

Peter Cooper Village and Stuyvesant Town.

The Suits

C. Robert Henrikson: Chairman, CEO, and President
William J. Wheeler: CFO
William J. Toppeta: President of International Business
William J. Mullaney: President of Institutional Business
Lisa M. Weber: President of Individual Business

The Stats

2007 sales: $54 billion
2007 net income: $7.3 billion
Market cap: $45.6 billion
Employees: 49,000
Locations: More than 990 offices in the United States and offices in 16 international regions

Major competitors: Prudential Financial, Inc., The Hartford Financial Services Group, Lincoln National Corp.

Largest operating units*:

Institutional Business......$21.5 billion
Individual Business ....$15.6 billion
Reinsurance.....................$5.7 billion
International ....$5.4 billion
Auto & Home..................$3.1 billion
Corporate and Other........$1.6 billion
*2007 sales

The Story

1863: A group of New York businessmen start the National Union Life and Limb Insurance Company to insure Civil War soldiers against wartime injury

1868: The company shifts its focus to the life insurance industry, targeting the middle-class consumer, and charters a new company—the Metropolitan Life Insurance Company

2000: MetLife, formerly a mutual company, launches its initial public offering

2001: MetLife Bank is a new entrant into the consumer bank sector

2005: Pulls in $1.2 billion from selling two of its New York skyscrapers, including the iconic Park Avenue MetLife building

2005: Travelers Life and Annuity is acquired from Citigroup

2006: In the biggest real estate deal in history, MetLife sells the Peter Cooper Village and Stuyvesant Town apartment complexes in New York City for $5.4 billion

2006: Pays $19 million to reach a settlement with the New York attorney general on an investigation of price fixing in the insurance industry; also this year, C. Robert Henrikson succeeds Robert Benmosche as MetLife's chairman, CEO, and president

2007: Acquires Safeguard Health Enterprises, a provider of dental and vision benefits products

The Skinny

Most important to recruiters: Communication skills, analytical skills, leadership skills

Selectivity: 1 of 16 applicants hired in 2006, down from 1 of 14 applicants hired in 2005

Diversity of entry-level workforce: 30% minority; 52% female

Facts to know:

- MetLife actively recruited on 225 U.S. undergraduate campuses during the 2006–2007 school year, but the company extended job offers on only 30 of those campuses.

- The company boasts a 3-year retention rate of 53% for its nonsales associates (as listed in the "Fast Facts" section of this profile), but the 3-year retention rate for sales associates is only 32%.

The Starting Gate

Undergraduate internships: 420

Duration of summer internship: 8 to 12 weeks

Average total compensation: $6,800

Interns by grade level:
Freshman 3%
Sophomore 32%
Junior..40%
Senior 25%

Interns who receive full-time job offers: 65%

Interns who are extended full-time job offers that accept: 94%

The Sliding Scale

Entry-level hires who had been interns: 38% in corporate and administrative departments; 82% in sales

Most important performance measurements in entry-level hire: Sales/revenue generation, customer satisfaction, productivity/efficiency

Entry-level hires receiving signing bonuses: None*

Average entry-level signing bonus: N/A*

Entry-level hires receiving performance bonuses: 87%*

Average performance bonus during first year: $1,190*

*Nonsales positions

The Stand-Out Perks

- 401(k) with company match of up to 4% of salary and co-funded pension

- Educational expenses reimbursement

- Full and partial graduate school sponsorship after 6 months of continuous service

- 17 paid vacation days

- Health plan with dental coverage

- Employee discounts

- Charitable gift match ($5,000)

The Skills

- One-day orientation involving an interactive e-learning program

- Formal leadership development program available for some new hires

- Formal mentorship program (10% of entry-level hires participate)

- Eight to twelve weeks of training available to new service and sales personnel

THE ENTRY-LEVEL SPOTLIGHT

Name: Anthony Sealey
Job: Business Analyst

Why MetLife is a top entry-level employer: *Before becoming a full-time employee [in Jersey City, NJ], I was an INROADS intern at MetLife for three consecutive summers and also worked during winter recess between semesters [at Seton Hall University]. The partnership between INROADS and MetLife is significant because it is centered on development, retention, and conversion of top talent into full-time associates. If MetLife did such a great job giving me opportunities to work on meaningful and challenging projects with their best people, then it was a common sense they would be an ideal place for building a career.*

Briefly describe your firm's work culture: *MetLife is a very close-knit company despite the large number of customers and employees. Valuable programs, benefits, and policies like flexible work arrangements, full tuition reimbursement, and performance management create an environment that allows employees to be effective.*

Advice for ambitious young employees on how to get noticed: *Reputation. Like a closely managed brand, your reputation speaks for the quality of work you do and the manner in which you do it. Having "grown up" at MetLife, I have also developed a network of mentors who, along the way, have guided my career to continually help me realize my potential. Even though MetLife is a large company, there is a tremendous potential to develop a large network of valuable relationships.*

Briefly describe a typical day: *Checking e-mail and voice mail first thing, then perhaps meeting with other associates to plan our next training session, participating in conference calls, or maybe meeting with my manager to discuss my development plan and assess the progress in relation to my objectives. After lunch, I might lead a meeting to draft business requirements for an IT project management solution or perhaps meet with my fellow INROADS alumni. My schedule is hectic but that's the only way I would have it.*

Nationwide

One Nationwide Plaza
Columbus, OH 43215
Phone: 614-249-7111
Fax: 614-249-9071
Web Addresses: www.nationwide.com;
www.nationwide.com/nw/careers/
    index.htm

The Company

- Nationwide is one of the largest diversified insurance and financial services organizations in the world. The company, which provides a full range of insurance and financial services, handles automobile, motorcycle, boat, homeowner's, life, and commercial insurance, as well as administrative services, annuities, mortgages, mutual funds, pensions, long-term savings plans, and health and productivity services.

- The sporty insurer is the title sponsor of the Nationwide Tour (PGA) and many Ohio-based sports teams (including Ohio State's athletics program), and it will take over a big NASCAR sponsorship in 2008.

- In 2005, Mothers Against Drunk Driving (MADD) and Nationwide teamed up to create THINK, a drinking prevention program for high school students. The program works to encourage teens to stay sober throughout the academic year. As of 2005, there were no alcohol- or drug-related fatalities

among the over 20.5 million students who committed to Nationwide Prom Promise (the predecessor program of THINK).

- Nationwide Financial Services (ticker: NFS), a subsidiary of Nationwide, is the only part of the company that is publicly traded. In the third quarter of 2007, Nationwide Financial's profit fell 9% from third-quarter 2006 earnings. However, Nationwide Financial's operational results improved, with company sales jumping 8% over the same quarter the year before.

The Suits

Jerry Jurgensen: CEO
Mark Thresher: President and COO
    of Nationwide Financial
Stephen Rasmussen: President and
    COO of Property and Casualty
    Insurance Operations

Patricia Hatler: Executive VP and CLO

Terri Hill: Executive VP and CAO

The Stats*

2007 sales (NFS): $4.5 billion

2007 net income (NFS): $626.8 million

Market cap (NFS): $6.9 billion*

Employees (companywide): 36,211

Locations: Headquartered in Ohio, with 490 offices across the United States

Major competitors: MetLife, New York Life Insurance, State Farm, Allstate

Largest operating units[†]:

Net Investment Income ....$2.3 billion
Policy Changes ....$1.4 billion
Other Income ....$601 million
Premiums ....$433 million
Net Realized Investment
   Gains/Losses ....–$165 million

*As of May 9, 2008; *BusinessWeek* data.
[†]2007 sales (NFS)

The Story

1925: The Ohio Farm Bureau Federation merges with the Farm Bureau Mutual Automobile Insurance Company, targeting auto customers in rural Ohio

1928: The growing company opens operations in West Virginia, Delaware, Maryland, Vermont, and North Carolina

1934: Moves into metropolitan areas and begins writing property insurance policies after purchasing a fire insurance company

1955: Changes name to Nationwide Insurance to reflect its steady expansion into 32 states

1978: Nationwide moves into One Nationwide Plaza; the 40-story structure is the largest office building in central Ohio

1996: Nationwide Financial Services becomes a publicly traded company

2007: Nationwide Bank opens to the public

The Skinny

Most important to recruiters: Communication skills, analytical skills, leadership skills

Selectivity: N/A

Diversity of entry-level workforce: N/A

Facts to know:

- Nationwide actively recruited at 21 U.S. undergraduate campuses during the 2006–2007 school year.

- Entry-level hires are formally evaluated twice a year and are eligible for their first internal job change after one year at the company.

- Out of Nationwide's 370 senior executives (VP and higher), 102 have been with the company for 20 years or more.

The Starting Gate

Undergraduate internships: 12

Duration of summer internship: 10 to 12 weeks

Average total compensation: $6,510

Interns by grade level:
Sophomore 8%
Junior..63%
Senior 8%
College graduate 21%

Interns who receive full-time job offers: 15%

Interns who have been extended full-time job offers that accept: 80%

The Sliding Scale

Entry-level hires who had been interns: N/A

Most important performance measurements in entry-level hire: N/A

Entry-level hires receiving signing bonuses: None

Average entry-level signing bonus: N/A

Entry-level hires receiving performance bonuses: None

Average performance bonus during first year: N/A

The Stand-Out Perks

- Educational expenses reimbursement ($2,250)

- Full and partial graduate school sponsorship

- 401(k), co-funded pension, and profit-sharing plan

- Charitable gift match ($5,000)

- Relocation compensation

- Employee discounts

The Skills

- One-day formal orientation that includes computer training, guest speakers, diversity exercises, and team-building exercises

THE ENTRY-LEVEL SPOTLIGHT

Name: Ashley Heilman
Job: Communications Coordinator

Briefly describe a typical day: *I support the communication and marketing efforts of Nationwide Better Health (NBH), the business entity of Nationwide that offers health and productivity solutions for employers. You can typically find me crafting internal communications or producing material to help strengthen the NBH brand and strategy. I also assist with media outreach, community involvement, customer communications, sales collateral, and market positioning efforts. I'm lucky to have an entry-level job that gives me great responsibility and experience.*

Fun quirk of the job: *On the Corporate Communications floor at Nationwide, we hold an activity every month that allows us to show off our creativity and have a little fun. From our "name your favorite song" board to a "who's that baby" contest, we learn a lot about each other—and laugh with each other!*

Why choose nationwide: *There are so many opportunities for growth at Nationwide. I went through our internship program as a college student. I was able to gain hands-on, practical work experience before I even graduated with my bachelor's degree. When I was offered my entry-level job, I felt Nationwide had prepared me for success as a professional.*

Advice for ambitious young employees: *Always give your honest opinion and be confident in your work. You never know who's paying attention to your efforts, so talk to your coworkers and be aware of your surroundings. If you can prove you're dependable, efficient, and reliable, people at Nationwide will want you on their team.*

New York Life Insurance

51 Madison Ave.
New York, NY 10010
Phone: 212-576-7000
Fax: 212-576-8145
Web Addresses: www.newyorklife.com;
www.newyorklife.com/careers

The Company

- New York Life Insurance Company is the largest mutual life insurance company in the United States and one of the largest life insurers in the world. New York Life's family of companies offers life insurance, retirement income, investments, and long-term care insurance. New York Life Investment Management LLC provides institutional asset management and retirement-plan services. Other New York Life affiliates provide an array of securities products and services, as well as institutional and retail mutual funds.

- New York Life also targets middle-income families and offers a wide variety of products catering to the needs of the younger family. Furthermore, it has college savings programs designed to meet the needs of this demographic.

- In the late 1980s, New York Life began a promising expansion into Asia and Latin America (regions where life insurance is still a rarity in many areas), capping its international ventures with its 1998 purchase of a Hong Kong–based life insurance company. Today the company's overseas arm is known as New York Life International.

👔 The Suits

Sy Sternberg: Chairman and CEO
Theodore Mathas: President and Chief Operating Officer
Gary Wendlandt: Vice Chairman of the Board and Chief Investment Officer

The Stats

2007 total revenue: $21.1 billion
2007 net income: $1.5 billion
Market cap: N/A
Employees: 13,580[*]
Locations: Subsidiaries and affiliates in China, Hong Kong, India, Argentina, Mexico, South Korea, and Taiwan[†]

Major competitors: Northwestern Mutual, MassMutual, Prudential, MetLife

Largest operating units[†]:
Premiums ....$9.9 billion
Net Investment Income....$8.9 billion
Fees—Universal Life and
    Annuity Policies ....$1.0 billion
Other Income ....$745.0 million
Net Investment Gains ..$627.0 million

*Figure does not include New York Life's 40,100 licensed agents.

[†]2007 sales; through New York Life International, LLC, the company's international arm

The Story

1841: The Nautilus Insurance Company is issued a charter to engage in business by a special act of the New York State Legislature

1845: Pliny Freeman and 56 other New York businessmen open Nautilus Insurance Company for business

1849: The Nautilus Insurance Company is renamed the New York Life Insurance Company

1892: Becomes the first insurer to organize a branch office system

1987: Acquires a controlling interest in Sanus Corp. Health Systems

1992: Launches an insurance joint venture in Indonesia, marking its expansion into Asia

1995: Settles a $65 million lawsuit with clients that accused the firm of persuading them to buy more expensive policies than necessary

2000: Joint venture with Max India allows New York Life's expansion into the Indian market

2002: Becomes the largest mutual life insurance company in America

The Skinny

Most important to recruiters: College GPA, leadership skills, communication skills

Selectivity: N/A

Diversity of entry-level workforce: 32% female; minority

Facts to know:

- Most entry-level employees begin in the two-year trainee program. While in the program, they receive performance-based salary increases every six months. At the conclusion of the program, they are eligible for annual merit raises.

- New York Life Insurance spends $85,300 on average in training a new life insurance agent in his or her first year.

The Starting Gate

Undergraduate internships: 667

Duration of summer internship: 10 weeks

Average total compensation: $9,800

Interns by grade level:

Freshman 1%

Sophomore 14%

Junior..36%

Senior 48%

College graduate 1%

Interns who receive full-time job offers: N/A

Interns who have been extended full-time job offers that accept: 3%

📟 The Sliding Scale

Entry-level hires who had been interns: 8%

Most important performance measurements in entry-level hire: Accountability, adaptability/flexibility, communication skills (oral and written)

Entry-level hires receiving signing bonuses: 100%

Average entry-level signing bonus: $2,000

Entry-level hires receiving performance bonuses: None

Average performance bonus during first year: N/A

The Stand-Out Perks

- Educational expenses reimbursement (immediate reimbursement)
- 10 paid vacation days
- Paid time off for religious observances
- Charitable gift match ($5,000)
- Employee discounts

The Skills

- Formal two-day orientation program that includes guest speakers, diversity exercises, team-building exercises, and a tour of the facilities
- Management Training Program for new agents, which lasts 50 to 156 weeks
- Formal mentorship program

THE RECRUITER SPOTLIGHT

Name: Elizabeth King
Job: Director of Talent Management

Advice for prospective young employees: *Although our primary focus is on life insurance, New York Life is a financial services firm that offers retirement income funding, investments, and long-term care insurance. This is important for prospective employees to know. Knowing about New York Life's values is also critical because it affords an understanding of how we do business and the culture at New York Life. The company's values of financial strength, integrity, and humanity have been the foundation for the decisions we have made for over 160 years.*

Why choose this industry: *We offer a career in a strong and stable industry. The life insurance industry is unique because our products empower people to provide for their future and offer the peace of mind that comes along with this financial security. The industry also offers a tremendous range of diverse career opportunities and movement, where employees can develop their technical skills and still be entrepreneurial.*

An interview "don't" to remember: *They [candidates] prepare for very specific questions in an interview, and when asked questions that are outside the realm of their preparation, they freeze. The result is that they can come across as inauthentic. I would rather have an authentic answer that is not as polished than a canned answer that is not indicative of the candidate's personality or abilities.*

Your take on video résumés: *I would recommend that applicants always submit a one-page résumé and cover letter because this is still the best way for recruiters to be able to quickly see an applicant's skills and accomplishments. Creative methods should be encouraged, though. These methods can be used to communicate one's accomplishments, skills, and interests in an innovative way. These skills and interests may also lend insight into where the candidate may fit within the organization.*

Northwestern Mutual

720 E. Wisconsin Ave.
Milwaukee, WI 53202
Phone: 414-271-1444
Fax: N/A
Web Addresses: www.nmfn.com;
www.careers.nmfn.com

The Company

- Insurance and financial services firm Northwestern Mutual, which is the largest direct provider of life insurance and pays more life insurance dividends to policy owners than any other company in the industry, markets itself as "the Quiet Company" to highlight the fact that it doesn't need to market itself at all.

- The private mutual company markets a product line of long-term care, disability, life, and health insurance, in addition to retirement plans that offer fixed and variable annuities. Under subsidiaries like Northwestern Mutual Investment Services and the Northwestern Mutual Wealth Management Company, it markets trust and brokerage services.

- Aiming to create a network of financial experts, the Northwestern Mutual Financial Network actively seeks new talent through its internship program and recruitment department. (A strong work ethic, relationship skills, and professionalism are all highly valued characteris-

FAST FACTS

"Best Places to Launch a Career" Rank: 84
"Best Internships" Rank: N/A
Full-Time Salary: $45,000–$49,999
Entry-Level Hires: 1,619
Top College Major: Business
3-Year Retention Rate: 17%
Stock Ticker: N/A (privately owned)

tics.) The company admits that starting out as a financial representative requires time, energy, and hard work.

The Suits

Edward J. Zore: President and CEO
John M. Bremer: COO and Chief Compliance Officer
Gary A. Poliner: Executive VP, Chief Investment Officer, and CFO
Marcia Rimai: Executive Vice President of Business Integration Services
Greg Oberland: Chief Information Officer

The Stats

2007 sales: $21.4 billion
2007 net income: $1 billion
Market cap: N/A
Financial representatives: 7,000
Locations: 350 offices across the United States

Major competitors: AIG, New York Life, Prudential

Policyowner Dividends Payable ....$5.0 billion
Policyowner Benefits Paid.............................$5.6 billion
Total Assets.................$156.5 billion

📖 The Story

1857: John Johnston founds a life insurance company in Janesville, Wisconsin, that will later become Northwestern Mutual

1888: The company's executive committee officially establishes Northwestern Mutual's credo: "The ambition of Northwestern has been less to be large than to be safe; its aim is to rank first in benefits to policyowners rather than first in size"

1918: 759 Northwestern Mutual policyowners lose their lives in World War I; the company pays their survivors $1.2 million in benefits

1933: Introduces annuities, Northwestern Mutual's first product line outside of life insurance

1955: Appoints Catherine Cleary to its board of trustees, making Cleary one of the first women to serve on the board of a major U.S. company

1966: Starts its college internship program

2000: Rebrands itself from Northwestern Mutual Life Insurance Company to Northwestern Mutual Financial Network

2001: Northwestern Mutual Wealth Management Company opens to provide trust services to the company's clients

2007: Northwestern Mutual celebrates its 150th anniversary

The Skinny

Most important to recruiters: Entrepreneurial spirit, communication skills, work experience

Selectivity: N/A

Diversity of entry-level workforce: 28% minority; 17% female

Facts to know:

- All of Northwestern Mutual's financial representatives are independent contractors, and their compensation is based on commission. Interns' income is also 100% derived from commissions and will, as a result, vary based on each individual's productivity.

- Although the majority of Northwestern Mutual's entry-level hires were business majors (60%), a fifth of them have a degree in the liberal arts.

🏇 The Starting Gate

Undergraduate internships: 1,653

Duration of summer internship: 12 weeks

Average total compensation: N/A

Interns by grade level:

Freshman 5%
Sophomore 25%
Junior...45%
Senior 20%
College graduate 5%

Interns who receive full-time job offers:
21%

Interns who are extended full-time job offers that accept: N/A

The Sliding Scale

Entry-level hires who had been interns: 13%

Most important performance measurements in entry-level hire: Quality, effort, customer satisfaction

Entry-level hires receiving signing bonuses: None

Average entry-level signing bonus: N/A

Entry-level hires receiving performance bonuses: None

Average performance bonus during first year: N/A

The Stand-Out Perks

- Because financial representatives are independent contractors, they arrange their own vacation time and holidays

- Automatic enrollment in two pension plans (defined benefit and defined contribution)

The Skills

- 15-day orientation program

- Leadership through Excellence and Development (LEAD) program, which lasts 104 weeks

- Formal mentorship program

The Sound-Off

- "The internship is more of a learning experience than doing work."
  —*Bentley junior**

- "Fewest holidays possible, salary levels lower than competing firms. However, good retirement benefits for those who've been here over 30 years (which is a large majority of the present staff)." —BW *Discussion Forum*

- "Why take a financial rep position? (1) Independence: you have the ability to run your own business and make your own hours. (2) Income: your income is determined only by your own ability to produce results. (3) Impact: you have the ability to make a lasting impact on someone's life, family, and business." —*Northwestern Mutual financial representative*

*Data: Universum Communications

THE SUPERSTAR SPOTLIGHT

Name: Cristi Stroud

Job: Managing Partner of the Southern New England Group

Describe a typical day: *I begin each day at the office before 7:00 a.m. I like getting an early start, as this allows me to review activities from the previous day, tie up any loose ends, and prepare for the day ahead. Most mornings I hold coaching meetings with new financial representatives to work on case development, and in the afternoons I meet with veteran representatives.*

Discuss your quick rise through the ranks: *From the beginning, I knew I wanted to be a managing partner, and I set very clear 5-year and 10-year goals to achieve this. I took advantage of every opportunity to learn more about Northwestern Mutual and our industry by attending as many conferences and seminars as possible. It was also important for me to push myself out of my comfort zone by building relationships and networking with various people in the company to learn more about their roles.*

Advice for ambitious young graduates: *My advice to others is to have an open mind about the financial services industry. Through relationship building with clients and others within the organization, I've witnessed exciting opportunities for entrepreneurial-minded professionals to advance quickly and achieve their goals. Most importantly, it is essential to find something that you are passionate about, both the job you are doing and the company you are doing it for. Passion is the fuel that will lead to success. I've found that passion at Northwestern Mutual.*

Progressive

6300 Wilson Mills Rd.
Mayfield Village, OH 44143
Phone: 440-461-5000
Fax: 800-456-6590
Web Addresses: www.progressive.com/
Progressive/aboutprog.asp;
jobs.progressive.com/

The Company

- The Progressive Group of Insurance Companies is the third-largest auto insurance group in the United States, offering professional liability insurance, as well as insurance for boats, motorcycles, RVs, and snowmobiles.

- Progressive is distinctive for pioneering an online insurance system that actually encourages consumers to "shop around," compare its rates with those of other providers, and buy policies live online.

- Progressive has an avant-garde approach to offices, furnishing its corporate facilities with over 6,500 works of fine art from the Progressive Art Collection.

- Progressive's third-quarter 2007 profit fell 27% from its third-quarter 2006 earnings. Although the company increased its number of policyholders by 3.9%, its earnings suffered as a result of a company decision to lower Progressive's auto policy rates in order to remain competitive with rivals.

The Suits

Glenn Renwick: CEO and President
Brian J. Passell: Group President of Claims
Charles E. Jarrett: Chief Legal Officer, Vice President, and Secretary
Brian C. Domeck: CFO

The Stats

2007 sales: $14.7 billion
2007 net income: $1.2 billion
Market cap: $13.4 billion
Employees: 27,000
Locations: On top of its 30,000 independent insurance agencies, Progressive has 475 claims offices across the United States
Major competitors: Allstate, GEICO, 21st Century, American Financial, Liberty Mutual
Largest operating units*:
Property and Casualty
Insurance....................$13.9 billion
*2007 sales

The Story

1937: Joseph Lewis and Jack Green form Progressive Mutual Insurance Company to issue vehicular insurance to drivers

1956: Progressive Casualty Company is formed to serve high-risk drivers

1965: Progressive Casualty and Progressive Mutual merge to become the Progressive Corporation

1971: Progressive becomes a publicly traded company and appears on the New York Stock Exchange under the stock ticker PGR

1994: Introduces Immediate Response Vehicles to serve customers at the scene of an accident

2003: Introduces concierge-level service, which allows customers to drop off their cars at Progressive after an accident and let the company handle any claims and/or repairs that must be addressed

2007: Company announces in June a 100-million-share buyback that will take place over the next two years

The Skinny

Most important to recruiters: Communication skills, analytical skills, leadership skills

Selectivity: 1 of 50 applicants hired in 2006, roughly the same as in 2005

Diversity of entry-level workforce: 37% minority; 56% female

Facts to know:

- In 2006, Progressive spent more than $36 million on training and development for its employees.

- In addition to an average hourly wage of $17.32, Progressive provides interns with a housing allowance and access to several entertainment options, such as tickets to baseball games, concerts, and amusement parks.

The Starting Gate

Undergraduate internships: 70

Duration of summer internship: 9 to 21 weeks

Average total compensation: $10,785

Interns by grade level:
Sophomore 7%
Junior..46%
Senior 28%
College graduate 19%

Interns who receive full-time job offers: 61%

Interns who are extended full-time job offers that accept: 70%

The Sliding Scale

Entry-level hires who had been interns: Zero

Most important performance measurements in entry-level hire: Leadership ability, effort, results

Entry-level hires receiving signing bonuses: 12%

Average entry-level signing bonus: $1,311

Entry-level hires receiving performance bonuses: N/A

Average performance bonus during first year: N/A

The Stand-Out Perks

- Educational expenses reimbursement (eligible for up to $2,000 to $5,250 after one year with the company; IT employees may be eligible for an additional $3,250)

- 401(k) with company match of up to 3% of pay

- Charitable gift match ($5,000)

- Relocation compensation

- Employee discounts

The Skills

- Formal two-day orientation program, including computer training, guest speakers, diversity exercises, team-building exercises, a tour of the facilities, review of emergency procedures, lunch with managers, and additional training specific to your business area

- Sales and Service Accelerated Supervisor Trainee Program, a formal leadership program for entry-level hires that lasts 36 weeks

- Leadership Rotational Program, a formal leadership program for entry-level hires consisting of three rotations and lasting 32 to 120 weeks

- Formal mentorship program

The Sound-Off

- "Progressive Insurance offers competitive pay, arranges group activities for the entire internship class, provides housing, and offers many interns full-time employment." —*Ohio State senior**

*Data: Universum Communications

THE RECRUITER SPOTLIGHT

Name: Jamie Bertone
Job: Director, Corporate and Executive Recruiting

Inappropriate recruiting behavior: *I'm always surprised when students show up at college career fairs in nonbusiness attire, like pajama pants and Ugg boots. It's never too early to start practicing good business etiquette!*

Why choose Progressive: *Progressive does not have the typical corporate hierarchy one might expect with a large corporation. It is filled with employees who never thought they would be working at an insurance company. It is a fast-paced, team-oriented environment that constantly challenges its employees to think differently and never be satisfied with the status quo. This is an environment where employees are celebrated—for the people they are, for the ideas they bring, and for the energy they invest.*

Advice for a young prospective employee: *At Progressive, the opportunities are endless. If you're smart, driven, and open to taking on new challenges, this is the type of company where you can move between business lines and job functions and learn while you go, while adding value, thanks to your various business experiences. Be open to new and different ideas and career paths once you are here. I never expected to be in the role I am in today, but I can't imagine not having taken the opportunity to learn and grow!*

Prudential Financial

751 Broad St.
Newark, NJ 07102
Phone: 973-802-6000
Fax: 973-367-6476
Web Addresses: www.prudential.com;
www.prudential.com/careers

The Company

- With $648 billion in assets (as of June 30, 2007), Prudential Financial Companies, which operates through its subsidiaries, is among the largest financial services institutions in the world. The Prudential Insurance Company of America, for instance, is one of the largest and most well-known life insurance groups in the United States.

- Headquartered in New Jersey since 1875, Prudential now has offices in Latin America, Europe, and Asia. It operates through two divisions: Insurance & Investments and International. Prudential offers a variety of services and products to individual and business customers worldwide, including annuities, mutual funds, real estate brokerage franchises, and retail securities brokerage services, through a joint venture with Wachovia.

- In 2006, Prudential agreed to pay more than half a billion dollars to the Securities and Exchange Commission (SEC) following an investigation into market-related activities

involving Prudential Securities, Inc. The company also acquired Allstate's variable annuity business that same year.

The Suits

Arthur F. Ryan: Chairman
Mark B. Grier: Vice Chairman of the International Division
John Strangfeld Jr.: CEO and President
Susan L. Blount: Senior VP and General Counsel
Richard J Carbone: Executive VP and CFO

The Stats

2007 sales: $34.4 billion
2007 net income: $3.7 billion
Market cap: $42.2 billion
Employees: 40,703
Locations: United States, Asia, Europe, Latin America

Major competitors: AIG, MetLife

Largest operating units:

Financial Services
(Insurance) ....$9.9 billion
Financial Services
(Investment) ....$7.3 billion
Financial Services
(International Insurance
and Investments) ....$8.9 billion
Financial Services (Corporate
and Other) ....$302.0 million
Closed Block Business ......$8.0 billion

The Story

1875: John Dryden creates a life insurance company in Newark, New Jersey

1878: Prudential's first branch office opens in Paterson, New Jersey

1896: The Rock of Gibraltar becomes Prudential's symbol

1937: Joins its peers at the first Million Dollar Round Table, a premier association of life insurance professionals

1960: Launches a $20 million urban redevelopment project to revitalize downtown Newark, New Jersey, the home of its headquarters

1997: Helps fund the New Jersey Performing Arts Center in downtown Newark

2000: Partners with a group of firms to invest in a $2 billion effort to revitalize Times Square in New York City

2001: The Prudential Insurance Company of America converts from a mutual life insurance company to a stock life insurance company; Pruden-

tial Financial takes over operations as parent company and goes public on the New York Stock Exchange

2006: Reaches a settlement following government investigations into market timing–related activities involving Prudential Securities and agrees to pay more than half a billion dollars to the SEC; acquires Allstate Financial's variable annuity business

The Skinny

Most important to recruiters: College major, communication skills, analytical skills

Selectivity: N/A

Diversity of entry-level workforce: 30% minority; 41% female

Facts to know:

- Maternity, paternity, and adoption leave is called "parental leave" at Prudential and is granted when an employee (or an employee's spouse) gives birth to or adopts a child. It includes 10 days of paid leave and up to 24 additional weeks of unpaid leave.

The Starting Gate

Undergraduate internships: 165

Duration of summer internship: 10 to 12 weeks

Average total compensation: $6,000

Interns by grade level:

Freshman 2%
Sophomore 2%
Junior..10%
Senior 85%
College graduate 1%

Interns who receive full-time job offers: 75%

Interns who are extended full-time job offers that accept: 50%

The Sliding Scale

Entry-level hires who had been interns: 30%

Most important performance measurements in entry-level hire: Learning ability, intelligence, productivity/efficiency

Entry-level hires receiving signing bonuses: 100%

Average entry-level signing bonus: $3,000

Entry-level hires receiving performance bonuses: 90%

Average performance bonus during first year: $2,000

The Stand-Out Perks

- Educational expenses reimbursement ($12,000)

- 19 paid vacation days

- On-site fitness facilities at some offices

- Charitable gift match ($5,000)

- Employee discounts

The Skills

- One-day orientation program

- Actuarial Leadership Development Program, which consists of five rotations and lasts 260 weeks

The Sound-Off

- "The transition from college to the corporate world was a breeze. The program offered many great opportunities to meet senior management, as well as my peers. Having about 20 recent college graduates like me in the program made the adjustment easier. The other rotational associates have the same questions as me, and we have helped each other answer them in the first few months. The work is challenging, but not overwhelming. Great networking opportunities, challenging work, and the promise of experiencing different aspects of this business have me looking forward to my next three years in this program—and hopefully a fulfilling career with this company after that." —*Prudential Finance Rotational Program participant*

THE RECRUITER SPOTLIGHT

Name: Jenna Washbourne
Job: Director of Staffing

Wackiest technique used by a job candidate: *An individual submitted his résumé by way of a singing telegram to our office. It was a neat and creative way of making an impression. However, a candidate with more job-related experience received the position.*

Advice for young prospective employees: *Be informed and do your homework—prepared candidates stand out. Show that you want the job enough to go the extra mile, so do some research. With the wealth of resources available on the Internet, research the history and philosophy of the company. Know the industry and the particular market for which you are interviewing. Be aware of any recent press or media announcements about the company.*

Types of experiences to highlight on a résumé: *Never assume that your experience is not relevant to the business world. For example, highlight how, during your summer job waiting on tables, you developed your customer service skills, and show how that would benefit Prudential. Companies are also interested in learning how students demonstrated leadership during their college years. If a student belonged to a fraternity or sorority, Prudential wants to know whether the student held a position of leadership within that organization. In addition, students who tout volunteer work in college might fare better during an interview if they can cite a fund-raising effort that they led. Last, consider highlighting your transferable skills, and show creativity.*

The Travelers Companies

385 Washington St.
Saint Paul, MN 55102
Phone: 651-310-7911
Fax: 651-310-3386
Web Addresses: www.travelers.com;
www.travelers.com/careers

The Company

- The Travelers Companies has long been an insurance industry trailblazer: in 1864, the company became the first company in America to insure against accidents, and in 1897, Travelers issued the first automobile insurance policy. A century later, Travelers launched the first insurance policy protecting individuals who use computers for online banking purposes.

- Travelers is one of the largest property and casualty insurance providers in the United States today, boasting 10,000 agency locations, 13,000 claims professionals, 30 field offices, and a 24-hour claim hotline. Its three business segments are Personal Insurance, Business Insurance, and Financial, Professional, and International Insurance.

- Travelers developed the industry's first catastrophe-response vehicles during the aftermath of Hurricane Andrew in 1997, calling them "claim offices on wheels."

🏁 FAST FACTS

"Best Places to Launch a Career"
  Rank: 37
"Best Internships" Rank: 36
Full-Time Salary: $35,000–$39,999
Top College Major: Business
3-Year Retention Rate: 45%
5-Year Retention Rate: 30%
Stock Ticker: TRV

The Suits

Jay Fishman: Chairman, CEO, and President
Charles Clarke: Vice Chairman
Irwin Ettinger: Vice Chairman
William Heyman: Vice Chairman and Chief Investment Officer
Jay Benet: Vice Chairman and CFO

The Stats

2007 sales: $26 billion
2007 net income: $4.6 billion
Market cap: $34.7 billion
Employees: 33,300
Locations: Significant operations in Hartford, Connecticut, and international offices in the United Kingdom, Ireland, and Canada
Largest operating units*:
Business Insurance..........$14.5 billion
Financial, Professional & International Insurance ..$3.9 billion
Personal Insurance...........$7.5 billion
Corporate ....$135 million
*2007 net written premiums

📖 The Story

1897: Travelers issues its first automobile insurance policy

1903: The company sets up a school to train its insurance agents

1936: Travelers launches a drivers' education program

1953: The first driver education automobile simulator is developed by Travelers

1956: Travelers sets up its own weather research center

2004: Travelers Property Casualty is acquired by the St. Paul Companies; the collective organization is named the St. Paul Travelers Companies

2007: A group of insurance companies, including Travelers, agrees to pay $2 billion in settlements from claims made after the destruction of the World Trade Center in order to speed up redevelopment at "Ground Zero"

2007: The St. Paul Travelers Companies changes its name to the Travelers Companies

The Skinny

Most important to recruiters: Analytical skills, leadership skills, college GPA

Selectivity: N/A

Diversity of entry-level workforce: 18% minority; 58% female

Facts to know:

- The company's Web site features a tool that is designed to help students determine which job opportunities at Travelers would best fit their college major.

- To acclimate its new hires to the company's culture, Travelers offers its entry-level workers rotational Leadership Development Programs (LDPs) in Actuarial Sciences, Human Resources, Financial Management, Information Technology, and Insurance Operations.

🏃 The Starting Gate

Undergraduate internships: 99

Duration of summer internship: 10 to 12 weeks

Average total compensation: $8,193

Interns by grade level:
Freshman 6%
Junior...15%
Senior 75%
College graduate 4%

Interns who receive full-time job offers: 50%

Interns who are extended full-time job offers that accept: 60%

📊 The Sliding Scale

Entry-level hires who had been interns: 42%

Most important performance measurements in entry-level hire: Team player, varies by position

Entry-level hires receiving signing bonuses: None

Average entry-level signing bonus: N/A

Entry-level hires receiving performance bonuses: None

Average performance bonus during first year: N/A

The Stand-Out Perks

- Educational expenses reimbursement
- Partial graduate school sponsorship
- 20 paid vacation days
- 401(k) plan with company match of up to 5% of salary
- Six to eight weeks of paid maternity leave

The Skills

- Orientation program with computer training and a tour of the facilities
- Half-week Leading by Personal Example program
- Actuarial Leadership Development Program (LDP), which consists of three rotations and lasts 156 weeks
- Formal mentorship program within the LDPs (5% of entry-level hires participate)

The Sound-Off

- "Travelers may be a good place to 'start' a career—when you're young and single. But it's not a good place to 'continue' your career. Since the merger with St. Paul, they wiped out many of their family-oriented benefits. For example, both companies offered paid adoption leave similar to maternity leave. The combined company totally eliminated it. They also stopped giving an adoption subsidy. Likewise, sick pay was scaled back considerably. Anyone with a chronic illness will have to use up their vacation time and essentially never have a vacation." —BW *Discussion Forum*

- "Travelers is a family-oriented company. While benefits may have changed to reflect the insurance industry standards over the last few years, nothing was really taken away; it was revised. We have FMLA that will help cover time away for adoption and chronic illness. The company also has short-term and long-term disability benefits. As far as sick time goes, a bank of paid leave days was given to cover sick, personal, family, and vacation days. You even have the option to buy five extra vacation days a year! The culture here is diverse and family-friendly, and I enjoy coming to work every day." —BW *Discussion Forum*

THE ENTRY-LEVEL SPOTLIGHT

Name: Andrew J. Evans

Job: Actuarial Leadership Development Program Participant

Why choose Travelers: *Travelers demonstrates its commitment to growing the company's future leaders through its support of the Leadership Development Programs. I know that the company values my professional development because of the training and actuarial exam support I receive. However, these are only a couple of the investments that are made to attract and keep top talent throughout the company.*

Best part of the job: *As part of the Actuarial Leadership Development Program, I have the opportunity to work in three one-year rotations. A few short weeks ago, I was in a totally different job in another area of the company. It is exciting to contribute in different capacities in different units while I learn about the business. I know that when I complete the rotations, I will be able to make an informed decision as to where I fit best within the organization.*

Weird/funny workplace encounter: *You have probably seen Travelers' recent television commercial with the concept that people no longer need luck (in the form of a lucky rabbit's foot) because Travelers provides products that stay in sync with their risks. Throughout the advertisement, the rabbits happily rehab their brightly colored, reattached feet, as people no longer need them as a lucky charm. Shortly after these commercials began airing, I checked my office mailbox, and imagine my surprise when I found a plush rabbit with a purple foot.*

CareerBuilder.com

200 N. LaSalle St., Suite 1100
Chicago, IL 60601
Phone: 773-527-3600
Fax: 773-527-2415
Web Addresses: www.careerbuilder.
com; www.careerbuilder.com/
share/aboutus/careers_main.aspx

The Company

- CareerBuilder.com is the United States' largest online job site and powers the online job search sites for over 1,400 partners, including MSN, AOL, and 150 newspapers. It also operates related sites, such as CBcampus.com for college recruiting, empleosCB.com for Hispanic workers, salary calculator CBsalary.com, and niche job site Sologig.com for independent contractors and freelancers.

- CareerBuilder.com is privately owned by media giants McClatchy, Tribune Co., Gannett Co., and Microsoft, which has a minority equity stake in the company.

- CareerBuilder.com gives job seekers access to over 1.5 million jobs, while employers have access to over 22 million unique visitors each month and a résumé database of over 25 million. CareerBuilder.com also utilizes a unique technology that automatically matches candidates' interests and experience with the most relevant job opportunities.

 **FAST FACTS**

"Best Places to Launch a Career" Rank: 91
"Best Internships" Rank: N/A
Full-Time Salary: Less than $35,000
Entry-Level Hires: 1,050
Top College Major: Business
3-Year Retention Rate: 29%
Stock Ticker: N/A (privately owned)

The Suits

Matt Ferguson: President and CEO
Brent Rasmussen: COO
Kevin Knapp: CFO
Mary Delaney: Chief Sales Officer
Eric Presley: Chief Technology Officer

The Stats

2006 sales: $672 million
2006 net income: N/A
Market cap: N/A
Employees: 1,800
Locations: 28 sales offices nationwide
Major competitors: Monster.com, Craigslist, Yahoo!, HotJobs
Largest operating units: N/A

The Story

1995: NetStart Inc., forerunner to CareerBuilder.com, is founded

1996: CareerBuilder.com is developed and the Web site is officially launched a year later

2000: Joins forces with Tribune and Knight Ridder

2001: Acquires Headhunter.net

2002: Gannett Co. joins Tribune and Knight Ridder to become an equal partner

2003: CareerBuilder.com establishes itself as industry leader in job postings

2004: Matt Ferguson becomes president and CEO

2004: Launches alliance with AOL and becomes the Internet service provider's exclusive job content provider

2005: Increases company exposure with Super Bowl commercial

2005: Launches alliance with MSN as its exclusive job content provider

2005: Takes the lead in traffic in the online recruitment industry

2006: CBcampus.com is created to serve college students and alumni

2006: McClatchy inherits partial ownership after acquisition of Knight Ridder

2006: CareerBuilder.com passes its largest competitor in U.S. revenue

2007: Microsoft takes a minority equity stake in CareerBuilder.com. In addition to powering the career site on MSN in the United States, Career-Builder is now doing so for key MSN international sites.

The Skinny

Most important to recruiters: Analytical skills, communication skills, references

Selectivity: 1 of 14 applicants hired in 2006

Diversity of entry-level workforce: 28% minority; 40% female

Facts to know:

- The company recently established a new summer internship program, Camp CareerBuilder, that teaches students about marketing, public speaking, and interviewing and résumé skills.

- CareerBuilder actively recruited on 30 U.S. undergraduate campuses during the 2006–2007 school year and extended job offers on 25 of those campuses.

 The Starting Gate

Undergraduate internships: 23

Duration of summer internship: 8 weeks

Average total compensation: $6,800

Interns by grade level: N/A

Interns who receive full-time job offers: N/A

Interns who are extended full-time job offers that accept: N/A

The Sliding Scale

Entry-level hires who had been interns: 1%

Most important performance measurements in entry-level hire: Learning ability, productivity/efficiency, customer satisfaction

Entry-level hires receiving signing bonuses: None

Average entry-level signing bonus: N/A

Entry-level hires receiving performance bonuses: 100%

Average performance bonus during first year: $7,500

The Stand-Out Perks

- 401(k) with company match to 3% of salary
- Profit-sharing program
- Educational expenses reimbursement ($10,000)
- Full and partial graduate school sponsorship
- 18 days of paid time off
- Health plan with dental and vision coverage
- Employee discounts

The Skills

- 10-day orientation, including computer training, guest speakers, team-building exercises, mentor shadowing, and lunches with company leaders
- High Performance Management program that lasts two weeks
- Three-year-long Leadership Development Program
- Formal mentorship program (50% of entry-level hires participate)

THE SUPERSTAR PROFILE

Name: Michelle Kossack

Job: Human Resources Operations Manager

Describe a typical day: *I'm currently managing the implementation of a new Human Resources Information System (HRIS), so my days have a variety of activities based upon each phase in the project. I have always been a multitasker, so I break up my days into very small time increments. Lately, I have been working on data-gathering spreadsheets, answering historical questions, composing communication to keep the project team up-to-date, writing new business processes, and taking care of normal day-to-day business, such as quarterly reviews.*

Best part of the job: *As a manager, one of my main responsibilities is to develop my team. Every quarter, I can contribute to my employees' attainment of their goals and then help them select new challenges for the next quarter.*

What keeps things interesting: *There are frequently humorous happenings around the office. . . . We tend to have a work hard/play hard environment. Wii, foosball, Ping-Pong tournaments, air hockey, burrito-eating contests, someone falling asleep in a massage chair during an employee appreciation event, a sales rep wearing a chimpanzee costume with a pink tutu—you name it, I've seen it!*

Advice for ambitious young employees: *Giving candid feedback, bringing innovative ideas to the table, taking on an attitude of entrepreneurship and owning their business—there are myriad ways to get noticed here.*

Best perks: *Employees can be reimbursed for items that enrich their wellness: gym memberships, smoking cessation programs, tennis lessons, marathon training programs, home gym equipment. CareerBuilder.com has also partnered with the Millennium Promise Organization, and employees can participate in educational and fund-raising activities to help eradicate extreme poverty.*

Google Inc.

1600 Amphitheatre Pkwy.
Mountain View, CA 94043
Phone: 650-253-0000
Fax: 650-253-0001
Web Addresses: www.google.com;
www.google.com/jobs

The Company

- Everyone's favorite Web search engine is one of the five most popular Web sites in the world, drawing 380 million global unique users each month. Google has sustained its growth by creating a steady stream of new products and making strategic acquisitions, such as its $1.7 billion purchase of leading Web video site YouTube in 2006.

- In 2004, Google took itself public at $85 a share—holding its initial public offering through an online auction to make its shares accessible to a broader audience—and saw its stock price jump to over $100 a share in its first day of trading on Nasdaq. The stock price has skyrocketed in the years since, to over $470 a share as of spring 2008.

- Google has doubled the size of its workforce annually over each of the past few years and is currently hiring approximately 500 new employees a month, many of whom are recent graduates in their mid- to late twenties.

FAST FACTS

"Best Places to Launch a Career" Rank: 5
"Best Internships" Rank: N/A
Top College Major: Computer science
Active Undergraduate Recruiting: 73 U.S. campuses
Reimbursement for Graduate School Expenses: Full
Average Work Week: 50
Stock Ticker: GOOG

The Suits

Dr. Eric Schmidt: Chairman of the Executive Committee and CEO
Larry Page: Cofounder and President of Products
Sergey Brin: Cofounder and President of Technology
Shona Brown: Senior Vice President of Business Operations

The Stats

2007 sales: $16.6 billion
2007 net income: $3.1 billion
Market cap: $216.3 billion
Employees: 16,805
Locations: Google's headquarters is in Mountain View, California, but the company has marketing and sales teams around the world, in North America, Europe, India, Australia, Asia, and Brazil
Major competitors: Yahoo!, MSN

Largest operating units*:

Advertising ....$16.4 billion
Licensing and other
  revenue....................$181.0 million

*2007 sales

📖 The Story

1998: Former Stanford graduate students Larry Page and Sergey Brin found Google Inc. in Menlo Park, California

2000: Google launches the Google Toolbar and Adwords, a user-activated ad program

2002: Google News is unveiled

2003: Pyra Labs and Blogger are acquired

2004: Google goes public; shortly thereafter, the company announces the launch of Gmail, a Web-based mail service that offers one gigabyte of free storage for each e-mail user (the file size has since been increased to two gigabytes)

2005: Google Earth, Google Talk, Google Book Search, and Google Blog Search are launched

2006: Acquires YouTube for $1.7 billion; Google Chat, the latest in workday diversions, is also born this year

The Skinny

Most important to recruiters: College major, college GPA, analytical skills

Selectivity: N/A

Diversity of entry-level workforce: N/A

Facts to know:

- Employees enjoy free lunches and onsite massage and yoga, among other unique, stand-out perks.

- The company's recruiting efforts are focused on computer science majors, but it also hires those with backgrounds in math, physics, and other engineering disciplines for technical roles. For all nontechnical roles, Google will consider all different types of majors.

- Job candidates are asked to complete an elaborate automated online application that includes questions pertaining to their behavior, attitude, personality, and background. (The company requests information dating back to high school.)

🏃 The Starting Gate

Undergraduate internships: N/A

Duration of summer internship: 10 to 26 weeks

Average total compensation: N/A

Interns by grade level: N/A

Interns who receive full-time job offers: 65%

Interns who are extended full-time job offers that accept: 90%

 **The Sliding Scale**

Entry-level hires who had been interns: N/A

Most important performance measurements in entry-level hire: N/A

Entry-level hires receiving signing bonuses: N/A

Average entry-level signing bonus: N/A

Entry-level hires receiving performance bonuses: 100%

Average performance bonus during first year: N/A

The Stand-Out Perks

- Educational expenses reimbursement ($8,000)

- Graduate school sponsorship

- Access to 401(k) with company match of 100% of the first $7,500 of base salary per year

- 15 paid vacation days during first year

- Employee discounts

The Skills

- Orientation program lasting anywhere from one day to two weeks that includes guest speakers and a tour of the facilities

- A formal mentorship program

The Sound-Off

- "Google should be number one [on *BusinessWeek*'s "Best Places to Launch a Career" list] by far, in my opinion. I was an intern there last summer, and I can tell you that it's the most fun and intellectually stimulating job in the world. Larry and Sergey, please hire me full time!" —BW *Discussion Forum*

- "At this point, your chances for advancement are the same as they are at a more mature company, like Intel. On top of that, when it was a much younger company, Google hired a bunch of young, inexperienced people who have now been promoted into positions they shouldn't be in. As a former employee and current stockholder, I want to see them clean house and weed out employees who still like to think of Google as their own little college geek frat where they can throw around buzzwords and phrases like 'thinking outside the box'." —BW *Discussion Forum*

THE RECRUITER SPOTLIGHT

Name: Arnnon Geshuri
Job: Director of Staffing

The wackiest technique used to get a job with Google: *A couple of examples come to mind. We had a brand new tennis shoe delivered to the office by messenger. Attached to the shoe was a note from the applicant explaining that she was trying to get a "foot in the door." Another applicant sent his résumé in the form of a singing telegram. The musical messenger walked into the lobby, was escorted right up to the recruiter's cubicle, and immediately began belting out a song about the applicant. Everyone in the surrounding offices stopped what they were doing and came out to partake in the midday entertainment.*

Advice for young prospective employees looking to join Google: *Get to know yourself, what you want in a career, and what you are passionate about. Research the company, get to know its values, and think through how Google aligns with your career goals and personal interests.*

Deutsche Bank

60 Wall St.
New York, NY 10004
Phone: 212-250-2500
Fax: N/A
Web Addresses: www.db.com;
www.db.com/careers

The Company

- The German banking chain has grown into a multinational firm specializing in investment banking, asset management, and retail banking. Corporate and private clients are served by over 1,700 offices in Europe, the Pacific, and North and South America.

- Notable subsidiaries include U.S.–based DWS Scudder, a large mutual fund manager, and RREEF Real Estate, a real estate manager with $84 billion in assets under management worldwide as of September 30, 2007. New York–based Deutsche Bank Securities is currently the only investment bank actually located on Wall Street.

- The turmoil in the U.S. financial markets has spread across the Atlantic, hitting European banking heavyweights such as Deutsche Bank and UBS. On April 1, 2008 Deutsche Bank announced it would write down 2.5 billion euros of loans and asset-backed securities. "Conditions have become signifi-cantly more challenging during the

last few weeks," noted the firm in a recent statement.

 ## The Suits

Josef Ackermann: Chairman of the Management Board and the Group Executive Committee
Herman-Josef Lamberti: COO
Anthony Di Iorio: CFO
Clemens Boersig: Chairman of the Supervisory Board
Hugo Banziger: CRO
Rainer Neske: Head of Private and Business Clients

The Stats

2007 sales: 30.7 billion euros
2007 net income: 6.5 billion euros
Market cap: 36.6 billion euros (as of April 11; Capital IQ)
Employees: 78,291*
*As of September 31, 2007

Locations: 1,700 offices located in 75 countries on the Asian, American, and European continents

Major competitors: Goldman Sachs, Credit Suisse, Lehman Brothers, Citigroup, JPMorgan Chase

Largest operating units†:

Corporate and Investment
Bank ....19.1 billion euros

Private Clients and Asset
Management ......10.1 billion euros

Corporate
Investments ....1.5 billion euros

†2007 sales

2001: Becomes the first German bank to list on the NYSE

2001: Cuts 2,600 jobs in conjunction with corporate restructuring

2006: $11.1 million fine is issued by U.K. regulators for market misconduct involving trading malfeasance in London; SEC investigates the tax filings of the bank; CEO Josef Ackermann goes on trial for receiving illegal bonuses during his employment at another firm. Ackermann ultimately settled for 3.2 million euros without admitting guilt.

The Story

1870: Georg von Siemens opens Deutsche Bank in Berlin, Germany

Late 1800s: Deutsche Bank finances Germany's electrification of the United States' and Ottoman Empire's railroad construction

1940s: The Allies split Deutsche Bank, which financed the Nazi Party, into 10 smaller banks; the bank becomes extinct in East Germany, which falls under Soviet control

1957: Ten branches are reassembled, and commercial banking operations resume

1989: Chairman Alfred Herrhausen, a symbol of big business, is killed by terrorists

1990: Herrhausen's successor, Hilmar Kopper, oversees Deutsche Bank's reestablishment in East Germany

The Skinny

Most important to recruiters: Communication skills, analytical skills, leadership skills

Selectivity: 1 of 20 applicants hired in 2005 and 2006

Diversity of entry-level workforce: 41% minority; 32% female

Facts to know:

• During the 2006–2007 academic year, Deutsche Bank actively recruited on 20 U.S. campuses and extended job offers on all 20 campuses.

The Starting Gate

Undergraduate internships: 262

Duration of summer internship: 10 weeks

Average total compensation: N/A

Interns by grade level:

Junior..100%

Interns who receive full-time job offers: 80%

Interns who are extended full-time job offers that accept: 67%

The Sliding Scale

Entry-level hires who had been interns: 32%

Most important performance measurements in entry-level hire: Productivity/efficiency, analytical skills, being a team player

Entry-level hires receiving signing bonuses: None

Average entry-level signing bonus: N/A

Entry-level hires receiving performance bonuses: 100%

Average performance bonus during first year: $24,000

The Stand-Out Perks

- Educational expenses reimbursement (18 credits per year)
- Access to 401(k) with company match of up to 4% of salary (fully vested after 60 months)
- Charitable gift match ($5,000)
- Relocation compensation ($10,000)
- Employee discount program

The Skills

- Formal one-day orientation program, including guest speakers and team-building exercises
- Global Market Analysts Induction, a formal 22-week leadership program held in London

The Sound-Off

- "Not only do they pay their interns hourly, but they also make a significant effort to ensure that the intern has as much experience as possible, e.g., client meetings, building models." —*Indiana University senior**
- "Deutsche Bank compensates up to $50,000 for a 10-week internship program. Compare that to $13,000 for the next best investment banking internship." —*Indiana University senior**
- "Deutsche Bank offers lots of different locations, which is important for students. They also focus on undergraduate students who are studying German, which makes it perfect for me." —*Virginia Tech junior**
- "Deutsche Bank pays overtime when other industry leaders do not for their summer interns." —*Princeton senior**

*Data: Universum Communications

THE RECRUITER SPOTLIGHT

Name: Kristina Peters

Job: Managing Director; Global Head of Graduate Recruitment & Employer Brand

Most unusual job-seeking tactics: *One student who accepted an offer wrote a "thank you" note on a real coconut and sent it to me (he had been honeymooning in Tahiti). One creative applicant sent me a small child's shoe along with his résumé. The shoe had a handwritten tag attached that read, "I just want to get my foot in the door." I still have the shoe in my office.*

Ultimate do/don't of applying for a job: *Ultimate "don't"—don't have any typos on your résumé or get the company name wrong in the cover letter. I am still surprised how many students either forget to change from a competitor's name in the letter or just spell our name incorrectly. This really sends a message about their attention to detail. Ultimate "do"—do your research on the company, the industry, and the position. Company Web sites are a great place to start, but don't stop there. Talk to current staff, former staff, classmates, etc. Research some of the independent career sites. Be in a position to demonstrate that you have really done your homework, beyond just cramming one night over a Web site.*

Why young job seekers should choose Deutsche Bank: *Deutsche Bank is intensely focused on attracting and developing a diverse pool of top talent—a strategy that is critical to how we grow our business and meet our clients' demands for product innovation and expertise. We run a truly global business and believe in the power of building global networks from day one. What does that mean if you are just starting out? An abundance of challenging career opportunities in a firm with global reach and a commitment to developing and retaining talent, all starting with market-leading, comprehensive training programs.*

Goldman Sachs

85 Broad St.
New York, NY 10004
Phone: 212-902-1000
Fax: 212-902-3000
Web Addresses: www.gs.com;
www.gs.com/careers/

The Company

- Among the largest, most prestigious financial services companies in the world, Goldman Sachs has produced its fair share of high-profile alumni, including Jon Corzine, who was elected to the U.S. Senate in 2000 and became the governor of New Jersey in 2005, and Henry Paulson, who became the secretary of the treasury in 2006.

- Goldman had some very uncharacteristic hedge-fund meltdowns that included a 22.5% loss in its Global Alpha hedge fund in August 2007. Another fund needed a $3 billion infusion from a group of investors, including Eli Broad and Hank Greenberg, to stay afloat. In typical Goldman fashion, the company recovered with through-the-roof third-quarter earnings, largely by systematically "shorting" the very same mortgage-related financial instruments that were wreaking havoc on competitors.

FAST FACTS

"Best Places to Launch a Career"
   Rank: 13
"Best Internships" Rank: 4
Full-Time Salary: $60,000–$64,999
Entry-Level Hires: Over 1,500
   (globally)
Top College Major: Business
3-Year Retention Rate: N/A
Stock Ticker: GS

The Suits

Lloyd C. Blankfein: Chairman and CEO
Gary D. Cohn: President and Co-COO
Jon Winkelried: President and Co-COO
David A. Viniar: Executive VP and CFO
John S. Weinberg: Vice Chairman

The Stats

2007 sales: $46 billion
2007 net income: $11.6 billion
Market cap: $91.5 billion
Employees: 30,522
Locations: The Americas, Europe, Asia, India, Japan, South Africa, United Arab Emirates
Major competitors: JPMorgan Chase, Merrill Lynch, Morgan Stanley

Largest operating units*:

Trading/Principal
Investments ....$31.2 billion
Investment Banking ....$7.6 billion
Asset Management/Security
Services ....$7.2 billion
*2007 sales

 The Story

1869: Marcus Goldman starts a commercial paper business in New York City

1882: Samuel Sachs joins Goldman to create Goldman, Sachs & Co.

1896: Goldman joins the New York Stock Exchange (NYSE) and launches its trading services

1956: Goldman begins offering its investment banking services

1970: The firm opens its first international office in London

1986: Goldman joins stock exchanges in London and Tokyo

1998: Because of market volatility, Goldman withdraws its plans to go public

1999: The firm goes public in a deal valued at approximately $4 billion

2000: Acquires NYSE specialist SLK

2003: Acquires financial planner Ayco; merges with Australian securities giant JBWere to form Goldman JBWere

2006: Posts Wall Street's largest profits ever; employee bonus pool tops $16 billion

The Skinny

Most important to recruiters: College GPA, leadership experience, work experience

Selectivity: N/A

Diversity of entry-level workforce: 48% minority; 37% female

Facts to know:

- Goldman Sachs University (GSU) offers employees formal training programs and 2,000 classroom and online courses on topics such as Products and Markets, Culture and Orientation, Diversity and Inclusion, Leadership and Management, and Professional Skills.

- Goldman targeted 40 schools and hired from over 150 schools for the 2006–2007 hiring season.

- Goldman's entry-level hiring was up 23% in 2007, and of those that were hired, 58% got their foot in the door as interns.

 The Starting Gate

Undergraduate internships: 911

Duration of summer internship: 8 to 12 weeks

Average total compensation: $11,538*

Interns by grade level:

Freshman 2%
Sophomore 13%
Junior..73%
Senior 12%

Interns who receive full-time job offers: 72%

Interns who are extended full-time job offers that accept: 73%

*Summer analyst (undergraduate intern) compensation varies by division. The most common summer analyst compensation ($60,000 per annum prorated for the 10 weeks interns spend in the program) appears above.

▦ The Sliding Scale

Entry-level hires who had been interns: 58%

Most important performance measurements in entry-level hire: Analytical skills, teamwork, leadership, communication skills, work ethic, commercial interest, and enthusiasm

Entry-level hires receiving signing bonuses: N/A

Average entry-level signing bonus: N/A

Entry-level hires receiving performance bonuses: N/A

Average performance bonus during first year: N/A

The Stand-Out Perks

- Educational expenses reimbursement (8 credits per semester)
- 18 paid vacation days, including 3 floating holidays
- Access to health plan that covers dental (for no extra cost) and vision

- Eligibility for profit-sharing plan
- 80 paid days of maternity leave and 20 paid days of paternity leave for entry-level employees; 40 paid days leave for adoptive parents
- Relocation compensation ($10,000)

The Skills

- 30-day orientation program, including computer training, guest speakers, team-building exercises, a tour of the facilities, products and markets training, and business-process skills training
- 10 hours of additional training annually
- Formal mentorship program

The Sound-Off

- "I interned there over the summer of 2006 and had a marvelous time. I learned a ton, and the people were very smart. I am looking forward to going back as a full-time employee after graduation." —*Johns Hopkins senior**
- "[On team building outings like bowling with free beer, wine, and pizza:] It's a fun way to relax after a day of bond pricing, which can get mentally taxing." —*Goldman Sachs financial analyst*

*Data: Universum Communications

THE RECRUITER SPOTLIGHT

Name: Aaron Marcus
Job: Global Head of Recruiting

Craziest job-seeker behavior: *I have heard stories of people traveling very long distances and coming to New York without an appointment, hoping to be seen for an interview. Although we admire the ambition and drive of these individuals, it's difficult for us to make allowances in these cases, because we see thousands of students each year on campus and schedule hundreds to come to the firm for interviews.*

Worst interview faux pas: *Getting the company name [wrong] is the worst. There is no reason not to know the name of the company you are interviewing with. Hopefully, candidates would realize if they said the wrong name or mentioned another firm and correct themselves to make a quick recovery.*

Career advice: *Meet the people of Goldman Sachs and other organizations to determine if there's a good cultural fit and if you can see yourself working with them. Additionally, the most important aspect of your first job is the learning you'll get through formal and informal training opportunities. Therefore, it's crucial to surround yourself with the best talent possible.*

Why choose Goldman: *Goldman Sachs provides students with the opportunity to build a strong skill set and solid foundation for a long-term career with the firm. This is accomplished while working in a collegial environment that provides training, mentoring, teamwork, and continuous business challenges.*

JPMorgan

JPMorgan Investment Bank
270 Park Ave.
New York, NY 10017
Phone: 212-270-6000
Fax: N/A
Web Addresses: jpmorgan.com;
jpmorgan.com/careers

The Company

- Global financial services firm
  JPMorgan has long maintained an
  elite position among top-tier investment banking and financial services
  firms. After its merger with the
  Chase Manhattan Corporation in
  2000, the company was renamed
  JPMorgan Chase & Co. Then, in
  2004, JPMorgan Chase & Co. and
  Bank One combined forces.

- The JPMorgan brand includes
  Investment Bank, Asset Management, Private Banking, Worldwide
  Securities Services, and One Equity
  Partners. The U.S. consumer and
  commercial banking businesses serve
  customers under the Chase brand.

- With backing from the Federal
  Reserve, JP Morgan made an emergency $2-per-share bid to buy com-
  petitor Bear Stearns when Bear
  Stearns founds itself on the brink of
  financial collapse in March 2008.
  In the weeks since, JP Morgan has
  raised the offer to $10 per share. As
  of mid-April, the deal is still pending though, and Bear Stearns' future

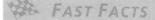

FAST FACTS

"Best Places to Launch a Career"
  Rank: 17
"Best Internships" **Rank:** 8
Full-Time Salary: $60,000
Entry-Level Hires: 305
Top College Major: Business
3-Year Retention Rate: N/A
Stock Ticker: JPM

(if it will have one) remains uncer-
tain.

The Suits

Jamie Dimon: Chairman and CEO
  of JPMorgan Chase
Michael J. Cavanagh: CFO and
  Executive VP of JPMorgan Chase
Steven D. Black: Co-CEO of
  JPMorgan Investment Bank
William T. Winters: Co-CEO of
  JPMorgan Investment Bank

The Stats

2007 sales: $74.8 billion (Investment
  Banking [IB]: $18.2 billion)*
2007 net income: $15.4 billion
  (IB: $3.1 billion)
Market cap: $146.6 billion
Employees: 180,667 (IB: 25,000+)
Locations: Offices in 50 countries+
Major competitors: Goldman Sachs,
  Merrill Lynch, Morgan Stanley,
  Lehman Brothers, Citigroup

Largest operating units*:

Investment Banking ......$18.2 billion
Retail Financial Services....$17.5 billion
Card Services..................$15.2 billion
Asset Management ....$8.6 billion
Treasury and Securities
    Services ....$6.9 billion
Corporate ....$4.2 billion
Commercial Banking........$4.1 billion
*2007 sales; reported on a managed basis

 The Story

1871: Firm is founded in New York City as Drexel, Morgan & Co. by J. Pierpont Morgan and Anthony Drexel

1895: Drexel, Morgan & Co. becomes J.P. Morgan & Co

1930s: Forced by the Glass-Steagall Act to operate as either a commercial or an investment bank, the firm chooses to position itself as a commercial bank; shortly thereafter, two partners split off to create the investment bank Morgan Stanley

1940: J.P. Morgan becomes a publicly traded company

1959: Firm merges with Guaranty Trust Company to create Morgan Guaranty Trust Company

1969: J.P. Morgan is set up as the parent company of Morgan Guaranty Trust Company, freeing the organization from the constraints of the Glass-Steagall Act and allowing the firm to expand further

2000: Merges with Chase Manhattan Corp. to become JPMorgan Chase & Co.

2006: JPMorgan Chase sells Chase Insurance for $1.2 billion

The Skinny

Most important to recruiters: Leadership skills, analytical skills, communication skills

Selectivity: 1 of 31 applicants hired in 2006, down from 1 of 24 applicants hired in 2005

Diversity of entry-level workforce: 47% minority; 38% female

Facts to know:

- All summer interns participate in a community service activity.

- JPMorgan has plans for a "green" renovation of its headquarters. The firm intends to achieve LEED-Platinum status, which, if carried out, will necessitate the largest certified conversion of an existing commercial building.

The Starting Gate

Undergraduate internships: 245

Duration of summer internship: 8 to 10 weeks

Average total compensation: $14,288*

Interns by grade level:
Sophomore 2%
Junior..8%
Senior 90%

Interns who receive full-time job offers: 80%

Interns who are extended full-time job offers that accept: 90%

*Estimate, inclusive of weekly salary of $1,154, one-time housing allowance of $2,000, and reimbursement for round-trip travel

The Sliding Scale

Entry-level hires who had been interns: 75% to 100%, based on program

Most important performance measurements in entry-level hire: Productivity/efficiency, sales/revenues, profitability/margin

Entry-level hires receiving signing bonuses: 100%

Average entry-level signing bonus: $2,500*

Entry-level hires receiving performance bonuses: 100%

Average performance bonus during first year: $68,000**

*Figure is for former interns only.
** For Investment Banking, Sales & Trading, and Research programs.

The Stand-Out Perks

- 401(k) with company match of up to 5% of salary

- Educational expenses reimbursement ($7,500)

- 20 paid vacation days; 8 paid personal days

- Relocation bonus of $10,000

- Charitable gift match ($1,000)

The Skills

- Intensive five- to eight-week global entry-level training programs for new hires in Investment Banking, Sales and Trading, and Research on core technical and professional skills

- Tutoring and mentoring programs

The Sound-Off

- "Pro: Everyone was amicable, easy work environment, opportunities to interview with different positions. Con: HR seems unorganized, desks/materials/passes were not set up." —*Operations, Management Services, & Technology intern*

- "I know the Bank One/Chase merger has been an ongoing topic, but … I have noticed that integration has finally taken full effect. While there may still be some culture clashing between the Investment Bank (predominantly JPMorgan) and the Commercial Bank (old Bank One), which will happen regardless of any merger, I have personally found no dilemmas in terms of attitude, people, or technical systems." —*JPMorgan Chase credit analyst*

THE RECRUITER SPOTLIGHT

Name: Barbara Smith
Job: Head of North America Investment Bank Recruiting

Most exciting recruiting development: *I love the fact that we have a number of freshmen and sophomores coming to our events. We've even started a special internship program for them called the JPMorgan Investment Bank Honors Program, which allows them to start interning with us before their junior year.*

Advice to young prospective employees: *Spend time at the firm or at our on-campus presentations to learn more about us; visit our Web site (jpmorgan.com/careers) and take part in some of our initiatives (such as our online trading game, FantasyFutures, or our socially responsible case competition, Good Venture) in order to get a sense of what we stand for and how we work.*

Tips on how to recover from being late for an interview: *Try to call the recruiter ahead of time to let him know that you are running late. Offer a sincere but brief apology at the outset (realizing that you are already short on time) and then focus on why you are there and not the fact that you were late for the meeting. I would also recommend sending a follow-up thank-you note with an apology.*

Why choose JPMorgan: *We call them the "Hot Six"—the top six reasons that people across levels, business groups, and geographies have joined and stayed at JPMorgan. The Hot Six are our scale, scope, and prestige; our reputation as a business innovator; our quality of training and development; the opportunity to make a personal impact; the exceptional quality of the work; and our spirit of cooperation and teamwork.*

Lehman Brothers

745 Seventh Ave.
New York, NY 10019
Phone: 212-526-7000
Fax: 212-526-8766
Web Addresses: www.lehman.com;
www.lehman.com/careers

The Company

- In its 158-year history, Lehman Brothers has grown from a small-time southern general store into one of the most powerful financial institutions in the world.

- Lehman currently employs over 28,000 people worldwide and provides financial services, including trading and research, investment banking, equity and fixed-income sales, and asset management; to governments, corporations, and high-net-worth individuals. Lehman takes its "One Firm" internal slogan seriously; every employee owns shares of company stock to foster a culture of collective teamwork.

- In the wake of competitor Bear Stearns' recent meltdown, Lehman has been the target of speculation that it will find itself in similarly dire financial straits due to limited access to capital. The firm has made recent moves to quash these rumors. On April 1, 2008 Lehman announced a $4 billion offering of convertible preferred stock after

receiving substantial interest from several key long-term clients and institutional investors. Lehman will use the proceeds to bolster capital and increase financial flexibility.

The Suits

Richard S. Fuld, Jr.: Chairman and CEO
Joseph M. Gregory: President and COO of Lehman Brothers Holdings and Lehman Brothers Inc.
Erin Callan: CFO
Thomas A. Russo: Executive VP, Chief Legal Officer, and Vice Chairman of Lehman Brothers Inc.

The Stats

2007 sales: $19.3 billion
2007 net income: $4.2 billion
Market cap: $34.7 billion
Employees: 28,556 (as of November 30, 2007)

Locations: Headquarters in New York, London, and Tokyo

Major competitors: Goldman Sachs, Merrill Lynch, Morgan Stanley

Largest operating units*:

Capital Markets..............$12.3 billion
Investment Banking ....$3.9 billion
Investment Management ..$3.1 billion

*2007 sales

The Story

1850: Henry Lehman, the owner of a general store in Montgomery, Alabama, is joined in the venture by his brothers Emanuel and Mayer to form Lehman Brothers

1860s: After the Civil War, the brothers move their business to New York, where they help establish the Cotton Exchange and begin selling railroad bonds

1929: When the stock market crashes, Lehman Brothers becomes a pioneer in innovative financing techniques, making capital readily available to desperate borrowers

1960: Begins overseas expansion, opening a new firm in Paris; offices in London and Tokyo follow a decade later

1977: The firm merges with Kuhn, Loeb & Co. to form Lehman Brothers Kuhn Loeb

1984: Lehman Brothers Kuhn Loeb is acquired by American Express and becomes part of Shearson Lehman Hutton

1993: The firm becomes independent through a public stock offering;

Lehman Brothers Holdings Inc. common stock commences trading on the New York and Pacific stock exchanges

2007: Buys a 20% stake in D.E. Shaw & Co.

2008: In March, files a $350 million lawsuit against Japanese trading house Marubeni to recover funds allegedly lost due to fraud

The Skinny

Most important to recruiters: Leadership skills, being a team player, analytical skills

Selectivity: N/A

Diversity of entry-level workforce: 39% minority; 35% female

Facts to know:

- The percentage of entry-level hires at Lehman who were formerly interns at the firm has risen steadily over the past few years. In 2005, 39% of new entry-level employees had been interns; in 2006, 46% were once interns; and in 2007, the percentage rose to 57%.

- While 40% of the recent-graduate hires in Lehman's analyst programs majored in business, 25% were economics majors, 17% majored in the liberal arts, and 9% studied computer science.

The Starting Gate

Undergraduate internships: 556

Duration of summer internship: 8 to 10 weeks

Average total compensation: $11,690

Interns by grade level:
Junior..4%
Senior 96%

Interns who receive full-time job offers: 87%

Interns who are extended full-time job offers that accept: 74%

The Sliding Scale

Entry-level hires who had been interns: 46%

Most important performance measurements in entry-level hire: Leadership ability, team player, analytical skills

Entry-level hires receiving signing bonuses: 99%

Average entry-level signing bonus: $12,000

Entry-level hires receiving performance bonuses: 100%

Average performance bonus during first year: $50,000

The Stand-Out Perks

- Educational expenses reimbursement
- Full and partial graduate school sponsorship

- 10 paid vacation days and time off for religious observance
- Charitable gift match ($2,000)
- Relocation compensation ($10,000)
- Employee discounts

The Skills

- Formal 35-day orientation program
- Several formal leadership programs offered
- Formal mentorship program (100% of entry-level hires participate)

The Sound-Off

- "Outstanding corporate culture, good [intern] salary level, great networking opportunities, and a great opportunity for a full-time position." —*New York University junior**

- "Management quality at the intermediate level is good by Street standards, but varies by group. Never choose a group without doing your homework to better understand which have reputations, good and bad. It's generally a positive, team-oriented culture with strong leadership." —*Former summer associate in Sales and Trading*

*Data: Universum Communications

THE RECRUITER SPOTLIGHT

Name: Larry Band

Job: Managing Director and Global Head of Recruiting and Programs

Advice for young prospective employees: *Dedicate time to researching the industry so that you can understand whether banking is the right career path for you. Additionally, recognize that there are many divisions and functions in an investment bank, and accordingly different types of jobs that are available to graduates. I am surprised that students often define working for an investment bank solely as working in the investment banking division. There are many other terrific opportunities at Lehman Brothers, including programs in our Capital Markets, Investment Management, and corporate areas (Finance, Information Technology, Operations, and so on).*

Tips on how to recover from interview faux pas: *It's human; it happens. In fact, most of the regular faux pas of everyday life—spilling coffee, not remembering another interviewer's division name—would not be considered something a candidate needs to redeem himself/herself from at Lehman Brothers. Additionally, we don't run "stress interviews," and someone's ability to "recover" from a faux pas is not a competency we consider or evaluate. Having said that, candidates should approach the Lehman Brothers interview as a formal business meeting. Certainly, someone's ability to remain composed after such non-faux pas situations (from our standpoint) is important.*

Why choose Lehman: *First, we offer new hires an opportunity to make an immediate and significant impact. We've experienced terrific momentum—a consistent track record of results, a winning management team—and this growth and success translate into responsibility. We feel that you will get more responsibility faster at Lehman Brothers than at any other firm. Second, we have an excellent culture. We value teamwork; we focus on getting the job done, not on individual glory; and we have achieved success without the unintended by-products, e.g., arrogance and attitude.*

Merrill Lynch & Co.

4 World Financial Center
250 Vesey St.
New York, NY 10080
Phone: 212-449-1000
Fax: 212-449-7461
Web Addresses: www.ml.com;
careers.ml.com

The Company

- A full-service financial services firm
  that manages client assets of
  approximately $1.7 trillion and
  includes the world's largest brokerage, Merrill Lynch is divided into
  two main business segments:
  Global Markets and Investment
  Banking Group (GMI) and Global
  Wealth Management (GWM).
  GMI provides sales and trading,
  investment banking, capital raising,
  and risk management services to
  corporations, governments, and
  institutions. Meanwhile, GWM
  includes Global Private Client
  (advisory wealth management services and products for high-net-
  worth individuals and small to
  midsize businesses) and Global
  Investment Management (management of the company's hedge funds
  and alternative investment tools).

- "Mother Merrill" (a nickname
  referring to Merrill's conservative,
  homey image) reported significant
  2007 third-quarter losses as a result

FAST FACTS

"Best Places to Launch a Career"
  Rank: 16
"Best Internships" Rank: 10
Full-Time Salary: $55,000–$59,999
Entry-Level Hires: 321
Top College Major: Business
3-Year Retention Rate: 44%
Stock Ticker: MER

of huge losses on subprime mortgages, asset-backed bonds, and
leveraged loans, forcing the company to take an $8.4 billion write-
down. CEO Stan O'Neal stepped
down on October 30, 2007, and
New York Stock Exchange CEO
John Thain was soon named as his
replacement.

The Suits

John Thain: Chairman and CEO
Rosemary T. Berkery: Vice Chair-
  person and General Counsel
Gregory J. Fleming: President and
  COO
Nelson Chai: CFO
Robert J. McCann: Vice Chairman
  and President of Global Wealth
  Management

The Stats

2007 sales: $11.3 billion
2007 net income: $8.6 billion
Market cap: $46 billion
Employees: 64,200
Locations: 38 countries worldwide
Major competitors: Goldman Sachs, Morgan Stanley, Credit Suisse
Largest operating units*:
Global Markets and Investment
    Banking........................$2.7 billion
Global Wealth
    Management ....$14.0 billion
*2007 sales

The Story

1914: Charles E. Merrill & Co. is founded; then it is renamed Merrill, Lynch & Co. a year later

1958: After merging with E.A. Pierce & Cassatt and Fenner & Beane in the early 1940s, the company is renamed Merrill Lynch, Pierce, Fenner & Smith (MLPF&S)

1971: MLPF&S launches its initial public offering with four million shares at a price of $1.75 per share

1973: Merrill Lynch & Co., Inc. is created as a holding company, with MLPF&S continuing to operate as a subsidiary

2003: Four former Merrill Lynch executives are indicted on charges of fraud for their alleged involvement in an Enron deal designed to inflate reported earnings; an appellate court later overturns all fraud convictions against the four former executives

2004: Merrill Lynch undergoes a series of acquisitions, buying Entergy-Koch LP and Mortgages Plc, among others

2005: Undertakes a global expansion initiative that includes signing a joint venture deal with Mitsubishi UFJ Financial Group

2006: BlackRock announces a merger with Merrill Lynch Investment Managers in exchange for a 49.8% stake in the joint company; Merrill Lynch reports record full-year net revenues and net earnings

The Skinny

Most important to recruiters: Analytical skills, leadership skills, creativity, communication skills

Selectivity: 1 of 38 applicants hired in 2006, down from 1 of 28 applicants hired in 2005

Diversity of entry-level workforce: 33% female; minority: N/A

Facts to know:

- Three out of four entry-level hires are former interns, and during an individual's first year with the company, Merrill Lynch will spend $10,000 training him or her.

- Each summer, Merrill Lynch holds a conference for female employees and interns at which five women business leaders take part in a moderated discussion on strategies and choices for women in the workplace.

The Starting Gate

Undergraduate internships: 393

Duration of summer internship: 10 weeks

Average total compensation: $12,000

Interns by grade level:
Freshman 1%
Sophomore 2%
Junior...7%
Senior 90%

Interns who receive full-time job offers: 80%

Interns who are extended full-time job offers that accept: 75%

 ## The Sliding Scale

Entry-level hires who had been interns: 75%

Most important performance measurements in entry-level hire: Analytical skills, productivity/efficiency, profitability/margin

Entry-level hires receiving signing bonuses: 100%

Average entry-level signing bonus: N/A

Entry-level hires receiving performance bonuses: 100%

Average performance bonus during first year: $25,000

The Stand-Out Perks

- 401(k), co-funded pension, and profit-sharing program
- Educational expenses reimbursement ($7,000)
- Partial graduate school sponsorship
- 15 paid vacation days, 4 paid personal days, 3 paid sick days, plus paid time off for religious observances

The Skills

- 25-day orientation program
- Global Markets Program (LDP), which lasts six weeks

The Sound-Off

- "Fairly good [internship] pay, excellent diverse workforce." —*Clark Atlanta University senior**
- "The company offers interns the opportunity to work on three different desks throughout the summer, giving them access to multiple areas of the bank." —*College of William & Mary senior**
- "Launching a career at a large bank like Merrill Lynch, you have the freedom to experiment and move literally scores of different places in hundreds of different positions to find what ignites your passion." —*Former Commodities Trading Group analyst*

*Data: Universum Communications

THE SUPERSTAR SPOTLIGHT

Name: Amit Rijhsinghani

Job: VP, Credit Trading Systems and Technology

Describe the most important part of your day (and how you became a VP so quickly): *It is to ensure that we are functioning as a well-orchestrated unit, from understanding what a trader wants to assessing our impact on finance, risk managers, and operations. The key to my success has definitely been surrounding myself with the right people and taking calculated risks. My goal is to seek out the smartest team, including a broad diversity of thought, and infuse energy and passion into them for a common cause. That's a winning team.*

Tips for young employees on getting ahead: *At the start of our careers, we can often afford to take more risks because we have fewer family pressures and social responsibilities. If you have suggestions, feel confident to speak up. You might not have the experience, but you have the energy and a fresh perspective. So capitalize on those.*

Advice on how to ace a Merrill Lynch interview: *Definitely do your research and show a practical approach to situations. Management is not impressed by throwing terms and definitions out of a textbook. Demonstrate the practical significance of what you have learned at school or [in] a previous job experience. If you don't know the answer to a question, it's better to admit it than to try to bluff your way through. I once asked a candidate in an interview a question for which she did not have the answer, but after the interview I got an e-mail from the candidate with the right answer. It was definitely impressive, as it showed that she cared and took the time to follow up and research the right answer.*

UBS AG

1285 Ave. of the Americas
New York, NY 10019
Phone: 212-713-2000
Fax: 212-713-1075
Web Addresses: www.ubs.com;
www.ubs.com/1/e/career_candidates.
html

The Company

- UBS is the world's largest personal wealth manager. Headquartered in Switzerland, the international bank serves clients ranging from high-net-worth individuals to corporate hedge funds. UBS's four global business groups are Global Wealth Management and Business Banking, Investment Bank, Global Asset Management, and Corporate Center.

- UBS has experienced its share of legal headaches over the past decade, including falsified accounting allegations (2003), a high-profile sex discrimination suit (2005), and, most recently, an analyst ratings scandal (early 2007) that led to the arrest of former UBS executive director Mitchell Guttenberg.

- UBS is in the process of eliminating 1,500 jobs as a result of the financial hit the company has taken during the recent credit crunch. However, UBS made a series of promising acquisitions in 2007 that may strengthen its portfolio.

FAST FACTS

"Best Places to Launch a Career"
  Rank: 42
"Best Internships" Rank: 26
Full-Time Salary: $55,000–$59,999
Entry-Level Hires: 263
Top College Major: Economics
3-Year Retention Rate: 80%
Stock Ticker: UBS

The Suits

Marcel Rohner: Group CEO and Chairman and CEO of the Investment Bank
Peter Kurer: Chairman
Raoul Weil: Chairman and CEO of Global Wealth Management and Business Banking
John Fraser: Chairman and CEO of Global Asset Management

The Stats*

2007 sales: $25.6 billion
2007 net income: –$5 billion
Market cap: $69.3 billion†
Employees: 78,140
Locations: With major offices in Switzerland, New York, Chicago, Connecticut, New Jersey, London, Tokyo, and Hong Kong, UBS also operates in more than 50 countries
Major competitors: Citigroup, Credit Suisse, HSBC, Deutsche Bank, Merrill Lynch

Largest operating units: N/A

*Sales, net income, and market cap data from *Business Week* Company Insight Center.

† As of May 9, 2008

The Story

1862: The Bank of Winterthur opens to manage trade and finance railroads in Switzerland

1893: The Bank of Winterthur merges with Toggenburger Bank, forming UBS, or the Union Bank of Switzerland

1946: Stays afloat during World War II as a result of Swiss neutrality; opens an office in Manhattan

1962: After several acquisitions in the 1950s, UBS grows to 81 branches

1967: Opens a full-service office in London

1970s: Establishes underwriting services outside of Switzerland

1991: Opens offices in Paris, Singapore, and Hong Kong

1995: UBS joins with Swiss Life to offer insurance products to clients

1996: The bank suffers its first-ever loss after writing off bad loans

1998: Union Bank of Switzerland merges with the Swiss Bank Corporation

1999: UBS buys Bank of America's European and Asian banking operations, as well as a U.S. real estate management firm

2000: Buys Paine Webber, prompting another companywide reorganization

2002: A "logic bomb," triggered by an unhappy Paine Webber employee, attacks the UBS computer system, deleting 1,000 files and causing $3 million in damage

2006: Acquires Piper Jaffray Companies' Private Client Services branch network

The Skinny

Most important to recruiters: Communication skills, leadership skills, work experience

Selectivity: 1 of 14 applicants hired in 2006, down from 1 of 10 applicants hired in 2005

Diversity of entry-level workforce: 52% minority; 42% female

Facts to know:

- The UBS trading floor in Stamford, Connecticut, is the world's largest securities trading floor. The 103,000-square-foot structure holds over 1,000 traders and other staffers who oversee about $1 trillion in transactions daily.

- Unlike its peers in the industry, many of whom offer only two- to three-year analyst programs for recent graduates, UBS offers a post-graduate training program that is 18 to 24 months in length.

The Starting Gate

Undergraduate internships: 228

Duration of summer internship: 8 to 12 weeks

Average total compensation: N/A

Interns by grade level:
Sophomore 9%
Junior...91%

Interns who receive full-time job offers: 75%

Interns who are extended full-time job offers that accept: 63%

The Sliding Scale

Entry-level hires who had been interns: 26%

Most important performance measurements in entry-level hire: Learning ability, sales/revenues, enthusiasm

Entry-level hires receiving signing bonuses: 100%

Average entry-level signing bonus: $8,500

Entry-level hires receiving performance bonuses: 100%

Average performance bonus during first year: $4,000

The Stand-Out Perks

- Educational expenses reimbursement

- Full and partial graduate school sponsorship

- 401(k) with company match of up to 4% of salary

- Charitable gift match ($2,500)

- Relocation compensation

- Employee discounts

The Skills

- Formal one-day orientation program, including guest speakers, diversity exercises, description of UBS businesses, and Human Resources policies and procedures

- Formal mentorship program (100% of entry-level hires participate)

The Sound-Off

- "UBS provides a 10-week internship with over a week spent on training, weekly intern events, mentors within and outside of the group, and speeches by executives in other business lines."
  —*University of Virginia senior**

- "I think UBS offers the best [internship] program because the company truly strives to turn interns into full-time employees. UBS wants to teach its interns and junior bankers, and allows them to be involved in the deal process." — *Georgetown University junior**

- "UBS trains you incredibly well while an intern, and you learn to do your job better than you would elsewhere. You learn if it's actually something you want to do."
  —*Columbia University senior**

*Data: Universum Communications

THE ENTRY-LEVEL SPOTLIGHT

Name: Brad Banken
Job: Institutional Equity Trader

A typical day at work: *My typical day starts around 6:15 a.m., when I start running the morning packets for the trading desk, which include internal and external research, as well as information on the general economic climate. Then I gather data from the events that occurred overnight in my space, speak with our research analysts about our stocks, and present relevant news and information in our morning meeting. After the meeting, I discuss our strategy with my mentors and put together an e-mail highlighting our views and events for the stocks I cover. Before the open, we call our clients to discuss our opinions with them. As the market opens, we make markets in our stocks, facilitate client orders, monitor dislocations and news, and provide advice to clients regarding the stocks in our sector. After the market closes, I help calculate the statistics for the entire desk and recap major trades we did in our space to help prepare for the next morning. Then, I usually leave around 6:00 p.m.*

Wacky/funny workplace story: *Last year my training program class [Banken, 23, started at UBS in July 2006, after graduating from the University of Chicago with a bachelor's in economics] helped organize a fundraiser around the holidays. As we were raising money across the trading room floor, the class felt that people were not completely in the holiday giving spirit. So the class went up to the catwalk overlooking the whole trading floor and sang—actually, belted out—two holiday carols. It was quite embarrassing, but we ended up raising close to $100,000 for eight different local charities.*

Boeing

100 N. Riverside Plaza
Chicago, IL 60606
Phone: 312-544-2000
Fax: 312-544-2082
Web Addresses: www.boeing.com;
www.boeing.com/employment/careers/

The Company

- Boeing is the leading aerospace company in the world. One of two manufacturers of large commercial jetliners, it makes 75% of the jets currently in operation. The company also designs and manufactures rotorcraft, electronic and defense systems, missiles, satellites, launch vehicles, and advanced information and communication systems. Furthermore, Boeing is a part of a consortium that operates the Space Shuttle and is the general contractor for the International Space Station.

- Boeing is currently at work on the 787 Dreamliner. Slated to debut in 2008 (although the company has announced delays that will push this back until 2009), the twin-engine plane is described as "super-efficient" and will carry 210 to 290 passengers on long-range flights.

- Over the past decade, Boeing has faced substantial challenges including scandals that have resulted in the resignation of two CEOs since 2003, billions of dollars of Air

"Best Places to Launch a Career"
 Rank: 14
"Best Internships" Rank: 35
Full-Time Salary: $50,000–$54,999
Entry-Level Hires: 1,016
Top College Major: Engineering
3-Year Retention Rate: 62%
Stock Ticker: BA

Force contracts lost due to misconduct, and increased competition from rivals such as Airbus. However, the tide has noticeably turned in the past few years under CEO Jim McNerney, a seasoned corporate leader who joined Boeing in 2005 after stints at GE and 3M.

The Suits

W. James McNerney, Jr.: Chairman, President, and CEO
James A. Bell: Executive VP of Finance and CFO
James F. Albaugh: Executive VP of Boeing and President and CEO of Integrated Defense Systems
Scott E. Carson, Executive VP of Boeing and President and CEO of Commercial Airplanes
Wanda K. Denson-Low: Senior VP of the Office of Internal Governance

The Stats

2007 sales: $66.4 billion
2007 net income: $4.1 billion
Market cap: $67.8 billion
Employees: 159,313
Locations: 70 countries, with major operations in Washington state, southern California, and St. Louis, Missouri
Major competitors: Airbus, Lockheed Martin, Northrop Grumman, BAE Systems, Inc., EADS, Raytheon
Largest operating units*:
Commercial Airplanes ....$33.4 billion
Integrated Defense
   Systems ....$32.1 billion
Boeing Capital Corp ..$815.0 million
*2007 sales

The Story

1919: The B-1 mail plane, a Boeing-designed commercial aircraft, takes off on its first flight

1941: Boeing B-17s fly into combat for the first time

1967: Delivers the first of more than 3,000 737 twinjets, the world's most popular jetliner

1987: Signs a contract to design the International Space Station

1996: Buys Rockwell aerospace and defense units to form Boeing North American

2003: Boeing is barred from competing for a contract with the U.S. Air Force after it's discovered that the company had unlawful access to documents belonging to its key competitor, Lockheed Martin

2003: Phil Condit resigns in the wake of a scandal involving his CFO, who was fired after illegally hiring an Air Force officer; Harry Stonecipher replaces Condit as President and CEO

2004: Signs a $6.4 billion U.S. Army contract to accelerate the system development and demonstration phase of the Future Combat Systems Program

2005: Jim McNerney is appointed CEO after Stonecipher resigns following a scandal involving a Boeing female executive

2006: Receives regulatory approval for United Launch Alliance, a joint venture with Lockheed Martin that positions Boeing as part of the largest provider of rocket services to the U.S. government

The Skinny

Most important to recruiters: Work experience, leadership skills, college major

Selectivity: 1 of 20 hired in 2006, down from 1 of 10 hired in 2005

Diversity of entry-level workforce: 39% minority; 29% female

Facts to know:

- Sixty percent of the company's top executives have been with Boeing for at least 20 years.

- Internship opportunities are available in areas that include Engineering, Science, Manufacturing,

Information Technology, Finance, Accounting, and Supply Chain.

The Starting Gate

Undergraduate internships: 1,009

Duration of summer internship: 10 to 12 weeks

Average total compensation: $8,980

Interns by grade level:
Freshman 3%
Sophomore 14%
Junior 49%
Senior 18%
College graduate 16%

Interns who receive full-time job offers: N/A

Interns who are extended full-time job offers that accept: N/A

The Sliding Scale

Entry-level hires who had been interns: 26%

Most important performance measurements in entry-level hire: Customer satisfaction, quality, productivity/efficiency

Entry-level hires receiving signing bonuses: 7%

Average entry-level signing bonus: $4,300

Entry-level hires receiving performance bonuses: 100%

Average performance bonus during first year: $2,500

The Stand-Out Perks

• Educational expenses reimbursement

• Full graduate school sponsorship

• Charitable gift match ($6,000)

• Relocation compensation

• Access to 401(k) with company match of up to 6% of salary

The Skills

• Formal one-day orientation program

• Business Career Foundation Program, which consists of one to six rotations and lasts two years

The Sound-Off

• "My internship was tailored to my abilities." —*University of Illinois junior**

• "The internship pay was great, and they have a high conversion of interns to full hires. They reimburse last year's tuition and give a lot of other benefits." —*UCLA senior**

*Data: Universum Communications

THE SUPERSTAR PROFILE

Name: Brian Moran

Job: Chief of Staff to the President and CEO of Boeing Integrated Defense Systems

Current job: *I am currently the Chief of Staff to the President and CEO for Boeing Integrated Defense Systems (IDS). IDS is Boeing's 72,000-person business unit that includes the company's total defense, government, intelligence, space, and communications capabilities. In this role, I help ensure the seamless operations of the president's office by interfacing with the company's senior leadership, as well as with external stakeholders.*

Stand-out accomplishment: *I applied for a Congressional Fellowship Program at the Brookings Institution in Washington, D.C. Once I was selected, Boeing granted me an educational leave of absence and facilitated the assignment to give me firsthand knowledge of the U.S. political process. During my time away from Boeing, I worked as a Legislative Fellow to a senior member of Congress, covering a variety of topics ranging from immigration to trade and 9/11.*

Briefly describe a typical day: *The dynamic nature of my job typically results in a series of "pop-up" meetings and requests that not only keep the job exciting, but also have taught me to make decisions quickly and to ask for help when needed. While a significant portion of my job is working from my office on providing actionable intelligence to a wide range of people, I try to spend at least one week per month visiting some of our major sites across the country to meet new people and to learn more about our wide range of products.*

Advice on how to rise through the ranks quickly: *Looking back, I never really worried about the next job, but instead focused on the job at hand. Meeting commitments and keeping promises, delivering results, making yourself an expert in your subject matter, seeking out mentors and coaches, sharing information and credit with others, and doing what's right for the company are all key ingredients for launching a good career—the rest will follow.*

General Electric

3135 Easton Turnpike
Fairfield, CT 06828
Phone: 203-373-2211
Fax: 203-373-3131
Web Addresses: www.ge.com;
www.gecareers.com

The Company

- Founded by Thomas Edison in 1890, General Electric (GE) has grown to include seven diverse business units: GE Money, GE Commercial Finance, GE Healthcare, GE Infrastructure, GE Consumer & Industrial, GE Enterprise Solutions, and NBC Universal.

- In 2001, after 20 years at the helm, longtime CEO Jack Welch hand-picked Jeffrey Immelt as his successor. Immelt has rigorously pushed for forward-thinking moves into biotech, emerging markets, and renewable energy, pouring billions into research and development spending. In 2006, GE filed 2,650 U.S. patents, an increase of 19% over 2001's numbers.

- GE's ambitious "ecomagination" campaign aims to increase annual revenue from environmentally friendly products to $20 billion by 2010. Significantly reducing greenhouse gas emissions is another goal.

- Despite earnings growth over recent years, GE's stock price has been

lackluster of late, only recently rebounding in 2007. However, GE's market value plummeted $47 billion after the company announced 2008 first-quarter profits from continuing operations had dropped 12% from a year earlier—the company's first quarterly-earnings decrease in five years—and cut its annual profit forecast.

The Suits

Jeffrey Immelt: Executive Chairman and CEO
Keith S. Sherin: Vice Chairman and CFO
Michael A. Neal: Vice Chairman and CEO of GE Commercial Finance
John G. Rice: Vice Chairman and CEO of GE Infrastructure
David R. Nissen: President and CEO of GE Money

The Stats

2007 sales: $173 billion
2007 net income: $22 billion
Market cap: $374.6 billion
Employees: 320,000
Locations: More than 100 countries worldwide
Major competitors: Citigroup, Philips Electronics, Siemens AG, Procter & Gamble, United Technologies
Largest operating units*:

Infrastructure ....$58 billion
Commercial Finance ....$34 billion
GE Money ....$25 billion
Healthcare ....$17 billion
NBC Universal.................$15 billion
Industrial ....$18 billion
*2007 sales

THE STORY

1890: Thomas Edison organizes his smaller business ventures into the Edison General Electric Company

1892: Edison Electric and Thomson-Houston are merged to form GE

1930: GE Plastics department is established

1978: Becomes the first organization in history to file for its 50,000th patent

1986: After its Radio Corporation of America (RCA) acquisition, GE becomes the parent company of television network NBC

1992: GE is convicted by the U.S. government of corrupt practices in weaponry sales to Israel

1998: Assets purchased from Toho Mutual Life Insurance are used to create GE Edison Life

2003: NBC and Vivendi Universal Entertainment are merged to form NBC Universal; GE owns 80% and Vivendi owns 20% of the new holding

2007: Saudi Basic Industries Corp. buys GE's Plastics unit for approximately $11 billion

The Skinny

Most important to recruiters: College major, college GPA, analytical skills

Selectivity: N/A

Diversity of entry-level workforce: N/A

Facts to know:

- GE has long been known as having top-notch leadership development training programs—80% of GE's CEOs got their start in its Financial Management Program.

- In 1995, then-CEO Jack Welch implemented "Six Sigma," an efficiency-focused business strategy developed at Motorola, and applied its principles to employee performance. Employees were grouped into the top 20%, the middle 70%, and the bottom 10%. Those in the bottom group were subject to performance improvement plans or termination. Today, the process has been modified to be less rigid, but GE continues to require performance plans.

The Starting Gate

Undergraduate internships: 2,200

Duration of summer internship: 8 to 12 weeks

Average total compensation: $10,000

Interns by grade level:
Freshman 1%
Sophomore 5%
Junior.......................................25%
Senior 66%
College graduate 3%

Interns who receive full-time job offers: 50%

Interns who are extended full-time job offers that accept: 85%

The Sliding Scale

Entry-level hires who had been interns: 50%

Most important performance measurements in entry-level hire: Analytical skills, leadership ability, creativity, team player

Entry-level hires receiving signing bonuses: 75%

Average entry-level signing bonus: $4,000

Entry-level hires receiving performance bonuses: None

Average performance bonus during first year: N/A

The Stand-Out Perks

• Full graduate school sponsorship

• Charitable gift match ($50,000)

• 401(k) savings plan with company match of up to 4% of salary

The Skills

• The three-day orientation program includes guest speakers, diversity exercises, team-building activities, and a tour of the facilities

• Formal Leadership Development Programs (LDPs), in Finance, Sales & Marketing, Human Resources, Communications, Information Technology, and Manufacturing/ Operations

• A formal mentorship program (99% of entry-level hires participate)

The Sound-Off

• "You [interns] work on value-adding projects. You get exposure to top executives. You get to network with many different employees. Compensation is good. They pay for housing and transportation, including a car." —*Bryant University senior**

• "I currently work for NBC Universal in the Burbank Studios. My program is set to groom top management. NBC's CFO, Lynn Calpeter, the FMP Program Manager, went through FMP herself." —*FMP participant, age 22*

*Data: Universum Communications

THE ENTRY-LEVEL SPOTLIGHT

Name: Leah Crider

Job: Nuclear safety analyst; GE-Hitachi Nuclear Energy Americas

Coolest part of the job: *Every day when I come into work, I know that I'm helping to supply power safely, without carbon emissions. I love being able to see the impact of my work.*

Tips for ambitious, young employees on getting noticed: *The young people who tend to get noticed at GE are those who reach out to other people. These people dream up new ideas and solutions to current problems; they share ideas with others and persevere to see them implemented.*

Coolest project on the job: *When I was still in the Edison Engineering Development Program, we gathered over 100 young engineers [into 10 groups] at a summit at GE Global Research. As part of a team-building project, each group of 10 received pieces of cardboard, pipe cleaners, tape, some mini-boxes of cereal, markers, paper clips, and the like. The group had 15 minutes to design a product and a brief ad campaign for any of GE's businesses. While the organic light-emitting diode safety vest, hot-air-balloon-delivered emergency survival kit, and solar-powered Universal Studios roller coaster were memorable, the "locomotion of the ocean" spiel really sold me. That group created a wave-driven generator that would dispose of trash in an environmentally friendly manner.*

Why GE is a top employer for recent graduates: *GE has many entry-level leadership programs that allow its employees to develop themselves and explore GE's businesses through rotational programs. We are fortunate that there are many supporters of these programs who are willing to serve as mentors, teachers, and role models.*

Ingersoll Rand

P.O. Box 0445
155 Chestnut Ridge Rd.
Montvale, NJ 07645
Phone: 201-573-0123
Fax: 201-573-3172
Web Addresses:
www.ingersollrand.com;
www.ingersollrand.com/careers/

The Company

- Ingersoll Rand (IR) has been "energized" in recent years. Formerly involved in the mining and construction markets, the Bermuda-based company has exited these markets and currently controls businesses in climate control, security, and industrial technologies, priding itself on creating products that optimize energy efficiently and for focusing on environmental safety. IR is the provider of diverse products that include Club Car golf carts, Hussmann refrigeration technologies, Schlage locks, Thermo King refrigeration equipment, and Kryptonite locks.

- Thanks to impressive growth in its international operations, not only did IR's third-quarter 2007 revenue increase nearly 10% over its third-quarter results in 2006, but the company also raised its year-end earnings forecast, despite softness in a U.S. market crippled by the housing slump. The company ultimately reported full-year 2007 net revenues of $8.8 billion, a 9% increase over 2006.

- In July 2007, IR agreed to sell its Bobcat utility equipment and attachments business to Doosan Infracore for $4.9 billion, part of the company's larger plan to move away from the heavy machinery business and focus on the climate control, industrial, and security markets.

👔 The Suits

Herbert L. Henkel: Chairman, President, and CEO
Timothy R. McLevish: Senior VP and CFO
Barry Libenson: VP and Chief Information Officer
Patrick Shannon: VP of Strategy and Business Development

The Stats

2007 sales: $8.8 billion
2007 net income: $4 billion
Market cap: $12.7 billion
Employees: 35,560
Locations: Operates in more than 20 countries
Major competitors: Emerson Electric Co., Johnson Controls Inc., Atlas Copco, Assa Abloy, United Technologies
Largest operating units*:
Climate Control
Technologies ....$3.4 billion
Security Technologies ......$2.5 billion
Industrial Technologies ....$2.9 billion
*2007 sales; 2007 financials unaudited

The Story

1871: Simon Ingersoll patents his steam-powered rock drill, then launches the Ingersoll Rock Drill Company

1872: The first Rand air compressor is introduced; shortly thereafter, the Rand & Waring Drill and Compressor Company is founded

1905: A merger between Rand & Waring and the Ingersoll Rock Drill Co. forms the Ingersoll-Rand Company

1925: Develops the first commercially successful diesel electric locomotive

1977: IR builds the world's fastest rescue drill for South African Chamber of Mines

1996: Acquires Steelcraft and Zimmerman International Corporation

2000–2003: Allegations surface that two IR foreign subsidiaries have collaborated with the Iraqi government and abused the United Nations' Oil for Food program (IR later settles with the U.S. government for $6.7 million and terminates the individuals implicated in the scheme)

2005: Acquires CISA, ITO, and Super-Ray

2007: Agrees to sell its Bobcat business to Doosan Infracore for $4.9 billion

The Skinny

Most important to recruiters: Leadership skills, college major, communication skills

Selectivity: N/A

Diversity of entry-level workforce: 46% minority; 43% female

Facts to know:

- Recent graduate hires have the option of utilizing the accelerated development program. The program trains and challenges young workers by giving them experience in multiple industries and geographies in order to gain a global perspective.

- IR actively recruited on 21 U.S. undergraduate campuses during the 2006–2007 school year and extended job offers on all 21 of those campuses.

The Starting Gate

Undergraduate internships: N/A

Duration of summer internship: N/A

Average total compensation: N/A

Interns by grade level: N/A

Interns who receive full-time job offers: N/A

Interns who are extended full-time job offers that accept: N/A

The Sliding Scale

Entry-level hires who had been interns: 17%

Most important performance measurements in entry-level hire: Productivity/efficiency, learning ability, being a team player

Entry-level hires receiving signing bonuses: 27%

Average entry-level signing bonus: $4,000

Entry-level hires receiving performance bonuses: 27%

Average performance bonus during first year: $1,000

The Stand-Out Perks

- Educational expenses reimbursement ($8,000)

- Full and partial graduate school sponsorship

- 15 paid vacation days

- Access to 401(k) with company match of up to 6% of salary and a cofunded pension

- Charitable gift match ($15,000)

- Relocation compensation

- Employee discounts on car rentals, gym memberships, cell phones/ service

The Skills

- Accelerated Development Program, a formal rotational leadership program for entry-level hires that consists of two to three rotations and lasts 96 to 138 weeks; graduates of program typically receive a double-digit raise

THE ENTRY-LEVEL SPOTLIGHT

Name: Michael Norelli
Job: Accelerated Development Program participant

Briefly describe your work: *Right after college I worked as a New Product Development Engineer and spent a lot of time at a manufacturing facility preparing for a product launch. Next, I worked in more of a Research and Development atmosphere, conducting tests and experiments in our lab. Currently, I am working in marketing, helping to put together business cases for potential new products. However, even within these three different experiences, every day is completely different from the next.*

Why choose Ingersoll Rand: *Our Accelerated Development Program rotates members through different divisions during their first two to three years. Not only does this give us a great foundation, but it also helps us determine the type of work we'd ultimately like to do. Young employees are constantly challenged and empowered to make an immediate impact on the organization. For instance, I went to upper management with a project proposal to help make Ingersoll Rand a more environmentally sustainable company, and they told me to run with it. Now I'm leading a cross-functional, multinational team working on the project. Talk about empowerment! Finally, our program allows direct interaction with senior business leaders. I have coworkers who have already presented to our CEO twice in their first two years with Ingersoll Rand. This past summer, I spent two days working on an innovation project with one of our business unit presidents.*

Tips for ambitious young employees: *Like anywhere else, results get noticed. Consistently meeting project objectives and beating deadlines will get a young person noticed in any field of work. Ingersoll Rand is not afraid to put its young employees on the front lines of important projects.*

Lockheed Martin

6801 Rockledge Dr.
Bethesda, MD 20817
Phone: 301-897-6000
Fax: N/A
Web Addresses:
www.lockheedmartin.com;
www.lockheedmartin.com/careers

The Company

- One of the world's biggest defense contractors, Lockheed Martin researches, designs, manufactures, and sustains advanced technology products and services. Its businesses span space, telecommunications, electronics, aeronautics, energy, and systems integration. Nearly 80% of Lockheed's business is with U.S. federal government agencies, including the U.S. Department of Defense.

- The largest provider of IT services, systems integration, and training to the U.S. government, Lockheed hired nearly 4,600 entry-level employees in 2006 alone (up from 3,983 in 2005) and is likely to continue aggressively recruiting young talent. Roughly 65,000 (or more than 40%) of its current employees are expected to retire by 2014.

- The maximum educational reimbursement at Lockheed is $15,000 annually for technical degrees and $10,000 annually for nontechnical degrees. However, participants in the company's Leadership Development Programs (LDPs) have no annual reimbursement limit.

The Suits

Robert J. Stevens: Chairman, President, and CEO
Bruce Tanner: Executive VP and CFO
Chris Kubasik: Executive VP of Electronic Systems
Ralph D. Heath: Executive VP of Aeronautics
Joanne Maguire: Executive VP of Space Systems

The Stats

2007 sales: $41.9 billion
2007 net income: $3 billion
Market cap: $43.5 billion
Employees: 140,000
Locations: Operates in 56 international and 939 domestic facilities, the latter of which are located in 457 U.S. cities and 45 U.S. states

Major competitors: Boeing, Northrop Grumman, Raytheon

Largest operating units*:

Electronic Systems..........$11.1 billion
Aeronautics ....$12.3 billion
Space Systems ....$8.2 billion
Information Systems & Global
    Services ....$10.2 billion

*2007 sales

The Story

1909 and 1913: Glenn L. Martin and the Loughead brothers, respectively, complete maiden voyages in their own flying machines, founding the two companies that will merge nearly 90 years later to form Lockheed Martin

1995: Lockheed Corporation merges with Martin Marietta Corporation, forming Lockheed Martin

1996: Lockheed purchases Loral's defense electronics and systems-integration businesses for $10 billion, forming a new joint venture

2001: Wins contract to build Joint Strike Fighter with an initial $200 billion order for 3,000 jets

2006: Rolls out its first combat-capable F-22 stealth fighter, which is destined for operations in the Pacific Rim; signs a $110 million contract to upgrade the C-130J Super Hercules transports flown by pilots in the United Kingdom, Australia, Italy, and Denmark; signs a $3.9 billion NASA contract to design and build its next spaceship, Orion

2007: Acquires RLM Systems Pty Ltd.

The Skinny

Most important to recruiters: College major, college GPA, work experience

Selectivity: 1 of 11 applicants hired in 2006, down from 1 of 10 applicants hired in 2005

Diversity of entry-level workforce: 30% minority; 30% female

Facts to know:

- Entry-level benefits have increased in a huge push to attract talented candidates, particularly those with engineering degrees.

- Need-based scholarships have been created to help low-income students get government security clearance.

The Starting Gate

Undergraduate internships: 1,857

Duration of summer internship: 3 to 19 weeks

Average total compensation: $7,572

Interns by grade level:

Freshman 4%
Sophomore 29%
Junior...25%
Senior 35%
College graduate 7%

Interns who receive full-time job offers: 60%

Interns who are extended full-time job offers that accept: 80%

The Sliding Scale

Entry-level hires who had been interns: 17%

Most important performance measurements in entry-level hire: Analytical skills, learning ability, creativity

Entry-level hires receiving signing bonuses: 20%

Average entry-level signing bonus: $2,235

Entry-level hires receiving performance bonuses: 7%

Average performance bonus during first year: $382

The Stand-Out Perks

- 401(k) plan with company match of up to 4% of salary

- 15 paid vacation days

- Charitable gift match ($10,000)

- Full and partial graduate school sponsorship

The Skills

- One-day orientation program that includes guest speakers and a tour of facilities and that is part of a 12-month continual orientation program in which the employee and manager meet and discuss career development and other issues

- Formal mentorship program (100% of entry-level hires participate)

- Leadership Development Programs (LDPs) in Finance, Operations, Engineering, HR, and Communications that consist of two to four rotations and last approximately 104 weeks

The Sound-Off

- "Every engineering employee is immediately eligible for $15,000 in education reimbursement. If you're in one of the leadership programs, Lockheed Martin will reimburse you the moment you pay. You're still working, so you get the benefits of getting a degree without that pesky poor-college-student status." —*Young Lockheed Martin employee*

- "One major problem is that performance has absolutely no bearing on pay or promotion. Every year you get an inflation increase, and when the specified number of years has passed, you get a promotion. The system rewards mediocrity and is very frustrating to high-performing engineers. If it wasn't for that, Lockheed Martin would be the perfect company." —*Lockheed engineer;* BW *Discussion Forum*

- "All employers have good and bad sides. I'm in Human Resources, and I've worked at Lockheed Martin, and I know that it's good for some people, like engineers, and bad for others, like [those in] Human Resources. My advice is to be wary. Find a company that's right for you. Don't pick one because of a name." —*Former Lockheed employee;* BW *Discussion Forum*

THE RECRUITER SPOTLIGHT

Name: Leslie Chappell
Job: Director of University Relations

Wackiest interview conducted: *A student showed up on time, but a bit dirty and not appropriately dressed. While surprised, we started the interview, and it turned out that he was a volunteer firefighter who had just returned from an emergency call. The student did a great job during the interview and didn't let his situation throw him off track. He also wove his firefighting experience and this most recent scenario into the interview questions.*

Why recent college graduates should choose Lockheed: *The exciting nature of our diverse business across the government sector. Whether it's working on the Joint Strike Fighter, the nation's next fifth-generation fighter aircraft, or developing a system that will capture all our nation's critical and essential records in an electronic format, the opportunities for challenging work that makes a difference in the lives of all citizens is at the heart of what we do.*

Worst interview offense: *I would say that getting the company name wrong is significant. The interview process is a time when both the interviewer and the interviewee are making assessments about fit, so it is best to be prepared by doing some research in advance.*

Northrop Grumman

1840 Century Park East
Los Angeles, CA 90067
Phone: 310-553-6262
Fax: 310-556-4561
Web Addresses:
www.northropgrumman.com;
www.careers.northropgrumman.com/

The Company

- Who manufactured the lunar module that carried astronauts to the moon's surface for the first time? Northrop Grumman, one of the world's leading defense and technology companies.

- Northrop Grumman operates in eight sectors—Electronic Systems, Information Technology, Integrated Systems, Mission Systems, Ship Systems, Newport News, Space Technology, and Technical Services—and has government, military, and commercial customers both in the United States and internationally. The company is the world's number one shipbuilder and the number three defense contractor, behind Lockheed Martin and Boeing.

- The diverse company has integrated 20 companies into its massive portfolio over the years, including Newport News Shipbuilding and TRW Incorporated.

The Suits

Ronald D. Sugar: Chairman and CEO
Wes Bush: President and COO
Robert W. Helm: Corporate VP of Business Development and Government Relations
James F. Palmer: Corporate VP and CFO
W. Burks Terry: Corporate VP and General Counsel

The Stats

2007 sales: $32 billion
2007 net income: $1.8 billion
Market cap: $26.6 billion
Employees: 120,000+
Locations: Corporate headquarters is in California, and the company also has a corporate office in Virginia
Major competitors: Lockheed Martin, Boeing

Largest operating units*:

Information and
    Services ....$12.6 billion
Aerospace ....$8.2 billion
Electronics.........................$6.9 billion
Ships ....$5.8 billion
Intersegment
    Eliminations ....–$1.5 billion

* 2007 sales

The Story

1907: U.S. President Theodore Roosevelt sends 16 battleships on an around-the-world voyage to demonstrate the United States' military might; Newport News has built 7 of these ships

1927: Ryan Aeronautical produces the *Spirit of St. Louis*, which Charles Lindbergh flies across the Atlantic

1930: Grumman Aeronautical Engineering Company is founded

1939: John K. "Jack" Northrop starts Northrop Aircraft Incorporated in Hawthorne, California

1940: The N-3PB patrol bomber, Northrop's first aircraft, is built

1941: A Westinghouse radar detects the attack on Pearl Harbor; its warnings go unheeded because of a high level of uncertainty about the new technology's reliability

1969: Grumman's Apollo Lunar Module lands on the surface of the moon

1994: Northrop acquires Grumman Corporation and forms Northrop Grumman

1996: Acquires the defense and electronics business of Westinghouse Electric Corp.

2001: Acquires nuclear-powered aircraft carrier and submarine designer Newport News Shipbuilding, as well as global electronics and IT enterprise Litton Industries

2007: Acquires signal processing and optoelectronic imaging provider Essex Corporation

The Skinny

Most important to recruiters: College major, college GPA, communication skills

Selectivity: N/A

Diversity of entry-level workforce: 32% minority; 33% female

Facts to know:

- Northhrop Grumman has a Wellness Program for its employees, as well as on-site health assessments, screenings, and counseling.

- As part of a new intiative aimed at providing alternatives to offshoring, Northrop Grumman recently began opening National Work Force Centers, which are cost-effective technology centers, across the United States.

The Starting Gate

Undergraduate internships: 770

Duration of summer internship: 6 to 16 weeks

Average total compensation: N/A

2006 interns by grade level:
Freshman 6%
Sophomore 17%
Junior...30%
Senior 42%
College graduate 5%

Interns who receive full-time job offers: 80%

Interns who are extended full-time job offers that accept: 94%

The Sliding Scale

Entry-level hires who had been interns: 17%

Most important performance measurements in entry-level hire: Analytical skills, team player, productivity/efficiency

Entry-level hires receiving signing bonuses: 17%

Average entry-level signing bonus: $2,792

Entry-level hires receiving performance bonuses: 1%

Average performance bonus during first year: $500

The Stand-Out Perks

- Full and partial graduate school sponsorship

- Educational expenses reimbursement

- 401(k) with company match of up to 4% of salary

- Charitable gift match ($5,000)

- Employee discounts on car rentals, gym memberships, and insurance

The Skills

- One-day orientation program

- Professional Development Programs in Engineering, Business Management, and Human Resources that consist of one to six rotations and last for 13 to 78 weeks; upon completion, participants typically receive a 5% to 10% raise

- Formal mentorship program (65% of entry-level hires participate)

The Sound-Off

- "Challenging and exciting internship work and decent pay." —*California Institute of Technology junior**

- "The interns are not just paper shufflers." —*North Carolina State-Raleigh sophomore**

- "Working in such a large company is overwhelming at first, but my program offers many opportunities to explore different career paths and network with management. Stay open to different opportunities that arise." —*Professional Development Program participant*

*Data: Universum Communications

THE SUPERSTAR SPOTLIGHT

Name: Tamra Johnson

Job: Flight Operations and Rehearsals Lead in Launch System Integration

Briefly describe a typical day: *My time is about evenly split between meetings and doing work at my desk. In that aspect, I think my day is typical of a lot of jobs. I think the unique aspect of my work is the actual subjects I deal with, including planning and conducting rehearsals to test and train a team on what will occur the day of a spacecraft launch. The rehearsals include more than 100 participants, so it's important that they are well developed and well planned. I lead two teams in these efforts, and the team members come from many organizations across the country. In addition to my regular job duties, I spend 5 to 10 hours each week on volunteering efforts to improve our organization. This includes several years that I spent helping with our new-hire networking group, CONNECT, and more recently, efforts to set up internal company forums.*

What's cool about your job: *My job is cool because I actually play a role in getting satellites into space. [Johnson, 28, has a BS in Aeronautical/ Astronautical Engineering from MIT and expects her Masters in Management Science & Engineering from Stanford in June 2009.] I've had the opportunity to witness a launch vehicle lifting off from the Earth, and it's an amazing thing to see and feel, knowing that it is about to leave the confines of our environment and be in space.*

Advice on how to rise through the ranks quickly: *I try to always be open to new opportunities, to not be afraid to try something even if it is outside my area of experience, and to always look at what I could bring to the group or the organization. I've always believed I can do anything I set my mind to, but I'm also aware of how important the help of others is in getting the job done correctly.*

Raytheon

870 Winter St.
Waltham, MA 02451
Phone: 781-522-3000
Fax: 781-522-3001
Web Addresses: www.raytheon.com;
www.rayjobs.com/

The Company

- Company trivia: Raytheon means "light of the gods."

- What do Doppler Weather Radar and microwave cooking have in common? Both were invented by Raytheon, one of the biggest defense contractors in the world. For nearly a century, Raytheon has been the source of a number of key innovations in technology, ranging from radio tubes to satellite systems to air traffic control devices. The company is also the number one missile producer in the world.

- In 2001 and 2002, the company lost $763 million and $640 million, respectively. In recent years, however, the company has been raking in record returns as the U.S. War on Terror has continued to escalate. Raytheon recorded a $365 million profit in 2003, and the company made an additional $3.8 billion over the next four years. The U.S. government accounted for 85% of Raytheon's sales in 2006.

FAST FACTS

"Best Places to Launch a Career"
  Rank: 28
"Best Internships" Rank: 18
Full-Time Salary: $60,000–$64,999
Entry-Level Hires: 1,082
Top College Major: Engineering
3-Year Retention Rate: 70%
Stock Ticker: RTN

The Suits

William H. Swanson: Chairman and CEO
Thomas M. Culligan: Executive VP of Business Development and CEO of Raytheon International
Keith J. Peden: Senior VP of Human Resources
Jay B. Stephens: Senior VP, General Counsel, and Secretary

The Stats

2007 sales: $21.3 billion
2007 net income: $2.6 billion
Market cap: $26.1 billion
Employees: 72,000
Locations: Offices in 18 countries, with global subsidiaries in the United Kingdom, Australia, and Canada
Major competitors: Boeing, Lockheed Martin, Northrop Grumman

Largest operating units*:

Missile Systems ....$5.0 billion
Space/Airborne Systems....$4.3 billion
Integrated Defense ....$4.7 billion
Network Centric Systems $4.2 billion
Intelligence Systems..........$2.7 billion
Technical Services ....$2.2 billion

*2007 sales; breakdowns do not include a $1.8 billion loss listed as "Corporate and Eliminations"

The Story

1922: Laurence K. Marshall, Vannevar Bush, and Charles G. Smith found the American Appliance Company in Cambridge, Massachusetts

1925: The American Appliance Company changes its name to Raytheon Company

1980: Purchases Grumman's Beech Aircraft division to diversify its holdings

1991: Raytheon secures an $800 million defense contract with the U.S. government to provide missiles during the Persian Gulf War

1997: Purchases both Texas Instruments' missile and defense electronics holdings and Hughes Electronics' defense business for a sum of over $12 billion

1998: 14,000 jobs are cut and 28 plants are closed as a result of weak company sales in Asia

2007: Raytheon Aircraft is sold to Hawker Beechcraft Corp. for $3.3 billion

The Skinny

Most important to recruiters: College major, college GPA, analytical skills

Selectivity: 1 of 17 applicants hired in 2006, up from 1 of 23 applicants hired in 2005

Diversity of entry-level workforce: 35% minority; 30% female

Facts to know:

• Raytheon has entry-level Leadership Development Programs in the following eight areas: Business Development, Communications, Contracts, Engineering, Financial, Human Resources, Information Technology, and Supply Chain.

• Over 40% of Raytheon's employees are engineers, and the company has implemented a number of programs—including the Fellows Program and the Technical Honors Program—to recognize stand-out contributions from these individuals. A select number of senior-level and young engineers are also invited to participate in the Engineering Mentorship Program.

The Starting Gate

Undergraduate internships: 897

Duration of summer internship: 10 to 14 weeks

Average total compensation: $8,952

Interns by grade level:

Freshman 9%
Sophomore 21%
Junior..37%
Senior 33%

Interns who receive full-time job offers: 92%

Interns who are extended full-time job offers that accept: 85%

⊞ The Sliding Scale

Entry-level hires who had been interns: 13%

Most important performance measurements in entry-level hire: Analytical skills, being a team player, productivity/efficiency

Entry-level hires receiving signing bonuses: 42%

Average entry-level signing bonus: $4,370

Entry-level hires receiving performance bonuses: 89%

Average performance bonus during first year: $1,200

The Stand-Out Perks

- Educational expenses reimbursement ($8,000)

- Full and partial graduate school sponsorship

- 401(k) with company match of up to 4% of salary

- Charitable gift match ($5,000)

- Relocation compensation ($6,600)

The Skills

- Formal one-day orientation program

- Leadership Development Program, which consists of one to three rotations and lasts 104 weeks

- Formal mentorship program (75% of entry-level hires participate)

The Sound-Off

- "The [internship] program allowed me to begin an engineering internship straight out of high school, which then became a summer co-op position after I completed my first year of college. This is great, because it means I have a job every summer." —*University of Alabama student**

- "Raytheon is a good place to work if you want stability. Pay is about average, and benefits are excellent. I put in only 40 hours, make my own schedule, and nobody cares, as long as you get things done. The company promotes work-life balance and emphasizes ethics. All employees get plenty of training as well." —BW *Discussion Forum*

- "My advice: work for one of these companies for a few years to gain some experience. If possible, move on to a small company that will value you more. I am now an independent consultant and love every minute of it!" —*Former Raytheon employee;* BW *Discussion Board*

*Data: Universum Communications

THE ENTRY-LEVEL SPOTLIGHT

Name: Enrique Santiago
Job: Systems Engineer II

The weirdest/funniest thing encountered at work: *Defense companies are known for their use of acronyms. It can really challenge a new hire, because everyone assumes that you know what they mean and uses them in meetings. Most times, you try to figure it out, but that can lead to confusion, as it did with me. I was sitting in a room with 12 other test engineers shortly after starting work, and all of them started talking about FTP. I was familiar with the FTP acronym . . . or so I thought. To me, it meant file transfer protocol. I couldn't understand why it was such a big part of our discussion, or why we were talking about breaking it up into sections. I thought we were a test team, not a software design group. I actually started to wonder if I was in the wrong meeting. They finally noticed my confused look and asked me if I knew what FTP meant. I said yes, thinking it meant file transfer protocol. In this setting, it actually meant Factory Test Procedure. The morale of the story: don't assume, and don't ever be afraid to ask if something doesn't seem right!*

Advice on how a young, ambitious employee can get noticed: *I'm part of the company's rotational engineering leadership development program. As a result, I get to network with fellow engineers across the enterprise. I also get greater exposure to the company's senior management, so I'm very lucky. But I've also seen plenty of examples of younger employees who aren't in the program who still manage to get noticed. They volunteer to take on added responsibility. They contribute at meetings—after all, a lot of what we're designing will be used by people our age. In some cases, we reverse-mentor more senior colleagues. Bottom line: if you're ambitious and you want to get noticed, there's no shortage of ways to do it at Raytheon.*

Wolseley

Wolseley North American Division
12500 Jefferson Ave.
Newport News, VA 23602
Phone: 757-874-7795
Fax: 757-989-2501
Web Addresses: www.wolseleyna.com;
www.wolseley.com/Careers/

The Company

- Wolseley plc is the world's largest specialist trade distributor of plumbing and heating products to professional contractors and a leading supplier of building materials in North America, the United Kingdom, and continental Europe. Group revenues for 2007 were approximately $31.6 billion.

- With a diversified product line, Wolseley delivers over 100,000 different items to meet consumer demand.

- Listed on both the London and New York Stock Exchanges, Wolseley straddles the Atlantic, reaching far into North America and all the way to Eastern Europe. For this reason, Wolseley maintains headquarters in Newport News, Virginia, as well as in Reading, England. Job seekers take note: if foreign language skills or an international outlook are atop your résumé, you can expect to fit in well at the globally minded Wolseley.

FAST FACTS

"Best Places to Launch a Career"
  Rank: 72
"Best Internships" Rank: 63
Full-Time Salary: $35,000–$39,999
Entry-Level Hires: 1,250
Top College Major: Business
3-Year Retention Rate: 60%
Stock Ticker: WOS

The Suits

John W. Whybrow: Chairman
Claude "Chip" A. S. Hornsby: Group
  CEO of Wolseley plc
Frank W. Roach: CEO North America
Robert H. Marchbank: CEO Europe
Stephen P. Webster: CFO

The Stats*

2007 WNA sales: $16.9 billion
2007 WNA net income: $821
  million
Market cap: $14.5 billion (as of July 31, 2007)
Employees: 41,240 (as of July 31, 2007)
Locations: Maintains 5,000 branches and operates in 28 countries
Major competitors: 84 Lumber Co., Saint-Gobain Building Distribution Ltd., Travis Perkins

Largest operating units:[†]
Ferguson ....$11.1 billion
Stock Building Supply ......$4.6 billion
Wolseley Canada CAD ....$1.2 billion
*Wolseley North American (WNA) Division *only*
except for market cap, which is Wolseley plc, and
locations, which are also global.
[†]2007 sales

The Story

1887: In Sydney, Australia, Frederick York Wolseley founds the Wolseley Sheep Shearing Machine Company, Ltd., after he produces a new sheep-shearing technology

1889: Wolseley relocates the company to Birmingham, England, broadening his focus to agricultural equipment and motorcar manufacturing

1901: After producing hundreds of cars, Wolseley sells all components of his auto businesses

1958: Wolseley merges with Geo H. Hughes, a wheel manufacturer, and the company is renamed Wolseley-Hughes

1979: Wolseley acquires John James Group of Companies Limited, now Pipe Center, which includes several manufacturing companies

1982: With its purchase of Ferguson Enterprises, Wolseley officially begins operating in the United States

2003: Purchases the fourth largest wholesale distributor of waterworks, wastewater, and storm drainage material in the United States

2005: North American functions consolidated under continental division

2006: Acquires over 50 more companies in Europe and North America as it continues its growth strategy

2007: Wolseley is now the leading distributor of heating and plumbing products, as well as the leading supplier of professional builders' products

The Skinny

Most important to recruiters: Communication skills, leadership ability, work experience

Selectivity: 1 of 10 applicants hired in 2006, down from 1 of 7 applicants hired in 2005

Diversity of entry-level workforce: 16% minority; 35% female

Facts to know:

- Wolseley actively recruited on 235 U.S. undergraduate campuses during the 2006–2007 school year and extended job offers on 143 of those campuses.

- Of Wolseley's 50 senior executives (VP level or higher), 20 have been with the company for 20 years or more.

The Starting Gate

Undergraduate internships: 75

Duration of summer internship: 10 weeks

Average total compensation: $5,000

Interns by grade level:
Sophomore 9%
Junior...12%
Senior 79%

Interns who receive full-time job offers: 72%

Interns who are extended full-time job offers that accept: 58%

The Sliding Scale

Entry-level hires who had been interns: 1%

Most important performance measurements in entry-level hire: Leadership ability, enthusiasm, customer satisfaction

Entry-level hires receiving signing bonuses: None

Average entry-level signing bonus: N/A

Entry-level hires receiving performance bonuses: 100%

Average performance bonus during first year: $2,250

The Stand-Out Perks

- 401(k) with company match of up to 3.5% of salary

- Full (dependent on maintaining a B grade average) and partial graduate school sponsorship and reimbursement for educational expenses

- Educational expenses reimbursement dependent on B grade average

- 8 paid vacation days, 8 paid holidays, and 5 paid sick days

- Relocation compensation

- Employee discounts

The Skills

- Four-day orientation program, including computer training, guest speakers, team-building activities, a tour of the facilities, and mentor pairing

- Trainee leadership program, which consists of 3 to 10 rotations and lasts 35 to 52 weeks

- Formal mentorship program (40% of entry-level hires participate)

THE RECRUITER SPOTLIGHT

Name: Denise Brown

Job: Director of Recruiting, Recognition, and Human Resources Acquisitions

Advice for prospective young employees: *Work hard, be proactive, be open-minded to new and different opportunities. The more open you are, the faster you will move up!*

If someone arrives late for an interview, how can that person redeem him- or herself?: *It certainly is a major faux pas to show up late for an interview, but a good/valid reason helps—and knocking my socks off in the interview can [help you] redeem yourself! Other faux pas include dressing inappropriately (always ensure that you understand the dress code) and not doing your homework (knowing nothing about the company you're interviewing with).*

Why choose Wolseley: *There are three great things about our company: the people, the culture, and the opportunities. We are a performance-based company, and there is enormous opportunity for someone who is energetic, excited, [and] a strong performer with a great work ethic. The opportunities grow exponentially when you are willing to relocate, as we have thousands of locations across North America. The people and culture are incredible: we are like a family, and not just at the local operation level, but [at] the corporation [level] as well. If you want to get up excited to go to work every day, and if you like working with your best friends, this is the place to be!*

California State Auditor

555 Capitol Mall, Ste. 300
Sacramento, CA 95814
Phone: 916-445-0255
Fax: 916-322-7801
Web Addresses: www.bsa.ca.gov;
www.bsa.ca.gov/opportunities

The Company

- The California State Auditor (Bureau of State Audits, or BSA) is an independent, nonpartisan auditing body that was created by the California legislature in 1993 to replace the Office of the Auditor General, which had operated since 1956. The types of audits conducted by the bureau are financial and compliance- and performance-related. The bureau also conducts investigations of improper activities of state employees. The bureau's audits are directed by statute or requested by the Joint Legislative Audit Committee—a 14-member bipartisan committee made up of seven senators and seven assembly members.

- The State Auditor appoints the Chief Deputy State Auditor, who assists the State Auditor and takes his or her place during any absence. Employees of the bureau are civil servants subject to the standards of the California Constitution.

- The State Auditor has access to the records, vouchers, and correspondence letters of all state and local

FAST FACTS

"Best Places to Launch a Career"
  Rank: 69
"Best Internships" Rank: 53
Full-Time Salary: $35,000–$39,999
Entry-Level Hires: 29
Top College Major: Business
3-Year Retention Rate: 25%
Stock Ticker: N/A (government agency)

agencies, public contractors, schools, and tax-funded bodies. Recent reports and investigations conducted by the State Auditor involve the California Indian gaming industry, Department of Housing and Community Development, Student Aid Commission, and Water Resources Control Board, to name a few.

The Suits

Elaine M. Howle: State Auditor
Doug Cordiner: Chief Deputy State Auditor
Debbie Meador: Chief of Legislative Affairs
Sharon Reilly: Chief Legal Counsel
Margarita Fernandez: Chief of Public Affairs
Philip J. Jelicich, John Collins, Kim Anderson: Deputy State Auditors

The Stats

2006 sales: N/A
2006 net income: N/A
Market cap: N/A
Employees: N/A
Locations: Sacramento, California
Major competitors: N/A
Largest operating units: N/A
Figures: If recommendations made by the bureau from July 1, 2001, through December 31, 2006, had been implemented properly, Californians would have saved $953 million, equaling a return of $10.50 for every dollar spent on state audit operations (from California State Auditor Biennial Report)
Jurisdiction: Public agencies and special districts in the state of California

The Story

1956: Auditor General's Office is established

1992: Auditor General's Office closes because of budget constraints

1993: California Senate Bill 37 is signed into law by the governor, establishing the Bureau of State Audits, which replaces the Auditor General's Office; whereas the Auditor General's Office was under the jurisdiction of the legislative branch, the new bureau, though a member of the executive branch, is exempt from executive oversight

The Skinny

Most important to recruiters: College major, analytical skills, communication skills

Selectivity: 1 of 27 hires in 2006, up from 1 of 35 in 2005

Diversity of entry-level workforce: 45% minority; 41% female

Facts to know:

- Employees are allowed to accrue up to 80 days of paid time off that can be used for maternity or paternity leave.

- The state of California does not currently provide any contribution to the 401(k) program for employees. It is 100% funded from employee contributions through payroll deduction. In addition, employees are also eligible to contribute to a 457(k) plan and have access to a co-funded pension.

- Employees are reimbursed for a CPA review course, and those who pass the exam receive a $4,800 bonus paid out over three years.

The Starting Gate

Undergraduate internships: 4

Duration of summer internship: 10 weeks

Average total compensation: $3,143

Interns by grade level:
Junior...25%
Senior 50%
College graduate 25%

Interns who receive full-time job offers: 75%

Interns who are extended full-time job offers that accept: 100%

The Sliding Scale

Entry-level hires who had been interns: 11%

Most important performance measurements in entry-level hire: Analytical skills, learning ability, team player

New hires majored in:

Business 31%
Computer Science 3%
Economics 24%
Science...7%
Other 35%*

*Other includes International Relations, Public Policy, Public Administration, and Political Science

Entry-level hires receiving signing bonuses: None

Average entry-level signing bonus: N/A

Entry-level hires receiving performance bonuses: 17%

Average performance bonus during first year: $850

The Stand-Out Perks

- Educational expenses reimbursement ($4,000)

- Partial reimbursement of graduate school expenses

- Employee discounts on gym memberships, cell phone service, insurance, and publications

- Access to a cofunded pension (fully vested after five years)

- 23 days of paid time off in first year

The Skills

- Formal three-day orientation program that includes guest speakers, computer training, team-building exercises, and tour of facilities

- Formal mentorship program (100% of entry-level hires participate)

THE ENTRY-LEVEL SPOTLIGHT

Name: Whitney Smith
Job: Auditor Evaluator

Describe a typical workday: *I'd say there are several types of "typical days" working here at the BSA. Depending on the assignment, you might be working out at a state agency conducting interviews with auditees and gathering documents, or be in the office, synthesizing information and discussing your findings with your team lead. For some travel audits, you may be living in a hotel for a week or more anywhere from San Diego to Crescent City, California, as you work with auditees located outside of the Sacramento area.*

Best part of the job: *I really enjoy the variety in our work. Our job is to understand government processes well enough to evaluate their effectiveness and recommend changes based on our findings. So your day-to-day tasks really do change as the audit develops. Also, audits generally last an average of about six months, so everyone is constantly dealing with completely different areas of state government with each new round of assignments.*

Discuss your workplace culture: *In my experience, the BSA approach to auditing encourages auditors to find a balance between completing your own assignments independently as you work to develop a sort of "expert knowledge" about your own specific aspects of the audit, and collaborating with the team to fit your piece into the larger whole to develop the larger "audit story." I always turn to my team members in working out an analytical challenge, and the office is generally buzzing with these kinds of informal discussions and conferences. The BSA hires a lot of smart young people from a wide variety of academic fields and work experiences, and that makes for a truly fascinating and often hilarious bunch of people to spend your lunch hour with.*

Advice to prospective young employees: *The audits we do here aren't just about crunching numbers; they demand a variety of skills, from interviewing auditees, to evaluating state law, to writing reports. At the same time, you can begin as an auditor here without any prior experience and really learn by doing once you're here. The BSA places a lot of emphasis on writing ability, and the task of drafting performance audit reports falls on all audit team members. The audit leads will know if you have excellent writing skills to offer, since you work directly with them during our extensive editing and risk review process.*

CIA

Office of Public Affairs
Washington, DC 20505
Phone: 703-482-0623
Fax: 703-482-1739
Web Addresses: www.cia.gov;
www.cia.gov/careers/

The Company

- Many things about the Central Intelligence Agency (CIA) are classified—from the department's budget to its number of employees—but what we do know about the highly secretive spy agency is that its primary purpose is to collect and evaluate intelligence for the U.S. government.

- The McLean, Virginia–based CIA Museum houses hundreds of rare Soviet and Stasi espionage artifacts. (Appropriately, though, because it is located in the CIA compound, it is not open to the public for tours.)

- The CIA has received a great deal of media attention, much of it unwanted, in recent years: Since the start of the millennium, the agency has come under fire for 9/11 and, later, for providing flawed intelligence on Iraq's weapons programs. All the negative press hasn't hurt the agency's appeal for job seekers, though: applications have increased dramatically since 9/11, and the CIA now receives over 100,000 applications a year.

 FAST FACTS

"Best Places to Launch a Career" Rank: 50
"Best Internships" Rank: 21
Full-Time Salary: N/A
Entry-Level Hires: N/A
Interns Who Receive Full-Time Job Offers: 74%
Top College Major: Liberal Arts
3-Year Retention Rate: 84%
5-Year Retention Rate: 76%

The Suits

Michael V. Hayden: Director
Stephen R. Kappes: Deputy Director
Michael J. Morell: Associate Deputy Director
John A. Kringen: Directorate of Intelligence

The Stats

2007 sales: N/A
2007 net income: N/A
Market cap: N/A
Employees: N/A
Locations: N/A
Major competitors: N/A
Largest operating units: N/A

The Story

1942: President Franklin D. Roosevelt appoints William J. Donovan as the first Coordinator of Information and the head of the Office of Strategic Services (OSS)

1945: The OSS and other war agencies are dissolved and their duties are assumed by the State and War Departments

1947: President Harry S. Truman signs the National Security Act and creates the CIA to aggregate intelligence in one organization

1975: Former President George H. W. Bush serves as head of the CIA until 1977; he is the only president ever to have held the post

1980: The Senate Select Committee on Intelligence and the House Permanent Select Committee on Intelligence are assigned to oversee the CIA by the Intelligence Oversight Act

2004: President George W. Bush signs the Intelligence Reform and Terrorism Prevention Act and creates the Director of National Intelligence position

2006: Michael V. Hayden becomes the eighteenth director of the CIA—and also the first military officer to hold the post in 26 years

The Skinny

Most important to recruiters: N/A

Selectivity: N/A

Diversity of entry-level workforce: 23% minority; 48% female

Facts to know:

- The CIA does not recommend any one academic track over another. Positions within the agency run the gamut from librarians to counterterrorism analysts and paramilitary operations officers. However, fluency in a foreign language and overseas travel are a plus.

- The agency offers several highly competitive programs for students considering a career in the intelligence field, including the Undergraduate Student Trainee (Co-op) Program, the Internship Program, the Graduate Studies Program, and the Undergraduate Scholarship Program, which is targeted at high school seniors and college sophomores.

The Starting Gate

Undergraduate internships: N/A

Duration of summer internship: 12 weeks

Average total compensation: N/A

Interns by grade level: N/A

Interns who receive full-time job offers: 74%

Interns who are extended full-time job offers that accept: 100%

The Sliding Scale

Entry-level hires who had been interns: 14%

Most important performance measurements in entry-level hire: Depends on occupation

Entry-level hires receiving signing bonuses: N/A

Average entry-level signing bonus: N/A

Entry-level hires receiving performance bonuses: N/A

Average performance bonus during first year: N/A

The Stand-Out Perks

- Full and partial graduate school sponsorship

- Educational expenses reimbursement

- 13 paid vacation days

- Access to 401(k) with company match of 5% of salary

- Relocation compensation

The Skills

- 4-day orientation program

- Formal mentorship program

The Sound-Off

- "The Central Intelligence Agency offers the best opportunities because they have co-op, internships, and scholarships, combined with job placement opportunities immediately after graduation." —*College senior**

- "Good internship program because there is a chance for a full-time job offer with the program. Also, it requires a high level of clearance that is very beneficial once obtained." —*James Madison sophomore**

- "Here are a few totally unclassified thoughts: interns/co-ops are probably treated better than full-time workers. You most likely get a TS/SCI clearance, which is both good and bad. If you want to get involved in government consulting, you've got a golden ticket. However, you'd better like the D.C. area (99% of the jobs are here), and it's hard to get any jobs outside of cleared consulting. Interviewers outside the TS world always worry that they won't be able to get you away from the cleared jobs. Cleared jobs pay better than almost any entry-level jobs. A lot of people either love or hate their experience at the agency. I didn't like what I was doing, but I was able to see and do things I'll never find at any other job. The CIA changed my career path from Wall Street to Washington, D.C." —*Former recent-grad employee*

*Data: Universum Communications

THE RECRUITER SPOTLIGHT

Name: Betsy Davis

Job: Chief of CIA's Recruitment and Retention Center

Faulty assumptions about the agency: *These are just a few of the myths that I have encountered [while recruiting] and had to dispel: (1) You'll never see your family and friends again. Not true. At the CIA, the work we do may be secret, but that doesn't mean your life will be, too. You will most likely work on location at CIA headquarters, experiencing a lifestyle that includes social and cultural activities in the nation's capital and the Virginia and Maryland suburbs. Your friends and family will still be part of your life every day, as they would be with almost any other career choice you make. (2) Hardly anyone ever makes it through the background check. Not true. Because of the CIA's national security role, there are specific qualifications that candidates must meet, but cutting class once or twice during your senior year of high school probably won't disqualify you. The fact is, it takes a while to go through the stringent process of completing the qualifications screening, medical exams, security procedures, and polygraph interview. We want to ensure that only the most qualified and committed individuals are selected. (3) If you don't speak a foreign language, forget about it. Not true. Sure, every CIA officer in the movies speaks fluent Farsi or Mandarin. In reality, most people who work at the agency aren't bilingual. But, if you need to be versed in a foreign language for a particular position, we'll teach you. In fact, the CIA has one of the most advanced foreign language teaching laboratories in the world, staffed by exceptional linguists and instructors. That said, if you currently possess superior foreign language skills, all the better. You can look forward to generous hiring bonuses, language awards, and additional pay for maintaining your linguistic skills.*

Why choose the CIA: *I believe young people today want to work for the CIA because they want to serve their nation and make a difference in the world. They see our mission as exciting yet challenging, and they want to be involved. Especially since the terror attacks of 9/11, we have had a dramatic increase in the number of applicants. We average over 100,000 applicants each year, with a majority of these people stating that it's their desire to work for national security.*

Peace Corps

1111 20th St. NW
Washington, DC 20526
Phone: 800-424-8580
Fax: 202-692-2901
Web Address: www.peacecorps.gov

The Company

- John F. Kennedy first mentioned the idea of a global army of young American volunteers in a 1960 University of Michigan presidential campaign speech, and he formally created the Peace Corps after he was elected. Kennedy's brother-in-law, Sargent Shriver, was appointed the agency's first director.

- Over the course of the Peace Corps' history, some 90,000 volunteers have been sent to 139 countries for 27-month assignments. In 2007, there was a 37-year high of 8,079 Peace Corps volunteers serving in the field.

- Volunteer assignments fall into the areas of education (36%), health/HIV/AIDS (21%), business development (15%), environment (14%), youth (6%), agriculture (5%), and other issues (4%).

- Volunteer Snapshot
Age: 27 (average) and 25 (median)
Marital Status: 93% single, 7% married
Education: 95% have at least an undergraduate degree; 11% have graduate studies or degrees

- In 2005, Peace Corps volunteers served in the United States for the first time when workers were sent to the Gulf Coast to assist the Federal Emergency Management Agency (FEMA) in the wake of Hurricanes Katrina and Rita.

The Suits

Ronald A. Tschetter: Director*
Josephine "Jody" K. Olsen: Deputy Director
Henry McKoy: Regional Director of Africa
Jay Katzen: Regional Director of Europe, Mediterranean, and Asia (EMA)
Allene Zanger: Regional Director of Inter-America and Pacific (IAP)

*Volunteered with his wife, Nancy, in India (1966–1968)

The Stats*

Employees: 8,079 volunteers and trainees
Locations: 74 countries currently served
Fiscal year budget: $330.8 million
*2008 data

The Story

1961: President John F. Kennedy creates the Peace Corps and names Sargent Shriver the agency's first director; Shriver sends the Peace Corps' first volunteers to Ghana and Tanzania

1981: Congress makes the Peace Corps an independent federal agency

1990s: Volunteers are sent to serve in Eastern Europe, the former Soviet Union, China, and South Africa for the first time

2004: President's Emergency Plan for AIDS Relief (PEPFAR) is formed; by May 2005, the Peace Corps has deployed its first group of 22 PEPFAR-funded volunteers to Zambia

2005: The organization's volunteers are sent to the Gulf Coast region to aid FEMA following Hurricanes Katrina and Rita

2007: Over 8,000 Peace Corps volunteers—the highest number since 1970—are serving around the world; also sends first volunteers to Cambodia and reopens its post in Ethiopia

The Skinny

Most important to recruiters: Leadership skills, volunteer activity and motivation, work experience

Selectivity: Roughly 1 out of 3 applicants selected as volunteeres in both 2006 and 2007

Diversity of entry-level workforce: 17% minority; 59% female

Facts to know:

- Volunteers are paid a fixed stipend based upon the prevailing wage in their host country.

- The Peace Corps offers returning volunteers job placement assistance and $6,000 to aid in making the transition back to life in the United States.

- Although a very active recruiter of recent graduates, the agency also recently launched a "50+" campaign that is aimed at enlisting members of the huge boomer population for overseas volunteer work as they begin retiring. An estimated 5% of current volunteers are over age 50; the Peace Corps' oldest volunteer is 80 years of age.

- The Peace Corps has some bold-faced names among its ranks. NBC's *Hardball* host Chris Matthews volunteered in Swaziland from 1968 to 1970; U.S. Senator Christopher Dodd was in the Dominican Republic from 1966 to 1968; and Wisconsin governor Jim Doyle and his wife Jessica served in Tunisia from 1967 to 1969.

The Sliding Scale

Entry-level hires who had been interns: N/A

Most important performance measurements in entry-level hire: Analytical skills, organizational skills, team player

Entry-level hires receiving signing bonuses: None

Average entry-level signing bonus: N/A

Entry-level hires receiving performance bonuses: None

Average performance bonus during first year: N/A

The Stand-Out Perks

- 24 paid vacation days

- Volunteer travel expenses to and from posts are paid in full by the Peace Corps

- Medical and any emergency travel expenses are paid in full by the Peace Corps

- Peace Corps Fellows/USA graduate fellowship program offering financial assistance to returning volunteers who wish to earn professional certification; master's or doctoral degrees in various subjects; also includes paid internships in underserved U.S. communities

- $6,000 toward transition to life back home after completing assignment

- Federal student loan deferment or cancellation (dependent on eligibility)

The Skills

- 90-day orientation program that includes language instruction, specific technical skills, and cross-cultural immersion in a community-based setting

- A formal leadership program for entry-level hires that have been with the agency for a year or less

- Formal mentorship program (100% of entry-level hires participate)

The Sound-Off

- "I was a Peace Corps volunteer prior to returning to MBA school and going corporate. I now manage a $4 billion retail services business. I must say that while I gave up a few years of income during my tour of duty, the experience provided me with an adaptability and thought diversity that are uniquely valuable among MBA candidates in the corporate world." —BW *Discussion Forum*

- "Not enough people have respect for America's most significant federal agency. None of the other employees can compare to the accomplishments of Peace Corps volunteers. We need more level-headed individuals out in the world, making a difference, not ruining this world." —BW *Discussion Forum*

THE SPOTLIGHT: A CONVERSATION WITH A YOUNG VOLUNTEER

Name: Courtney Phelps
Job: Youth Development Mobilizer

Describe your assignment: *I am a Peace Corps Masters International student and thus am working on finishing my thesis project during my service in Cape Verde. Being placed both at a center for disadvantaged and often traumatized girls and at a general Youth Center, my role has primarily been to provide much-needed support for the understaffed and underfunded Girls' Center and to try to link the already well-functioning Youth Center to the Girls' Center. My primary activities include organizing and planning field trips and hikes for the girls, planning a participatory photography project for community change with the girls, creating a volunteer corps using young adults from the Youth Center to come lead activities and sports with the girls, making family/domestic visits with the social worker, teaching English at the Youth Center, and training the monitors who work with the girls at the center, among other secondary activities.*

Discuss the adjustment: *Learning the local language (Kriolu) was a key part of my integration into the community and Cape Verdean culture, so I took every opportunity to practice speaking and trying to communicate. Teaching children new games and asking them to teach me theirs was an excellent way for me to learn about different methods of communication and social interaction. Another good way to learn about the intricacies of Cape Verdean culture was to participate in as many local activities, festivals, celebrations, and cultural events as possible. The first several months were spent patiently and attentively observing everything and everyone, trying all new foods, and taking my cues from the Cape Verdeans around me.*

Why the work's rewarding: *The relationships I have built with the girls at the center I work at. I adore them and their big smiling faces, and I love hearing "Tia!" (an affectionate term for people they care about) every day.*

A memorable experience: *Working with a particular young woman with severe clinical depression whom I grew close to within my first six months at the site. Being with her every day taught me so much about the work I want to do, the person I want to be, and what I am and am not capable of. Her strength in dealing with her condition gave me strength and challenged me in ways I have never been challenged before.*

Teach for America

315 W. 36th St., 6th Floor
New York, NY 10018
Phone: 212-279-2080
Fax: 212-279-2081
Web Addresses:
www.teachforamerica.org;
www.teachforamerica.org/online/
info/index.jsp

The Company

- In 1990, recent college graduate Wendy Kopp founded Teach for America (TFA), basing the nonprofit's model on a prototype she had developed for her senior thesis at Princeton. Since its inception, over 17,000 recent college graduates have joined TFA, which dispatches these "corps members" to teach in underserved communities for two-year commitments.

- TFA is on track to meet a growth plan to more than double in size, from 3,500 members in 2005 to 7,500 members by the end of the decade.

- TFA's skeptics argue that bright, enthusiastic 21-year-olds, many of whom have had little or no prior teaching experience, aren't ready for such tough teaching assignments. However, in a 2007 survey conducted by Policy Studies Associates, 95% of the principals from the schools that TFA serves said that they felt that corps members are as effective as other beginning teachers in terms of performance and impact on student achievement.

The Suits

Wendy Kopp: Founder and CEO
Matthew Kramer: President and Chief Program Officer
Elisa Villanueva Beard: Chief Operating Officer
Aimee Eubanks Davis: Chief People Officer
Kevin Huffman: Chief Growth and Development Officer

The Stats

Employees: More than 5,000 corps members
Locations: Over 1,000 schools in 26 regions across the United States
Major competitors: N/A
Largest operating units: N/A

Fiscal year 2007 operating budget:
$77 million
Fiscal year 2008 operating budget:
$120 million

The Story

1989: Princeton senior Wendy Kopp develops the idea for TFA in her senior thesis at Princeton; a seed grant Kopp secures from the Mobil Corporation brings her nonprofit to life

1990: Kopp and a small staff start TFA; 500 college graduates are selected from 2,500 applicants and placed in teaching positions in six regions across the United States

1993: TFA helps shape AmeriCorps, the federal national service initiative, and becomes a member of the Ameri-Corps national service network

1995: Hundreds of former corps members gather at Teach for America's first alumni summit to celebrate the organization's first five years

1997: The first annual TFA Week features business, political, and entertainment leaders who teach in corps members' classrooms

2001: TFA is named by First Lady Laura Bush as one of the five organizations she will actively support during her husband's tenure as president of the United States

2002: TFA forms its first corporate partnership with the Wachovia Corporation

2005: TFA successfully completes it five-year growth plan, expanding from 15 to 22 sites and from 1,500 to 3,500 corps members; Alumnus Jason Kamras is named National Teacher of the Year, the first Washington, D.C., teacher ever to win the award

2007: Commits to launching a new organization that will support entrepreneurs in other countries who are trying to implement the TFA model locally

The Skinny

Most important to recruiters: Leadership skills, proven record of achievement, the ability to influence others, strong critical thinking, perseverance in the face of past obstacles

Selectivity: 1 of 6 applicants hired in 2007, up from 1 of 8 applicants hired in 2006 and 2005

Diversity of entry-level workforce: 28% minority; 73% female

Facts to know:

- Teach for America selected less than 20% of its over 18,000 applicants. In aggregate, the applicants represented 5 to 10 percent of the senior classes at 90 colleges and universities, including Princeton, Harvard, Yale, the University of Michigan, Morehouse, Spelman, and Howard.

- More than 100 graduate and education schools help support TFA by providing prospective corps members with benefits such as two-year deferrals, scholarships, course credits for their TFA experience, and application waiver fees.

- TFA has also forged partnerships in recent years with 16 employers, including Deloitte, Google, and General Electric, all of whom allow recent hires to defer their job offers so that they can spend two years teaching.

- Although not all TFA alums continue teaching, more than two-thirds are currently working or studying full time in the field of education.

The Stand-Out Perks

- 50 paid vacation days and 25 paid holidays during first year

- Educational expenses reimbursement ($4,725)

- Employee discounts

The Skills

- Preinstitute independent work, a series of independent assignments before summer institute that encourage corps members to reflect upon the task that they will soon undertake

- Regional induction, a five-day program that provides corps members with an overview of their new region; networking opportunities with other corps members and alumni; and information on TFA's mission and values

- Summer institute, a rigorous five-week training program where corps members develop foundational teaching skills and knowledge

- Regional orientation, which consists of training sessions that help corps members establish clear goals for their students' achievement, plan for instruction, and collect and interpret data so as to be continually aware of their students' improvement

- Ongoing professional development, a formal leadership development and coaching program that lasts throughout corps members' two-year commitment (100% of entry-level hires participate)

The Sound-Off

- "Those in New York City (the largest part of the corps) and outside have very different experiences, given the reforms going on in New York City schools, from what I understand. What I love about teaching is that I'm gaining skills I can use in every profession, and I feel like I'm making a real and immediate impact on the kids in my class." —*TFA corps member*

THE RECRUITER SPOTLIGHT

Name: Elissa Clapp
Job: Senior VP, Recruitment

Advice for prospective corps members: *Joining Teach for America is a life-changing experience. The work is challenging but incredibly rewarding, as it gives corps members a personal strength that helps them increase their long-term impact. In two years, you have the opportunity to affect the life prospects of students in low-income communities by helping them attain an excellent education. Regardless of the field TFA alumni choose after their two-year commitment, the skills they acquire as corps members help them succeed in future endeavors. Furthermore, TFA has built strong relationships with more than 100 top-ranked business, law, medicine, and public policy graduate schools and education schools, which offer TFA alumni benefits, including two-year deferrals, scholarships, course credits, and application fee waivers. We also have partnerships with a number of leading employers that value the leadership skills and experiences that distinguish TFA corps members, including JPMorgan, Morgan Stanley, McKinsey, Google, and Goldman Sachs. Our graduate school and professional partnerships demonstrate how highly TFA alumni are regarded after their time in the classroom.*

Wackiest interview techniques encountered: *As part of the final interview process, TFA applicants are asked to teach a five-minute lesson on the subject of their choice. Some years ago, an applicant stood up in front of the room, announced that he was going to do a demonstration, and threw himself on the center table, writhing around on his stomach and wildly flailing his arms and legs. At the end of this spectacle, we were told that we had just witnessed an "insect simulation." You really do learn something every day.*

U.S. Department of State

2201 C St., NW
Washington, DC 20520
Phone: 202-647-4000
Fax: N/A
Web Addresses: www.state.gov;
www.state.gov/careers

The Company

- The U.S. Department of State, a body of the Executive Branch, is the official representative of the United States in foreign countries. Diplomacy, women's issues, nonproliferation, and free trade are among the many issues handled by the numerous Department of State ambassadors, consuls, and diplomats that are stationed throughout the world. The Department of State is also the government body that takes care of Americans traveling or living abroad.

- Diplomats go through a rigorous application process, including the Foreign Service Officer Test and interview (where knowing a second language is extremely helpful). All officers, domestic or foreign, must receive a security clearance as well, the level of which depends on the type of information the officer handles.

- The Department of State's Bureau of Educational and Cultural Affairs sponsors the Fulbright program,

which gives academic grants to scholars wishing to conduct research overseas.

The Suits

Condoleezza Rice: Secretary
John Negroponte: Deputy Secretary
Henrietta Fore: Director of U.S. Foreign Assistance and U.S. Agency for International Development Administrator
Patrick Kennedy: Under Secretary for Management
R. Nicholas Burns: Under Secretary for Political Affairs

The Stats

Employees: 57,434*
Locations: U.S. Department of State has a presence (embassies, consulates, and missions) in over 180 countries. The agency had 167 embassies, 64 consulates general,

and 21 consulates as of January 15, 2008.

*Includes direct hire foreign service and civil service personnel and all foreign service nationals.

The Story

1776–1778: Benjamin Franklin acts as the first U.S. diplomat, appealing to France in an effort to gain its support of the American Revolution

1789: Congress passes "An Act to provide for the safe keeping of the Acts, Records, and Seal of the United States, and for other purposes"; the passage of this law causes the Department of Foreign Affairs to be renamed the Department of State

1790–1793: Thomas Jefferson is the first secretary of state

1830–1860: The Department of State pursues expansion through the Louisiana Purchase and the Indian Treaty and Removal Act

1918: President Woodrow Wilson presents his "Fourteen Points" to Congress to lay out his plans for peace in Europe after World War I

1942: The United Nations is created

1947: The National Security Act is signed, creating the Central Intelligence Agency; Secretary of State George C. Marshall issues the Marshall Plan, the aim of which is to rebuild Europe

1985: The Reagan Doctrine, detailing President Ronald Reagan's intolerance for communism abroad, aims to push back Soviet influence in the world

2007: Undergoes scrutiny for the major delay in passport production and has since added staffers and facilities to its passport operations in preparation for the 2008 travel season

The Skinny

Most important to recruiters: Judgment, communication skills, leadership skills, the 12 dimensions, which can be found at www.careers.state.gov/specialist/selection.html

Selectivity: 1 of 26 applicants hired in 2006, down from 1 of 25 applicants hired in 2005

Diversity of entry-level workforce: 20% minority; 51% female (Foreign Service Officer)

Facts to know:

- In 2006, the gross payment per employee who qualified for the Department of State's Student Loan Repayment Program was $4,600. The department anticipates that the 2007 amount will be $6,000.

- Liberal arts majors are actually in demand at the Department of State. In 2006, 45% of new entry-level hires and 62% of interns were liberal arts majors.

The Starting Gate

Undergraduate internships*: 1,547

Duration of summer internship: 10 weeks

Average total compensation†: $4,400

Interns by grade level[‡]:

Junior...22%
Senior 39%
College graduate 39%

Interns who receive full-time job offers[§]: N/A

Interns who are extended full-time job offers that accept: N/A

*Includes spring, summer, and fall
[†]This is average compensation for paid internships only (some internships are unpaid)
[‡]All Department of State internships require a minimum of 60 college credits for consideration
[§]One must take the Foreign Service Officer test to become a Foreign Service Officer

The Sliding Scale

Entry-level hires who had been interns: N/A

Most important performance measurements in entry-level hire: Intelligence, analytical skills, leadership ability, and 12 dimensions (see "The Skinny" section)

Entry-level hires receiving signing bonuses: N/A

Average entry-level signing bonus: N/A

Entry-level hires receiving performance bonuses: N/A

Average performance bonus during first year: N/A

The Stand-Out Perks

- Educational expenses reimbursement
- Relocation compensation
- Fitness facilities and employee day care at most locations
- Housing and paid education for children of employees living and working overseas

The Skills

- Formal orientation program
- Career Entry Program, which consists of approximately six rotations and lasts 104 weeks
- Formal mentorship program (86% of entry-level hires participate)

The Sound-Off

- "Help in finding housing abroad, generous pay for an internship. Very professional, stable and friendly environment. Also, some challenging tasks." —*University of Michigan junior**
- "We have a culture that sees time spent in training as a 'vacation' from real work, as opposed to a way to improve job performance. This attitude has changed somewhat recently, but we have a long way to go." —BW *Discussion Forum*

*Data: Universum Communications

THE SUPERSTAR SPOTLIGHT

Name: Michael G. Singh

Job: Senior Director for the Middle East and North Africa; National Security Council

Describe your career trajectory: *I joined the Foreign Service in May 2000 and was sent to Tel Aviv, Israel, where I worked from 2001 to 2002 on consular and economic issues and as staff aide to the U.S. ambassador. From there, in 2003, I went to the State Department Operations Center, which is a 24/7 operations and crisis management office that serves the secretary of state. Then, in 2004, I was asked to serve as a special assistant to Secretary of State Colin Powell, and then to Secretary Condoleezza Rice when she succeeded General Powell in 2005. After serving in the secretary's office, I was seconded to the National Security Council in November 2005. I initially served as the National Security Council Director for Syria, Lebanon, Egypt, and North Africa, then was made the director for Iran, and, finally, in April 2007, I was promoted to the position of Senior Director for the Middle East and North Africa. In this job, I coordinate U.S. policy for the Middle East, from Morocco to Iran (but excluding Iraq, which is handled by a separate office here).*

Briefly describe a typical day: *I start a typical day here by receiving an intelligence briefing and reviewing the latest press and diplomatic reporting. Following a staff meeting chaired by the National Security Advisor or his deputy, I usually spend the bulk of the day meeting with foreign diplomats and officials, chairing or attending meetings between the various government agencies to discuss U.S. policy, and drafting or reviewing policy papers that are intended for the president, the national security advisor, or other senior officials.*

The best part of your job: *The chance to serve my country and to work closely with a highly talented and hard-working group of people who are dedicated to public service. Plus, every now and then I get to participate in a meeting with the president in the Oval Office, an experience that never gets old.*

Internal Revenue Service

U.S. Internal Revenue Service
1111 Constitution Ave., NW
Washington, DC 20224
Phone: 800-829-1040
Fax: N/A
Web Addresses: www.irs.gov;
jobs.irs.gov/home.hmtl

FAST FACTS

"Best Places to Launch a Career"
  Rank: 70
"Best Internships" Rank: 73
Full-Time Salary: $35,000–$39,999
Top College Major: Business
3-Year Retention Rate: 90%
5-Year Retention Rate: 80%
Stock Ticker: N/A

The Company

- The Internal Revenue Service (IRS) is a bureau under the U.S. Department of the Treasury. The commissioner and chief counsel are the only two members of the bureau who must be appointed by the president and confirmed by the Senate.

- The mission of the IRS is to apply tax law. In doing so, the IRS works both to educate taxpayers on the rules and regulations to which they are subject and to enforce the actual payment of these taxes.

- The IRS came under Government Accountability Office (GAO), fire in 2007 for mismanaging paper case files. The GAO (a body of the legislature) cited several District Court cases in which the lack of IRS paperwork cost the government $40,000 per case. The GAO said that 10% to 14% of all IRS paper case files were missing during GAO audits of the bureau, and up to 19% of paper case files were missing when the Treasury Inspector General conducted a separate, random audit of the IRS. (In all fairness, the GAO, which completes numerous reports on the IRS each year, has also given the agency more favorable reviews on a number of other occasions.)

The Suits

Linda E. Stiff: Acting Commissioner
Nina E. Olson: National Taxpayer Advocate
Donald L. Korb: IRS Chief Counsel
Frank Keith: Chief Communications and Liaison
Sarah Hall Ingram: Chief Appeals

The Stats

The IRS collected $2 trillion in taxes in 2004.

The IRS spent $0.44 for every $100 collected in 2005.

The Story

1862: To finance the Civil War, President Abraham Lincoln and Congress enact an income tax and develop the position of commissioner of Internal Revenue to oversee its collection

1872: Lincoln's income tax is repealed

1894: The income tax is revived, only to be deemed unconstitutional by the U.S. Supreme Court the following year

1913: The Sixteenth Amendment to the Constitution is ratified, giving Congress authority over the issue of income tax

1918: The top income-tax rate rises to 77%, but drops dramatically in the following postwar period

1950s: The Bureau of Internal Revenue is renamed the Internal Revenue Service (IRS) as more professionals come on board the bureau's staff

1998: The IRS Restructuring and Reform Act is passed; the IRS undergoes a drastic modernization, modeling itself after the private sector to better handle customer services (i.e., taxpayer education)

The Skinny

Most important to recruiters: College major, communication skills, analytical skills

Selectivity: N/A

Diversity of entry-level workforce: 51% minority; 69% female

Facts to know:

- The IRS casts its entry-level hiring net wide, actively recruiting on nearly 400 U.S. undergraduate college campuses.

- The number of annual training days for entry-level employees depends upon the position. The range is from 10 weeks for revenue agents to 13 weeks for revenue officers to six months for special agents.

The Starting Gate

Undergraduate internships: 684

Duration of summer internship: 8 weeks

Average total compensation: $3,520

Interns by grade level:
Sophomore 1%
Junior..1%
Senior 9%
College graduate 89%

Interns who receive full-time job offers: N/A

Interns who are extended full-time job offers that accept: N/A

The Sliding Scale

Entry-level hires who had been interns: 6%

Most important performance measurements in entry-level hire: Learning ability, productivity/efficiency, organizational skills

Entry-level hires receiving signing bonuses: None

Average entry-level signing bonus: N/A

Entry-level hires receiving performance bonuses: 100%

Average performance bonus during first year: N/A

The Stand-Out Perks

- Educational expenses reimbursement

- Access to co-funded pension and 401(k) with company matching up to 5% of salary (fully vested after 60 months)

- Employee discounts

The Skills

- Formal one-day orientation program

- Frontline Leader Readiness Program, which consists of two to four rotations and lasts eight weeks

The Sound-Off

- "The co-op program is geared toward a full-time experience with the IRS, and the pay is competitive." —*CUNY Baruch senior**

- "Once the probationary period is over, you are permitted (to a certain extent) to make your own hours and manage your case work/inventory in the way that best fits you. You could be in the field a whole day one day, in the office the next, and so forth." —*27-year-old IRS Revenue Officer*

- "The employees that you write about (recruited at colleges/college graduates) are offered professional positions that come with flexibility in the work schedules, some level of empowerment, and decent opportunities to advance. The 'call-site' employees I work with are normally hired as seasonals, have little job empowerment, and have little flexibility in work schedules . . . the morale is low." —BW *Discussion Forum*

- "I love my job because it is always full of challenges, and no single day is like any other." —*IRS Supervisory Revenue Officer*

*Data: Universum Communications

THE SUPERSTAR SPOTLIGHT

Name: April Zins

Job: Midwest Exam Area Technical Advisor; Small Business/ Self-Employed Division

Describe your job: *At the IRS, there is something new and different every day. With every position I have held within the IRS, each day has presented a new challenge in working with a variety of taxpayers, IRS employees, and/or programs. As a Revenue Agent, each case I worked had a different issue and different type of taxpayer. As a Group Manager, each day presented different issues and challenges. In all the IRS jobs I have held, I have been expected to work independently, make decisions, solve problems, and help people—both inside and outside the IRS. It is exciting and [gives you] a sense of accomplishment to feel that you can "make a difference."*

Discuss your rise through the ranks: *Learning what opportunities are available throughout the IRS and having the opportunity to work in different positions helped me progress. I was open to new assignments and responsibilities that broadened my knowledge. For example, I have been an on-the-job instructor for several waves of new Revenue Agent hires, and I have been a classroom instructor. I also participated in the redesign of the Revenue Agent training process for new hires. I was willing to move beyond my "comfort zone" and accept more responsibility.*

Tips for ambitious young employees: *The IRS has a wide variety of positions available. You are able to stay within the organization but work at different jobs throughout your career. The IRS is the perfect place for young, motivated individuals to work because of the variety and opportunities available.*

U.S. Patent & Trademark

Madison Buildings (East and West)
600 Dulany St.
Alexandria, VA 22314
Phone: 571-272-8400 (Office of Public
Affairs)
Phone: 703-305-8231 (Office of Human
Resources)
Web Addresses:
www.uspto.gov/index.html#;
jobsearch.usajobs.opm.gov/a9pto.asp

The Company

- An agency under the U.S. Department of Commerce, the U.S. Patent and Trademark Office (USPTO) states that its foremost goal is to promote the progress of science and innovation by issuing patents and registering trademarks. A patent provides inventors with exclusive rights to their creations for a limited time. A trademark is a word, name, symbol, or device that is used in the trade of goods to indicate the source of the goods and to distinguish them from the goods of others.

- The USPTO encourages technological advancement by issuing patents, which provide incentives to invent, invest in, and disclose new technology. In its registration of trademarks, the USPTO assists businesses in protecting their investments, promoting quality goods and services, and safeguarding consumers against confusion and deception in the marketplace.

- The USPTO's Office of International Relations works with the World Intellectual Property Organization, the World Trade Organization, and other international bodies to promote a fair exchange of ideas globally and to secure U.S. property interests abroad. USPTO is working with other government agencies and the private sector on the STOP! initiative, which was created to combat trade in pirated and counterfeit goods. STOP! is the most comprehensive U.S. government-wide initiative of its kind.

The Suits

John Dudas: Under Secretary of Commerce for Intellectual Property and Director of USPTO

Margaret J. A. Peterlin: Deputy Under Secretary of Commerce for Intellectual Property and Deputy Director of USPTO

Lynne G. Beresford: Commissioner for Trademarks

Sharon Marsh: Deputy Commissioner for Trademark Examination Policy

John J. Doll: Commissioner for Patents

The Stats*

Employees: 8,000

Locations: A campus-style setting in Alexandria, Virginia

Total patents issued: 183,187

Total trademarks registered: 147,118

Total patents issues since 1790: Over 7.5 million

Total active trademark registrations: 1,322,155

*Fiscal year 2006

The Story

1788: The U.S. Constitution is ratified and includes a clause (now referred to as the "Intellectual Property Clause" or the "Patent/Copyright Clause") in Article 1, Section 8, Clause 8, that states: "Congress shall have the Power . . . To Promote the Progress of Science and useful Arts, by securing for limited Times to Authors and Inventors the exclusive Right to their respective Writings and Discoveries"

1790: President George Washington signs the first patent bill

1870: The first law concerning trademarks is enacted

1946: Congress passes the Trademark Act of 1946, creating the current trademark registration system employed by the USPTO

1991: Under the Omnibus Budget Reconciliation Act (OBRA) of 1990, the USPTO becomes 100% funded by user fees

1999: The American Inventors Protection Act establishes the USPTO as an agency with performance-based attributes (for example, a clear mission statement, measurable services, a performance measurement system, and predictable sources of funding)

The Skinny

Most important to recruiters: College major, college GPA, work experience

Selectivity: 1 of 14 applicants hired in 2006, down from 1 of 12 applicants hired in 2005

Diversity of entry-level workforce: 54% minority; 40% female

Facts to know:

- Entry-level hires are required to have an extremely technical skill set in engineering or the sciences. Individuals with law degrees who are newly hired by the USPTO as patent and trademark attorneys are also included in this profile's entry-level hiring data.

- The vast majority of the USPTO's new hires are patent examiners, who are required to complete a formal training program (32 weeks in length) that is delivered through the Patent Training Academy. This program provides all of the skills training required to become a fully productive patent examiner. The training includes coursework in the use of both patent information systems and technology associated with key elements of the patent examiner position.

The Starting Gate

Undergraduate internships: N/A

Duration of summer internship: 8 to 13 weeks

Average total compensation: $1,692

Interns by grade level: N/A

Interns who receive full-time job offers: 1%

Interns who are extended full-time job offers that accept: 100%

The Sliding Scale

Entry-level hires who had been interns: None

Most important performance measurements in entry-level hire: Learning ability, analytical skills, productivity/efficiency

Entry-level hires receiving signing bonuses: 43%

Average entry-level signing bonus: $8,200

Entry-level hires receiving performance bonuses: 100%

Average performance bonus during first year: $2,000

The Stand-Out Perks

- Educational expenses reimbursement ($5,000)

- Full and partial graduate school sponsorship

- Employee discounts

- On-site child care

- Transportation subsidy up to $100

The Skills

- Formal one-day training program, including guest speakers and a tour of the facilities

- Patent Training Program, which lasts 32 weeks (see "Facts to Know" section), and Department of Commerce Aspiring Leadership Commerce Program, which lasts 52 weeks

THE ENTRY-LEVEL SPOTLIGHT

Name: Brandon Hoffman
Job: Patent Examiner

Briefly describe your workplace culture: *The atmosphere is very relaxed in that the higher-ups (supervisors, directors, and others) do not hover around us while we attempt to do our job. They understand that we are just coming out of school, most likely are moving to a new area, and are trying to adapt to the whole idea of working a real job. On the flip side, anytime you would like help, your immediate supervisor is always just down the hall, plus your colleagues are always willing to help. Quality is of the utmost importance, which is why every case an examiner turns in gets reviewed by a supervisor. As you progress up the corporate ladder, the amount of time spent on reviewing your cases goes down, until eventually they are reviewed only by you. The atmosphere here is very relaxed—there is time to walk the halls and chat with friends, and there is time to be at your desk working.*

Weirdest/funniest thing about the job: *Other than the people (you have to remember, we have over 6,000 engineers and scientists running around our buildings), it would be the applications themselves. Sometimes people have just a little bit too much time and money on their hands, which makes for a funny day at the office.*

Describe a typical day: *The first thing I do is pick up (not literally, since it is all electronic) an application and read through the specification, claims, and drawings to get an understanding of what the applicant is trying to get a patent on. After reading, I formulate a search strategy using our own in-house searching tools to try to find other patents or publications that cover the same thing, or at least close enough to raise some doubt. Once I find some good "prior art" (prior because it has to be filed before the applicant's application is filed), I write up an "office action" that explains to the applicant why he or she is or is not getting a patent for this invention. This process takes three days, if you are a new hire, to about a day and a half if you have been here for four years. Additional responsibilities include interviews with the inventors (or their representatives, aka attorneys).*

Abbott Laboratories

100 Abbott Park Rd.
Abbott Park, IL 60064-3500
Phone: 847-937-6100
Fax: N/A
Web Addresses: www.abbott.com;
www.abbott.com/careers

The Company

- The global health-care giant specializes in pharmaceuticals (HIV treatment Kaletra, arthritis and Crohn's disease drug HUMIRA), medical devices (glucose monitors, stents), nutritional products (Ensure, Similac), and diagnostic equipment (PathVysion, a molecular breakthrough in breast cancer treatment).

- Early results for the Xience stent have been promising, and the company hopes that this will be a future blockbuster product pending FDA approval which could occur as early as the second quarter of 2008. One question mark for the company is migraine drug Depakote, a product that may face stiff competition when some of its patents expire in July 2008.

- Abbott offers low-cost HIV drugs to 114 countries, providing them at no profit in the 69 least developed of these nations.

The Suits

Miles D. White: Chairman and CEO
Thomas Freyman: Executive VP of Finance and CFO
Laura Schumacher: Executive VP and General Counsel

The Stats

2007 sales: $25.9 billion
2007 net income: $4.4 billion (excluding items)
Market cap: $86.8 billion
Employees: 65,000
Locations: More than 100 locations internationally
Major competitors: Merck, Pfizer
Largest operating units*:
Pharmaceuticals..............$14.6 billion
Nutritionals ....$ 4.4 billion
Diagnostics ....$3.2 billion
Vascular...........................$1.7 billion
*2007 sales

The Story

1900: Abbott is officially founded as the Abbott Alkaloidal Company by physician Dr. Wallace C. Abbott, one of the founders of modern pharmacy

1910: Establishes its first European agency in London; opens branches in New York, San Francisco, Seattle, Toronto, and India

1916: Acquires its first synthetic medicine, which is used on World War I battlefields to clean wounds

1929: Abbott becomes a publicly traded company

1964: Acquires M&R Dietetic Laboratories, a maker of infant formula, which eventually becomes Abbott's nutrition division

1973: Forms a diagnostics division; introduces Ensure, the first adult medical nutritional supplement

1985: Wins approval to market the world's first diagnostic test for AIDS

2003: Stirs up controversy when it raises the price for AIDS drug Norvir fourfold in the United States; is accused of price gouging by some consumer groups

2006: Acquires Guidant's vascular business and Kos Pharmaceuticals

The Skinny

Most important to recruiters: Leadership skills, work experience, communication skills

Selectivity: 1 of 17 applicants hired in 2006, roughly the same as 2005

Diversity of entry-level workforce: 23% minority; 53% female

Facts to know:

- The internship program offers several additional extracurricular activities, including a sports league and volunteer program. Interns have direct access to senior Abbott staff, including the CEO. Housing is provided, and barbecues for interns and managers are held once a week.

- Almost 90 percent of Abbott's U.S. workforce utilizes some type of flexible work option, including part-time schedules, job shares, flex hours, or telecommuting.

The Starting Gate

Undergraduate internships: 216

Duration of summer internship: About 12 weeks

Average internship compensation: $15,000 (includes housing, transportation, and expenses)

Interns by grade level:
Freshman 6%
Sophomore 6%
Junior...60%
Senior 7%
College graduate 21%

Interns who receive full-time job offers: 59%

Interns who are extended full-time job offers that accept: 44%

The Sliding Scale

Entry-level hires who had been interns: 33%

Most important performance measurements in entry-level hire: Productivity/efficiency, quality, team player

Entry-level hires receiving signing bonuses: 21%

Average entry-level signing bonus: $6,500

Entry-level hires receiving performance bonuses: 100%

Average performance bonus during first year: $3,700

The Stand-Out Perks

- Educational expenses reimbursement ($7,000)

- Full graduate school sponsorship for junior-level employees

- 401(k) plan, cofunded pension, and profit-sharing plan

- Relocation compensation

- Employee discount program

The Skills

- Formal orientation program including computer training, guest speakers, diversity exercises, team-building exercises, review of company values and ethics/compliance expectations, and a tour of facilities

- Managers and new employees create 30-, 60-, and 90-day Internet-based development plans

- Young management hires are eligible for a one-week Abbott New Leader Program

- A formal mentorship program

The Sound-Off

- "Good [internship] compensation, plus housing and meals and car. Plus I learned more than I ever thought possible." —*Miami University junior**

- "One of the biggest pros in my first 3 months working at Abbott is the exposure I got to upper-level employees. I have had the opportunity to engage in a one-on-one discussion with the CFO of our company... Another pro is that I get to travel." —*Financial Professional Development Program participant (age 23)*

*Data: Universum Communication

THE ENTRY-LEVEL SPOTLIGHT

Name: Fabiola Salcedo
Job: Professional Development Program participant

Discuss your experience in the Professional Development Program (PDP): *Abbott's PDP allows recent college graduates to rotate through different positions before choosing a specific job and career path. I am on my last rotation, helping to manage financial operations at an Abbott Nutrition plant in Columbus, Ohio, that manufactures infant formulas such as Similac and adult nutritional supplements such as Ensure. Previously I had the opportunity to work in different divisions across Abbott. I was also able to work in several different locations, including Abbott's headquarters in suburban Chicago and an R&D and manufacturing site in Germany.*

Best part of the job: *Having exposure to different types of managers and groups within Abbott has helped me become more flexible and adaptable. . . . Beyond my daily duties, Abbott's PDP also offers great training opportunities; each member is provided with coursework ranging from ethics courses to presentation skills and database training. There are also a lot of opportunities to interact with and learn from senior leaders at Abbott. Additionally, there are leadership opportunities for program participants; for example, currently I am the chair for the Welcoming Committee, which strives to provide a smooth transition for new PDP participants. Also, PDP members get together to give back to the community through volunteering.*

What's next: *I will soon be starting a new position as a financial analyst supporting Abbott Nutrition's EAS brand, which markets science-based sports nutrition products.*

Eli Lilly

Lilly Corporate Center
893 S. Delaware
Indianapolis, IN 46285
Phone: 317-276-2000
Fax: 317-276-4878
Web Addresses: www.lilly.com;
www.lilly.com/careers

The Company

- Eli Lilly and Co. is the name behind many commercial pharmaceuticals, including Cymbalta (depression), Byetta (diabetes), and Cialis (erectile dysfunction). Eli Lilly is also a leader in the veterinary pharmaceuticals industry. It acquired Ivy Animal Health in 2007, to bolster the market presence of its own Elanco Animal Health division.

- In 2007, Eli Lilly settled with 18,000 patients who had lodged complaints about schizophrenia drug Zyprexa's harmful side effects.

- To date, Eli Lilly has over 40 drugs in development, including treatments for patients suffering from Alzheimer's disease, diabetes, and cancer. It is also working to defend its patents on Strattera (which accounted for $500 billion in sales in 2006) in U.S. courts and other product patents abroad. Intellectual property rights infringements (particularly by China) continually

FAST FACTS

"Best Places to Launch a Career"
   Rank: 32
"Best Internships" Rank: 66
Full-Time Salary: $55,000–$59,999
Entry-Level Hires: 574
Entry-Level Female Hires: 62%
3-Year Retention Rate: 68%
Stock Ticker: LLY

threaten Eli Lilly's position as a top world pharmaceutical producer.

The Suits

Sidney Taurel: Chairman
John Lechleiter: President and CEO
Steven Paul: President of Lilly Research Laboratories and Executive VP of Science and Technology
Robert Armitage: Senior VP and General Counsel
Gino Santini: Senior VP of Corporate Strategy and Business Development

The Stats

2007 sales: $18.6 billion
2007 net income: $3 billion
Market cap: $60.6 billion
Employees: 40,600 (20,400 in the United States)
Locations: Medicines marketed in 143 countries; research facilities in 9 countries; testing conducted in 60 countries worldwide

Major competitors: GlaxoSmith-
Kline, Pfizer, Amgen, AstraZeneca,
Merck, Novartis, Bristol-Meyers
Squibb

Largest operating units*:
Pharmaceuticals...............$17.6 billion
Animal Health................$996 million
*2007 sales

The Story

1876: Union Colonel Eli Lilly founds
Eli Lilly and Co. with $1,300

1923: Introduces Iletin, the world's first
commercially available insulin product

1947: Introduces DES, a drug designed
to prevent miscarriages; although the
drug commands 70% of its market, by
1971, is linked to cervical cancer in its
patients and is removed from the market

1952: Becomes the first company to
supply the Salk polio vaccine in bulk

1986: Releases revolutionary depression treatment Prozac

2002: Settles litigation with eight states
after 600 customers' e-mail addresses
are accidentally disclosed

2003: Creates a public-private partnership with the World Health Organization (WHO) to address the expanding
global crisis of multi-drug-resistant
tuberculosis (MDR-TB)

2004: After Strattera (attention-deficit/
hyperactivity disorder drug) is linked to
liver problems, Lilly begins to put a
warning label on the product

2006: Cymbalta (depression drug)
becomes one of only a handful of med-

icines to reach $1 billion in sales in just
its second year on the market

2006: Becomes the first pharmaceutical company to post all clinical trial
results online

2007: Acquires privately held Hypnion
to gain access to new insomnia medicines; also acquires ICOS and gains
Cialis in the process

2007: Evitsta, originally an osteoporo-
sis drug, is approved as a preventative
measure for breast cancer in post-
menopausal women

The Skinny

Most important to recruiters: College
GPA, leadership skills, college major

Selectivity: N/A

Diversity of entry-level workforce:
21% minority; 62% female

Facts to know:

- Eli Lilly actively recruited on 79
  U.S. undergraduate campuses during the 2006–2007 school year and
  made job offers on 38 of those campuses.

- Almost half of Lilly's top executives
  (VP and above) have been with the
  company for 20 years or more.

The Starting Gate

Undergraduate internships: 165

Duration of summer internship: 12
weeks

Average total compensation: $9,500

Interns by grade level: N/A

Interns who receive full-time job offers: N/A

Interns who are extended full-time job offers that accept: N/A

The Sliding Scale

Entry-level hires who had been interns: 10%

Most important performance measurements in entry-level hire: N/A

Entry-level hires receiving signing bonuses: None

Average entry-level signing bonus: N/A

Entry-level hires receiving performance bonuses: None

Average performance bonus during first year: N/A

The Stand-Out Perks

- Educational expenses reimbursement

- Partial graduate school sponsorship

- 12 paid vacation days

- Company fitness center staffed with professional exercise specialists

- Access to 401(k), with company match of up to 6% of salary, cofunded pension, and profit-sharing plan

- Charitable gift match ($10,000)

- Relocation compensation

The Skills

- Formal one-day orientation

- Lilly Initial Financial Leadership Program, which lasts 24 weeks

- Formal mentorship program (100% of entry-level hires participate)

The Sound-Off

- "They pay [interns] competitively, assign real projects, and have a multitude of events scheduled throughout the summer." —*Purdue senior**

- "They do a very good job of providing the necessary information and resources. At the end of your internship, you present to high-level executives." —*Michigan State senior**

*Data: Universum Communications

THE RECRUITER SPOTLIGHT

Name: Nancy E. Lange
Job: Director of U.S. Recruiting and Staffing

Why choose Eli Lilly: *At Lilly, employees find a collaborative environment that supports their contributions to our growing portfolio of products. Our future depends on a global community of people with diverse skills to help pioneer pharmaceutical innovation. Each employee's part in our efforts to develop health-care solutions makes a difference in the lives of our patients around the world.*

The wackiest technique used to get a job: *On more than one occasion, candidates have sent me a shoe, usually with a résumé inside. The tag line used was "wanted to get my foot in the door" in all cases. It's funny; the first time I received a shoe was in 2001, and it was a black wingtip. Most recently, I received a bright blue flip-flop. Because our policy states that in order to be considered for a position at Lilly, candidates must submit their résumé online, I'm not sure what the outcome was for the creative "shoe" candidates.*

Interview mistake to avoid: *We occasionally have candidates who give the answers they believe we want to hear rather than share their true experiences, or who are afraid to share any past mistakes with us for fear of being judged rather than have the mistake looked on as a learning experience. As long as you can demonstrate learning from something that didn't go as well as expected, don't hesitate to share it during an interview.*

Impressive prior work experience: *Our traditional jobs require the traditional experiences/majors—finance, marketing, biologists, information technology professionals, chemists, statisticians. What may be surprising to people are the degrees of the people we hire to be part of our sales force. We have found a variety of degrees to be relevant beyond those of business, MBA, or PharmD [Doctor of Pharmacy]. Many of our successful sales representatives have psychology, political science, and other liberal arts degrees.*

Johnson & Johnson

One Johnson & Johnson Plaza
New Brunswick, NJ 08933
Phone: 732-524-0400
Fax: 732-214-0332
Web Addresses: www.jnj.com;
www.jnj.com/careers

The Company

- Known for its baby products, Johnson & Johnson (J&J) also counts Tylenol, Motrin, Band-Aid, Neutrogena, and Splenda among its thousands of products. J&J owns 250 companies worldwide and is split up into three business segments: consumer, medical devices and diagnostics, and pharmaceutical.

- In 1982, after seven people died from ingesting cyanide-laced Tylenol, Johnson & Johnson responded by recalling over 30 million bottles of Tylenol and bringing the product back to market a few months later in tamper-proof packaging. This Tylenol recall is still regularly lauded as a best practices example in good management.

- Johnson & Johnson has long been known for its philanthropic efforts, which date back to the supplies it sent to victims of the 1906 San Francisco earthquake. The company has earned accolades in recent years for its sustainable environmental practices.

FAST FACTS

"Best Places to Launch a Career"
  Rank: 24
"Best Internships" Rank: N/A
Full-Time Salary: $55,000–$59,000
Entry-Level Hires: 479
Top College Major: Business/economics
3-Year Retention Rate: 70%
Stock Ticker: JNJ

The Suits

William C. Weldon: Chairman and CEO
Dominic J. Caruso: CFO
Christine A. Poon: Vice Chairperson
Russell C. Deyo: VP, General Counsel, and Chief Compliance Officer

The Stats

2007 sales: $61.1 billion
2007 net income: $10.6 billion
Market cap: $190.9 billion
Employees: 119,200
Locations: 57 countries around the world
Major competitors: Abbott, Merck, Pfizer
Largest operating units*:
Pharmaceuticals..............$24.9 billion
Medical Devices/
    Diagnostics ....$21.8 billion
Consumer Goods ....$14.5 billion
2007 sales

The Story

1887: Johnson & Johnson (J&J) is founded in New Brunswick, New Jersey

1893: Johnson's Baby Powder is introduced

1920: Earle Dickson invents Band-Aid brand bandages, which will remain one of J&J's most popular products for decades

1944: The company goes public on the New York Stock Exchange

1950s: Enters the pharmaceutical business with its acquisition of McNeil Laboratories

1974: Acquires Dr. Carl Hahn Company in Germany

1986: Acquires LifeScan, Inc., a manufacturer of glucose-monitoring products

1991: J&J's no-calorie sweetener Splenda is introduced

1994: Acquires Neutrogena Corporation

1998: The acquisition of orthopedic product manufacturer DePuy, Inc., is the largest in the company's history

2003: Acquires OraPharma, Inc.

2006: Acquires Pfizer Consumer Healthcare

The Skinny

Most important to recruiters: Leadership skills, communication skills, college major

Selectivity: N/A

Diversity of entry-level workforce: 38% minority; 59% female

Facts to know:

- A minimum GPA is required for many of J&J's Leadership Development Programs. A second language or experience living abroad is also highly desirable.

- Among the health-care and pharmaceutical companies on *Business-Week*'s list of "Best Places to Launch a Career," J&J spends the most on training new entry-level hires: $6,000 a head.

The Starting Gate

Undergraduate internships: 873

Duration of summer internship: 12 weeks

Average total compensation: $8,000

Interns by grade level:
Freshman 5%
Sophomore 10%
Junior..35%
Senior 50%

Interns who receive full-time job offers: N/A

Interns who are extended full-time job offers that accept: N/A

The Sliding Scale

Entry-level hires who had been interns: N/A

Most important performance measurements in entry-level hire: Productivity/efficiency, organization skills, customer satisfaction

Entry-level hires receiving signing bonuses: 40%

Average entry-level signing bonus: $3,000

Entry-level hires receiving performance bonuses: 100%

Average performance bonus during first year: $2,500

The Stand-Out Perks

- Educational expenses reimbursement
- Partial graduate school sponsorship
- 10 paid vacation days
- Access to 401(k) and cofunded pension
- Charitable gift match
- Relocation compensation (average contribution of $20,000)
- Employee discounts

The Skills

- Formal two-day orientation program that includes computer training, tour of facilities, enrollments, meeting with team members and business partners, lunch and dinner, and review of security procedures

- Information Technology Leadership Development Program, which consists of three rotations and lasts 104 weeks

- Formal mentorship program (30% of entry-level hires participate)

The Sound-Off

- "It is a six-month [internship] program, pays well, [has] housing compensation, [is a] good reference, [and has a] good intern-to-employee turnover." —*Butler junior**

- "Johnson & Johnson offers an internship program that allows each intern to undertake and complete a project on their own with the assistance of a senior mentor. They also finish the project with a presentation to senior leadership." —*Ohio State senior**

- "Johnson & Johnson offers a challenging co-op program that challenges students with real work, rather than run-around projects." —*Arizona State senior**

- "Johnson & Johnson offers a great internship program because of the possibility of the company paying for future education." —*Michigan State senior**

*Data: Universum Communications

THE RECRUITER SPOTLIGHT:

Name: Irene De Nigris
Job: Director, Global University Recruitment

Most memorable recruiting moments: *Several situations come to mind, [like] a time when a candidate wanted to stand out, so he came to the interview dressed as a clown (he stood out, but for the wrong reason), a time when a candidate came to the interview with a parent as a reference, [and] a time when a candidate brought a specialty food he had made to the interview to share with the recruiter.*

Worst interview offense: *Getting a company's name wrong in the interview is the worst, followed by a ringing cell phone. Arriving late can be excusable if there is a good reason. I want to know that a candidate made a conscious effort to interview with my company, so not knowing the company name is bad. A ringing cell phone is just rude, unless there is an emergency phone call the candidate is waiting for (wife having a baby, someone undergoing surgery, or something similar). Although I want candidates arriving on time, sometimes there are issues beyond their control. If a candidate is going to be more than several minutes late, he should call, advise what is causing the delay, and find out if the interviewer will still be able to conduct the interview if he is late.*

Why candidates should choose Johnson & Johnson: *The company's size and decentralized structure allow them to have the best of both worlds through working in a small entrepreneurial environment at one of our 250 operating companies in 57 countries, along with the big company impact of Johnson & Johnson.*

Merck

One Merck Dr.
Whitehouse Station, NJ 08889
Phone: 908-423-1000
Fax: 908-735-1253
Web Addresses: www.merck.com;
www.merck.com/careers

The Company

- Merck discovers, develops, manufactures, and markets vaccines and medicines that are then distributed in 140 countries. Areas of focus include Alzheimer's, cardiovascular disease, diabetes, vaccines, obesity, oncology, and pain and sleep disorders.

- In the fall of 2004, Merck yanked blockbuster arthritis drug Vioxx from store shelves after an internal study found that it increased the risk for heart attacks and strokes. Afterwards, the company was hit with over 27,000 lawsuits; it recently announced a $4.9 billion agreement that would settle the vast majority of the claims filed in the United States. (At the same time, Merck found itself facing patent expirations on several popular drugs, including cholesterol lowering Zocor in June 2006 and Fosamx in February 2008.)

- In May 2005, company veteran Richard Clark became CEO, implementing changes in strategy that included putting employees in

FAST FACTS

"Best Places to Launch a Career"
   Rank: 49
"Best Internships" Rank: N/A
Full-Time Salary: $60,000–$64,999
Entry-Level Hires: 887
On-Campus Recruiting: 94 schools
Dress Code: Business casual
Stock Ticker: MRK

much closer contact with patients and doctors.

- Merck received FDA approval for five new drugs in 2006, the most notable of which are Januvia, a cutting-edge diabetes drug available in one-a-day form, and Gardasil, the first vaccine for cervical cancer.

The Suits

Richard T. Clark: Chairman, President, and CEO
J. Chris Scalet: Senior VP of Global Services and Chief Information Officer
Peter N. Kellogg: Executive VP and CFO
Kenneth C. Frazier: Executive VP and President of Global Human Health
Peter S. Kim: President of Merck Research Laboratories
Bruce Kuhlik: Senior VP and General Counsel

The Stats

2007 sales: $24.2 billion
2007 net income: $3.3 billion
Market cap: $126.5 billion
Employees: 59,800
Locations: Offices, 28 manufacturing sites, 11 research facilities, and products sold in 140 countries in North America, Latin America, the Middle East, Asia, and Europe
Major competitors: Bristol-Myers Squibb, Pfizer, Sanofi-Aventis
Largest operating units*:
Pharmaceuticals..............$20.1 billion
Vaccines ....$3.8 billion
All Other ....$162.0 million
Corporate.....................$97.0 million
*2007 sales

📖 The Story

1891: George Merck organizes Merck & Co. in New York City

1899: Merck introduces (also known as *Merck's Manual of the Materia Medica—The Merck Manual*) a compact, handy medical reference guide that quickly gains popularity with those in the medical profession

1903: Merck opens a plant in Rahway, New Jersey

1933: Merck opens its first research lab

1942: First dose of penicillin is manufactured by Merck's Rahway lab

1944: Company develops the steroid Cortisone

1958: Merck releases an antihypertensive drug called Diuril

1987: Develops and donates Mectizan to halt the progression of river blindness in Africa

1997: Stocrin and Crixivan are launched for the treatment of HIV/AIDS

2004: Vioxx is pulled from the marketplace after being linked to heart attack and stroke risks

2006: Acquires Sirna Therapeutics; also launches five promising new medicines and vaccines, including diabetes drug Januvia and cervical cancer vaccine Gardasil

The Skinny

Most important to recruiters: College major, analytical skills, leadership skills

Selectivity: N/A

Diversity of entry-level workforce: N/A

Facts to know:

- Merck sweetened its vacation package in 2007 in an attempt to more effectively attract young talent.

- Although the average salary range for a new entry-level hire is in the $60,000 to $65,000 range, 14% of these hires earn $65,000 to $69,999, and 16% earn $70,000 and above.

- Merck's philanthropic efforts include increasing access to medications and a nonprofit branch that publishes neutral health information.

The Starting Gate*

Undergraduate internships: 194

Duration of summer internship: 10 to 12 weeks

Average total compensation: N/A

Interns by grade level:
Freshman ....N/A
Sophomore.................................N/A
Junior...18%
Senior 50%
College graduate 10%

Interns who receive full-time job offers: N/A

Interns who are extended full-time job offers that accept: N/A

*Note: Merck tracks only a portion of its interns.

The Sliding Scale

Entry-level hires who had been interns: N/A

Most important performance measurements in entry-level hire: Productivity/efficiency, quality, analytical skills

Entry-level hires receiving signing bonuses: N/A

Average entry-level signing bonus: N/A

Entry-level hires receiving performance bonuses: N/A

Average performance bonus during first year: N/A

The Stand-Out Perks

- Full and partial graduate school sponsorship

- 15 paid vacation days

- 401(k) with company match of up to 4.5% of salary and co-funded pension

- Charitable gift match

- Relocation compensation

The Skills

- Formal one-day orientation program

- Merck Manufacturing Development Program (MMDP), a formal rotational program that lasts 52 weeks

- Formal mentorship program

The Sound-Off

- "Merck offers a $5,000 stipend along with the internship." —*Georgia Tech junior**

- "Merck & Co. helps the students [interns] with everything from transportation to housing. In addition, it provides fun and educational activities in which the interns can engage." —*Arizona State junior**

- "Merck has a well-established [internship] program with assigned mentors and a series of workshops and seminars designed specifically for college interns." —*California Institute of Technology undergraduate**

- "I like Merck's internship program because it includes compensation as well as money to help pay tuition for the following school year. It also offers assistance finding housing and a large number of potential locations." —*Rensselaer Polytechnic sophomore**

*Data: Universum Communications

THE SUPERSTAR SPOTLIGHT

Name: Jason Johnson
Job: Senior Director of Molecular Informatics

Briefly describe your position and a typical day on the job:
I work at Merck's Seattle site, which is primarily focused on the application of genomic tools and technologies to help discover new medicines. The department that I lead develops new genomics methods, applies them in partnership with Merck therapeutic teams, and creates software tools to provide broader access across Merck. Much of my job now is collaboratively developing and implementing strategic plans for the role of informatics and genomics in the company's future.

Discuss the best part of your job: *The best thing about my job is that I get to work on one of the most fascinating scientific puzzles—the biological meaning of the human genome—and apply this research to one of the most meaningful problems—alleviating the burden of disease. It's definitely a rewarding situation to be surrounded by so many smart people that care so much about what they are working on.*

Advice for recent graduates just starting out: *In many areas of biotech and pharmaceutical research, things move so fast that, in my opinion, much—if not most—of the work that needs to happen doesn't fall cleanly into someone's job description, but falls between groups and roles. The people who figure out what the company really needs and act on it, reaching out to collaborate with other groups, become leaders quickly.*

St. Jude Medical

One Lillehei Plaza
St. Paul, MN 55117
Phone: 651-483-2000
Fax: 651-482-8318
Web Addresses: www.sjm.com;
www.sjm.com/careers/careerindex.aspx

The Company

- St. Jude Medical designs, manufactures, and distributes medical devices for heart and neurological conditions. The company was named after founder Manuel Villafana's newborn son Jude, who suffered from a life-threatening condition that required multiple operations. Villafana wanted to thank his son's talented surgeons as well as supportive friends and family members—many of whom had prayed to St. Jude, the patron saint of hopeless causes—for their continued support.

- St. Jude has a global-minded growth strategy. In 2007, the company began construction on phase one of an expansion of its global headquarters. Over 40% of its 2007 sales came from outside of the U.S., and the company's International Division recently established an international college recruiting program.

- In 2004 and 2005, several cardiac device companies including St. Jude, Medtronic, and Guidant came under scrutiny for several bypass and defibrillator devices that malfunctioned. Although St. Jude emerged relatively unscathed—its software flaw was comparatively minor, and the company diligently pledged to more closely scrutinize devices during production and manufacturing—recent concerns about a lead wire in its Riata defibrillator surfaced in November 2007.

- In fall 2007, St. Jude's restructured its management and moved a handful of executives to new roles in order to accommodate growth. St. Jude's also launched over 20 new ICD and pacemaker products during 2007, and overall revenues increased 14% over 2006. (The fourth quarter of 2007 was its first quarter ever with over $1 billion in sales.)

The Suits

Daniel J. Starks: Chairman, CEO, and President
John C. Heinmiller: CFO and Executive VP
Eric S. Fain: President of Cardiac Rhythm Management
Joseph H. McCullough: Group President
Michael T. Rousseau: Group President

The Stats

2007 sales: $3.8 billion
2007 net income: $559 million
Market cap: $13.9 billion
Employees: 12,000
Locations: Locations in more than 130 countries, with 20 operating and manufacturing facilities around the world (including in Brazil, Puerto Rico, Sweden, and the United States)
Major competitors: Medtronic, Boston Scientific, Abbott Labs, Johnson & Johnson, Pace Medical, Cordis, Biosense Webster
Largest operating units*:
Cardiac Rhythm
    Management ....$2.4 billion
Cardiovascular ....$790.0 million
Atrial Fibrillation ....$410.0 million
Neuromodulation........$210.0 million
*2007 sales

The Story

1976: St. Jude Medical is founded in St. Paul, Minnesota

1977: First implant of St. Jude Medical mechanical heart valve

1982: Obtains approval from the U.S. Food and Drug Administration (FDA) to sell mechanical heart valves in the United States

1994: Acquires Pacesetter, Inc., a Siemens AG pacemaker company

1996: Acquires tissue valve company Biocor

2000: One millionth St. Jude Medical mechanical heart valve implanted

2004: Obtains FDA approval for cardiac resynchronization therapy, a high-voltage device that is inserted into the human body like a regular pacemaker but that contains an extra lead to stimulate the heart's left ventricle; St. Jude's also acquires Irvine Biomedical, a catheter company

2005: Acquires Advanced Neuromodulation Systems (ANS), a neuromodulation device company

2006: Cardiac surgery and cardiology divisions of the business are combined into the Cardiovascular Division

The Skinny

Most important to recruiters: Teamwork skills, communication skills, analytical skills
Selectivity: 1 of 3 applicants hired in 2006, up from 1 of 5 applicants hired in 2005

Diversity of entry-level workforce: 52% minority; 39% female

Facts to know:

- St. Jude's 5-year retention rate is 97%, the highest among the nearly 100 companies in *Business Week*'s "Best Places to Launch a Career" ranking.

- The University-Planned Career Development Training programs are integrated university programs that allow employees to complete either a master's degree or a certificate or module for career progression on site. They can complete an MBA, an MS-BMS (Biotech Management Sciences), or an MS-MTM (Technical Management).

The Starting Gate

Undergraduate internships: 89

Duration of summer internship: 10 to 12 weeks

Average total compensation: $9,600

Interns by grade level:
Senior 90%
College graduate 10%

Interns who receive full-time job offers: 75%

Interns who are extended full-time job offers that accept: 98%

The Sliding Scale

Entry-level hires who had been interns: 60%

Most important performance measurements in entry-level hire: Integrity, intelligence, creativity

Entry-level hires receiving signing bonuses: None

Average entry-level signing bonus: N/A

Entry-level hires receiving performance bonuses: 10%

Average performance bonus during first year: $2,600

The Stand-Out Perks

- Educational expenses reimbursement ($5,000)

- Partial graduate school sponsorship

- 401(k) and profit-sharing plans

- Charitable gift match ($1,000)

- Relocation compensation

- Employee discounts

The Skills

- Formal one-day orientation program, including a tour of the facilities, benefits information, company overview, and so on

- The largest division (located in California) has a formal rotational program for entry-level hires

- University-planned Career Development Training program

- Formal mentorship program for entry-level hires in some divisions

THE SUPERSTAR SPOTLIGHT

Name: Angela Craig
Job: VP, Corporate Relations

Describe a typical day at work: *There is no typical day in Corporate Relations. That's what makes it interesting. One minute we're developing an integrated investor relations and communications strategy, and the next we're reviewing the impact of a specific piece of pending legislation. One minute I'm talking to an analyst about our earnings, and the next I'm developing ideas to raise general awareness of sudden cardiac death. It's terrific.*

Best part of your job: *The variety of the role and knowing that the company I work for exists to help and serve people. It's very gratifying.*

Career advice based on your own success: *I was hired as a VP here at 33 years old. The key to my success at both organizations where I have served as a senior executive was finding good mentors who ultimately championed my career, being honest and realistic about what I did and did not yet know as a young leader, and working hard every single day to help the organization achieve success. Ambition is a great asset if the focus of that ambition is team or organizational success.*

Describe the work environment/culture: *The culture at St. Jude Medical is focused on achieving success in the marketplace against some very large competitors by doing the right things in the right ways. There is never any question about whether we will be successful. Sometimes we suffer setbacks, but the culture here is to immediately look for another highway that will get us where we are going faster.*

Helpful interview tips: *The most impressive candidates that I see spend hours poring over information on my company beforehand, and they know our business as well as any outsider can before they walk through the door. This level of knowledge helps them answer questions in a sophisticated way that usually ends up putting them at the head of the pack.*

Kohl's

N56 W17000 Ridgewood Dr.
Menomonee Falls, WI 53051
Phone: 262-703-7000
Fax: 262-703-6143
Web Addresses: www.kohls.com;
kohlscareers.com/001KCareers/
index.htm

The Company

- Kohl's has grown from a single Wisconsin brick-and-mortar store into a nationwide department store chain with over 900 locations. The retailer offers both exclusive lines and established apparel and home product brands at discounted prices, and it also touts its spacious, easy-to-navigate, well-lit stores, which average 86,500 square feet in size.

- Kohl's expects to open 70–75 new stores in 2008, including its first units in the Miami/Fort Lauderdale/West Palm Beach market. Although a difficult retail market has led to disappointing financial results recently (2007 net sales grew 5.6% over the year before, but net income decreased by 2.2%), the company is still poised for growth. Kohl's celebrated the largest grand opening in its history by launching 80 new stores on a single day in October 2007.

- To compete with rivals that have introduced lower-cost lines from

top designers, Kohl's has contracted couture wedding gown designer Vera Wang to produce a women's collection called "Simply Vera" that debuted in fall 2007. Other recent partnerships include a line for women inspired by *Elle* magazine and a licensing agreement to carry Tony Hawk's line of clothing for young men.

👔 The Suits

R. Lawrence Montgomery: Chairman and CEO

Kevin Mansell: President and Director

Thomas Kingsbury: Senior Executive VP

Wesley McDonald: Executive VP and CFO

Richard Schepp: Executive VP, General Counsel, and Secretary

Jule Gardner: Executive VP and Chief Marketing Officer

The Stats

2007 sales: $16.5 billion
2007 net income: $1.1 billion
Market cap: $14.4 billion
Employees: 125,000
Locations: 929 stores in 47 states; distribution centers in Missouri, Texas, Georgia, New York, Wisconsin, California, and Virginia
Major competitors: J.C. Penney, Target, Old Navy, Fashion Bug, Sears, Macy's
Largest operating units: N/A

The Story

1962: The Kohl family opens its first store in Brookfield, Wisconsin

1978: The department store is acquired by BATUS Retail Group, which expands Kohl's from 10 to 39 stores throughout Wisconsin, Illinois, and Indiana during the period it owns the company

1986: Kohl's is purchased by a group of investors led by its own senior management

1992: Kohl's becomes a publicly traded company and begins a period of aggressive expansion, opening 11 new stores in 1993, 18 in 1994, and 22 in both 1995 and 1996

1997: Opens 32 new stores; moves into the Washington, D.C., Philadelphia, and Pittsburgh markets

2003: Having already expanded into the Southeast, Northeast, and South Central United States, Kohl's opens 28 stores in California, giving it a true coast-to-coast presence

2004: Increases holdings in California to 62 stores, making it Kohl's largest state; by the end of the 2004 fiscal year, Kohl's is operating 637 stores in 40 states

2005: Opens 95 new stores, including its first locations in Florida

2006: Adds 85 new locations and expands its collection of exclusive lines with the introduction of Tony Hawk and Chaps for Women and Boys

2007: Kohl's 23,000-square-foot design office opens in the heart of New York City's Garment District

The Skinny

Most important to recruiters: Communication skills, leadership skills, analytical skills

Selectivity: 1 of 20 applicants hired in 2006, down from 1 of 17 applicants hired in 2005

Diversity of entry-level workforce: 25% minority; 60% female

Facts to know:

- Kohl's offers internships in merchandising, product development, advertising/marketing, logistics, store administration, finance, real estate, information systems, merchandise presentation, design, and management.

- Kohl's actively recruited on 65 U.S. undergraduate campuses during the

2006–2007 school year and extended job offers on 60 of those campuses.

 The Starting Gate

Undergraduate internships: 143

Duration of summer internship: 10 weeks

Average total compensation: $5,000

Interns by grade level:
Sophomore 5%
Senior 95%

Interns who receive full-time job offers: 75%

Interns who are extended full-time job offers that accept: 65%

The Sliding Scale

Entry-level hires who had been interns: 50%

Most important performance measurements in entry-level hire: Learning ability, sales/revenue, analytical skills

Entry-level hires receiving signing bonuses: 100%

Average entry-level signing bonus: $2,000

Entry-level hires receiving performance bonuses: None

Average performance bonus during first year: N/A

The Stand-Out Perks

- Educational expenses reimbursement ($3,000)

- Partial graduate school sponsorship

- 15 paid vacation days

- Charitable gift match ($500)

- Relocation compensation

- Employee discounts on car rentals, gym memberships, cell phones/ service, insurance, cultural events, and publications

- Corporate office features on-site dry cleaning, day care, auto repair, and other such services

The Skills

- Formal two-day orientation program includes computer training, guest speakers, diversity exercises, team-building exercises, and tour of facilities

- Merchandise Analyst Trainee Program, a formal leadership program for entry-level hires that lasts 12 to 20 weeks

THE RECRUITER SPOTLIGHT

Name: Telvin Jeffries
Job: Executive VP, Human Resources

Advice for young job seekers: *We look for candidates who had balance in college between academics, work experience (summer jobs, internships, or after-school work), and extracurricular activities (clubs and volunteer organizations). Students who are heavily focused on academics alone sometimes lack strong people skills. A well-rounded student with strong leadership potential will probably have a successful transition.*

Why choose Kohl's: *Kohl's offers immediate responsibility and the opportunity to make an impact. We have individualized development programs and a collaborative and team-focused environment. Our company continues to grow. We have approximately 100 stores opening annually ... this brings with it career growth opportunities across the company. We have people who have all types of academic backgrounds, and we recruit people from most industries.*

Wackiest technique a job seeker has used: *One time someone sent us a shoe in a box with the words, "I am the right fit." While we didn't hire the candidate, we did grant an interview because of the creativity and boldness used.*

Faux pas to avoid: *Sometimes candidates forget that the interview process is a two-way street. We are interviewing them, and they are interviewing us. While it's important that you present yourself well, you need to be your authentic self. It's important that candidates come prepared to compete by selling themselves (communication), are ready to share their experiences (balance), and are able to differentiate themselves from the other candidates.*

Whether video résumés are ever a good idea: *In a field like acting or a visual media field, video résumés might be appreciated, but given the volume of résumés that we receive, recruiters are generally not able to appreciate the effort that might go into producing the video. I think, for now, a professional letter and résumé via the Web or U.S. mail is still a good bet.*

Macy's, Inc.

7 W. 7th St.
Cincinnati, OH 45202
Phone: 513-579-7000
Fax: 513-579-7555
Web Addresses: www.macys.com/;
www.macysjobs.com/macys

The Company

- Macy's, Inc., the nation's largest operator of department stores, is made up of two very different chains—midlevel retailer Macy's and its upscale counterpart Bloomingdale's.

- The retailing giant has hosted New York City's annual Macy's Thanksgiving Day Parade since 1924 and the city's Fourth of July fireworks extravaganza since 1976.

- In 2005, Macy's, Inc. (then called Federated) doubled in size when it acquired the May Department Stores Company. Federated sold May's Lord & Taylor, David's Bridal, and Priscilla of Boston stores and rebranded the remaining May's locations with the Macy's name. Unexpected merger costs hurt the company's financials, and its stock price dropped 25% in a year (October 2006–2007).

- Macy's, Inc. is divided into 10 retail divisions: Bloomingdale's, Macy's East, Macy's Florida, Macy's Midwest, Macy's North, Macy's Northwest, Macy's South, Macy's West, Macy's Home Store, and macys.com. It also has five support divisions specializing in systems, credit, logistics, marketing, and corporate services.

FAST FACTS

"Best Places to Launch a Career"
  Rank: 25
"Best Internships" Rank: 31
Full-Time Salary: $35,000–$39,999
Entry-Level Hires: 435
Top College Major: Business
3-Year Retention Rate: 65%
Stock Ticker: M

The Suits

Terry J. Lundgren: Chairman, President, and CEO
Thomas G. Cody: Vice Chair
Thomas L. Cole: Vice Chair
Janet E. Grove: Vice Chair
Susan D. Kronick: Vice Chair

The Stats

2007 sales: $26.3 billion
2007 net income: $893 million
Market cap: $11.2 billion
Employees: 182,000
Locations: 853 retail stores in 45 U.S. states, the District of Columbia, Puerto Rico, and Guam

Major competitors: Lord & Taylor, Nordstrom, JC Penney

Largest operating units*:
Department Stores ....N/A

*2007 sales

🔲 The Story

1858: R.H. Macy & Co. is founded when its namesake opens a fancy New York City–based dry goods store

1929–1930: Federated Department Stores is created when Abraham & Straus of Brooklyn, New York; Filene's of Boston, Massachusetts; F&R Lazarus & Co. of Columbus, Ohio; and Bloomingdale's of New York City merge and become one company

1945: Federated acquires Foley's, then makes the transition from holding-company to operating-company status to accommodate the company's rapid expansion

1976: Federated acquires Rich's, a retailer based in Atlanta, Georgia

1980: The Federated Foundation, a charitable trust, is established by Federated to give back to the community

1988: Real estate developer Robert Campeau buys Federated

1990: Federated files for bankruptcy

1992: Federated regains its financial footing

1994: R.H. Macy & Co. is acquired by Federated

2005: The May Department Stores Company, a former rival, is acquired by Federated

2006: Federated becomes Macy's Inc. and sells off its Lord & Taylor, David's Bridal, and Priscilla of Boston stores

The Skinny

Most important to recruiters: Analytical skills, communication skills, leadership skills

Selectivity: 1 of 20 applicants hired in 2006, down from 1 of 17 applicants hired in 2005

Diversity of entry-level workforce: 30% minority; 69% female

Facts to know:

- When Margaret Getchell was promoted to the position of store superintendent in 1866, Macy's, Inc., made history as the first retail store to hire a female executive.

- Macy's was among the first major corporate sponsors to support the fight against AIDS, launching an HIV/AIDS awareness campaign called "Passport" in 1982 and raising over $25 million for the cause in the years since.

🔲 The Starting Gate

Undergraduate internships: 274

Duration of summer internship: 10 weeks

Average total compensation: $5,600

Interns by grade level:

Sophomore 10%

Junior..20%

Senior 70%

Interns who receive full-time job offers: 77%

Interns who are extended full-time job offers that accept: 67%

▦ The Sliding Scale

Entry-level hires who had been interns: 26%

Most important performance measurements in entry-level hire: Leadership ability, sales/revenue, analytical skills

Entry-level hires receiving signing bonuses: None

Average entry-level signing bonus: N/A

Entry-level hires receiving performance bonuses: None

Average performance bonus during first year: N/A

The Stand-Out Perks

- Employee merchandise discounts at Macy's and/or Bloomingdale's stores

- Educational expenses reimbursement

- Unlimited time off for religious observances

- Charitable gift match ($22,500)

- Relocation compensation

- Employee discounts on gym memberships, cell phone service, insurance, cultural events

The Skills

- Formal five-day orientation program, including guest speakers, diversity exercises, team-building exercises, tour of facilities, and computer training

- Performance Through People, a formal, 10-week leadership program

- Formal mentorship program (90% of entry-level hires participate)

The Sound-Off

- "Macy's West is a structured, split internship exposing interns to two crucial aspects: management and buying." —*University of California, Berkeley senior**

- "Macy's West [internship] is half management and half buying, so it is like you are having two internships in one summer. It gives you an opportunity to see both sides of the retail industry to decide which one you are a better fit with." — *University of Arizona senior**

*Data: Universum Communications

THE ENTRY-LEVEL SPOTLIGHT

Name: John Rabold

Job: Assistant Buyer in Macy's South Division

Macy's as an entry-level employer: *The training program the company has created is second to none and really helps develop young professionals into experienced merchants in a short period of time. As a company, Macy's practices exactly what it says it stands for—by being completely loyal, extremely determined to be the best, and being focused on a genuine "team-first" philosophy.*

Work environment: *Macy's South [in Atlanta, Georgia] has a very diverse workforce that includes—in my opinion—a very caring and friendly group of professionals who work together as a cohesive unit. The atmosphere is young and fresh and completely oriented toward giving customers fashion and trends in every merchandise category.*

Best aspect of job: *I really enjoy dealing with different apparel vendors and seeing how the retail industry truly works behind the scenes. It is definitely cool to get firsthand insight into new fashion assortments long before they are introduced to the public. It's also very nice working toward the company's goal of delivering fashion and affordable luxury to our customers.*

Advice for young job seekers: *A person can get noticed by taking initiative with his or her business and truly applying what was learned during training. Young employees can also help themselves by consistently being on time— even early—to all meetings and work-related events. Feeling comfortable and confident in giving suggestions or your opinion in meetings is also a great way to be noticed.*

Walgreen Co.

200 Wilmot Rd.
Deerfield, IL 60015
Phone: 847-914-2500
Fax: 847-914-2804
Web Addresses: www.walgreens.com;
www.walgreens.com/about/careers/
default.jsp

The Company

- Walgreens is the nation's largest pharmacy retail chain by sales, serving nearly 5 million customers daily. Leading the drugstore industry in retail sales and profits last year, the company plans on opening 550 new stores in fiscal year 2008. It is currently expanding its healthcare services beyond traditional pharmacy through Walgreens Health Services, its managed care division, and Take Care Health Systems, a wholly owned subsidiary that manages convenient care clinics located in drugstores.

- The company's rich history includes notable benchmarks that range from inventing the malted milkshake to being one of the very first American companies to establish profit-sharing and pension plans.

- To maintain the neighborhood appeal of a corner druggist, Walgreens still opens all of its new stores on street corners. The company also remains steadfastly United States–focused in an age of

global expansion: though Walgreens bought Mexican retailer Sanborn's in 1943, it sold the asset in 1984 and hasn't invested in international ventures since.

The Suits

Jeffrey A. Rein: Chairman and CEO
Gregory D. Wasson: President and COO
Mark A. Wagner: Executive VP of Store Operations
Trent E. Taylor: Executive VP and President of Walgreens Health Services

The Stats

2007 sales: $53.8 billion
2007 net income: $2 billion
Market cap: $37.8 billion
Employees: 226,000
Locations: 5,997 stores in 48 U.S. states and Puerto Rico

Main competitors: Rite-Aid, Target, CVS, Wal-Mart

Largest operating units*:
Retail Drug Stores ....$53.8 billion
*2007 sales

The Story

1901: Charles R. Walgreen Sr. buys the Chicago drugstore where he works as a pharmacist and renames it Walgreens

1909: The second Walgreens store opens

1916: Nine Walgreens stores are incorporated as Walgreen Co.

1922: Walgreens invents the malted milkshake

1926: The 100th Walgreens store opens in the Chicago metro area

1927: Walgreen Co. becomes a publicly traded company

1939: Charles Walgreen Jr. takes over as the company's president

1943: Opens a nonprofit store in the Pentagon that is in operation until the 1980s

1950: Begins building self-service instead of clerk-service stores and becomes the largest self-service retailer in the United States by 1953

1969: Charles Walgreen III becomes president

1982: Next-day photofinishing is made available chain-wide

1992: Opens its first store with a drive-through pharmacy

2006: Acquires Happy Harry's drugstore chain

2007: Acquires Take Care Health Systems

The Skinny

Most important to recruiters: Communication skills, leadership skills, analytical skills

Selectivity: N/A

Diversity of entry-level workforce: 46% minority; 68% female

Facts to know:

- This profile includes data only on employees who were hired or promoted to entry-level assistant manager or staff pharmacist positions. Corporate office entry-level positions aren't included. By this definition, 75% of employees are assistant store managers, who start out at approximately $35,000 a year, and 25% of entry-level hires are pharmacists, who start out in the $70,000 salary band.

- Of Walgreens' 79 senior executives (VP level or above), 60 have been there for 20 years or more.

The Starting Gate

Undergraduate internships: 2,092

Duration of summer internship: 10 weeks

Average total compensation: N/A

Interns by grade level: N/A

Interns who receive full-time job offers: N/A

Interns who are extended full-time job offers that accept: N/A

The Sliding Scale

Entry-level hires who had been interns: N/A

Most important performance measurements in entry-level hire: Customer satisfaction, leadership ability, analytical skills

Entry-level hires receiving signing bonuses: N/A

Average entry-level signing bonus: N/A

Entry-level hires receiving performance bonuses: N/A

Average performance bonus during first year: N/A

The Stand-Out Perks

- Educational expenses reimbursement ($16,500 for pharmacy students)

- Child-care facilities typically available at corporate headquarters

- Employee discounts

The Skills

- Formal orientation program

- Management Training Program, a formal eight-week leadership program

- Formal mentorship program for entry-level hires

The Sound-Off

- "I had the best mentor one could ask for, who tailored the [internship] program to include my career goals. I was able to practice my management/leadership skills and apply my degree to help the store gain competitiveness in the area." —*Former intern*

- "If you get to store manager, Walgreens is a good career, [because] you're making pretty good money—with big bonus potential—and you're basically running your own store. The best tip I could give someone looking at getting there is to be very "buddy buddy" with your district manager, the rest of the district staff, and all other store managers in your district. Also, try starting in a region where Walgreens is building stores, since most of the time a store manager position opens up because of [the opening of a] new store." —*Former retail management intern*

THE SUPERSTAR SPOTLIGHT

Name: Gary Nephew

Job: District Pharmacy Supervisor

Promotions: *I started as an intern in the last year of pharmacy school in 2004, got promoted to staff pharmacist, then pharmacy manager, and I am now a district supervisor watching over 28 stores.*

Briefly describe a typical day: *There isn't really a typical day, but a normal day would include store visits. We go to a store and look over operations. I normally get to two to three stores per day, meet with pharmacy managers and technicians, and go over operations and what they can do to improve. Then there's hiring and discipline and all sorts of fun stuff.*

Best part of the job: *I get to interact with our corporate headquarters and people in the stores. Interaction with a lot of people is definitely the coolest thing.*

Advice for ambitious young students interested in pharmacy: *Be prepared, and ask lots of questions [during your interview]. I definitely talked to many people who were in the positions that I had been trying to interview for. I also had good trainers. The other advice I would give [once you've gotten the job] is to ask a lot of questions. As a staff pharmacist, I tried to learn how to be a pharmacy manager, and when I was a pharmacy manager, I tried to learn how to be a district supervisor.*

Cisco Systems

170 W. Tasman Dr.
San Jose, CA 95134
Phone: 408-526-4000
Fax: 408-526-4100
Web Addresses: www.cisco.com;
www.cisco.com/go/universityjobs.com

The Company

- Cisco is the world's leading network equipment maker. Since the company's inception, Cisco engineers have been leaders in the development of Internet Protocol (IP)-based networking technologies. The company's core development areas include routing and switching, as well as advanced technologies such as application networking, data center, digital media, IPICS, mobility, security, storage networking, TelePresence, unified communications, and video.

- The company recently received some unwanted media criticism for selling routers to China that could be individually configured to block specific Web sites. However, Cisco maintains that these are the same routers sold worldwide and weren't preconfigured to restrict access.

- Cisco's business has been centered around selling routing, switching, and firewall services to large corporations. However, the company has made notable moves into

FAST FACTS

"Best Places to Launch a Career" Rank: 77
"Best Internships" Rank: N/A
Full-Time Salary: N/A*
Entry-Level Hires: 646
Top College Major: Engineering
Maximum Annual Education Reimbursement: $7,500
Management Training Program: Yes
Stock Ticker: CSCO
*57% make $70,000 and above (includes Masters and Ph.D. candidates)

the personal networking arena with acquisitions including Linksys (2003), which manufactures routers for small businesses and homes and Scientific Atlantic (2006), which specializes in digital/cable television and home broadband networking.

The Suits

John T. Chambers: Chairman and CEO
Dennis D. Powell: Executive VP and CFO
Randy Pond: Executive VP of Operations, Processes, and Systems
Charles H. Giancarlo: Executive VP and Chief Development Officer
Richard Justice: Executive VP of Operations and Business Development

The Stats

2007 sales: $34.9 billion
2007 net income: $7.3 billion
Market cap: $164.2 billion
Employees: 63,050
Locations: Operates in 76 countries and has offices in 24; it is headquartered in San Jose, California
Major competitors: Juniper Networks, Nortel, Siemens
Largest operating units*:
Switches ....$12.5 billion
Advanced Technologies ....$8.1 billion
Routers ....$6.9 billion
Service.............................$5.5 billion
Other ....$2.0 billion
*2007 sales

The Story

1984: Stanford University computer scientists Len Bosack and Sandy Lerner invent a multiprotocol router and found Cisco Systems; the company is named for San Francisco, gateway to the Pacific Rim

1986: Hires first employee

1990: Goes public with Nasdaq stock exchange ticker CSCO

1998–1999: John Chambers meets with China's then-president Jiang Zemin to discuss the nation's telecommunications future; Cisco purchases optical transport companies Cerent and Monterey Networks, for a combined $7.4 billion acquisition

2000: Becomes the world's most valuable company at the zenith of the dot-com boom; makes motion picture history by successfully transmitting the first film ever over the Internet—20th Century Fox's animated adventure film, *Titan A.E.*

2003: Acquires Linksys, the popular manufacturer of broadband and wireless routers for small businesses and homes, in an effort to extend Cisco's reach into the home

2006: Purchases Scientific Atlanta, a Georgia-based company specializing in digital/cable television and home broadband networking, further extending its reach into the personal networking arena

2007: Acquires web conferencing company WebEx for $3.2 billion

The Skinny

Most important to recruiters: Communication skills, leadership skills, analytical skills

Selectivity: N/A

Diversity of entry-level workforce: N/A

Facts to know:

- The Cisco Networking Academy, a comprehensive e-learning program, provides students with Internet technology skills. Since its creation in 1997, over 1.6 million students in 163 countries have enrolled at more than 10,000 academies.

- Cisco doubled its entry-level hires in 2007, to 646—and 9 out of every 10 new hires were former interns.

The Starting Gate

Undergraduate internships: 332

Duration of summer internship: 12 weeks

Average total compensation: N/A

Interns by grade level:
Freshman 9%
Sophomore 19%
Junior...44%
Senior 20%
College graduate 8%

Interns who receive full-time job offers: N/A

Interns who are extended full-time job offers that accept: N/A

The Sliding Scale

Entry-level hires who had been interns: 85%

Most important performance measurements in entry-level hire: Leadership ability, sales/revenue generation, learning ability

Entry-level hires receiving signing bonuses: N/A

Average entry-level signing bonus: N/A

Entry-level hires receiving performance bonuses: N/A

Average performance bonus during first year: N/A

The Stand-Out Perks

• Educational expenses reimbursed ($7,500 undergraduate; $10,000 graduate)

• Partial graduate school sponsorship

• Relocation compensation

• On-site cafes, free snacks and beverages, and health screenings

The Skills

• One-day orientation program

• "Cisco-Choice" program for some entry-level engineers

• Associate Sales Representative and Associate Systems Engineer (ASR/ASE) Training Program, which lasts 26 to 52 weeks

• Human Resources Leadership Program, which consists of two to four rotations and lasts two years

The Sound-Off

• "As for benefits (i.e., life and health insurance, stock options, salary, etc.), Cisco *far* exceeds the top 50 companies listed [for 'Best Places.']" — *Young Cisco employee*

• "Best internship offer that I received in the form of compensation, benefits, and overall importance. I really feel like I am a part of the company and have learned a lot." —*San Jose State University senior**

*Data: Universum Communications

THE ENTRY-LEVEL SPOTLIGHT

Name: Jennifer Overgaag
Job: Systems Engineer

Briefly describe a typical day: *On a typical day, I will start by checking e-mails and taking care of administrative tasks. Then, depending on what I have scheduled that day, I will head out to customer meetings. I love interacting with our customers, so this is my favorite part of the day. Between meetings, I will find a coffee shop or cafe and work on follow-up from my meetings. I also try to block off a few hours each week for personal development, to keep up-to-date with new technologies and Cisco Solutions.*

Best part of the job: *No two days are the same, and I am interacting with new people constantly. This keeps me on my toes, because I never know who I will meet next or what questions they will be asking of me as their systems engineer. I also really enjoy working with other members of my team. Every day I am impressed with their skill level and their willingness to help out when I have a question. Since my first day, I have been extremely impressed with Cisco's philanthropic focus and commitment to giving back. I very seldom meet a coworker who is not involved in the community; I really like that.*

Advice for young job seekers interested in Cisco: *They say that starting a job at Cisco is like trying to drink from a fire hose. If you are able to manage your time effectively and absorb the stream of new information being given to you, you will definitely get noticed.*

Dell

One Dell Way
Round Rock, TX 78682
Phone: 512-338-4400
Fax: N/A
Web Addresses: www.dell.com;
www.dell.com/careers

The Company

- Founded by young college dropout Michael Dell in 1984, Dell quickly grew into one of the world's largest PC makers by utilizing a revolutionary direct sales model that cut out the middleman and allowed customers to order computers—and choose which bells and whistles they wanted on their PC—directly over the phone and the Internet. Dell then built the units from scratch, an approach that cut down on overhead. Using a similar sales approach, Dell has aggressively expanded into the server and printer markets over the past decade.

- Despite its many early successes, Dell has taken a number of hits in the past five years, including a massive recall that was issued when faulty Sony batteries used in 2.7 million Dell laptops caused the computers to overheat and catch fire. In 2007, founder Michael Dell parted ways with longtime first lieutenant Kevin Rollins, who had been appointed CEO in 2004 when Dell stepped down, and reinstalled himself in the role.

FAST FACTS

"Best Places to Launch a Career" Rank: 61
"Best Internships" Rank: N/A
Full-Time Salary: $50,000–$54,999
Entry-Level Hires: 1,425
Top College Majors: Finance, Engineering
3-Year Retention Rate: N/A
Stock Ticker: DELL

The Suits

Michael S. Dell: Founder, Chairman, and CEO
Donald J. Carty: Vice Chairman and CFO
Paul D. Bell: Senior VP and President of Americas

The Stats

2007 sales: $57.4 billion
2007 net income: $2.6 billion
Market cap: $54.9 billion
Employees: 82,200
Locations: 51 countries, with corporate headquarters in Texas, Singapore, and the United Kingdom
Major competitors: Hewlett-Packard, Lenovo, Apple
Largest operating units*:
Desktop PCs ....$19.8 billion
Mobility ....$15.5 billion
Software and Peripherals ..$9.0 billion
Servers and Networking....$5.8 billion

Enhanced Services ....$ 5.1 billion
Storage ....$2.3 billion
*2007 sales

The Story

1984: Michael Dell founds Dell Computer Corporation

1987: Dell opens a subsidiary in the United Kingdom, expanding the company internationally

1988: The company goes public

1991: Unveils the first of the Latitude line of laptop computers

1996: Dell introduces a new way to buy PCs when it allows customers to buy their computers directly from the company at Dell.com; Dell makes the Standard & Poor's 500 Index and then branches out into the server business

1999: Surpasses Compaq as the leading seller of personal computers in the United States

2001: Achieves a number-one ranking in global market share for the first time

2003: The company name is changed to Dell Inc. to reflect its growing product line

2005: Faulty motherboard capacitors on some Dell computers cause $300 million in losses

2006: Acquires hardware manufacturer Alienware

2007: Investors file class-action lawsuits against Dell, claiming that the company withheld information regarding faulty hardware; Michael Dell returns as CEO

The Skinny

Most important to recruiters: Communication skills, leadership skills, work experience

Selectivity: N/A

Diversity of entry-level workforce: 56% minority; 32% female

Facts to know:

• Though many of Dell's current internship openings are in the company's home base of Texas, it has additional opportunities nationwide for MBA students and young professionals.

• Prospective candidates can stay up to date on Dell's University Relations news on its blog at http://direct2dell.com/one2one/archive/category/1034.aspx.

 ## The Starting Gate

Undergraduate internships: 74

Duration of summer internship: 12 weeks

Average total compensation: N/A

Interns by grade level:
Junior...5%
Senior 30%
College graduate*.......................65%

*The interns listed as "college graduates" are mostly MBA-level candidates based on the need of the company at the time. Dell has since shifted to a higher mix of undergraduates.

Interns who receive full-time job offers: 80%

Interns who are extended full-time job offers that accept: 45%

The Sliding Scale

Entry-level hires who had been interns: 35%

Most important performance measurements in entry-level hire: Leadership ability, analytical skills, being a team player

Entry-level hires receiving signing bonuses: 100%

Average entry-level signing bonus: $4,000

Entry-level hires receiving performance bonuses: 100%

Average performance bonus during first year: $4,000

The Stand-Out Perks

- Educational expenses reimbursement ($3,000)

- Full and partial graduate school sponsorship

- Charitable gift match ($3,000)

- Relocation compensation

- Employee discounts

The Skills

- Formal one-day orientation program

The Sound-Off

- "Allowed for highly visible project work for interns that was extremely cross-functional in nature." —*Penn State senior**

- "Dell offers challenging [internship] assignments with diverse departmental opportunities, as well as the chance to see a monumental shift in marketing/manufacturing focus within a prestigious company." —*Michigan State senior**

*Data: Universum Communications

THE RECRUITER SPOTLIGHT

Name: Sherri Sides
Job: University Relations Manager

Advice for young prospective employees: *Do the homework and understand the company objectives, financials, and challenges. This will help candidates articulate why they are interested in working for Dell. While still in school, they should also gain work experience through internships—if not directly at Dell, then anywhere that will allow them to develop the skills and experience needed to stand out. And they should apply directly to the Dell job postings at www.dell.com/careers. Students enrolled on campuses where Dell recruits have a great opportunity to learn about the company by attending sponsored events and signing up for interviews through their career center. They can also get involved with professional associations through their campus student organizations. Many Dell employees participate in these groups, which is a great way to network.*

Interview faux pas a candidate should avoid: *(1) Being late. It sends a bad message about a candidate's interest in the company, and one can never take back that first impression. (2) Chewing gum. This is distracting and isn't appropriate in an interview. (3) Parents at the interview. Take charge of the interview process and avoid getting parents involved at this stage. Companies want to know that candidates are self-reliant and in charge of their careers. (4) Demonstrating poor body language during the interview process. It's not impressive and shows a lack of interest.*

Why young job seekers should choose Dell: *Dell is an exciting place to grow new careers. The environment is fast-paced, innovative, and always changing. We do not have the typical bureaucratic, hierarchical mentality; instead, employees are encouraged to look for opportunities to improve the company and are given the freedom to run with great ideas. We are a meritocracy, so the team is rewarded based on performance. I would recommend Dell to anyone who wants to work in a fun, challenging environment that is driven to win.*

Hewlett-Packard

3000 Hanover St.
Palo Alto, CA 94304
Phone: 650-857-1501
Fax: 650-857-5518
Web Addresses: www.hp.com;
www.jobs.hp.com

The Company

- Hewlett-Packard (HP) has been on the forefront of communications technology since 1939; many consider the Palo Alto-based company to be the founder of Silicon Valley. In 2006, HP—a maker of LaserJet printers, printing supplies, and desktop PCs—became the world's largest IT corporation in terms of sales when it passed IBM in annual revenue.

- HP can trace its humble beginnings to the Palo Alto, CA garage where cofounders Bill Hewlett and David Packard teamed up to work on ideas for sound equipment aids. HP ultimately created some of the first-ever oscillators to be used in a "modern" movie theater.

- Former HP chairman and CEO Carly Fiorina, one of the country's first high-profile female chief executives, resigned on February 9, 2005, in part because of HP's rocky performance following a controversial 2002 merger with Compaq that she helped push through.

- In 2006, several HP officials were charged with committing fraud and identity falsification after it emerged that they'd hired investigators to illegally spy on certain reporters and HP board members in order to pinpoint the source of press leaks. CEO Mark Hurd, who had already spearheaded an impressive post-Fiorina turnaround, didn't let the controversy throw him. HP continued posting impressive financial results and the stock price surged by approximately 25% over the next year. Recent big deals include a seven-year contract with NASA; Hurd was also named "*BusinessWeek*'s 2007 Business Person of the Year."

The Suits

Mark Hurd: Chairman, CEO, and President
Todd Bradley: Executive VP of the Personal Systems Group
Jon Flaxman: Executive VP and Chief Administrative Officer
Michael Holston: Executive VP, General Counsel, and Secretary
Vyomesh (VJ) Joshi: Executive VP of the Imaging and Printing Group

The Stats

2007 sales: $104.3 billion
2007 net income: $7.3 billion
Market cap: $130 billion
Employees: 172,000
Locations: Though its major operations and headquarters are located in California, HP operates in more than 170 countries and has several hundred offices located globally
Major competitors: Intel, Sun, IBM, Dell
Largest operating units*:
Personal Systems ....$36.4 billion
Imaging/Printing............$28.5 billion
Enterprise Storage and
   Services ....$18.8 billion
HP Services ....$16.6 billion
HP Software ....$2.3 billion
HP Financial Services ......$2.3 billion
Corporate
   Investments ....$762.0 million
Corporate...................–$1.4.0 billion
*2007 sales

The Story

1939: Bill Hewlett hatches the idea for a low-cost device to measure audio frequencies in his master's thesis at Stanford. He teams up with David Packard in a Palo Alto garage (now a California historic landmark) and the two even bake paint in Lucile Packard's oven after which, she jokes, "the roast beef never tastes quite the same."

1948: Offers insured pension plan for employees with at least five years loyalty to HP

1957: HP is taken public at $16 a share

1964: HP's atomic clocks, engineered to maintain accurate time for 3,000 years, garner praise

1968: Introduces the first scientific desktop calculator, calling the device a "personal computer"

1972: Unveils the world's first handheld scientific calculator; becomes "first U.S. electronics firm to be invited to China for trade discussions"

1984: Sells first thermal InkJet and LaserJet printers for desktops

1999: HP creates a spin-off company, Agilent Technologies, to take over the company's non-computer-related businesses; Agilent becomes Silicon Valley's largest initial public offering ever

2002: Merges with Compaq; creates first tablet PC

2005: CEO Carly Fiorina resigns, and Mark Hurd is appointed the new CEO

2007: Earnings jump 17% over 2006; HP is awarded a seven-year NASA contract worth up to $5.6 billion

The Skinny

Most important to recruiters: College major, analytical skills, communication skills

Selectivity: N/A

Diversity of entry-level workforce: 36% minority; 32% female

Facts to know:

- Throughout its history, HP has been a pioneer in employee benefits. HP was one the first organizations to offer companywide "disaster" health insurance, stock grants to employees, and a "telecommuting" option to its workers.

The Starting Gate

Undergraduate internships: 605

Duration of summer internship: 10 to 12 weeks

Average total compensation: $13,071

Interns by grade level:
Freshman 7%
Sophomore 7%
Junior...15%
Senior 30%
College graduate 41%

Interns who receive full-time job offers: 44%

Interns who are extended full-time job offers that accept: 40%

 ## The Sliding Scale

Entry-level hires who had been interns: 33%

Most important performance measurements in entry-level hire: Productivity/efficiency, analytical skills, sales/revenue

Entry-level hires receiving signing bonuses: 10%

Average entry-level signing bonus: $8,750

Entry-level hires receiving performance bonuses: 100%

Average performance bonus during first year: $8,400

The Stand-Out Perks

- Educational expenses reimbursement ($5,000)

- Charitable gift match ($1,000)

- Relocation compensation

- Employee discounts

The Skills

- Formal two-day orientation program that includes computer training, guest speakers, diversity exercises, team-building exercises, and tour of facilities

- Offers Human Resources Management Associate Program, which is rotational and lasts 72 weeks

THE SUPERSTAR SPOTLIGHT

Name: Daniel Puga

Job: Research and Development Director—IPG Enterprise Software

Briefly describe a typical day: *My organization is spread across several geographies, both in the United States (Roseville, California; Boise, Idaho; and Austin, Texas) and overseas (Bangalore, India, and Porto Alegre, Brazil). My time is typically spent in the following areas: (1) Meetings to discuss the portfolio and roadmap of our products and solutions to ensure that we have our resources deployed in the right areas to get our solutions to market with the right business models. (2) Meetings to evaluate the current status of development activities that are currently underway and to ensure that we can proactively remove barriers and adjust to ensure a successful delivery. (3) Meetings with customers to understand and solve their current issues and to identify opportunities for future solutions. (4) Meetings with key partners both inside and outside the company. (5) Mentoring discussions and looking for our next great leaders within our organization and looking at opportunities for them to grow.*

Your quick rise through the ranks: *Early in my career, I let my manager know what my career goals were. We had an in-depth conversation about what that meant, and that it wouldn't happen by accident. I needed to begin developing myself if I expected to achieve those goals. He encouraged me to go back for my MBA [Northwest Nazarene University], which really opened my eyes to leadership and business management. I have also tried to ensure that I stay coachable and learn as much as I can from the people around me. I also looked at other leaders whom I would like to emulate.*

Advice for young professionals: *Make sure your management team is aware of your career goals. When opportunities come around, it is critical that your management team knows you and considers you for those opportunities. Seek out mentoring. Do your job with passion, integrity, and humility. People need to trust in your integrity. Humility ties in with integrity. When you make a mistake, you have to be willing to take responsibility for it, learn, and move on. Always hire great people, and get them in the right roles!*

Intel

2200 Mission College Blvd.
Santa Clara, CA 95054
Phone: 408-765-8080
Fax: 408-765-9904
Web Addresses: www.intel.com;
www.intel.com/jobs

The Company

- Intel is the nation's longstanding leader in semiconductor technology; the company manufactures and sells the microprocessors (as well as network cards, flash memory, motherboard chips, and more) used in desktops, laptops, and computer servers. PC makers Dell and Hewlett-Packard are Intel's largest corporate clients, accounting for 35% of the company's total sales.

- Intel and competitor Advanced Micro Devices (AMD) began the first of many clashes in the mid-1980s, engaging in a heated seven-year legal battle over whether upstart AMD was allowed to make copies of Intel's industry-dominating microprocessor chip. (In 1995, AMD was awarded the right to license Intel's software.)

- Despite making a little-seen (and little-understood) product, Intel is one of the most recognizable brands on the planet thanks to its innovative "Intel Inside" campaign (launched in 1991). Thousands of

Intel's PC-maker customers are licensed to display a sticker with Intel's name and logo, ensuring that the company name is prominently displayed on millions of Intel-powered machines.

The Suits

Craig Barrett: Chairman
Paul Otellini: President and CEO
Andy Bryant: Executive VP and Chief Administrative Officer
Sean Maloney: Executive VP, General Manager of the Sales and Marketing Group, and Chief Sales and Marketing Officer
Arvind Sodhani: Executive VP and President of Intel Capital
David Perlmutter: Executive VP and General Manager of Mobility Group

The Stats

2007 sales: $38.3 billion
2007 net income: $6.9 billion
Market cap: $155.9 billion
Employees: 86,300
Locations: Corporate offices and production centers are located in over 50 countries in North and South America, Europe, and Southern Asia
Major competitors: AMD, Sun Microsystems, Texas Instruments, Hewlett-Packard
Largest operating groups*:
Digital Enterprise
    Group ....$20.3 billion
Mobility Group..............$14.7 billion
All Other.........................$3.3 billion
*2007 sales

The Story

1968: Three engineers—Robert Noyce, Gordon Moore, and Andy Grove—from Fairfield Semiconductor form Intel (INTegrated ELectronics) in Mountain View, California

1971: Intel releases the 4004 microprocessor

1981: Intel's 8088 chip is chosen for IBM's Personal Computer

1998: Intel releases the Celeron processor

2000: Releases the Pentium 4 processor

2000: Recalls hundreds of thousands of motherboards with defective chips and cancels production of low-cost microprocessors for budget PCs

2001: Management announces phase-out of consumer electronics operations

2005: Begins supplying Apple with chips for Macintosh

2005: Joins with Micron Technologies to develop IM Flash Technologies

2006: Because of market share losses, cuts $1 billion from spending and terminates 1,000 management jobs

2007: Wins contract to supply Sprint-Nextel with technologies for its WiMAX network-based infrastructure; puts $2.5 billion into a wafer fabrication plant in Dalian, China

The Skinny

Most important to recruiters: College major, college GPA, work experience

Selectivity: 1 of 8 applicants hired in 2006, down from 1 of 5 applicants hired in 2005

Diversity of entry-level workforce: 49% minority; 29% female

Facts to know:

• In 2006, Intel invested $380 million in employee training and development.

• Philanthropic initiatives include Intel Teach® programs which have trained nearly 5 million teachers in over 40 nations on how to use technology to help students learn, and Intel Learn® educational programs for elementary and high school students in developing countries.

The Starting Gate

Undergraduate internships: 1,710

Duration of summer internship: 12 weeks

Average total compensation: $16,000

Interns by grade level*:

Freshman 1%
Sophomore 3%
Junior..10%
Senior 26%
College graduate 60%

*All information in this section includes graduate-level interns. Half of the interns listed as "college graduates" are currently candidates for an advanced degree.

Interns who receive full-time job offers: 58%

Interns who are extended full-time job offers that accept: 78%

The Sliding Scale

Entry-level hires who had been interns: 21%

Most important performance measurements in entry-level hire: Team player (other traits depend on the business and the job requirements)

Entry-level hires receiving signing bonuses: 35%

Average entry-level signing bonus: $7,033

Entry-level hires receiving performance bonuses: 100%

Average performance bonus during first year: $1,600

The Stand-Out Perks

- 15 paid vacation days and 10 paid holidays
- Educational expenses reimbursement
- 401(k) and Supplemental Retirement Program, where company contributes between 7% and 12.5% of salary (approximately 8% in recent years) in profit sharing
- Charitable gift match ($10,000)
- Relocation compensation ($21,000)
- 65 days paid maternity leave

The Skills

- One- to two-day orientation program
- Rotation Engineer and Business Program, which consists of three to four rotations and lasts 52 weeks
- Formal mentorship program (75% of entry-level hires participate)

The Sound-Off

- "Good compensation; expect interns to perform to new-hire standards. They train you but inform you they are not there to hold your hand." —*Penn State student**
- "I took on two real, full-time engineering projects in three months. I learned more in those months interning than in a year of school." —*Arizona State senior**

*Data: Universum Communications

THE SUPERSTAR SPOTLIGHT

Name: Leyla Najafi
Job: Program Manager/Systems Engineer

Briefly describe your work culture: *To summarize: work hard, play hard. The culture at Intel is very fast-paced. People are motivated and driven to get things done. And it definitely helps that the people here are incredibly smart. The schedules and requirements force you to quickly learn how to multitask. Another aspect of the culture is the egalitarian mindset. Intel really pushes for this.*

Best part of the job: *I work in a group called Digital Health, which focuses on improving health care through the use of technology. That in itself is very cool: to know that your work is going to improve people's lives! I'm currently working on some independent-living technologies by managing some aspects of a user trial and providing system engineering support. I'm currently working on some independent-living technologies by managing some aspects of a user trial and providing system engineering support [Najafi, age 23, received a BS in mechanical engineering from the University of California, Berkeley]. And it's great to know that I'm going to make an impact because it's not busywork.*

Tips for ambitious young employees: *A big part of it is not only doing a good job and working hard, but making sure to communicate that. Communicating what you're doing not only to your manager, but to your peers and sometimes even your second-level manager (if appropriate) can make a difference. Take advantage of the fact that you're new, and if anything doesn't make sense, seek to understand it. One thing that I've heard successful people at Intel say is that you don't want to just point out that something is wrong, but try to find a solution. Being new, we are more likely to question certain processes and steps that are taken, which can bring about a positive change (such as simplifying required steps or saving money).*

IBM

1 New Orchard Rd.
Armonk, NY 10504
Phone: 800-426-4968
Fax: 914-765-7382
Web Addresses: www.ibm.com;
www.ibm.com/employment/

The Company

- Information technology giant, International Business Machines Corporation (IBM), operates through three business segments: Systems and Financing, Software, and Services. "Big Blue" (a popular nickname for IBM) is shifting its focus to the software and services arenas. IBM's software business was just 20% of the company's total revenue in 2006, but it contributed 40% of total profits. The company expects half of its profits to come from software by 2010.

- IBM employs five Nobel Prize winners. On top of that, Big Blue filed for more new U.S. patents than any other company last year—an accomplishment it has achieved for 14 years in a row.

- In May 2007, IBM unveiled Project Big Green, whose purpose is to redirect $1 billion in funds annually to business practices that will decrease the company's carbon footprint.

⚑ FAST FACTS

"Best Places to Launch a Career"
   Rank: 4
"Best Internships" Rank: 9
Full-Time Salary: $60,000–$64,999
Entry-Level Hires: 1,962
Top College Major: Computer science
3-Year Retention Rate: 90%
Stock Ticker: IBM

👔 The Suits

Samuel J. Palmisano: Chairman, President, and CEO
Mark Loughridge: CFO, Senior VP
Ginni Rometty: Senior VP of Global Business Services
Mike Daniels: Senior VP of Global Technology Services
Doug T. Elix: Senior VP and Group Executive of the Sales and Distribution Group

The Stats

2007 sales: $98.8 billion
2007 net income: $10.4 billion
Market cap: $149 billion
Employees: 386,558
Locations: Operates in 170 countries, including the United States, Australia, Canada, Germany, China, Denmark, India, Italy, Japan, South Korea, the Netherlands, England, Hong Kong, Poland, Singapore, Sweden, and France

Major competitors: EDS, Hewlett-Packard, Microsoft

Largest operating units*:

Global Technology
Services ....$36.1 billion
Systems and Technology ..$21.3 billion
Software ....$20.0 billion
Global Business Services ..$18.0 billion
Global Financing..............$2.5 billion
Other ....$842.0 million

*2007 sales

📖 The Story

1911: Three companies merge to become the Computing-Tabulating-Recording Company

1924: Changes its name to International Business Machines Corporation (IBM)

1937: Makes history when it becomes one of the first companies to offer paid vacations

1944: Introduces Mark I, the Automatic Sequence Controlled Calculator, which weighs in at nearly five tons, measures over 50 feet in length, and is the first machine to compute long calculations automatically

1957: Invents the first computer disk storage system

1969: IBM computers are present on Apollo 11 and aid in humans' first steps on the moon; the U.S. government also begins a sweeping, 13-year antitrust investigation of IBM this year

1976: Installs the IBM 3800, which is the first printer to utilize both lasers and electrophotography

1981: Introduces the IBM Personal Computer (PC)

1985: Uses "token-ring architecture" to connect computers, printers, and other equipment in large buildings

1992: Introduces the ThinkPad, one of many versions of its signature notebook computer

1997: Chess champ Garry Kasparov loses his first match ever to IBM supercomputer Big Blue

2004: Launches the World Community Grid, the world's largest public computing grid

2005: Sells PC division to Lenovo for approximately $1.3 billion

2007: Unveils nanotechnology breakthrough

The Skinny

Most important to recruiters: Analytical skills, leadership skills, communication skills

Selectivity: 1 of 70 applicants hired in 2006, up from 1 of 75 applicants hired in 2005

Diversity of entry-level workforce: 42% minority; 40% female

Facts to know:

- On any given day, over 40% of IBM's workforce is working virtually (from home, on the road, or at a client location).

- On "Think Fridays," employees develop skills and meet with mentors.

The Starting Gate

Undergraduate internships: 2,805

Duration of summer internship: 10 to 12 weeks

Average total compensation: $15,000

Interns by grade level:
Freshman 4%
Sophomore 15%
Junior...39%
Senior 22%
College graduate 20%

Interns who receive full-time job offers: 50%

Interns who are extended full-time job offers that accept: 88%

The Sliding Scale

Entry-level hires who had been interns: 24%

Most important performance measurements in entry-level hire: Analytical skills, leadership ability, customer satisfaction

Entry-level hires receiving signing bonuses: 55%

Average entry-level signing bonus: $2,000

Entry-level hires receiving performance bonuses: 92%

Average performance bonus during first year: $1,500

The Stand-Out Perks

• Full graduate school sponsorship

• Educational expenses reimbursement

• 15 paid vacation days

• 401(k) plan with company match of up to 6% of salary (IBM makes an automatic 1% contribution, regardless of participation in plan)

The Sound-Off

• "There were lots of others interns to interact with at and after work. I got exposure to other business areas and was considered for full-time employment." —*Clarkson University senior**

• "The company only cares about the bottom line.... The managers only care about their potential bonuses.... If IBM has a management training program, it's news to me." —BW *Discussion Board*

• "The culture, resources, image, products, locations, events, and other factors . . . make IBM a great place to intern." —*University of Puerto Rico student**

• "It's heavily bureaucratic, and IT commands the company. . . Young employees spend a ton of time on the bench." —*Young IBM employee*

*Data: Universum Communications

THE RECRUITER SPOTLIGHT

Name: Julie Baskin Brooks
Job: Staffing Leader for the Americas

Wackiest behavior by job seeker: *A candidate approached the IBM booth at a job fair with a magnetic white board that served as his résumé. He had completed the résumé using magnetic words and phrases and was prepared to tailor it on the spot if we did not see the skills we needed.*

Whether someone can redeem him- or herself if late for an interview: *Absolutely—being honest with a plausible and valid explanation is the best way to redeem oneself. We all recognize that things happen that are beyond an individual's control.*

Other interview faux pas that candidates should avoid: *Lying, not being prepared, poor humor, poor hygiene, overdressed or underdressed, revealing clothing, sharing inappropriate stories, talking inappropriately about current or former employees, and overconfidence to the point of arrogance.*

Why choose IBM: *IBM provides opportunities for people who are willing to stretch themselves, take calculated risks, and want to be part of an evolving organization. As a leader in technology and innovation, we're a global company offering a world of opportunities to be part of something big and make your mark.*

Microsoft

One Microsoft Way
Redmond, WA 98052
Phone: 425-882-8080
Fax: 425-706-7329
Web Addresses: www.microsoft.com;
www.microsoft.com/careers

The Company

- Microsoft is not only the architect
  of the Windows software used for
  some 92% of personal computers
  worldwide, but also boasts a diverse
  tech portfolio that includes a gaming console, an MP3 player, and
  myriad Web products. However, its
  empire has been threatened by a
  number of innovations from key
  competitors—ranging from Nin-
  tendo's Wii gaming system to
  Google's formidable search engine
  and ever-growing stable of Internet
  offerings. Microsoft, which still
  remains the world leader in software
  services, is hardly ready to back
  down in the other arenas. In February 2008, it announced an unso-
  licited takeover bid for search engine
  Yahoo!, which fended off these
  unwanted advances until Microsoft
  withdrew its offer in early May.

- Over the years, Microsoft has bat-
  tled antitrust complaints in places
  ranging from the United States to
  Europe, and even Korea. In 2001,
  Microsoft successfully overturned a
  U.S. judge's order on appeal that

FAST FACTS

"Best Places to Launch a Career"
  Rank: 6
"Best Internships" Rank: N/A
Full-Time Salary: $70,000 and above
Entry-Level Hires: 1,350
Top College Major: Computer science
3-Year Retention Rate: 75%
Stock Ticker: MSFT

would have forced the company to
break itself up.

- In July 2008, Bill Gates will transition out of a day-to-day role in the
  company to devote more time to
  his charitable work through the Bill
  & Melinda Gates Foundation.

The Suits

William H. Gates III: Chairman
Steven A. Ballmer: CEO
B. Kevin Turner: COO
Ray Ozzie: Chief Software Architect
Craig Mundie: Chief Research and
  Strategy Officer

The Stats

2007 sales: $51.1 billion
2007 net income: $14.1 billion
Market cap: $333.1 billion
Employees: 78,565 (as of June 30,
  2007)
Locations: Headquarters in Washington State

Major competitors: Google, Apple, IBM, Oracle

Largest operating units*:
Microsoft Business..........$16.4 billion
Server and Tools ....$11.2 billion
Client ....$14.8 billion
Entertainment & Devices..$6.1 billion
Online Services Business ..$2.5 billion
Unallocated and Other..$141.0 million
*2007 sales

The Story

1975: High school pals Bill Gates and Paul Allen establish Microsoft in Albuquerque, New Mexico

1981: Microsoft becomes an incorporated company, and IBM releases a personal computer using the Microsoft MS-DOS 1.0 operating system

1986: Corporate headquarters are moved to Redmond, Washington, and the company's stock goes public

1989: The earliest version of the Microsoft Office suite is released

1995: Windows 95 is introduced

1998: A formal antitrust complaint is filed against Microsoft by the U.S. Department of Justice

2001: Windows and Office XP are launched; the company also introduces its first gaming console, called Xbox, this year

2006: Bill Gates announces that he will minimize his role at the company beginning in 2008 in order to devote more time to his foundation and philanthropic work

2007: Windows Vista and the 2007 Microsoft Office suite are introduced

2008: Launches a bid to buy Yahoo!; withdraws its $47.5 billion offer in May

The Skinny

Most important to recruiters: Analytical skills, individual excellence, work experience

Selectivity: N/A

Diversity of entry-level workforce: 38% minority; 27% female

Facts to know:

- Roughly 90% of entry-level employees are given private offices. Microsoft also offers a fitness club membership to its employees.

- Microsoft provides emergency backup day care. Other parental-related perks include paid maternity leave (up to 60 days) and paid paternity leave (up to 20 days), adoption assistance, "Babies and You" seminars, external parenting resources, and "new mother" rooms on campus.

The Starting Gate

Undergraduate internships: 1,113

Duration of summer internship: 12 to 24 weeks

Average total compensation: N/A

Interns by grade level:

Sophomore 4%

Junior...24%

Senior 72%

Interns who receive full-time job offers: N/A

Interns who are extended full-time job offers that accept: N/A

🎛 The Sliding Scale

Entry-level hires who had been interns: 23%

Most important performance measurement in entry-level hire: Performance against commitments

Entry-level hires receiving signing bonuses: 17%

Average entry-level signing bonus: $4,438

Entry-level hires receiving performance bonuses: 100%

Average performance bonus during first year: $6,000

The Stand-Out Perks

- Educational expenses reimbursement ($7,500)

- 25 paid vacation days

- On-site cafeterias, Ping-Pong tables in every lobby, and free premium Starbucks coffee; discounts on software and financial services

- Charitable gift match ($12,000)

The Skills

- Three-day orientation program that includes guest speakers, instruction on benefits enrollment, and a business overview

- Managing at Microsoft, an online course for employees interested in learning how to lead in the company; and Exploring Management, a one-day conference available to attendees nominated by their managers

- Formal mentorship program (30% of entry-level hires participate)

The Sound-Off

- "Great quality of work, great work-life balance, a great deal of intern-related events—very strong! I had a great summer." —*University of Pennsylvania senior**

- "Working at Microsoft allows me to test the latest software before it's released to the public. Bugs from beta software can be frustrating, but at least I can help fix a problem before it reaches hundreds of millions of customers." —*Microsoft financial analyst*

- "Microsoft has a really great internship program. It's not only for engineers, but also for business-focused students as well. During the summer, interns are even invited to Bill Gates's house for dinner!" —BW *Discussion Forum*

*Data: Universum Communications

THE RECRUITER SPOTLIGHT

Name: Scott Pitasky
Job: General Manager of Staffing

Interview faux pas, like a ringing cell phone: *It's not a deal breaker if your cell goes off by accident. The key is to relax and not get overly stressed about a small hiccup such as this. Things like this happen. What we look for is how you react in the moment. If it totally derails your thinking and causes you too much stress, then that might be a concern for how you would deal with other challenges on the job. If you apologize and simply get back on track with the thoughtful discussion that was underway, then you'll be fine.*

Most impressive job-candidate behavior: *Earlier this year, we had a candidate from Michigan whom we offered to fly out to Seattle for an interview. However, because of some recent medical problems with his ears, this person was unable to fly. But that didn't stop him. Without hesitation, he packed his camper and hit the road with his dog, Amber. He made stops every 600 miles or so and continued his journey across the nation to Seattle to interview with us. I love this story because it shows the amazing lengths people will go to in order to follow their passion.*

Why choose Microsoft: *You will work alongside incredibly smart and passionate people who truly enjoy what they do. They thrive on tackling some of the biggest and most interesting challenges in our industry and driving new innovation and cutting-edge technology that has a broad impact around the world. The breadth of opportunity at Microsoft is unmatched—from using technology to find a cure for malaria, to developing new platforms for the way millions will play games, to taking on entirely new areas, like robotics.*

Motorola

1303 E. Algonquin Rd.
Schaumburg, IL 60196
Phone: 847-576-5000
Fax: 847-576-5372
Web Addresses: www.motorola.com;
www.motorolacareers.com/

The Company

- Though most people recognize Motorola for its pocket-sized, ultra-modern MOTORAZR V3 phone, the company has been responsible for a number of audio electronics innovations in the past 80 years. It developed one of the first handheld two-way radios, which became the standard on battlefields during World War II, and created one of the first commercially successful car radios. Roughly 35 years ago, Motorola also created the world's first portable cell phone.

- The company is a pioneer in the field of management theory, having invented a statistically based, efficiency-focused business strategy called "Six Sigma" in 1986, which has been put into use by hundreds of corporations.

- Motorola's earnings plummeted from $3.7 billion in 2006 to a $49 million loss in 2007. The "mobile services" segment has experienced the sharpest decline. Motorola—which has come under heavy fire

FAST FACTS

"Best Places to Launch a Career"
 Rank: 87
"Best Internships" Rank: 59
Full-Time Salary: $50,000–$54,999
Entry-Level Hires: N/A
Top College Major: Engineering
3-Year Retention Rate: N/A
Stock Ticker: MOT

from angry shareholders including activist investor Carl Icahn, who owns roughly 6% of the company—has announced it will spin off its ailing wireless handset division and create two separate publicly-traded companies in 2009. The search is underway for a CEO to run this new cell phone handset company, which will include the RAZR phone and other wireless devices.

The Suits

Gregory Q. Brown: President and CEO
Paul J. Liska: Executive VP and CFO
Patricia B. Morrison: Executive VP and Chief Information Officer
A. Peter Lawson: Executive VP, General Counsel, and Secretary
Gene Delaney: President of Government and Public Safety

The Stats

2007 sales: $36.6 billion
2007 net income: Loss of $49 billion
Market cap: $36.6 billion
Employees: 66,000
Locations: Approximately 73 countries, with major operations in Brazil, China, Germany, Malaysia, Mexico, Singapore, Taiwan, the United Kingdom, and the United States
Major competitors: Samsung, Nokia
Largest operating units*:
Mobile Devices ....$19.0 billion
Home and Networks
  Mobility ....$10.0 billion
Enterprise Mobility
  Solutions ....$7.7 billion
*2007 sales

The Story

1928: Paul and Joseph Galvin form the Galvin Manufacturing Corporation

1930: Galvin Manufacturing Corporation creates the first car radio, which is branded with the name "Motorola"—a combination of "motorcar" and "ola"—which is used to imply sound in motion

1943: Devises walkie-talkies; company goes public

1947: Company changes its name to Motorola

1955: Adopts the stylized modern "M" logo that still is used today

1963: Develops the first "truly rectangular" color television tube, which becomes the industry standard

1969: Uses a transponder to transmit the first words spoken on the moon to Earth

1984: Begins selling the world's first portable cellular phones

1986: Invents the Six Sigma Quality Process, which is used to reduce defects and improve the quality of business processes

1996: Releases the world's smallest and lightest phone at the time, the StarTAC Wearable Phone

2004: Introduces the MOTORAZR V3

2008: Announces it will split itself into two separate publicly-traded companies

The Skinny

Most important to recruiters: College major, leadership skills, college GPA, relevant experience

Selectivity: N/A

Diversity of entry-level workforce: N/A

Facts to know:

• New hires can apply for a new position after a year; if they have their manager's approval, they may do so in even less time.

• Motorola offers co-ops in addition to internships. Co-ops are full-time opportunities that are 16 weeks in length and take place during either the spring or the fall semester. Most universities provide some semester credit for co-op terms.

The Starting Gate

Undergraduate internships: 714

Duration of summer internship: 12 weeks

Average total compensation: N/A

Interns by grade level: N/A

Interns who receive full-time job offers: 40%

Interns who are extended full-time job offers that accept: 90%

The Sliding Scale

Entry-level hires who had been interns: N/A

Most important performance measurements in entry-level hire: Analytical skills, productivity/efficiency, leadership ability

Entry-level hires receiving signing bonuses: N/A

Average entry-level signing bonus: N/A

Entry-level hires receiving performance bonuses: N/A

Average performance bonus during first year: N/A

The Stand-Out Perks

- Educational expenses reimbursement
- New-graduate loans
- 22 paid vacation days
- Employee discounts

- 401(k) plan with company match of up to 4% of salary

The Skills

- One-day orientation program that includes guest speakers and a tour of the facilities
- Formal mentorship program

The Sound-Off

- "I have been with [Motorola] for 5 semesters and 2 summers. I have had the opportunity to work on many engaging projects and have consequently learned a lot." —*University of Illinois senior**

- "The company assigns the interns important projects, which helps them with problem solving and business skills." —*Penn State junior**

- "A great place for recent graduates. They give you a lot of responsibility from the start and have a great mentor program to help you adjust… Motorola encourages a healthy lifestyle with extremely flexible hours… Managers are attentive to training and tracking new hires' progress. Creativity is celebrated, and new ideas are recognized. Even with the senior leadership, new hires have a voice." —*Entry-level Motorola employee*

*Data: Universum Communications

THE ENTRY-LEVEL SPOTLIGHT

Name: Seun Phillips
Job: Electrical Engineer (Audio)

Briefly describe your company's culture: *People at Motorola are smart and laid back—and they love to have fun. My group and I work hard, but we also know how to have fun at the same time. We try to get together as much as possible, whether it be to grab some lunch, go to a sporting event, or grab a quick drink after work.*

Weirdest/funniest thing encountered on the job: *My friends' perceptions of how all employees at Motorola are swimming in phones. I probably get at least one request a week for a phone and/or Motorola accessory. Contrary to what people believe, just because one works for Motorola does not mean that one can distribute phones like candy. The requests seriously keep me laughing. Keep them coming, my friends!*

Describe a typical day: *I come in [between] 8:30 a.m. and 9 a.m. and immediately log into my computer to check my e-mail. My coworker and I will get a glass of water to start off our day. It's like a ritual—if one of us does not come in on any given day, we feel like there is something missing. My primary job responsibility at Motorola is to handle all audio issues/concerns pertaining to our current project. This involves numerous tests, meeting with suppliers, meeting with the audio experts at Motorola, and thinking outside the box about what music experience customers want. Depending on the day, I will either play basketball/volleyball and/or work out with my coworkers during lunch or after work. Go to bed, wake up, and repeat, with a little twist here and there.*

AT&T

175 E. Houston St.
San Antonio, TX 78205
Phone: 210-821-4105
Fax: 210-351-2071
Web Addresses: www.att.com;
www.att.jobs

The Company

- AT&T Inc. has come full circle. The one-time telecom monopoly was broken up into smaller regional companies after losing a government antitrust suit in 1984, only to become the world's largest telecom company once again following a 2006 merger with BellSouth, giving AT&T consolidated ownership of Cingular Wireless and Yellow-pages.com. In recent years, AT&T has expanded the services available to its over 100 million customers to include high-speed Internet and wireless capabilities.

- The company branded itself "the new AT&T" after the 2006 merger and announced that it will begin offering future services, such as "U-verse"—a technology that uses Internet Protocol (IP) to deliver television, Internet, and voice telephone to the consumer in one package.

- The new AT&T also secured the exclusive rights to sell Apple's iPhone until 2012. However, some members of Congress, as well as

consumers, have derided the move as anticompetitive.

- Is it 1984 all over again? Not quite. With cable-based providers increasingly going head to head with the telecom giants on a number of fronts, it's an extremely competitive time to be in the market. The battle is being waged in the courtroom—and also the R&D lab—making the industry a scary but exciting field for recent grads who want to be on the cutting edge of communications technology during a period of flux and change.

The Suits

Randall L. Stephenson: Chairman and CEO
Richard G. Lindner: Senior Executive VP and CFO
John T. Stankey: Group President of Telecom Operations

Wayne Watts: Senior Executive VP and General Counsel
William A. Blase Jr.: Senior Executive VP of Human Resources

The Stats

2007 sales: $118.9 billion
2007 net income: $12 billion
Market cap: $252.1 billion
Employees: 303,700
Locations: Retail locations throughout the United States; communications in the United States, Puerto Rico, and the U.S. Virgin Islands
Major competitors: Verizon, Sprint Nextel, Qwest, Cox Communications
Largest operating units*:
Wireline ....$64.0 billion
Wireless...........................$38.6 billion
Directory Assistance ....$4.8 billion
Other ....$11.6 billion
*2007 sales

The Story

1876: Alexander Graham Bell invents the telephone

1984: The Bell System is divested, and AT&T does away with its local telephone operations but maintains its long distance and manufacturing branches; Southwestern Bell and BellSouth are two of the seven regional companies created after the divesture

1997: Pacific Telesis Group is acquired by SBC Communications Inc. (formerly Southwestern Bell)

1998: SBC acquires Southern New England Telecommunications

1999: SBC acquires Ameritech Corporation

2005: SBC Communications Inc. acquires AT&T Corp. to form "the new AT&T"

2006: AT&T and BellSouth merge, consolidating ownership of Cingular Wireless and Yellowpages.com

The Skinny

Most important to recruiters: College major, college GPA, leadership skills

Selectivity: 1 of 14 hired in 2006, up from 1 of 18 hired in 2005

Diversity of entry-level workforce: 35% minority; 29% female

Facts to know:

- AT&T's Summer Management Program (SMP) is designed for undergraduate/graduate students who are within one year of graduation.

- AT&T has a policy whereby employees are given a specific number of vacation days based on their years of service, plus an additional seven personal days each year.

The Starting Gate

Undergraduate internships: N/A

Duration of summer internship: 10 to 12 weeks

Average total compensation: N/A

Interns by grade level:
Freshman 5%
Sophomore 20%
Junior...28%
Senior 20%
College graduate 27%

Interns who receive full-time job offers: N/A

Interns who are extended full-time job offers that accept: N/A

The Sliding Scale

Entry-level hires who had been interns: 17%

Most important performance measurements in entry-level hire: Leadership ability, team player, learning ability

Entry-level hires receiving signing bonuses: N/A

Average entry-level signing bonus: N/A

Entry-level hires receiving performance bonuses: N/A

Average performance bonus during first year: N/A

The Stand-Out Perks

- Educational expenses reimbursement ($5,250)
- Charitable gift match ($15,000)
- Relocation compensation (depending on situation)
- Employee discounts
- Free health, dental, and vision plan

The Skills

- Most new hires attend either a classroom or Web-based orientation that lasts approximately four hours, which is part of a larger initial training program that lasts an average of six weeks
- AT&T Sales Apprentice Program, which lasts a maximum of 24 weeks
- The Leadership Development Program (LDP) is a rotational program that lasts from 24 to 28 months
- Formal mentorship program

THE RECRUITER SPOTLIGHT

Name: Scott Grant
Job: Associate Director of Management Staffing

Wackiest interview technique you've encountered: *At a job fair in Texas, an applicant walked up to the AT&T booth and proceeded to sing a song about his qualifications for employment. He sang the song "My Girl," originally performed by The Temptations. Instead of the words "I've got sunshine on a cloudy day," he sang "I've got experience that you'll want today." The song was very entertaining and lasted for nearly two minutes. Unfortunately, the individual's skills were not a match for any of our open positions, but he was applauded and received an "A" for effort.*

Why choose AT&T: *Operating globally under the AT&T brand, AT&T is recognized as the leading worldwide provider of IP-based communications services to businesses and the leading U.S. provider of wireless, high-speed Internet access, local and long-distance voice, and directory publishing and advertising services. AT&T employs the most talented individuals from all backgrounds and perspectives to provide products and services that meet its customers' needs.*

Sprint Nextel

2001 Edmund Halley Dr.
Reston, VA 20191
Phone: 703-433-4000
Fax: 703-433-4343
Web Addresses: www.Sprint.com;
www.sprint.com/careers

The Company

- Sprint Nextel is the product of Sprint's 2005 acquisition of Nextel Communications, a merger that combined the respective number three and number five U.S. wireless service providers. Over three-quarters of the company's sales are from its wireless services, which include a 49% stake in U.K.–based call provider Virgin Mobile.

- Sprint Nextel lost 300,000 customers in 2006 and was forced to cut 5,000 full-time jobs in 2007. The company is banking on a number of new partnerships, including a joint venture with Time Warner and Cox to deliver cable, home phone, and wireless access in one package; and its newly formed partnership with Intel, Samsung, and Motorola to develop WiMAX technologies.

- The firm's most distinctive offering to its customers is its walkie-talkie capability, which allows direct communication between users in select Western Hemisphere countries, or to up to 20 other users simultaneously.

FAST FACTS

"Best Places to Launch a Career"
  Rank: 46
"Best Internships" Rank: 25
Full-Time Salary: $50,000–$54,999
Entry-Level Hires: 150
Top College Major: Engineering
3-Year Retention Rate: 63%
Stock Ticker: S

The Suits

Dan Hesse: President and CEO
William G. Arendt: Acting CFO
Keith Cowan: President of Strategic Planning and Corporate Initiatives
Paget L. Alves: Acting President of Sales & Distribution
John A. Garcia: Acting Chief Marketing Executive

The Stats*

2007 sales: $40.1 billion
2007 operating income: $1.4 billion
Market cap: $37.3 billion
2006 Employees: 60,000
Locations: Retail locations throughout the United States, as well as former Nextel divisions and other Sprint Nextel affiliates in the Philippines, Argentina, Brazil, Mexico, and Peru
Major competitors: AT&T Mobility, T-Mobile, Verizon, ALLTEL

Largest operating units[†]:

Wireless...........................$34.7 billion

Wireline ....$6.5 billion

*Unaudited results

†2007 sales; unaudited

The Story

1899: Jacob Brown and his son Cleyson found Brown Telephone Company in Abilene, Kansas

1925: Brown Telephone Company is incorporated into United Telephone and Telegraph

1965: After a period of losses and inactivity, United Utilities (it changed its name during the Depression) buys North Electric, an independent producer of phone equipment

1970: SPRINT (Southern Pacific Railroad Intercommunications) is formed

1972: United Utilities becomes United Telecommunications

1983: Sprint is acquired by General Telephone and Electronics (GTE), forming GTE Sprint Communications

1985, Following the breakup of AT&T, United Telecommunications buys GTE's 50% share of GTE Sprint, creating U.S. Sprint

1998: Sprint and Internet provider Earthlink combine their Internet units

1998: Sprint assumes ownership and management control of Sprint PCS, its wireless joint venture with TCI, Cox Communications, and Comcast

2000: Sprint and MCI Worldcom abandon their planned merger because of the U.S. Department of Justice's unfavorable terms

2005: Sprint acquires Nextel Communications to form Sprint Nextel

The Skinny

Most important to recruiters: Analytical skills, communication skills, college GPA

Selectivity: 1 of 9 applicants hired in 2006, down from 1 of 6 applicants hired in 2005

Diversity of 2006 internship class: 68% minority; 35% female

Facts to know:

- An award-winning Military Recruitment Program that includes a guarantee that Sprint will pay the difference between military pay and salary if an employee is called to active military duty (their family also continues receiving benefits).

- Employees who work at Sprint Operations headquarters in Overland Park, Kansas, have access to an Employee Health Center—as do their spouses and dependents (age 16 and up).

The Starting Gate

Undergraduate internships: 94

Duration of summer internship: 10 to 12 weeks

Average total compensation: $9,838

Interns by grade level:
Sophomore 9%
Junior...20%
Senior 65%
College graduate 6%

Interns who receive full-time job offers: 80%

Interns who are extended full-time job offers that accept: 85%

The Sliding Scale

Entry-level hires who had been interns: 25%

Most important performance measurements in entry-level hire: Learning ability, effort, revenues/sales

Entry-level hires receiving signing bonuses: 91%

Average entry-level signing bonus: $1,314

Entry-level hires receiving performance bonuses: 100%

Average performance bonus during first year: $529

The Stand-Out Perks

- Educational expenses reimbursement ($5,250)

- 15 paid vacation days

- 401(k) plan with company match of up to 5% of salary

- Charitable gift match ($5,000)

The Skills

- Two-day orientation program, including guest speakers, a tour of the facilities, diversity exercises, team-building exercises, and exposure to company executives

- New College Hire Development Program, which consists of three rotations and lasts 104 weeks

- Formal mentorship program (100% of entry-level hires participate)

The Sound-Off

- "Sprint is [a] paid[internship] and it will allow me to see what actually goes on in a business to business setting. I will be able to go on sales calls and learn firsthand." —*James Madison student**

- "The corporate culture at Sprint is very relaxed, and the people are friendly. Participating in programs such as the New College Hire Development Program (NCHDP) gives you the opportunity to learn about different aspects of Sprint and network with many high-level executives. The possibilities for career development are endless." —*NCHDP analyst**

*Data: Universum Communications

THE SUPERSTAR SPOTLIGHT

Name: Steve Kezirian
Job: VP, Telesales

Describe a typical day: *I find myself in a number of broad cross-functional meetings that address numerous issues. It may sound like a lot, but I like to limit my meetings to around 65% of each day. During the remainder of the time, I respond to e-mails and voicemails, and I spend more informal time with less senior team members. Lastly, I spend approximately 50% of my time on the road (and the other 50% in one of our two major locations in Overland Park, Kansas or Reston, Virginia).*

Your rise through the ranks: *Fresh out of school [Harvard University graduate] and new to both telecom and Sprint, I was given an opportunity to help manage the marketing rollout of our new high-speed wireless data service. In this capacity, I was exposed to various individuals from across the organization. Not only did this experience provide a crash course in "wireless," but it also provided me with insight into the structure, needs, and overall nuances of our matrix organization. Since then, I have focused on two things: working for individuals who will continue to nurture my professional development, and seeking out "stretch" assignments that will provide significant responsibility and/or take me out of my own comfort zone.*

Advice on how to communicate with higher-ups: *Know your audience! Often, when speaking with a higher-level employee, individuals tend to get mired in the specific details of their own jobs. Rather, I would try to envision what it is like to have the senior person's job, and engage in a discussion around the "bigger picture." Doing so will give you insight into the types of issues senior people deal with on a daily basis and provide for better discussion on the ways the overall business can be improved.*

Your company's culture: *The merger between Sprint and Nextel combined two separate cultures. Since then our company has been working to develop a new culture that embodies elements of the past and helps define ourselves as we move forward. While I believe this process is still unfolding...many things have remained constant since I joined Sprint. Specifically, I feel the company continues to put its employees first when making decisions.*

Verizon

140 West St.
New York, NY 10007
Phone: 212-395-1000
Fax: 212-571-1897
Web Addresses: www.verizon.com;
www.verizon.com/jobs

The Company

- Verizon, which is a fusion of the words *veritas* and *horizon,* has three distinct business units: Wireless, Business, and Telecom. "America's most reliable wireless network" (Verizon's tag line) is the largest domestic wireless company in terms of total revenues, data revenues, and retail customers, serving over 62 million wireless customers around the country.

- Verizon is facing another potentially daunting competitor—the Web. The increasing availability of Internet calling options poses a very real threat to Verizon's residential phone business. On the other hand, the Internet has provided the company with an attractive market of broadband customers, both business and residential.

- Last year, Verizon filed suit against Vonage, a provider of the popular Voice over Internet Protocol (VoIP) calling option, alleging that it had violated various Verizon patents. Vonage has been ordered to pay Verizon $58 million.

FAST FACTS

"Best Places to Launch a Career"
  Rank: 38
"Best Internships" Rank: 32
Full-Time Salary: $35,000–$39,999
Entry-Level Hires: 35,072
Top College Major: Business
3-Year Retention Rate: 60%
Stock Ticker: VZ

The Suits

Ivan Seidenberg: Chairman and CEO
Dennis F. Strigl: President and COO
Doreen A. Toben: Executive VP and CFO
John G. Stratton: Executive VP and CMO

The Stats

2007 sales: $93.5 billion
2007 net income: $6.9 billion (before special items)
Market cap: $126.3 billion
Employees: 235,000
Locations: Operations in over 140 countries
Major competitors: AT&T, Sprint Nextel, Qwest
Largest operating units*:
Verizon Telecom ....$31.9 billion
Verizon Business ....$21.2 billion
Verizon Wireless ....$43.9 billion
*2007 prior to intra-company eliminations

The Story

1984: Bell Atlantic Corporation is founded after the forced breakup of American Telephone & Telegraph (AT&T), which had lost a huge antitrust lawsuit; the new company inherits seven of AT&T's Bell Operating Companies

2000: Verizon is created when Bell Atlantic and General Telephone and Electronics merge

2001: Ends a partnership with FLAG Telecom in order to expand its own European network

2004: Verizon Communications is added to the Dow Jones Industrial Average

2005: Unveils video service FiOS TV; to reduce debt, Verizon begins selling off "nonstrategic" shares that it holds in other companies, like Cable and Wireless and Eurotel Praha; also sells off its wireline access lines in certain parts of the country

2005: Verizon makes a $6.5 billion bid for MCI; increases its bid to roughly $8.5 billion after rival Qwest expresses interest in MCI

2006: MCI and Verizon merge

The Skinny

Most important to recruiters: Analytical skills, leadership skills, communication skills

Selectivity: N/A

Diversity of entry-level workforce: 49% minority; 45% female

Facts to know:

• Verizon will match charitable contributions of up to $10,000 annually. The maximum reimbursement for housing- and moving-related relocation expenses is even more impressive ($40,000 to $100,000). Although entry-level employees are technically eligible for this amount, their maximum is usually lower ($8,000 to $15,000), depending upon their salary band.

• In addition to the 6% company match provided in Verizon's 401(k) plan, employees may receive an additional company contribution of as much as 3% of base salary based on company performance.

 **The Starting Gate**

Undergraduate internships: 233

Duration of summer internship: 6 to 16 weeks

Average total compensation: $8,100

Interns by grade level:
Sophomore 10%
Junior..30%
Senior 60%

Interns who receive full-time job offers: 80%

Interns who are extended full-time job offers that accept: 77%

The Sliding Scale

Entry-level hires who had been interns: 1%

Most important performance measurements in entry-level hire: Productivity/efficiency, customer satisfaction, analytical skills

Entry-level hires receiving signing bonuses: None

Average entry-level signing bonus: N/A

Entry-level hires receiving performance bonuses: 100%

Average performance bonus during first year: $4,500

The Stand-Out Perks

- Educational expenses reimbursement ($8,000)

- 10 paid vacation days and 7 paid holidays during first year with company

- Employee discounts

The Skills

- Five-day orientation program

- Formal leadership development programs, including the Financial Talent Acquisition Program, which consists of one to three rotations and lasts 52 weeks, and the Leadership Excellence and Development Program, which lasts 104 weeks

- Formal mentorship program (20% of entry-level hires participate)

The Sound-Off

- "Verizon has made this big attempt to move as many positions as possible overseas, mainly to India. It also keeps reducing the benefits. Here are the things we have lost since 2002: overtime pay, off-site training, and pension plan." —BW *Discussion Forum*

- "Verizon rewards its employees with very competitive salaries, a performance-based bonus program, stellar health-care benefits, a very generous 401(k) plan that ranks in the top 5% of all companies, and a number of other benefits." —*Verizon recruiting employee*

THE RECRUITER SPOTLIGHT

Name: Odesa G. Stapleton
Job: Director of Talent Management

Ultimate do/don't when applying for a job at Verizon: *Do provide accurate, truthful answers to questions on the job application. Do be punctual: arrive 10 minutes early for the interview, and be nice to any greeter you encounter along the way. Do dress appropriately, as first impressions are very important. Don't chew gum, fidget, or slouch during the interview. Candidates should avoid using slang, making negative comments about prior supervisors and/or coworkers, and being overly aggressive in responding to questions. Additionally, candidates should be certain that cell phones and pagers are turned off during interviews.*

Why choose Verizon: *Young people who come to Verizon will find that telecommunications is a very exciting industry. There is something exciting for every tech-savvy, Gen-Y new hire to look forward to each day. Verizon is a Fortune 15 company with a start-up culture. We have almost 240,000 employees who are truly team players. This is a place where ideas and values are appreciated at all levels.*

C.H. Robinson

C.H. Robinson Worldwide
14701 Charlson Rd.
Eden Prairie, MN 55347
Phone: 952-937-8500
Fax: 952-937-6714
Web Addresses: www.chrobinson.com;
www.chrobinson.com/careers

The Company

- C.H. Robinson is one of the largest third-party logistics companies in the world, using its relationships with railroads, trucking companies, ocean carriers, and airlines to manage the transportation of over five million shipments for its 25,000 customers annually. Its customers primarily specialize in food/beverage, manufactured, and retail items. C.H. Robinson also offers supply chain management services and produce sales and distribution, including third-party licensed and proprietary branded (Mott's, Welch's, etc.) and nonbranded products. C.H. Robinson continues to expand its international freight forwarding network through recent acquisitions in India, Germany, Italy, and China.

- In 2007, C.H. Robinson celebrated its tenth anniversary as a publicly traded company, a period in which it exceeded its long-term growth target of 15% with average annual earnings per share growth of just under 23%.

- Legend has it that, prior to forming C.H. Robinson in 1905, Charles H. Robinson ran off with famed sharpshooter Annie Oakley.

The Suits

John Wiehoff: Chairman, President, and CEO
Chad Lindbloom: VP and CFO
Tom Mahlke: VP and CIO
Jim Butts: VP
Scott Satterlee: VP

The Stats

2007 sales: $7.3 billion
2007 net income: $324.3 million
Market cap: $9.2 billion
Employees: 7,332
Locations*: 218 offices in the Americas, Asia, and Europe
Major competitors: DHL, DB Logistics, UPS Supply Chain Solutions, FedEx Trade Networks, CEVA Logistics

Largest operating units[†]:

Transportation .... $6.0 billion
Sourcing .... $1.3 billion
Information Services ....$45.5 million

*As of the end of 2007 third quarter
†2007 sales

📖 The Story

1905: Charles H. Robinson combines his produce brokerage with Nash Brothers'

1913: Nash Finch buys C.H. Robinson and expands its business operations into Illinois, Texas, Minnesota, and Wisconsin

1976: Employees buy out Nash Finch's shares, and the company becomes 100% employee-owned

1980: The passage of the Motor Carrier Act deregulates the U.S. transportation industry

1990: C.H. Robinson International, Inc., is formed, expanding Robinson's services as an international freight forwarder (ocean, air, and customs brokerage)

1993: Establishes a presence in Europe through partial ownership of Transeco, a French motor carrier; also opens offices in Mexico City and Venezuela

1997: Becomes a publicly traded company

1998: Buys Argentina-based Comexter Transportation group; also expands its LTL (less-than-truckload) business by acquiring Preferred Translocation Systems

1999: Buys U.S.-based American Backhaulers and France-based Norminter

2003: Is charged with three separate counts of wrongful death in connection with the involvement of its drivers in multivehicle accidents

2004: Expands into China with purchase of China-based freight forwarding company; acquires U.S.–based FoodSource, FoodSource Procurement, and Epic Roots for a total of $270 million

2005: Buys two freight forwarders in Italy and Germany

2006: Acquires Payne, Lynch and Associates and India-based freight forwarder Triune

2007: Acquires LXSI Services; opens an office in Singapore

The Skinny

Most important to recruiters: Communication skills, leadership skills, work experience, entrepreneurial spirit

Selectivity: N/A

Diversity of entry-level workforce: 24% minority; 41% female

Facts to know:

- After having been with the company for 6 to 12 months, an employee is invited to attend the New Employee Seminar (NES), which is held at C.H. Robinson's corporate headquarters in Eden Prairie, a nearby suburb of Minneapolis.

- C.H. Robinson's corporate offices have unique, open floor plans with shared workspaces and low-walled cubicles.

 ## The Starting Gate

Undergraduate internships: 198

Duration of summer internship: 12 weeks

Average total compensation: $4,600

Interns by grade level: N/A

Interns who receive full-time job offers: 60%

Interns who are extended full-time job offers that accept: 50%

The Sliding Scale

Entry-level hires who had been interns: N/A

Most important performance measurements in entry-level hire: Customer satisfaction, productivity/efficiency, sales/revenue

Entry-level hires receiving signing bonuses: None

Average entry-level signing bonus: N/A

Entry-level hires receiving performance bonuses: N/A

Average performance bonuses during first year: N/A

The Stand-Out Perks

- Access to a 401(k) with a company match of up to 4%

- Eligible for annual company profit sharing on January 1 or July 1 immediately following one year of employment

- Employee discounts on car rentals, gym memberships, cell phone service, and insurance

- Charitable gift match ($250)

The Skills

- New employees are assigned a mentor, who coordinates a six-month training program for the new hire

- QuickStart is C.H. Robinson's proprietary program for new Transportation Sales Representatives and consists of approximately six hours of instruction at a branch location and two weeks of on-site training

THE SUPERSTAR SPOTLIGHT

Name: Katie Andrews
Job: Transportation Salesperson

Briefly describe the company culture: *You're working in a fast-paced environment, relying on your team, making big decisions, and having fun! Be prepared to become close friends with your coworkers—it will happen. The atmosphere is open and dynamic, and you're definitely part of a team here. Our work is challenging; the company's flat organizational structure gives us vital responsibilities and the ability to make an impact on the company. We are given significant responsibilities early on in our careers and are able to make a difference for our customers, our carriers, and ourselves.*

The most enjoyable part of your job: *The company spends a lot of time and money on training and development. You decide your future here; what you put in, you will get back in return. My job is cool because it's not the typical, dull office setting. It is loud and competitive; there is no monotony—no "syllabus"—and we are not micromanaged. We are exposed to many facets of the business. We're valued as employees, empowered early on in our careers, and trusted to successfully carry out the day-to-day business actions and develop our relationships with our customers, carriers, and coworkers. We have a direct impact on the success of the company. I also think it's pretty cool how involved our company is in the community. Last year, Team Robinson was the largest team in the Minnesota Multiple Sclerosis (MS) 150—a 150-mile bike ride through northern Minnesota that raises money for MS. Our CEO and two of the VPs participated, along with 160 other riders.*

Weirdest/funniest thing encountered on the job: *Every year our company has a week of events that raises money for five different charitable organizations, called Robinson Cares Week. The theme last year was "Be a Robinson Hero." To kick off the week and create awareness, actors dressed as Superman, Cat Woman, and Wonder Woman ran through the building shouting, "Do you want to be a Robinson Hero?" and handed out agendas of the week's events. It was hilarious. At C.H. Robinson, we like to have fun while at the same time working hard. It was a creative and unique way to create awareness and generate interest.*

DHL

1200 South Pine Island Rd.
Suite 140–145
Plantation, FL 33324
Phone: 954-888-7114
Fax: 954-888-7310
Web Addresses: www.dhl.com;
www.dhl.com/careers

The Company

- DHL is the global market leader in international express, overland transport, and air freight. It is also number one in ocean freight and contract logistics. Its specialty divisions include DHL Express, DHL Freight, DHL Global Forwarding, DHL Exel Supply Chain, and DHL Global Mail.

- In 2002, DHL was purchased by Deutsche Post World Net, a global logistics group with over 500,000 employees in more than 225 countries and territories. Deutsche Post World Net is headquartered in Bonn, Germany, and its brands include DHL, Deutsche Post, and Postbank. DHL's United States and international America's headquarters are based in south Florida.

- DHL has developed a global network of DHL disaster response teams, which provide air cargo and warehousing services at airports close to the scene of major sudden-onset natural disasters. After the

2005 South Asia tsunami, DHL provided free charter flights carrying relief supplies and land transport, as well as monetary donations. DHL also engages in various sustainability-related efforts. In 2007 the company even launched the DHL YES Awards to recognize young social entrepreneurs in five different countries who have been working to achieve the United Nations' Millennium Development Goals.

The Suits*

Hans Hickler: CEO
John Cameron: Executive VP of Operations
Ian Clough: Executive VP and CFO
*DHL Express USA

The Stats*

2007 sales: 63.5 billion euros
2007 profit from operating activities: 3.2 billion euros
Market cap: N/A
Employees: 470,123
Locations: More than 225 countries and territories; U.S. corporate headquarters in Florida; many operations in Africa, Asia, and Europe—namely in Germany and Sweden
Major competitors: DB Logistics, FedEx, UPS, Nippon Express, CEVA Logistics
Largest operating units[†]:
Logistics .... 25.7 billion euros
Mail .... 15.5 billion euros
Express .... 13.9 billion euros
*Financial data for Deutsche Post-world Net
[†] 2007 sales

The Story

1969: Partners Adrian Dalsey, Larry Hillblom, and Robert Lynn found DHL in San Francisco

1972: First office in United Kingdom opens, marking company's foray into European business

1977: First German office opens in Frankfurt

1979: Begins delivering packages; before, only documents were sent

1986: Becomes first express company in the People's Republic of China

1998: Deutsche Post World Net buys a stake in DHL

2000: Deutsche Post World Net becomes a publicly traded company

2002: Deutsche Post World Net completes purchase of DHL; DHL is now 100% owned by DPWN

2002: DHL Boeing 757 collides with Russian aircraft Tupolev Tu-154, killing the 757's pilots and 69 people aboard the Tu-154, most of them Russian children

2003: With the acquisition of Airborne Express, DHL becomes third-largest express company in the United States; DHL pilots successfully land an Airbus A300 after being fired upon by Iraqi insurgents and are given an award for the feat by the Flight Safety Foundation

2005: Deutsche Post World Net acquires Exel, a company of over 100,000 employees offering transport and logistics solutions

2006: Creates approximately 1,000 new jobs by securing the contract to operate the United Kingdom's National Health Service Supply Chain

2007: DHL partners with Polar Air Cargo, providing guaranteed access to airlift capacity for the next 20 years, enhancing DHL's trans-Pacific capabilities

2008: DHL in the United States announces a partnership with Walgreens, which will more than double the DHL U.S. retail presence in 2008

The Skinny

Most important to recruiters: Communication skills, knowledge of DHL, work experience, college GPA

Selectivity: 1 of 25 applicants hired in 2006

Diversity of entry-level workforce: 54% minority; 47% female

Facts to know:

- DHL has an ongoing internship program that runs all year long.

- To brush up on the logistics industry (and impress your interviewer), take Deutsche Post World Net's online quiz: http://www.dpwn.de/dpwn?lang=de_EN&xmlFile=2008119.

The Starting Gate

Undergraduate internships: 85

Duration of summer internship: 12 to 26 weeks

Average total compensation: $15,600*

Interns by grade level: N/A

Interns who receive full-time job offers: 40%

Interns who are extended full-time job offers that accept: 100%

*Six-month internships only.

 ## The Sliding Scale

Entry-level hires who had been interns: 4%

Most important performance measurements in entry-level hire: Varies with business units and positions

Entry-level hires receiving signing bonuses: 10%

Average entry-level signing bonus: N/A

Entry-level hires receiving performance bonuses: 100% are eligible

Average performance bonus during first year: N/A

The Stand-Out Perks

- Educational expenses reimbursement ($3,000)

- Access to 401(k) with company match (fully vested after five years)

- Charitable gift match

- Relocation compensation

- Employee discounts

The Skills

- Formal one-day orientation program that includes computer training (additional orientation programs depend on position: sales employees participate in a 5-week training program; employees at corporate offices 1/2 day; interns 3 hours)

THE ENTRY-LEVEL SPOTLIGHT

Name: Pooja Shambhu
Job: Sales Training Specialist

Describe your role at DHL: *I started my career at DHL as an account representative in Atlanta, GA. During my first year and a half at DHL, I successfully brought in new business and was promoted to the sales training specialist position in January 2005. As a sales trainer, I have had the opportunity to work on projects ranging from the EU-U.S. exchange program to the DHL new hire sales and reseller sales training programs.*

On starting out in the recent graduate sales training program: *It was a warm welcome. We were greeted by the CEO. I learned about DHL—the products we sell—but more importantly, I learned how to sell those products. It's easy to just be book smart, but when you don't have the sales background, you need a baseline to work off of. How do I become a consultant to my customer instead of someone who just prints out rates and gives it to them? We had real-world simulations where DHL brought in "pretend" customers with whom we had to build relationships, assess needs, present a DHL solution and, finally, win their business.*

On the transition from trainee to sales rep: *Of course there is that anxiety, but the first time I went all on my own, the feeling was unbelievable. I think it was two weeks and I won my first account. Most of the time, unless your manager accompanies you, you're on your own. You have a base salary, and you can make commission over that. It definitely drives you to do better. It requires a lot of self-motivation.*

Enterprise Rent-A-Car

600 Corporate Park Dr.
St. Louis, MO 63105
Phone: 314-512-5000
Fax: 314-512-4706
Web Addresses: www.enterprise.com;
www.enterprise.com/careers

The Company

- Enterprise Rent-A-Car is North America's largest car rental agency and one of the country's largest privately held companies. CEO Andrew C. Taylor is the son of Enterprise founder Jack Taylor.

- Enterprise has a unique, from-the-ground-up management training system that has been in place since the company was founded in 1957. Young hires learn every aspect of the business, from manning the rental desk to scrubbing down vehicles. They're rewarded with a promotion after only 8 to 10 months, and some are even managing their own branch within their first two years.

- In 2007, Enterprise marked its fiftieth anniversary with a pledge to plant 50 million trees in 50 years at a cost of $50 million in today's dollars. Additional environmental initiatives include a fleet of fuel-efficient "FlexFuel" vehicles, gas/electric hybrid rentals, and financial support of alternative fuel research.

FAST FACTS

"Best Places to Launch a Career"
  Rank: 26
"Best Internships" Rank: 40
Full-Time Salary: Less than $35,000
Entry-Level Hires: 7,500
Top College Major: Business
Interns Who Receive Full-Time Job
  Offers: 85%
Stock Ticker: N/A (privately owned)

The Suits

Andrew C. Taylor: Chairman and CEO
Donald Ross: President and Vice Chairman
Pamela Nicholson: Executive VP and COO
William Snyder: Executive VP and CFO
Lee Kaplan: Senior VP and Chief Administrative Officer

The Stats

2007 sales: $9.5 billion
Employees: 66,000
Locations: Over 7,000 offices in the United States, Canada, the United Kingdom, Ireland, and Germany
Major Competitors: Hertz, Dollar, Thrifty, Avis

The Story

1957: Jack Taylor starts a one-shop rental car company called Executive Leasing Company in St. Louis, Missouri

1969: The company expands beyond St. Louis and is renamed Enterprise

1980: Enterprise creates its National Reservation Center, allowing customers to call a toll-free number to reserve a vehicle

1989: The organization undergoes one last name change to Enterprise Rent-A-Car

1993: The first international office opens in Windsor, Canada, sparking an expansion to approximately 400 Canadian locations and 475 locations in the United Kingdom, Ireland, and Germany

1995: Enterprise's first on-site airport location opens at Denver International Airport; the organization has grown to over 230 airport locations globally

1999: Enterprise Rent-A-Truck opens; the new business provides customers with commercial truck rentals (cargo vans, trucks, etc.) and has grown to include 120 locations nationwide

2007: Enterprise celebrates 50 years in the rental car business and acquires rival Vanguard Car Rental, owner of the National Car Rental and Alamo Rent-A-Car brands

The Skinny

Most important to recruiters: Leadership skills, work experience, communication skills

Selectivity: 1 of 33 applicants hired in 2005 and 2006

Diversity of entry-level workforce: 35% minority; 39% female

Facts to know:

- Enterprise recently rolled out a new extensive formal mentorship program for U.S. employees who have been with the company for at least a year or who have been recently promoted to a Management Assistant position. An informal support network is available to first-year employees not yet eligible.

The Starting Gate

Undergraduate internships: 2,000

Duration of summer internship: 10 to 12 weeks

Average total compensation: $5,000

Interns by grade level:
Junior..20%
Senior 80%

Interns who receive full-time job offers: 85%

Interns who are extended full-time job offers that accept: 50%

The Sliding Scale

Entry-level hires who had been interns: 9%

Most important performance measurements in entry-level hire: Leadership ability, work experience, communication skills

Entry-level hires receiving signing bonuses: N/A

Average entry-level signing bonus: N/A

Entry-level hires receiving performance bonuses: 20%

Average performance bonus during first year: $8,000

The Stand-Out Perks

- Employee discounts on car purchases, clothing, electronics and travel equipment

- 50% charitable gift match to the United Way

The Skills

- Five-day orientation program that includes discussions about company history and ethics, computer training and guest speakers

- Management Training Program, which lasts 32 to 52 weeks

- Formal mentorship program (25% of entry-level hires participate)

The Sound-Off

- "You're [an intern] treated like a regular, full-time employee." —*Purdue senior**

- "I'm a brand-new manager-in-training. . . . Sure, I work 50-plus hours a week, but the rewards are that much greater in the end. You work hard, you play hard." —BW *Discussion Forum*

- "Not a job most people can handle. I am 23, but working for Enterprise has made me feel 40." —*Enterprise employee*

- "I began my career on the business management (accounting) track, and it was phenomenal. With hard work, you quickly work your way up. A fantastic culture and there is a lot of interaction between the branch managers and even senior executives." —BW *Discussion Forum*

- "You don't need a college degree to work behind the counter at Enterprise, and wasting your initial career on such a position will set you back compared those who took positions that offered transferable skills." — BW *Discussion Forum*

- "I learned more about how to run a business in my first year at Enterprise than in the couple of years that it took to finish my master's degree. It's not a job for everyone— you work a lot of long hours and wash cars in a suit—but I was promoted six times with substantial pay increases during my first two years." —BW *Discussion Forum*

*Data: Universum Communications

THE SUPERSTAR SPOTLIGHT

Name: Karsten Summers
Title: Regional VP for Enterprise—Seattle, Washington

Describe your experience at Enterprise: *I have the pleasure of working for a company that operates by the values on which it was founded. We make our decisions based on "what is the right thing to do for our customers and our employees?" Following this simple principle, I have found great success at Enterprise. This has afforded me the chance to hold a position at 32 years old that most, if they get the opportunity at all, do not have until much later in life. I am involved with all aspects of running a business, from training and development, to real estate, to accounting and risk management. There is never a dull moment.*

Most unexpected lost-and-found item: *One of my employees in Los Angeles picked up a car left at a body shop by the customer. As she did the check-in to verify the condition of the vehicle, she opened the trunk to find that the customer had left her pet snake in the trunk.*

Any advice for ambitious young professionals? *Our company is filled with those who have an entrepreneurial spirit. . . . Fortunately, we have a business model that rewards hard work and recognizes successful and solid performance, allowing employees to advance at a pace that suits their skills and abilities. Because we promote from within, there are so many places your career can take you at Enterprise.*

Norfolk Southern Corp.

3 Commercial Pl.
Norfolk, VA 23510
Phone: 757-629-2600
Fax: 757-664-5069
Web Addresses: www.nscorp.com;
www.nscorp.com/nscportal/nscorp/
  JobSeekers/

The Company

- Norfolk Southern Railway, the main subsidiary of Norfolk Southern Corporation, transports coal, automotive products, chemicals, paper, clay, and forest products via 21,000 miles of railroad throughout the eastern United States. Its intermodal service uses rails and the open roads to deliver customer goods by train and truck.

- The company is expecting more rail business in the future as a result of the high cost of fuel, ever more crowded highways, and budding environmental consciousness (related to fuel and emissions).

- Norfolk Southern Corporation is currently upgrading its key rail corridors and infrastructure, as it views intermodal transport as a key means of growth.

FAST FACTS

"Best Places to Launch a Career" Rank: 90
"Best Internships" Rank: 13
Full-Time Salary: $50,000–$54,999
Entry-Level Hires: 277
Top College Major: Business
3-Year Retention Rate: 53%
Stock Ticker: NSC

The Suits

Wick Moorman: Chairman, President, and CEO
Stephen Tobias: Vice Chairman and COO
Debbie Butler: Executive VP of Planning and CIO
James Hixon: Executive VP of Law and Corporate Relations
Mark Manion: Executive VP of Operations

The Stats

2007 sales: $9.4 billion
2007 net income: $1.5 billion
Market cap: $19.9 billion
Employees: 30,541
Locations: Route miles in Washington, D.C., and 22 of the United States' eastern states
Major competitors: CSX, Union Pacific, Burlington Northern Santa Fe, trucking companies

Largest operating units*:

General Merchandise........$5.2 billion
Transport of Coal ....$2.3 billion
Intermodal ....$1.9 billion

*2007 sales

📖 The Story

1827: The South Carolina Canal and Rail Road (a predecessor of the Southern Railway, which is a predecessor of Norfolk Southern) is chartered

1833: Norfolk Southern's predecessor opens a 136-mile line to Hamburg, South Carolina, making it the world's longest railway

1881: E. W. Clark, a Philadelphia-based banker, buys Atlantic, Mississippi, and Ohio and renames it Norfolk and Western

1982: Southern Railway and Norfolk and Western merge to form Norfolk Southern

1985: Acquires North American Van Lines, a large motor carrier

1986: Launches Triple Crown Service, which features trailers that operate over both the road and the rail

1987: Drops bid to acquire Piedmont Aviation and enter the airline business

1997: When Norfolk Southern rival CSX bids for Conrail, Norfolk Southern makes a counteroffer; the result is a 58/42 split in ownership of Conrail between Norfolk Southern and CSX, respectively

1998: Sells North American Van Lines

1999: Completes transaction to operate part of Conrail, but problems occur during integration

2000: A voluntary agreement ends a class-action lawsuit alleging race discrimination in Norfolk Southern's promotion practices; the company agrees to improvements, including various diversity initiatives

2007: Shortly after Norfolk Southern's employees are named the safest in the nation for the 17th consecutive year in 2005, nine people die in South Carolina when chlorine gas is leaked into the atmosphere by colliding Norfolk Southern trains

The Skinny

Most important to recruiters: Communication skills, leadership skills, college major

Selectivity: 1 of 20 applicants hired in 2006, up from 1 of 25 applicants hired in 2005

Diversity of entry-level workforce: 33% minority; 27% female

Facts to know:

- While over 50% of entry-level hires earn between $45,000 and $55,000 in their first year, a lucky few from this recent grad pool (5%) earn over $70,000.

- The company's relocation policy for most new hires provides a lump sum of $3,700 for homeowners ($2,500 for renters) for home finding and temporary living. The policy also covers the cost of moving household goods, 30 days of storage, spouse and family assistance, and travel expenses.

- Norfolk Southern actively recruited on 48 U.S. undergraduate campuses during the 2006–2007 school year and extended job offers on 43 of these campuses.

The Starting Gate

Undergraduate internships: 186

Duration of summer internship: 12 to 16 weeks

Average total compensation: $9,972

Interns by grade level:
Freshman 1%
Sophomore 30%
Junior..22%
Senior 47%

Interns who receive full-time job offers: 7%

Interns who are extended full-time job offers that accept: 100%

The Sliding Scale

Entry-level hires who had been interns: 7%

Most important performance measurements in entry-level hire: Effort, learning ability, leadership ability

Entry-level hires receiving signing bonuses: 1%

Average entry-level signing bonus: $3,000

Entry-level hires receiving performance bonuses: 100%

Average performance bonus during first year: $2,581

The Stand-Out Perks

- Educational expenses reimbursement ($5,250)
- Partial graduate school sponsorship
- Charitable gift match ($35,000)
- Employee discounts on gym memberships, cell phones/service, and cultural events

The Skills

- Formal five-day orientation program including guest speakers, diversity exercises, team-building exercises, and a tour of the facilities
- Operation Supervision Training is a rotational leadership program lasting 26 weeks
- Management Training is a rotational leadership program lasting 60 weeks
- Formal mentorship program (100% of entry-level hires participate)

THE RECRUITER SPOTLIGHT

Name: Juan Cunningham
Job: Director of Management Staffing

Why choose Norfolk Southern: *We have an extensive 15-month training program for our college hires. We invest heavily in the development of our management trainees so that their personal level of success can be maximized. We provide ample opportunities for advancement. An employee can literally change professions and still stay within Norfolk Southern. For instance, an employee in Accounting may be able to eventually work in Human Resources, or an operations supervisor may pursue a career in Marketing.*

Why choose the railroad industry: *This industry combines the best of the old and the new. The railroad transportation industry is a vital part of the economy; most goods consumed in America are moved by rail at some point during their route. Our industry has thrived for a couple of centuries by providing a necessary service. This is not just your father's railroad; today's railroad is leveraging emerging technologies to better serve customers and compete. As an industry, we provide exceptional pay and benefits and afford new hires a steady, secure work environment with plentiful opportunities. As highways become more congested and fuel prices remain high, railroads offer a competitive service, and the forecast looks promising.*

Wackiest job applicant behavior encountered: *I once had a candidate deliver a bouquet of cookies to my office with his résumé attached. While it was certainly a creative approach, we did not hire the individual because his background was not suitable for our needs.*

Unexpected skills/majors you're looking for in an ideal young hire: *It might surprise some folks to know that a railroad company, which relies heavily on operations management, hires math majors. We have found the analytical skills possessed by math majors to be ideal for many of our positions. Problem-solving abilities are critical for people working in our company.*

Southwest Airlines

2702 Love Field Dr.
Dallas, TX 75235
Phone: 214-792-4000
Fax: 214-792-4200
Web Addresses: www.southwest.com;
www.southwest.com/careers/

The Company

- Originally launched as a small, local air carrier offering service between Dallas, Houston, and San Antonio, Southwest Airlines has expanded to 64 cities in 32 states across America. Long considered a "discount pioneer," Southwest has adopted a "short routes, high frequency" strategy and flies out of mostly secondary airports, adding only a handful of major airports in the past decade to appeal to business travelers.

- Southwest has continually raised the bar for customer care, launching a same-day air freight delivery service and successful customer-focused promotions, like Senior Fares. The airline recently instituted a new bingo-style boarding system, however, which has received mixed reviews.

- Southwest, which has seen its stock price lag in recent years, is currently trying to cut costs by slowing growth and offering buyouts to some veteran workers. On the upside, 2007 third-quarter net income more than tripled over third-quarter 2006 earnings,

FAST FACTS

"Best Places to Launch a Career"
  Rank: 79
"Best Internships" Rank: N/A
Full-Time Salary: Less than $35,000
Entry-Level Hires: 2,304
Most Important Applicant Trait: Fun-loving attitude
Stock Ticker: LUV

although full-year 2007 results ultimately fell short of the company's earnings goal.

- Southwest selected ticker symbol LUV because it is based out of Love Field in Dallas, Texas.

The Suits

Herbert D. (Herb) Kelleher: Founder and Chairman
Gary C. Kelly: Vice Chairman and CEO
Colleen C. Barrett: President and Corporate Secretary
Laura H. Wright: CFO and Senior VP of Finance
Ron Ricks: Executive VP of Law, Airports, and Public Affairs

The Stats*

2007 sales: $9.9 billion
2007 net income: $645 million
Market cap: $9 billion

Employees: 34,378

Locations: Flies to 64 cities in 32 states across America

Major competitors: Continental Airlines, Inc., AMR Corp., JetBlue Airways Corp.

Largest operating units†:

Passenger ....$9.5 billion
Freight ....$130.0 million
Other ....$274.0 million

*2007 financials unaudited

†2007 sales

The Story

1967: Texans Rollin King and Herb Kelleher found Air Southwest to offer air routes between Dallas, Houston, and San Antonio

1971: Newly renamed Southwest Airlines, the company makes its first scheduled flight after a legal battle over its right to become a regional carrier

1979: The new Wright Amendment restricts flights from Love Field (the home of Southwest Airlines) to select states

1987: Debuts its frequent-flier program, the precursor to its Rapid Rewards program

1993: Adds Baltimore as its first East Coast service destination

1995: Introduces a ticketless reservation system to cut costs

1996: Adds service to Florida, and also begins online ticket sales

2001: Southwest's Colleen Barrett becomes the first woman president of a major airline

2001–2002: Remains profitable despite the hits to the airline industry after the terrorist attacks of September 11, 2001

2003: Closes call centers in Dallas, Little Rock, and Salt Lake City to minimize costs; more than 2,000 workers are asked to either relocate or accept a severance package

2006: The Wright Amendment is modified, permitting direct service between Love Field and previously restricted states

The Skinny

Most important to recruiters: Fun-loving attitude

Selectivity: N/A

Diversity of entry-level workforce: N/A

Facts to know:

- Southwest employees and their immediate family members have a "fly free" policy. They are immediately eligible to receive space-available travel privileges, and they even get discounted flights from other carriers.

- Southwest's unapologetically enthusiastic corporate culture can be explained by the three traits it expects of employees: (1) a fun-loving attitude, (2) a servant's heart, and (3) a warrior spirit.

The Starting Gate

Undergraduate internships: 63

Duration of summer internship: 9 weeks

Average total compensation: N/A

Interns by grade level: N/A

Interns who receive full-time job offers: N/A

Interns who are extended full-time job offers that accept: N/A

The Sliding Scale

Entry-level hires who had been interns: N/A

Most important performance measurements in entry-level hire: Fun-loving attitude

Entry-level hires receiving signing bonuses: None

Average entry-level signing bonus: N/A

Entry-level hires receiving performance bonuses: None

Average performance bonus during first year: N/A

The Stand-Out Perks

- 401(k) with company match of up to 7.3% (fully vested after 5 years)

- 8 hours of paid sick/personal time off per month

- Employee discounts

- 90 days of paid maternity leave

The Skills

- Formal one-day orientation program, including guest speakers, diversity exercises, team-building exercises, a tour of the facilities, company history and culture overview, health benefits, retirement information, and customer service

- Manager-in-Training Program, a rotational, formal leadership program for entry-level hires that lasts 12 to 32 weeks

The Sound-Off

- "The internship is paid, and you get to sit in on real meetings and learn a great deal about the company." — *University of Central Florida junior**

- "[Internships provide] diverse exposure to the industry and the cut-throat aviation market, as well as competitive training. All-around experienced personalities make the airline a corporate, as well as a social, success." —*Embry Riddle Aeronautical University sophomore**

- "We hire for attitude and train for aptitude. We treat one another as a family, and we take care of each other through thick and thin. It's a great concept, because if we keep our employees happy, it will reflect on our customers every day on the job." —*Southwest flight attendant*

*Data: Universum Communications

THE ENTRY-LEVEL SPOTLIGHT

Name: David J. Garcia
Job: Flight Attendant (Orlando)

Why choose Southwest: *One of the main reasons I believe Southwest Airlines is a top entry-level employer is our prestigious reputation in the aviation industry. Everyone I meet that learns I work for Southwest always tells me that "Southwest is a great company to work for!" Southwest has a powerful reputation, with a history of success and profitability, and I am very proud to be a part of that.*

Best part of job: *It is different from any other job out there. Many of my friends took jobs with large firms in the accounting, engineering, and marketing fields, and they enjoy what they do, but they envy the flexibility and variety I have with my occupation. I get to travel the United States and come into contact with so many people on a day-to-day basis. It's amazing and unlike anything else out there.*

Staying on your toes: *Handling disgruntled customers is always an interesting experience, but I think that the funniest things that I have encountered were pranks and jokes played by fellow coworkers. In any job, the "rookies" tend to get picked on a little bit, and it is the same in our profession. Whether it's changing drink orders, making false wake-up calls, or findng holes in the coffee cups, it's all in good fun.*

Career advice: *The greatest thing about working for Southwest Airlines is that we are allowed to express ourselves and our personalities freely. In fact, this is highly encouraged at Southwest. With that, if you continue to be yourself and shine at doing what you do best, you'll get noticed.*

Union Pacific

1400 Douglas St.
Omaha, NE 68179
Phone: 402-544-5000
Fax: 402-501-2133
Web Addresses: www.up.com;
www.unionpacific.jobs

The Company

- The number one freight carrier in the United States, Union Pacific (UP) covers over 32,000 route miles in 23 states—mainly transporting coal, industrial goods, and chemicals—and owns 26,500 miles of rail. UP also offers intermodal transportation, combining rail transport with truck or air services, logistics management, and supply chain management software, which it distributes and integrates for its clients.

- In 1997, the federal government reviewed UP due to several fatal accidents and uncovered defects in its rail safety, including overworked employees and mechanical flaws. In response, the company hired more workers, added new carriers, and decentralized its operations to fix these conditions over the next few years. In the late 1990s, UP began offering lower rates to attract new customers and build more volume, which has resulted in a boom in business. In fact, more than half of UP's current long-term contracts

have been inked since the company began lowering its rates.

- Famed Warren Buffett-led investment fund Berkshire Hathaway is a shareholder in Union Pacific (although it reduced its stake in fall 2007). Union Pacific's stock price increased by over 25% during 2007. UP has also put a substantial amount of money into building more railroad track in order to increase the company's shipping capacity. However, UP's CEO has warned that further company growth—including its planned railway upgrades—could be put in jeopardy if railroad prices are reregulated as a result of the passage of pending antitrust legislation.

The Suits

James Young: Chairman, President, and CEO
Dennis Duffy: Executive VP of Operations
Charles Eisele: Senior VP of Strategic Planning
Robert Knight: Executive VP of Finance and CFO
John Koraleski: Executive VP of Marketing and Sales

The Stats

2007 sales: $16.3 billion
2007 net income: $1.9 billion
Market cap: $33 billion
Employees: 50,089
Locations: Railroad track in 23 states, primarily in the Western United States
Major competitors: Burlington Northern Santa Fe, CSX, American Commercial Lines, Ingram Industries, Norfolk Southern, Pacer International
Largest operating units*:
Industrial Products ....$3.1 billion
Energy...............................$3.1 billion
Intermodal ....$2.9 billion
Agricultural ....$2.6 billion
Chemicals ....$2.3 billion
Automotive ....$1.5 billion
Other ....$767.0 million
*2007 sales

The Story

1862: The U.S. Congress charters the Union Pacific Railroad (UP) to construct part of the Transcontinental Railroad

1872: The *New York Sun* breaks the "Credit Mobilier" scandal: it is reported that UP officials have been pocketing profits made during the construction of the Transcontinental Railroad

1893: UP goes bankrupt as a result of the lasting financial effects of the scandal

1897: UP is bought by a syndicate that includes E. H. Harriman

1913: The Supreme Court upholds antitrust legislation and forces UP to sell its subsidiaries

1930s: Offers trucking transport services for the first time

1970s: Begins producing gas and oil

1989: Joins with Blackstone Group to buy Chicago and North Western (CNW) Railways

1995: Purchases CNW in full

1996: After a lengthy acquisition, UP controls Southern Pacific (SP)

2001: Finally fully integrates SP trains and operations into its operations

2006: Reorganizes operating structure into Northern, Southern, and Western Spheres

The Skinny

Most important to recruiters: Analytical skills, leadership skills, communication skills

Selectivity: N/A

Diversity of entry-level workforce: N/A

Facts to know:

- Union Pacific was one of 50 companies listed as a 2007 military-friendly employer by *G.I. Jobs* magazine.

- In 2007, UP received an "Energy Innovators Award" from U.S. Energy Secretary Samuel Bodman for making energy efficiency a priority at its Omaha, Nebraska, headquarters.

The Starting Gate

Undergraduate internships: 350

Duration of summer internship: 8 to 12 weeks

Average total compensation: $9,000

Interns by grade level:
Freshman 1%
Sophomore 15%
Junior..52%
Senior 30%
College graduate 2%

Interns who receive full-time job offers: N/A

Interns who are extended full-time job offers that accept: N/A

The Sliding Scale

Entry-level hires who had been interns: N/A

Most important performance measurements in entry-level hire: Productivity/efficiency, profitability/margin, leadership ability

Entry-level hires receiving signing bonuses: 5%

Average entry-level signing bonus: $5,000*

Entry-level hires receiving performance bonuses: 75%

Average performance bonus during first year: $3,500

*Operating Management Training Program hires only.

The Stand-Out Perks

- Educational expenses reimbursement ($3,500)

- Partial graduate school sponsorship

- Charitable gift match

- Relocation compensation

- Employee discounts

The Skills

- Formal orientation program, including computer training, guest speakers, diversity exercises, team-building exercises, and a tour of the facilities

- Formal mentorship program (100% of entry-level hires participate)

THE SUPERSTAR SPOTLIGHT

Name: Michael Beatie

Job: Senior Project Manager of Cost and Profit Systems

Why choose Union Pacific: *It is a very stable and secure company that offers interesting work. When I joined Union Pacific Railroad, I was able to start in a department that was ideal for my education and previous experience. I have gained a solid foundation in the business and industry while having the opportunity to migrate into other challenging functions and projects. This company does a great job of recognizing and rewarding its employees. I started as a senior analyst in Finance. In a couple of years, I was promoted to a senior project manager.*

Briefly describe your firm's work culture: *A diverse, dynamic environment that emphasizes safety, ethics, and efficiency. There is great cohesiveness within my department and across functional areas.*

Describe a typical day at work: *My job consists of providing various analyses, working on projects, and maintaining financial systems while supporting our Marketing and Operations departments. I am the cost and profit project manager for our Agricultural Business Group. A typical day for me begins with maintaining a checklist of items that I need to accomplish and planning a daily schedule. Throughout the day, I respond to various requests for costing analyses, research, and support that affect marketing and operational decisions. In addition, I am always involved in projects to enhance our systems, procedures, and reports. So, I usually schedule and attend meetings while working with other team members to accomplish various tasks. I also produce various internal financial reports. A typical day for me is usually pretty fast-paced and exciting.*

UPS

55 Glenlake Pkwy., **NE**
Atlanta, GA 30328
Phone: 404-828-6000
Fax: 404-828-7666
Web Addresses: www.ups.com;
www.ups.managehr.com/index.html

The Company

- In the past 100 years, UPS has grown from a small-time messenger company to the largest package deliverer in the world, serving 7.9 million customers in 200 countries and territories around the globe.

- The company's fleet of delivery aircraft is so vast that UPS effectively owns the eighth-largest airline in the world. Aside from delivering packages, the company is also a global leader in specialized transportation, as well as supply chain and logistics services.

- Despite a stagnant domestic transportation market as a result of the weakened U.S. economy, not only did UPS's third-quarter 2007 profits rise 3% over 2006's earnings during the same period, but the company's performance beat analysts' estimates on the strength of the growing international business. Its supply chain and freight business also performed strongly. Thus far, 2008 hasn't been so promising. In April 2008, UPS lowered its first-

quarter earnings estimate. The company's ongoing challenges include a reduction in domestic package volume in the weakened U.S. economy and the significant increase in fuel prices.

The Suits

D. Scott Davis: Chairman and CEO
Kurt Kuehn: Vice Chairman and CFO
David P. Abney: Senior VP, COO, and President of UPS Airlines
David A. Barnes: Senior VP and CIO
Alan Gershenhorn: Senior VP of Sales and Marketing Group Manager

The Stats

2007 sales: $49.7 billion
2007 net income: $447 million*
Market cap: $74.3 billion
Employees: 427,700 worldwide
Locations: World headquarters in Atlanta, Georgia

Major competitors: Deutsche Post, FedEx, US Postal Service

Largest operating units[†]:
Package Operation ....$41.3 billion
Supply Chain and Freight ..$8.4 billion

*Includes the impact of the $6.1 billion payment to withdraw 45,000 employees from the Central States Pension Plan.

[†]2007 sales

The Story

1907: Jim Casey founds the American Messenger Company in Seattle, Washington

1919: Casey expands his company's service area to Oakland, California, and changes its name to the United Parcel Service

1975: Becomes the first delivery company capable of serving every address in 48 states; two years later, UPS expands its capacity and is able to deliver to addresses in all 50 states

1985: Air delivery goes international between the United States and six European nations

1999: UPS goes public on the New York Stock Exchange

2001: Acquires Mail Boxes, Etc. and iShip, a developer of Web-based technology used to process small package shipments

2005: Acquires Overnite, which expands its North American ground freight services

Most important to recruiters: Leadership skills, communication skills, analytical skills

Selectivity: 1 of 5 applicants hired in 2006, down from 3 of 5 applicants hired in 2005

Diversity of entry-level workforce: 30% minority; 29% female

Facts to know:

- UPS's campus recruiting efforts are particularly widespread: the company says that it searches for job candidates at almost every U.S. college and university campus (both two- and four-year degree institutions).

- 3- and 5-year retention rates for entry-level employees are an impressive 94% and 93%, respectively.

 The Starting Gate

Undergraduate internships: 776

Duration of summer internship: 12 weeks

Average total compensation: $9,300

Interns by grade level:
Freshman 7%
Sophomore 16%
Junior...29%
Senior 28%
College graduate 20%

Interns who receive full-time job offers: N/A

Interns who are extended full-time job offers that accept: N/A

The Sliding Scale

Entry-level hires who had been interns: 74%

Most important performance measurements in entry-level hire: Leadership ability, team player, enthusiasm

Entry-level hires receiving signing bonuses: N/A

Average entry-level signing bonus: N/A

Entry-level hires receiving performance bonuses: N/A

Average performance bonus during first year: N/A

The Stand-Out Perks

- 23 paid vacation days

- 401(k) plan with company match of up to 3% of salary (immediately vested)

- Salary increase of 2% to 5% at 6 months

- Annual incentive bonus of up to the equivalent of two months' salary that can be awarded as 50% restricted stock and 50% cash, all company stock, or deferred into the employee's 401(k) plan

- Educational expenses reimbursement ($5,250)

The Skills

- 10-day orientation program that includes professional/personal development and lessons on the principles of successful leadership, management, and effective communication skills

- A formal leadership program that lasts an employee's entire management career; development activities include internal and external training courses and rotational assignments

The Sound-Off

- "As a co-op participant, I had the opportunity to redesign and rewrite a fairly visible Web site used by the internal communications department. Managers are always focused on developing their employees to ensure that they move up in the corporation." —*UPS programmer*

- "It's almost like a family business, where you treat each other with respect and open-mindedness at all times, even though there will be challenges that push the limits of your tolerance." —*UPS corporate pricing analyst*

- "I worked at UPS for a number of years, and it is not a company that you will stay with. The reason is simple: high school–educated managers, no flexibility in work schedule, and getting a day off is like pulling teeth. Oh, and during Christmas, full-time managers are required to work 50 hours a week." —BW *Discussion Forum*

THE SUPERSTAR SPOTLIGHT

Name: Keisha Lee Cavil
Job: Workforce Planning Manager

Describe a typical day: *There really is no "typical" day, because we are faced with different challenges from one day to the next. But, as a routine, I try to spend the first 30 minutes of the day in my office without engaging with anyone while I check e-mails, voicemail, and my calendar. This allows me to focus and strategize my game plan before stepping onto the field.*

Best part of your job: *What I like best about being a workforce planning manager is that I am able to be a part of bringing new talent to UPS. At the same time, I provide employment opportunities in our community.*

Rising through the ranks: *The only thing that I can honestly say that I have done is to pursue my education and dedicate myself to various job assignments that I have been given. The credit must be given to UPS, because I've been given the opportunity to work among professionals who have been great mentors.*

Advice for ambitious young professionals: *Understand that having a life outside of your professional goals provides a balance that can help you focus. Never allow yourself to be discouraged when faced with adversity.*

Describe the workplace culture: *The UPS culture as I see it is about teamwork and a commitment to improvement in our business, in our community, and in the world. I feel this is done through maintaining the traditional values the company was built on while at the same time staying aware of current global trends.*

FOUND THE COMPANY?
NOW LAND THE JOB.

Learn how with the resources at the *BusinessWeek* Managing Channel.

CUSTOMIZE YOUR JOB SEARCH
- Compare employers based on criteria you select, from salary and perks to training and 401(k) plans.
- Explore in-depth profiles of nearly 100 top employers.

TAP INTO YOUR COMMUNITY
- Connect and share experiences with fellow students and recent grads.
- See what your peers think in Universum's annual survey of +40,000 U.S. undergraduates.

LEARN FROM OTHERS' EXPERIENCES
- Get career advice for young professionals in our "Starting Out" column.
- Hear from new hires on the job.

Go to businessweek.com/managing/career/